DETESTABLE AND
WICKED ARTS

DETESTABLE AND WICKED ARTS

NEW ENGLAND AND WITCHCRAFT IN THE EARLY MODERN ATLANTIC WORLD

PAUL B. MOYER

CORNELL UNIVERSITY PRESS

Ithaca and London

First published 2020 by Cornell University Press

Library of Congress Cataloging-in-Publication Data

Names: Moyer, Paul Benjamin, 1970– author.
Title: Detestable and wicked arts : New England and witchcraft in the early modern Atlantic world / Paul B. Moyer.
Description: Ithaca [New York] : Cornell University Press, 2020. | Includes bibliographical references and index.
Identifiers: LCCN 2019050798 (print) | LCCN 2019050799 (ebook) | ISBN 9781501751059 (hardcover) | ISBN 9781501751615 (paperback) | ISBN 9781501751066 (pdf) | ISBN 9781501751073 (ebook)
Subjects: LCSH: Witchcraft—New England—History—17th century. | Witchcraft—Great Britain—History—17th century.
Classification: LCC BF1576. M69 2020 (print) | LCC BF1576 (ebook) | DDC ss364.1/88—dc23
LC record available at https://lccn.loc.gov/2019050798
LC ebook record available at https://lccn.loc.gov/2019050799

To Bridget and Ethan

CONTENTS

Maps, Figures, and Tables

Maps

Figures

Tables

PREFACE

                          I have been teaching about witchcraft and witch-hunting in the early modern era (ca. 1450–1750) for well over a decade. After exploring other scholars' works on these topics with students for several years, I promised myself that I would author my own study about the time and place that first got me interested in the history of occult crime: seventeenth-century New England. I have now met that pledge.

I wrote this book because there is a need for it. It is easy for historians to forget that for most people witchcraft is an esoteric subject where sensationalism usually triumphs over more sophisticated understandings. Members of the general public mistakenly connect witchcraft in the past with the modern-day Wicca religion or hold wildly exaggerated notions of witch-hunting where executions numbered in the hundreds of thousands. The study of occult crime in early New England suffers an additional disability in that the Salem witch crisis of 1692 so dominates the popular imagination that it has become a stand in for the region's wider history of witchcraft even though it was in many ways outside the norm of witch-hunting in the Puritan colonies. For all these reasons, allegations of occult crime in early New England deserve a fresh look, and my primary objective has been to provide an engaging exploration that brings together existing scholarship on this topic and offers some new interpretations. Arguably the most comprehensive and influential book in the field is John Demos's 1982 landmark work, *Entertaining Satan: Witchcraft and the Culture of Early New England*. Two other foundational studies—Richard Weisman's *Witchcraft, Magic, and Religion in 17th-century Massachusetts* and Carol Karlsen's *The Devil in the Shape of a Woman*—followed in 1984 and 1987 respectively. There have been some notable additions to these books such as Richard Godbeer's *The Devil's Dominion* (1992), Elizabeth Reis's *Damned Women* (1997), and Emerson Baker's *The Devil of Great Island* (2007), but the initial trio continue to dominate thinking about witchcraft in New England. However, propelled by an outpouring of scholarship over the last few decades on occult crime in the Old World, understandings of witchcraft have evolved since Demos, Karlsen, and Weisman published their works more than a generation ago. Moreover, these three seminal studies were very much products of the New Social History of the 1970s and 1980s and its romance with anthropology, sociology, and psychology. Although this interdisciplinary approach produced brilliant insights, it also resulted in books marked by a clinical tone and penchant for jargon that can make them a challenging read. Thus, while certainly building on these works, I have attempted to produce a book that is more plainspoken and accessible.

Besides looking back to long-standing interpretations of witchcraft in New England, this study takes advantage of more recent scholarship on occult crime in early modern Europe that has enriched our understanding of how concerns over magical mischief intersected with gender, class, religion, and the law.[1] For a long time, historians stressed the divergence of elite and folk views on the occult and tended to see witch-hunting as a process imposed from above. Newer studies on European witchcraft have broken down these dichotomous views and reveal a greater level of give and take between common folk and elites when it came to witch beliefs and shared responsibility for witch-hunting—my book follows their lead.[2] Links between witch prosecutions and the rise of the state is another current focus of investigation.[3] Such a consideration might seem more appropriate for Europe—which witnessed the rise of large, centralized polities during the period of the witch hunts—than the Puritan colonies with their relatively lean and rudimentary institutions of governance. Nevertheless, the judicial institutions New Englanders deployed against black magic did not emerge out of thin air, but drew on European precedents, meaning that insights concerning how different types of Old World judicial systems did, or did not, facilitate witch-hunting are certainly applicable to the New World. Likewise, the analysis of the relationship between religion and witch-hunting in Europe also sheds light on the prosecution of occult crime in the Puritan colonies. Early on in the analysis of European witch hunts, scholars tried to determine whether the Catholic Church or any of the varieties of Protestantism that sprang up in the sixteenth century promoted witch prosecutions more vigorously than the others. While such efforts have fallen out of fashion, historians continue to explore how witch-hunting may have intertwined with the upheavals produced by the Protestant Reformation and Catholic Counter-Reformation, and their findings are relevant to the study of witchcraft in the seventeenth-century English Atlantic.[4]

Writing this book required me to make a number of decisions concerning sources and evidence. At the heart of studies of witchcraft stand legal documents—formal complaints, transcriptions of interrogations, indictments, and depositions—generated by the prosecution of suspected occult criminals. These materials can be frustratingly short on detail or present full-bodied narratives ripe for analysis; but no matter how talkative or tight-lipped, they invariably feature idiosyncratic spelling, capitalization, and punctuation that can make reading them a challenge. So, when quoting contemporary documents, I have modernized spelling and capitalization, added punctuation as needed, and removed excessive abbreviations. Records of witchcraft cases are also frequently incomplete and involve ordinary people who often left behind few traces. Accordingly, while I avoid interpretations at odds with the evidence, I have made informed inferences when I felt confident that the historical record was strong enough to support them. Thus the pages that follow contain words such as *likely*, *probably*, and *possibly* that indicate where my analysis rests on evidence that is not wholly conclusive.

A final word concerning witches. During the early modern era there was far more fear of witchcraft than actual witches. In a literal sense witches did not exist because to be a witch was to exercise magical power—defined here as a person's ability to effect change in the world through supernatural means—and there is not a shred of credible evidence that magic (except whatever psychosomatic effects it may have) works. While this leaves open the possibility of people *believing* that they could wield magic, it appears that the vast majority of those persecuted for occult crime were not witches in thought or deed, and certainly not in the sense that the authorities envisioned them. European demonologies defined a witch as a person who obtained supernatural powers by forming a pact with Satan, a belief that has little to no foundation in reality. That being said, it is clear that people attempted to perform various sorts of helpful, "white" magic that some early modern Europeans condemned as acts of witchcraft. Moreover, it seems that folk only rarely attempted to perform harmful, black magic and even fewer still did so on a regular basis. In short, with a few exceptions, those brought to book for witchcraft were innocent of the charge.

This book would not have been possible (and nearly as good) without the assistance of many people. I would like to express my appreciation to those who read drafts of this work while it was on its journey toward publication. They include my wife, Christine, who reviewed my initial manuscript and provided me with valuable feedback; and my colleague, Jamie Spiller, who read a later version and did yeoman service in helping me to hone and clarify its prose.

I would be remiss if I did not also extend my thanks to the people at Cornell University Press for all of their help in making this book a reality.

My editor, Michael McGandy, did a wonderful job shepherding it through the publishing process and was a constant source of good suggestions and sensible advice. I should also express my gratitude to the anonymous readers who reviewed my manuscript for the press. Their deep knowledge of witchcraft and witch-hunting in early New England came through loud and clear in their expert commentary and was invaluable to me as I revised my monograph.

Finally, I would like to recognize two groups of students who helped me to test this book in the classroom in the spring semester of 2018: Nate Bogal, Ryan Bristow, Shelly Burgess-DeFrance, Glenn Dowdle, Griffin Everly, Alan Gowans, Hailey LaRosa, Ryan Offen, Wendi Parisi, Will Roote, Danielle Simmons, Margo Smith, and Jake Tynan who took my undergraduate research seminar on New England witchcraft; and Matt Ballard, Emily Bouchard, Harry DeVoe, Dan Gall, Rebecca Healy, Ginny Huber, Katie Krantz, Casey Maves, Jordan McElligott, Lyndsey Richards, and Shei Valerio-Sanchez in my graduate seminar on witchcraft in the early modern Atlantic World.

DETESTABLE AND
WICKED ARTS

Introduction

The Devil in New England

On October 2, 1665, Ralph and Mary Hall of Setauket, Long Island, stood trial before New York's Court of Assizes for the capital crime of practicing the "detestable and wicked arts, commonly called witchcraft." The couple had purportedly employed dark powers to murder George Wood and his "infant child." According to the indictment, the magical assault started the previous Christmas and continued until their victims "mortally sickened" and died. After hearing the charges against them, both husband and wife pleaded not guilty.[1]

This was probably not the Halls' first run-in with accusations of occult crime. In June 1664, Setauket's town court heard a defamation complaint from Ralph Hall on behalf of his wife against a "Mr. Smith"—probably the wealthy Quaker Richard Smith who founded the nearby settlement of Smithtown. The court noted that the defendant had "not sufficiently made good what he hath said of" Mary Hall and ordered him to pay her "five marks." Surviving records do not specify the words Smith spoke against Goody (short for Goodwife) Hall; but considering future events, it is quite likely that they imputed her as a witch. Luckily for the Halls, their second and more serious encounter with witchcraft mentioned above resulted in a pair of acquittals. None of the witness testimony brought against the couple survives, but it clearly was not sufficient to convict and condemn them to death. After reviewing the case, the jury found "nothing considerable" against Ralph Hall; and though they felt that there were "some suspicions by the evidence" against Mary, none of it was sufficient "to take away her life." In the end, the two went free on the condition that Goodman Hall put up a bond to guarantee that his wife would appear at each session of the assizes so the court could monitor her future behavior.[2]

Following their release, the Halls returned to Setauket, but soon after sold their property there and moved to Great Miniford's Island (present-day City Island in the Bronx). The couple likely made the move to distance themselves from any suspicions of witchcraft that lingered after their trial and to be closer to New York City so that they could more easily attend the assizes held there. Goodman Hall dutifully brought his wife to each session of the court until New York governor Richard Nicolls, seeing "no direct proofs nor further prosecution of them since," released him from this obligation in 1668.[3]

Though the witchcraft trial of Ralph and Mary Hall unfolded under New York's jurisdiction, the people involved in the episode and the culture out of which it grew were firmly rooted in New England. The charges against them have much in common with cases of occult crime in the Puritan colonies, including the attribution of mysterious illnesses and deaths to black magic. Setauket, the place where suspicions against the Halls took shape, had been settled by New Englanders who came across Long Island Sound in the mid-1650s and was formally attached to the colony of Connecticut in 1661. Just three years later, English forces under James Duke of York conquered the Dutch colony of New Netherland and rechristened it New York. In the political shake-up that followed, Setauket and the rest of Long Island fell from Connecticut's grasp and ended up within the boundaries of the new colony. Like their neighbors, the Halls' path to Long Island took them through New England. Both of them emigrated from England to Massachusetts before 1649 (it is unclear if they married before or after their arrival in the New World) and were in Setauket by 1664 when Connecticut declared Ralph Hall a freeman and identified him as a resident of the town. That he earned this status indicates that Goodman Hall was a property owner and a man without serious blemish to his reputation, although that was soon to change.[4]

Witchcraft accusations were a sensational but somewhat regular part of life in early New England, and several of those involved in Ralph and Mary Hall's prosecution for black magic had previous encounters with allegations of occult crime. Fourteen years before he sued Richard Smith for defaming his wife (probably for witchcraft), Goodman Hall found himself on the receiving end of a slander suit in Massachusetts when Thomas Crauly accused him of "saying he [Crauly] called Robert Sawyer's wife a witch."[5] Thomas Baker, the foreman of the grand jury that indicted the Halls in 1665, was also a key figure in the witchcraft trial of Elizabeth Garlick of Easthampton, Long Island, in 1658. As a magistrate for the town, he recorded depositions and accompanied the accused to Hartford where she stood trial.[6] One of the Halls' supposed victims, George Wood, also had a previous brush with occult crime. Before taking up residence in Setauket, he lived in Saybrook, Connecticut, where in 1661 two neighbors with whom he had a contentious relationship, Nicholas and Martha Jennings, were arrested for witchcraft but escaped conviction. Last, Dr. Thomas Pell, the proprietor of Great Miniford's Island where the Halls took refuge after their trial, was connected to the Fairfield, Connecticut, witchcraft cases of Goody Basset in 1651 and Goody Knapp in 1653, both of which resulted in convictions and executions. Dr. Pell's wife Lucy led a committee of women who examined Knapp for signs of witchcraft and may have served in a similar capacity during Basset's trial. The doctor appears to have regretted his spouse's role in the proceedings since he cancelled all debts owed to him by the husbands of the executed women, and lingering guilt over their deaths may explain why he provided the Halls refuge after they sought to escape from the witchcraft suspicions that fell over them in Setauket.[7]

What happened to Ralph and Mary Hall after the governor of New York released the latter from her court-ordered surveillance in 1668 remains a mystery. As with many suspects, they were humble folk whose lives before and after their run-in with the charge of witchcraft left few marks on the historical record. However, a 1673 tax assessment from Hampstead, Long Island, includes a "Ralph Haull" who possessed a modest estate of seven acres, several cows, a hog, and two horses.[8] If this is the same Ralph Hall who lived in Setauket in 1665, then it appears that he and his wife remained people of relatively limited means who continued the pattern of geographic mobility they established earlier in their marriage. It is unclear if suspicions of witchcraft continued to haunt the Halls, but there is no indication that they ever again faced legal action for the crime.

The trial of Ralph and Mary Hall forms part of a much larger story of witchcraft in Europe and its Atlantic colonies during the early modern era (roughly the period between 1450 and 1750). During this period, approximately 100,000 Europeans faced prosecution for occult crime and as many as half of them lost their lives as a result. The years between the mid-sixteenth and mid-seventeenth centuries saw the peak of witch-hunting, with the Holy Roman Empire (and specifically Germany) as its geographic center. The Halls' birthplace, England, had a more restrained history when it came to the battle against magical mischief. During the early modern period, some

2,000 witch prosecutions and somewhere under 500 executions occurred there. Closer to home, Ralph and Mary Hall were two of the roughly 240 people formally accused of witchcraft in seventeenth-century New England, of whom 35 went to the gallows.[9] Any phenomenon that lasted so long, involved so many people, covered such a vast expanse of geography, cost so many lives, and so profoundly involved the efforts of civil and ecclesiastical authorities deserves attention.

Witchcraft—the idea that people can harness supernatural forces in order to cause injury to others, the fear it sparked, and the resulting efforts to identify and punish alleged occult criminals—opens a valuable window onto the experience and outlook of early modern Europeans. In light of modern-day science, it is difficult to accept that people wielded magical power of any sort, and there is no credible evidence that the wilder imaginings concerning witches—that they engaged in mass meetings at which they worshiped the Devil and participated in grisly rituals—have any foundation in fact. Nevertheless, most early modern Europeans believed it, and how they acted on that belief speaks to important social, religious, intellectual, and judicial dynamics and developments that framed their lives.

Why early modern Europeans believed in witchcraft and engaged in witch-hunting is complicated and varied across space and time. At the most elemental level, however, they allowed people to explain the unexplainable, account for misfortune, and take vengeance on those who supposedly wronged them. As for why certain individuals became subjects of suspicion and legal action for witchcraft, the answer often lay in interpersonal conflict. When individuals, families, and factions fell to feuding with one another, accusations of occult mischief sometimes followed. Of course, this did not come to pass every time people fell out with one another. However, when conditions were right, it became possible for individuals to see their enemies as malevolent figures who harnessed the dark forces of the occult. In sum, witchcraft and witch-hunting was born of conflict and misfortune, guilt and loss.

Witchcraft and witch-hunting in early New England grew out of a set of factors that played out on a local, regional, and transatlantic level. Personal misfortune and everyday disputes between neighbors intertwined with suspicions of black magic and offer up a rich seam for understanding the social context of occult crime.[10] Since none of the testimony from the 1665 witchcraft trial of Ralph and Mary Hall survive, it is impossible to reconstruct the interpersonal frictions that contributed to their case. If other, better-documented witchcraft cases in New England are any guide, however, then there was likely some sort of preexisting contention between the Halls, their accusers, and their purported victim, George Wood. Of course, personal conflict and loss were facts of life long before prosecutions for occult crime started in New England and continued after they stopped and cannot alone account for why witch trials emerged or ended.

Likewise, religious, political, and economic instability on a regional level had an impact on witchcraft suspicions and prosecutions. They created an atmosphere where fear and anxiety heightened concerns over black magic and almost invariably involved civil and ecclesiastical leaders who were key figures in witchcraft trials.[11] Such factors shaped Goodman and Goodwife Hall's run-in with witchcraft. In the years preceding their trial, Long Island settlements like Setauket were caught up in wider regional tensions and instabilities. Rumors and later the reality of war between England and Holland cast its shadow over Long Island as its communities found themselves on the front lines of conflict between the New England colonies and the Dutch colony of New Netherland. Next, in the wake of England's conquest of the Dutch possession, Long Island fell from Connecticut's orbit and came under the authority of the newly formed colony of New York. It is impossible to say exactly how these events may have shaped the lead-up to the Halls' witchcraft trial, but one thing is for certain: the fact that the couple was tried under New York law rather than Connecticut's certainly had an impact on their prosecution.

A transatlantic perspective is also vital to deciphering the battle against black magic in the Puritan colonies. Seventeenth-century New England maintained strong ties with England and other parts of its empire. The movement of people and ideas remained vibrant beyond the Great Migration of the 1630s when thousands of Puritans left the motherland and made new homes for themselves in its colonies. Parliament's victory during the English Civil War of the 1640s brought thousands of Puritan colonists back to Britain, while the collapse of the pro-Puritan commonwealth and the restoration of Charles II sent Puritans fearful of Royalist reprisals scurrying to England's imperial hinterlands.[12] In addition, clergymen and other intellectually minded Puritans across the empire kept abreast of the latest publications and corresponded with one another.[13]

The timing, tempo, and texture of witch prosecutions in New England can only be fully understood when placed in context with witch-hunting across England's Atlantic empire. Like New England, Britain and Bermuda witnessed a surge in witch trials during the mid-seventeenth century. England's Civil War and the social and political revolutions it set in motion reverberated across its colonial possessions in the 1640s and 1650s, triggering this wave of witch prosecutions. Likewise, the restoration of the monarchy in 1660 produced further rounds of instability and witch fears. Intertwined with these upheavals was a spiritual outlook linked to the religious reform movement known as Puritanism, which also helped create an environment ripe for witch-hunting across the English-speaking world. In addition, witch scares in one part of England's empire helped to spark them in others, and witch-hunting procedures developed in the mother country spread to its colonies. These transatlantic factors certainly had a bearing on the witchcraft episode that ensnared Ralph and Mary Hall. The previously mentioned instabilities of war and changing political jurisdictions that buffeted Setauket and helped to create conditions conducive to witch-hunting had their origins in imperial initiatives that originated in England. Moreover, the judicial procedures and rules of evidence that governed the couple's trial and led to their acquittal were firmly rooted in a body of English witch lore and jurisprudence that spanned England's overseas empire.

Thus, the story of witchcraft in early New England is part of a broader tale of a campaign against black magic across the English Atlantic and especially those parts of it where Puritans predominated.[14] This "Puritan Atlantic" includes the New England colonies of Plymouth, Massachusetts Bay, Connecticut, and New Haven (but not more heterodox Rhode Island). Beyond the North American mainland, it also embraces Bermuda and the short-lived colonies of Providence Island off the coast of Nicaragua and Eleuthera in the Bahamas as well as those portions of the British Isles, such as East Anglia and English settlements in Ireland, where Puritans held sway.[15] These places witnessed relatively high rates of witch trials and convictions, while other parts of the English empire experienced little witch-hunting activity. Virginia and Maryland, for example, saw only a handful of accusations, a few legal proceedings, and only one execution related to occult crime.[16]

The mid-seventeenth century, more specifically the years between 1640 and 1670, furnishes the best opportunity to explore the local, regional, and especially transatlantic contexts of witchcraft and witch-hunting in the Puritan colonies. While an examination of this period cannot present a comprehensive history of occult crime in the region, it does provide an understanding of witchcraft beliefs and the social dynamics of witch-hunting. Since occult lore did not change that much in New England across the seventeenth century, a look at its witchcraft episodes between 1640 and 1670 provide an excellent window into the colonists' views on black magic. Likewise, there was a great deal of continuity in terms of the judicial procedures employed in witchcraft trials and the sorts of people suspected of magical mischief. Therefore, the analysis of occult crime in

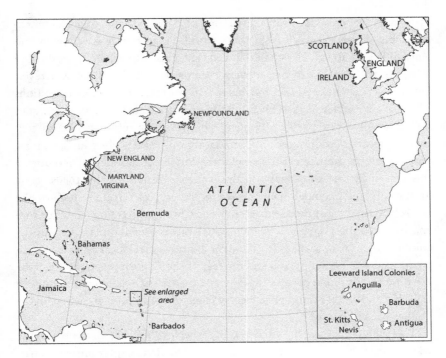

MAP 1.   The English Atlantic, ca. 1660

New England before 1670 can effectively illuminate its entire history of witch prosecution.

Examining New England's earliest witch trials also provides a necessary corrective to the analysis of occult crime in the region. Witchcraft episodes in the Puritan colonies during the mid-seventeenth century have received less scrutiny than those that marked its later years, especially the infamous Salem witch crisis of 1692. Indeed, in the popular imagination Salem has become a stand-in for a broader understanding of the battle against black magic in the Puritan colonies. Yet the Salem hunt is an outlier in New England's history of witch prosecution in terms of its scale, geographic reach, and the behavior of the judicial officials who conducted it. Whereas the vast majority of witchcraft cases in New England involved one or, at most, two suspects and the inhabitants of a single community, the Salem panic ensnared more than 150 people from across northeastern Massachusetts and Maine. Moreover, while New England judges had been cautious in their approach to the prosecution of occult crime in the preceding decades, the special court established to deal with the crisis aggressively promoted the witch hunt.[17] Thus, an exploration of years before 1670 promotes a more balanced understanding of New England witchcraft by shifting attention away from the extraordinary evens of 1692.

Finally, the period illustrates three sorts of ties that bound together witch-craft episodes in the English-speaking world. First, there were popular and learned beliefs about the occult that traveled across the ocean from the Old World to the New. Next, major events such as the English Civil War rever-berated across the Atlantic and helped to promote or inhibit conditions conducive to witch fears. Third, witch-hunting campaigns and techniques linked the disparate parts of England's empire. The mid-seventeenth cen-tury is especially well suited to illuminating this third sort of linkage, for a witch-hunting campaign that spanned the English Atlantic occurred during this period. It first took shape in the war-torn Britain of the 1640s, grew in intensity and extended its reach across the empire through much of the 1650s, and finally lost momentum in the 1660s. Although English witch lore and transatlantic events still shaped witchcraft prosecutions in the Puritan colonies after 1670, there was no longer a direct correlation between witch prosecutions in New England and the rest of the English empire. Indeed, by the time the Puritan colonies experienced the massive Salem witch hunt in 1692, judicial witch-hunting had largely fallen out of fashion elsewhere in the English-speaking world.

This then is the story of witchcraft in early New England and its ties to the wider seventeenth-century English Atlantic. The first chapter presents a nar-rative of witch-hunting in New England between the late 1630s and 1670 and begins the process of placing it in the broader context of the English Atlantic. From there, the remaining six chapters trace the process by which cases of occult crime took shape. Along the way, they illuminate the transatlantic dimensions of witch prosecutions in the Puritan colonies and, more broadly, answer questions essential to understanding the phenomenon of witch-hunting in the early modern period. The first step in stamping out occult mischief was its identification as a crime, and so chapter 2 tackles the ques-tion "What is witchcraft?" by exploring the various ways New Englanders envisioned it. A second critical stage involved the identification of witch sus-pects, and chapters 3 and 4 address this issue by outlining the traits that char-acterized the accused and exploring why New Englanders associated them with occult crime. In particular, chapter 4 details how witch fears intersected with gender constructs. The fifth chapter further delves into the dynamics of accusation and investigates what motivated people to denounce others as witches. Not all witchcraft cases were alike, and chapter 6 brings into focus witch panics that stood apart in terms of their scale and intensity from more ordinary instances of occult crime. In addition, it sheds light on a variety of accuser who often helped trigger such episodes: supposedly bewitched indi-viduals whose distinct social profile and startling symptoms of supernatural affliction distinguished them from other victims of black magic. The final chapter explains why some witch suspects went free while others went to the gallows by dissecting the terminal phase of many witchcraft cases: the judicial process that transformed informal suspicions against the accused into formal, criminal prosecutions.

Factors that shaped alleged cases of occult crime in New England, the broader English Atlantic, and Europe during the early modern era framed Ralph and Mary Hall's encounter with witchcraft in 1665. Contemporary understandings of black magic, widely held witch stereotypes, and well-worn judicial procedures helped to bring the couple under scrutiny for supernatural mischief, precipitated their arrest, and eventually led to their trial and acquittal. Although no documents survive that give details about the charges against the Halls, their case likely fell in line with a general pattern found in Europe and its New World colonies in which witch fears and accusations grew out of a dense thicket of interpersonal relationships and conflicts. In other words, tensions between the Halls and their neighbors were probably at the root of couple's run-in with witchcraft. However, beyond these local social dynamics, it was also a product of forces that operated on a regional and transatlantic level. Ralph and Mary Hall's arrest had much to do with the fact that they lived in a community established and inhabited by people from New England, a place with a well-established penchant for witch-hunting. In addition, although the Halls were almost certainly not aware of it, ideas and trends that reverberated across the English Atlantic powerfully shaped the beliefs and institutions that informed their case and helped determine its outcome.

CHAPTER 1

"Hanged for a Witch"

Witch-Hunting in New England before 1670

Alice Young of Windsor, Connecticut, appears to have been the first person executed for witchcraft in New England. Only fragments of information on her case remain. One reference to Young's trial appears on the flyleaf of a diary kept by Windsor's town's clerk, Matthew Grant, which reads, "May 26, [16]47, Alice Young was hanged." Exactly why she suffered this fate would have remained an open question if it were not for a curt entry from the same year in a journal kept by Massachusetts governor John Winthrop: "One _____ of Windsor arraigned and executed at Hartford for a witch." Though it did not include a name, the governor's note is doubtless an allusion to Young. There were only two people from Windsor hanged in 1647, and the other one was the John Newberry who went to the gallows after being convicted of bestiality.[1] These couple of lines constitute the entire surviving record of New England's first documented witch hanging. The exact nature of the charges against Young, the names of those who provided testimony, and what they said all remain a mystery.

Although the passage of time has scoured away the particulars of Alice Young's witch trial, some information can be gleaned about her life. She was probably the wife of John Young, a man of humble means who purchased land in Windsor in 1641 and later sold it in 1649 before relocating to Stratford, Connecticut, where he died in 1661. The timing of his relocation—shortly following Alice's execution—gives the appearance of a man trying to make a new start after losing his wife to the charge of witchcraft in his previous place of residence. If Goodman Young hoped that the move would erase his family's association with black magic, then it failed. In 1677 Thomas Beamon of Springfield, Massachusetts, the son of Alice (Young) Beamon, sued a man for saying that "his mother was a witch, and he looked like one." Beamon's mother was almost certainly a daughter of Alice Young. Not only did she bear her mother's name, but she and her children continued to suffer the stigma of witchcraft.[2]

What is clear about Young's execution is that it marked the beginning of an intense period of witch-hunting in New England. Authorities there initiated legal action against fifty-seven suspected witches between 1638 and 1670. Several were repeat offenders and so there was a total of sixty-five proceedings for occult crime during this period. Out of these episodes, forty-two resulted in full-blown trials and eighteen of these ended in convictions. Except for three lucky individuals who had their verdicts overturned, all those found guilty died at the end of a rope. These numbers represent a minimum, for there might have been more prosecutions of which no trace survives. For instance, the records of the New Haven Colony between 1649 and 1653 are missing, and there is a chance that they contain evidence of additional legal actions related to occult mischief. Moreover, before the 1660s New England's judicial systems lacked guidelines for the systematic recording of court proceedings, which increases the chance that some early cases may not show up in written sources. Nevertheless, the combination of surviving court documents, colonists' diaries, and books concerning New England's early witchcraft episodes penned later in the seventeenth century makes it unlikely that many early cases have been missed.

There were other activities related to witchcraft before 1670 besides these prosecutions. This includes seven documented instances where suspicions of witchcraft did not lead to any legal action, and there were undoubtedly many more such informal accusations that have not left a paper trail. Surviving records also indicate that there were nineteen slander suits involving imputations of witchcraft, which serves as a reminder that not all litigation related to occult crime involved the prosecution of the accused and that sometimes it was accusers who found themselves on trial.[3] There are no clear instances of vigilante action, such as mob assaults or lynching, against witch suspects during this period, and it is quite possible that none took place. This dearth of extralegal activity can be attributed to the premium the Puritans placed on order and respect for authority and the fact that there was no need for individuals to take the law into their own hands since the courts provided a means to punish witches. Indeed, the only documented attack on a witch suspect occurred in 1684 at a time when New England's justices were very reluctant to prosecute cases of occult crime. The incident took place when Mary Webster of Hadley came under suspicion for witchcraft and "a number of brisk lads" from the town dragged her from her home, hung her up until she was almost dead, cut her down, and then buried her in a snowbank. The woman miraculously survived the brutal attack.[4]

Putting aside the witchcraft accusations related to the highly unusual Salem witch crisis of 1692, which dwarfs every other episode of witch-hunting in the Puritan colonies, the legal actions related to occult crime that took place between 1638 and 1670 represent just over two-thirds of such cases in seventeenth-century New England. Most striking, all but one of the region's sixteen witch executions not related to the Salem crisis took place by 1670. In addition, the witchcraft trials that took place before this year produced a 40 percent conviction rate, while the thirty non-Salem prosecutions that took place between 1671 and 1699 resulted in only three guilty verdicts (two of which the courts eventually overturned).[5] In sum, New England's earliest decades of witch-hunting stand out in terms of their rates of prosecution, conviction, and execution.

When analyzed as a year-by-year progression of events, it becomes clear that witch-hunting in Puritan colonies before 1670 unfolded in several phases. The first, which ran from the late 1630s, when accusations of occult crime first began to surface in the courts, until late in the following decade, was a prologue to a much more intense period of witch-hunting. The second phase, covering 1647 to 1656, saw the rapid growth and peak of witch prosecutions. During the third, spanning 1657 to 1661, witch-hunting lost some momentum. This pause was only temporary, however, and the Hartford witch panic and its aftermath marked a return to witch-hunting between 1662 and 1665. The final phase, which saw a sharp decline in cases of occult crime, ran from the mid-1660s to decade's end.

While conditions in New England certainly shaped this course of events, the region's history of witch-hunting also intersected with developments beyond its borders, and so accounting for its changing contours requires an analysis that extends across the Atlantic. Historian John Demos developed a model for understanding ups and downs in witch-hunting that can be put to good use here. He argues that various factors served to generate or inhibit fears of the occult. In particular, Demos contends that "witchcraft proceedings and episodes of conflict did not appear together, in the same time and place; instead they waxed and waned, in alternative sequence." In its most basic terms, disputes ranging from wars to religious controversies distracted folk from the threat of witchcraft and consumed energies that

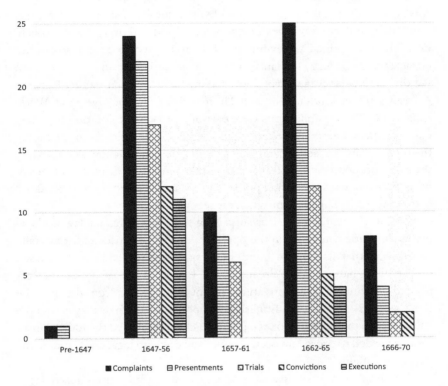

FIGURE 1.1 Witch-hunting in New England up to 1670

could have otherwise gone toward prosecuting occult crime. Demos notes, however, that in the aftermath of conflict—especially ones that fractured communities—accusations of witchcraft often returned with a vengeance. He also observes that "harms"—epidemics, crop failures, and other large-scale misfortunes—and "signs"—earthquakes, comets, or other unusual phenomena interpreted as God's efforts to communicate his divine displeasure—could trigger witch fears.[6] These factors played out on a local, regional, and transatlantic level.

Foundations, 1638–47

New England's colonists came from a land with a long history of witchcraft belief and decades of state-sponsored efforts to stamp out occult crime.

England passed witchcraft statutes in 1542, 1563, and 1604 that made the practice of black magic a civil crime. The final law was the most aggressive in terms of the punishments it mandated, which is not surprising since it was enacted during the reign of James I who published *Daemonologi* in 1597, a treatise that decried witches as servants of Satan and urged their prosecution. The book joined a growing body of English works concerning occult crime, including Henry Holland's *A Treatise against Witchcraft* (1580), William Perkins's *Discourse of the Damned Art of Witchcraft* (1608), Alexander Robert's *A Treatise of Witchcraft* (1616), and Thomas Cooper's *The Mystery of Witchcraft* (1617). These publications were part of a broader exploration of witchcraft that gained momentum among intellectuals in mainland Europe during the fifteenth and sixteenth centuries, and like their continental counterparts, their authors addressed the threat posed by witches and the proper means to bring them to justice. England put these laws and learned texts to good use and produced its fair share of witch prosecutions.[7]

In light of this heritage, it is surprising that New England saw no legal proceedings for witchcraft in the opening decades of settlement, especially considering that its Puritan immigrants saw themselves as God's chosen people doing battle against sin and Satan. Indeed, many of the ingredients needed for witch prosecutions were present in the region from the time the first colonists came ashore. English witch beliefs made their way across the Atlantic with the Puritan pioneers; they quickly established the judicial institutions needed to prosecute occult crime, and drew up legal codes that made it a capital offense.[8]

New England's laws against witchcraft, however, went unused for a decade. It is often difficult to determine why something did not happen, and such is the case when trying to figure out why so much time passed before a witch was brought to book. One likely reason is that the Puritan colonists were simply distracted by the demands of settlement, and hunting witches took a back seat to clearing land, building communities, and securing them from possible attack by Natives or competing European powers. In addition, stamping out religious dissent among the settler population occupied the attention of authorities.[9] Events back in the mother country also served to consume the energies of any would-be witch hunters. The 1630s witnessed a downward spiral in relations between King Charles I and Parliament, and this smoldering political crisis erupted into civil war in 1642. Anxious about loved ones back home and fearing that Parliamentarian forces (with whom the Puritans were aligned) might succumb to the king's army, New Englanders also worried about being drawn into the war if it spread across the empire. The conflict triggered other problems for the Puritan colonies, including economic dislocation and a surge in return migration to England that sapped their population.[10]

There are additional factors that may have inhibited witch-hunting during New England's first decades of settlement. The main migration to New England took place in the 1630s, a decade characterized by a lull in witch-hunting back home, meaning that hauling suspected black magicians into court may not have been a vital part of many colonists' Old World experience. Timing may also be relevant in another way. It is possible that the opening years of colonization were free of prosecutions for occult crime because such events commonly grew out of tensions that were years in the making. In other words, during the 1620s and 1630s, New England's fledgling settlements were not mature enough to have developed the layers of personal conflict and suspicion that generated witchcraft accusations.[11] Then again, perhaps it was the Puritan settlers' religious faith that inoculated them from witch scares in the early years of colonization. They may have believed that their status as God's chosen people gave them a level of protection against the Devil and his minions. More likely, the fact that the initial wave of migrants to New England was a largely self-selected group with a common background and set of values may have worked to mitigate the sorts of frictions that often sparked witchcraft episodes.[12]

Just because the courts were free of witch trials does not mean that Puritan colonists put aside their fears that people in their midst might have been guilty of black magic. More often than not such feelings went undocumented; however, witchcraft suspicions related to Massachusetts's Antinomian Controversy of 1636–38 have left a paper trail. To quickly sum up this complicated episode, it pitted the authorities against religious dissidents they labeled "Antinomians," meaning "opposed to the law." Reverends John Cotton and John Wheelwright, Anne Hutchinson, and Henry Vane (who served as the colony's governor in 1637) led the challenge to Massachusetts's civil and ecclesiastical leadership. Those in charge of the colony accused the dissenters of making the blasphemous claim that those who had received God's grace were free from civil law and able to supplant the Bible with revelations received directly from God. Anne Hutchinson was doubly offensive to those in charge: not only did she hold heterodox views but upended gender hierarchies by leading prayer meetings attended by both men and women. The upshot of all this was that the government vigorously suppressed the Antinomians. Their leaders faced banishment (Reverends Wheelwright and Hutchinson), left the colony of their own free will (Vane), or returned to the orthodox fold (Reverend Cotton).[13]

Rumors of witchcraft emerged in the aftermath of the Antinomian Controversy when accusations of occult misdeeds began to swirl around one of

Anne Hutchinson's followers, Jane Hawkins. As it had done with her mentor, Massachusetts banished Hawkins in 1638 and warned her not "to question matters of religion."[14] By this time, a strong connection existed between witchcraft and heresy in Europeans' minds, and Hawkins's ties to the Antinomians probably helped stoke fears that she was a witch. Her close association with the group's outspoken Jezebel, Anne Hutchinson, fit another facet of the witch stereotype, for many early modern Europeans saw witchcraft as primarily a female crime and believed that women commonly shared knowledge of the black arts with others of their sex.[15]

Reinforcing suspicion against Hawkins was her work as a medical practitioner. In a time and place where trained physicians were few and far between, local folk, most often women, filled the breach. Any housewife had at least a cursory knowledge of folk cures, while some women pursued medicine as a vocation. Others, such as Jane Hawkins, combined general medical services with the work of a midwife. Though the notion that midwifes were habitual targets of witchcraft accusation is an exaggeration, there was an association between witchcraft and the healing arts more broadly. In both Europe and the New World, healers ran afoul of witchcraft accusations when people began to view their activities in a malevolent light, for in an age when there was no clear line between medicine and magic, people believed that those with the power to cure also possessed the power to harm.[16]

Hawkins's troubles started after she aided fellow Hutchison disciple Mary Dyer during childbirth in October 1637. The baby was stillborn and quietly buried. In March 1638, right around the time that church officials excommunicated Anne Hutchinson, word spread that Dyer's dead child had been a monster. Massachusetts opened up an investigation during which they questioned both Hutchinson (who was also present at the birth) and Hawkins. According to Governor John Winthrop, the latter eventually admitted that the child:

> was of ordinary bigness; it had a face, but no head, and the ears stood upon the shoulder and were like an ape's; it had no forehead, but over the eyes four horns, hard and sharp . . . the eyes standing out, and the mouth also; the nose hooked upward; all over the breast and back full of sharp pricks and scales . . . it had two mouths, and in each of them a piece of red flesh sticking out; it had arms and legs as other children; but, instead of toes, it had on each foot three claws, like a young fowl, with sharp talons.

The authorities had the child's body exhumed and, "though it were much corrupted" by decomposition, an examination confirmed most of Hawkins's testimony. Winthrop also reported that when the deformed child "died in the mother's body, (which was about two hours before the birth,) the bed whereon the mother lay did shake, and withal there was such a noisome savor, as most of the women were taken with extreme vomiting and purging." The governor's sensational (and doubtlessly embellished) account includes a number of features—the shaking bed and unbearable stench—conventionally found in demonic possession narratives. The implication of all of this was clear: Dyer's monstrous birth was evidence that diabolical forces were at work.[17]

Dyer's devilish delivery cast suspicion on her midwife, Jane Hawkins. After news of the strange birth leaked out, Governor Winthrop stated that "she grew into great suspicion to be a witch" because of her medical activities. Indeed, before she left the colony, the General Court ordered her not to "meddle in surgery, or physic, drinks, plasters, or oils." The governor also claimed that Hawkins's reputation as a witch had traveled with her from the mother country, asserting that she "had much familiarity with the devil in England, when she dwelt at St. Ives, where divers ministers and others resorted to her and found it true."[18]

John Winthrop cast the shadow of witchcraft over Anne Hutchinson as well. In his journal he recounted a story about a Mr. Hales, "a young man very well conceited of himself and censorious of others," and a Mr. Collins, a "young scholar" who had preached in the West Indies before making his way to New England. In 1640 the pair went to "Aquiday" (Aquidneck), Rhode Island, where they quickly fell under the sway of Anne Hutchinson, who had taken up residence there after her banishment from Massachusetts. The two men's conversion to Hutchinson's heretical views was so rapid that Winthrop reasoned it "gave cause of suspicion of witchcraft," as did the report that she, like Mary Dyer, "was delivered of a monstrous birth" after leaving Massachusetts.[19]

Rise, 1647–56

New England's drought of witch prosecutions came to an end in 1647. Twenty-four formal complaints, nineteen trials, twelve convictions, and eleven executions for witchcraft happened in that year and the nine that followed it. Thus, of the two dozen legal actions initiated during this time span, half resulted in guilty verdicts and, with one exception, hangings. In sum, the years between 1647 and 1656 constituted the most active and deadly period of witch prosecution in New England until the Salem crisis of 1692.[20]

Map 2.   New England, ca. 1660

In Massachusetts thirteen formal complaints concerning witchcraft during this period led to nine trials, five convictions (one of which was later reversed), and four executions. The first person accused of the crime in the colony was also the first to hang for it. In the same year that Connecticut sent Alice Young to the gallows, Massachusetts officials tried, convicted, and executed Elizabeth Kendall of Cambridge after she was accused of bewitching a child to death. In the following year, Thomas and Margaret Jones of Charlestown faced the charge of witchcraft. While Goody Jones ultimately hanged, her husband's case never went to trial.[21] Hugh and Mary Parsons of Springfield found themselves the targets of witchcraft proceedings in 1651–52. Though a jury acquitted the wife, a court shortly thereafter sentenced her to death for the nonmagical murder one of her children. Goodman Parsons was convicted, but Massachusetts authorities later reversed the verdict. Around the same time, Alice Lake of Dorchester was tried, convicted, and hanged as a witch. Another two cases—those of Alice Stratton of Watertown and John Bradstreet of Rowley—unfolded in 1652, but neither resulted in a trial.[22] A year later, Jane Collins of Lynn was taken into custody for magical misdeeds upon the complaint of Enoch Coldam. Jane's husband, Christopher, had previously sued Coldam for slandering her with imputations of witchcraft and did so again after Coldam issued his complaint. It appears that neither Coldam's accusation nor Goodman Collins's defamation suit proceeded any further, and Jane Collins went free. In 1655 Goody Batchelor of Ipswich was formally accused, but her case does not seem to have resulted in any additional legal action. Two other purported witches, Jane Walford of Portsmouth and Eunice Cole of Hampton, stood trial and managed to escape conviction in 1656. In that same year, Anne Hibbins of Boston also faced prosecution as a witch; however, unlike Walford and Cole, she hanged for the crime.[23]

Connecticut stands out as the most aggressive witch-hunting colony during the late 1640s and early 1650s. With only a fraction of the population of Massachusetts, it was the site of seven trials, and all those who went before a jury suffered conviction and death at the gallows. Though Alice Young was the first victim of this deadly purge, her shadowy case says little about the dynamics of occult crime in the colony. More revealing is the prosecution of Mary Johnson, the second person to face the charge of witchcraft in Connecticut. Johnson was a servant living in Wethersfield when she came under suspicion in 1648.[24] Although no documents related to her witchcraft trial survive, the Reverend Cotton Mather recounted Johnson's case forty years later in his book, *Memorable Providences*. The reverend, who perhaps had access to materials that no longer exist, reported that Mary admitted that she had covenanted with the Devil and that he "was wont to do her many services," including chores such as cleaning ashes out of the fireplace and driving hogs out of her master's fields.[25]

Why Johnson confessed to being a witch—whether she truly believed she had given her soul to the Devil or provided a confession under duress—remains a mystery. According to Mather, Johnson further admitted to "the murder of a child, and that she had been guilty of uncleanness [meaning sexual indiscretions] with men and devils." If this version of events is accurate, then, with her conscience burdened with such sins, Johnson may have buckled under pressure and come to believe that she had gone one step further and committed the ultimate transgression of becoming a witch. Whether this was the case or not, references to sex with the Devil or demons, while relatively common in parts of Europe, were extremely rare in New England, making Johnson's testimony rather singular. The unusual aspects of her confession may be a product of the conditions under which she made it. Mather mentions that Hartford minister Samuel Stone took "great pains to promote her conversion unto God" and, in addition to seeking the young woman's redemption, could have possibly encouraged the demonic references in her confession in order to promote a more religiously charged understanding of witchcraft. Similarly, Mather may have embellished the story of Mary Johnson's witchcraft trial in order to combat what he and other clergymen in late-seventeenth century New England perceived as a decline in popular piety. Simply put, by publicizing cases of diabolical witchcraft, the reverend provided evidence of the Devil's existence and, by extension, God's.[26]

After the executions of Young and Johnson, prosecutions for occult crime in Connecticut continued apace during the first half of the 1650s. In 1651 John and Joan Carrington of Wethersfield came under suspicion. Not much is known about this couple's case other than that they were tried and hanged. In the same year that the Carringtons went to the gallows, a Goody Bassett of Stratford stood trial as a witch, confessed, and suffered the same fate. Just two years later, the neighboring town of Fairfield became the scene of another witch scare when residents lodged a complaint against the wife of Roger Knapp. She eventually went to trial and, as one person later recalled, "hanged for a witch." The case grew out of the earlier prosecution of Goody Bassett, for before her execution she allegedly claimed that there were three other witches in the area besides herself, thus keeping folk on edge and undoubtedly helping to stoke suspicions against Goody Knapp. Lydia Gilbert of Windsor was the last person accused of witchcraft in Connecticut before 1657. Charged with using black magic to cause the death of Henry Stiles, with frightening predictability she was tried, convicted, and executed.[27]

During its existence, the New Haven colony only opened witchcraft proceedings against three people, and all of these cases took place in the early 1650s. Elizabeth Godman, who first appeared in a New Haven court in 1653 as a plaintiff in a slander suit against others whom she claimed had marked her as a witch, came before the magistrates two years later to answer charges for occult crime. Though many prominent members of the colony testified against her, the evidence they presented did not merit a guilty verdict, and Godman got off with a stern warning. In the same year, Nicholas Bayley and his wife, a couple with an unsavory reputation, came before New Haven's highest court on two occasions after being accused witchcraft. The justices were suspicious of the pair but, again, the evidence against them was less than conclusive, and they let the couple go free on the condition that they left the colony.[28] Though these sorts of outcomes were uncommon in New England before 1656, they would become more frequent in the years that followed.

This bout of witch-hunting in the 1640s and 1650s was not limited to the Puritan colonies but extended across the English empire. The origins of this transatlantic witch hunt lay in the British Isles. After decades of relative judicial inactivity with regard to witchcraft, authorities there began to haul suspected occult criminals before the courts in the 1640s. This trend first took shape in Scotland in 1643 and by mid-decade the impulse to hunt down witches had spread south across the border into England. Between 1645 and 1647 the largest and deadliest English witch hunt broke out when fears of the occult swept across East Anglia. Encouraged by the self-styled witch finders Matthew Hopkins and John Stearne, people accused around three hundred

MAP 3.   England's mid-seventeenth century witch hunts

people of occult misdeeds and hanged about a third of them. Other major witch panics occurred in Scotland in 1649–50, the late 1650s, and 1661–62, while England experienced sizeable hunts in Northumberland in 1649–50 and Kent in 1652. All of these scares grew out of a backdrop of popular anxiety and institutional disarray produced by the English Civil War.[29]

The shockwaves of Britain's midcentury witch hunts rippled across the English Atlantic. Bermuda experienced its own campaign against black magic when the islands' residents, divided by the same religious and political fissures that fueled conflict in the mother country, took legal action against a dozen suspected witches in the 1650s and executed five of them.[30] Likewise, England's witch panics inspired New England's spate of prosecutions in the 1640s and 1650s. Indeed, Massachusetts's officials referenced the methods Hopkins and Stearne used in East Anglia during the 1648 witchcraft case of Margaret Jones.[31]

While it is often difficult to determine exactly how knowledge of Britain's Civil War–era witch hunts made their way across the English Atlantic, the sinews of empire that served to convey such news are more readily apparent. The civil and clerical elite of the Puritan colonies maintained a lively correspondence with friends throughout the English-speaking world in which they engaged in religious debates, discussed politics, and conveyed information about witchcraft. Governor John Winthrop of Massachusetts and Governor John Winthrop Jr. of Connecticut, for example, exchanged scores of letters with associates scattered across the English Atlantic. Such communication networks joined together people separated by hundreds of miles of ocean. Thus, when Bermuda experienced religious discord in the mid-1640s, Massachusetts's General Court declared a "day of humiliation" (prayer and fasting) in order to express sympathy for their like-minded brethren on the islands. Likewise, the Bay Colony pronounced several colonywide fast days in the 1640s in reaction to troubling news coming out of war-torn England. In addition to personal correspondence, books and pamphlets coursed through the empire after censorship laws fell into disuse during the Civil War. This stream of printed materials included a number of treatises on witchcraft, including Matthew Hopkins's *The Discovery of Witches* (1647) and John Stearne's *A Confirmation and Discovery of Witchcraft* (1648), both of which provided information on the East Anglian witch hunt.[32]

People also traveled back and forth across the Atlantic spreading news of witchcraft as well as witch-hunting know-how. Several members of Bermuda's civil and ecclesiastical leadership had been in England during the massive East Anglian witch panic of 1645–47 and could draw on their knowledge of the episode during their colony's own offensive against occult mischief in the 1650s. The itinerant Puritan minister Francis Doughty was another individual who helped to spread witch-hunting across the English Atlantic. Born in Bristol, he made his way to Massachusetts in the late 1630s where he served a congregation at Taunton. In 1641 he went to Rhode Island and shortly thereafter to western Long Island where he became pastor to several English settlements within the Dutch colony of New Netherland. Doughty moved once again in 1655, this time to serve as the minister of Hungers Parish on Virginia's Eastern Shore. It was here that he helped instigate one of that colony's few witchcraft cases when he accused a local resident of performing black magic (the identity of the suspect and the outcome of the case have been lost). In the late 1650s, the reverend left Virginia and became pastor to a church in Charles County, Maryland. Here he once again became involved in litigation related to witchcraft when John Mitchell initiated a slander suit against him for spreading rumors that Mitchell's wife was a witch.[33] Likewise, a bevy of Scots Calvinist clergymen (who immigrated to North America in the 1650s from a land known for its aggressive efforts to root out occult criminals) brought a witch-hunting impulse to the New World. Among these men was the Reverend David Lindsay who became the pastor of Wicomico Parish in Northumberland County, Virginia, in 1655. In the following year he helped to initiate a witchcraft accusation against William Harding that resulted in his trial, conviction, and banishment.[34]

Personal relationships also spread witch-hunting across the English empire. James Hopkins, father of the notorious witch finder Matthew Hopkins, was a friend of Massachusetts governor John Winthrop. In light of this, it is possible that Winthrop took an interest in the younger Hopkins's efforts to fight occult crime and imported his witch-hunting methods to the colony. Indeed, during the witchcraft case of Margaret Jones, the governor recommended that Massachusetts officials employ Hopkins's witch-finding techniques.[35]

In a similar vein, John Haynes, an early governor of both Massachusetts and Connecticut, and a man who stood out for his uncompromising stance against crime even among Puritans not noted for their easygoing attitude toward misbehavior, oversaw the latter colony's deadly spree of witch trials in the late 1640s and early 1650s. Haynes possessed ties with the fellow witch-hanging judge Sir Robert Rich, Earl of Warwick. Warwick was a Puritan aristocrat deeply involved in colonial ventures throughout the English Atlantic between the 1620s and late 1650s, including those in Bermuda and Connecticut. He was also a key figure in the East Anglian witch hunt, and he helped push the panic forward when he presided over a court held at Chelmsford in 1645 that convicted a number of the accused. Before he migrated to the New

FIGURE 1.2 Matthew Hopkins, the "Witch Finder General," with two confessing witches giving the names of their familiar spirits. From Matthew Hopkins, *The Discovery of Witches* (London, 1647). Division of Rare and Manuscript Collections, Cornell University Library.

World, Haynes lived just a short distance from the Earl's manor at Inworth and traveled in the same circle of prominent Essex County Puritans.[36]

Moreover, a significant proportion of the Puritan Atlantic's civil and ecclesiastical leaders (several of whom became involved in witch trials) were educated at Cambridge's Emmanuel College where they rubbed elbows with one another and partook of a liberal education that exposed them to matters

FIGURE 1.3　Robert Rich, Second Earl of Warwick, portrait by Anthony van Dyke, 1632–41. Image copyright: The Metropolitan Museum of Art. Image Source: Art Resource, NY.

of theological importance such as witchcraft. Thus, their alma mater ended up serving as a veritable academy of defense against the dark arts.[37]

Ordinary folk also transported beliefs about occult crime and how to combat it across the Atlantic. A high proportion of New England's colonists came from southeastern England, a region with a long history of witch-hunting that became the epicenter of the nation's largest witch scare in the mid-1640s. Moreover, widespread literacy among Puritans supported communication networks able to carry news and writings on witch hunts. The forced overseas migration of thousands of prisoners of war in 1650 and 1651 after England crushed Scottish resistance to Parliamentarian rule also helped spread witch fears throughout the empire. These involuntary colonists came from a country that possessed a deadly history of witch-hunting, and hundreds of them ended up in Massachusetts, Bermuda, and other colonies that experienced a wave of witch prosecutions in the 1650s. John Stewart, one of the Scottish prisoners of war sent to the Americas, was in Springfield, Massachusetts, during the witchcraft trials of Hugh and Mary Parsons. In addition, indentured servants Hugh Dudley, Edward Foster, and James Wells arrived in the town in 1650 and may have had a similar provenance. Though none of these men gave testimony against the Parsons, they may have participated in their trials in less obvious ways. At the minimum, they would have had a rich store of occult lore with which to help fuel witch fears in the community. In Bermuda the links between witch-hunting and the Scottish diaspora are more transparent. When John Middleton stood trial for witchcraft there in 1653, the main witness against him was John MacKeraton, a Scots prisoner from the Battle of Worcester.[38]

Regardless of how information about witchcraft circulated, the 1640s and 1650s was a tumultuous time for the English Atlantic and provided ideal conditions for witch-hunting to take root. The English Civil War, which started in 1642, brought a decade of instability and destruction that directly contributed to the outbreak of the East Anglian hunt of 1645–47. The disruption of regular judicial institutions combined with wartime tensions to ignite the massive panic. In keeping with the hypothesis that witch-hunting and other forms of human conflict did not usually occupy the same space, the witch panic took place during a pause in military conflict. Besides the role it played in triggering specific episodes of witch-hunting, the Civil War served to bring witchcraft back into public focus. With a wartime breakdown of censorship, English presses produced a torrent of publications on the occult. Moreover, Parliamentarian polemicists took to associating the Royalist cause with black magic. For example, they spread the story that a dog belonging to the king's trusted lieutenant, Prince Rupert, was actually a demonic spirit and that his successes on the battlefield were the result of a diabolical allegiance.[39]

Conflict in the mother country and troubles closer to home helped trigger New England's frenzy of witch-hunting at midcentury. As members of a larger Puritan movement aligned with Parliament, the colonists were keenly aware of the military and political struggles in England. That they largely stood outside of the conflict and could only look on with anxious concern was especially conducive to the rise of witch fears, for New Englanders avoided the direct confrontations that could have diverted their attention from occult crime. In the Puritan colonies, the prospect of war with Dutch New Netherland produced a growing apprehension about the future in the early 1650s. Fighting never actually broke out, meaning that while rumors of war heightened colonists' anxieties, there was no active conflict to distract them from setting their sights on suspected witches. The colonists also dealt with a number of other collective misfortunes at this time. In 1647, the same year that they hanged their first witch, New England experienced a deadly bout of epidemic disease; and a life-threatening illness again ran its course through the region in 1650. In both the Old World and the New, epidemics set the stage for witch fears and witch-hunting.[40]

A transatlantic campaign of godly reform was another factor that helped to trigger New England's deadly spate of witch prosecutions. Across Europe, the Reformation and Counter-Reformation ignited a drive to promote public piety and punish those who failed to fall in line. The impulse toward godly reform was not the property of any one denomination but marked both the Catholic Church and various Protestant sects. It fueled witch-hunting by creating an atmosphere in which behaviors once perceived as only antisocial or criminal became seen as immoral and even diabolical. Pious reformers saw sinners not just as failed Christians, but enemies of God who were apt to join Satan's ranks. By the seventeenth century, the confluence of godly reform and witch-hunting had taken root in the British Isles. Scotland's hardline Calvinist Covenanters who held sway over the land in the 1640s played a major role in sparking the decade's large-scale witch hunts. South of the border, militant Puritanism helped to stoke the witch panic that spread across East Anglia. Indeed, this same region had been the focus of the Puritan iconoclast William Dowsing who went around to parish churches smashing statues, breaking stain-glass windows, and destroying anything that even hinted of Papist imagery. This idol hunter thus paved the way for the witch hunters Matthew Hopkins and John Stearne.[41]

Religious reformers extended their campaign of moral discipline across the English Atlantic. Colonies controlled or dominated by Puritans—such as Bermuda and those in New England—proved fertile ground for these efforts and were the same places that experienced the highest levels of witch-hunting in the 1650s. The arrival of godly reform in New England took on concrete form when ministers from Massachusetts and Connecticut drew up the Cambridge Platform of 1648. It mostly dealt with church governance but also stressed that it was the duty of civil officials to maintain public morality by punishing religious crimes such as heresy, blasphemy, and of course witchcraft.[42]

Pause, 1657–61

Anne Hibbins's 1656 witchcraft trial marked the end of New England's witch-hanging spree and the start of a new phase of moderation in the prosecution of occult crime. Anne and her husband, William, settled in Boston in the early 1630s. Mr. Hibbins was a prominent merchant who served as a deputy to the Massachusetts General Court in 1641–42 and then as a higher-ranking assistant from 1643 to 1654. As the wife of a member of the colony's elite, Anne Hibbins earned the honorific "Mrs." at a time when people reserved it for women of rank. She appears to have been a quarrelsome and controversial person—so much so that the Boston church she belonged to excommunicated her in 1641. Mrs. Hibbins's husband died in 1654, and the following year she found herself under arrest for witchcraft.[43] She stood trial and a jury found her guilty, but the presiding judges disagreed with their verdict. The case then went to Massachusetts's General Court, which served as both the colony's legislature and highest court of appeal. Under pressure from a "popular clamor" to convict Hibbins, it ended up supporting the jury's decision and sent her to the gallows. It is unclear why the justices initially challenged the jury's findings. They may have been averse to the idea of executing someone of their own rank or simply dissatisfied with the evidence. No matter what the explanation, there was some degree of foot-dragging by the government in endorsing a guilty verdict.[44]

A similar reluctance on the part of the authorities to convict suspected occult criminals characterized a string of prosecutions in the years following Hibbins's execution. Between 1657 and early 1662, Massachusetts initiated five legal actions for witchcraft but none resulted in convictions.[45] The first involved William Brown of Gloucester, who by all appearances was a contentious man constantly at odds with his neighbors. Margaret Prince was one of them, and in 1657 she testified that Brown's magical malice resulted in "her child's death and her own weakened condition," emphasizing that before her husband came into conflict with the accused, she "was as lusty [healthy] as any woman in the town." In spite of such accusations, the authorities declined to bring Brown to trial. Two years later John Godfrey made the first of several appearances before the bar for witchcraft; and as with all the instances that followed, he was acquitted. Two more witchcraft episodes occurred in Massachusetts in 1659 with similar results. Winifred and Mary Holman of Cambridge stood trial for committing acts of occult mischief but went free, as did Elizabeth Bailey of York (in present-day Maine). The following year Winifred Holman was again arrested for witchcraft, but the complaint did not result in a trial.[46]

The story was much the same in Connecticut. During the late 1650s and the opening years of the 1660s, only four witchcraft cases came before the courts and none led to a conviction. Elizabeth Garlick faced trial in Hartford in 1658 for bewitching a young woman to death. After hearing the testimony gathered against Goody Garlick, a jury found her not guilty.[47] This outcome broke Connecticut's 100 percent conviction rate for cases of occult crime and inaugurated a period during which the courts proved unwilling to send the accused to the gallows. This newfound caution was on display in three other witchcraft episodes in Saybrook. In 1659 a resident of the town whose name has been lost faced a complaint for witchcraft and came before a grand jury, but the proceedings ended there. Two years later, Nicholas and Margaret Jennings suffered arrest on the same charge. The pair went to trial and a jury found them not guilty, though they let the couple know that they were "strongly suspect."[48]

Several developments help to explain this temporary lull in guilty verdicts. First, new judicial procedures and leadership (discussed in chapter 7) helped to blunt the successful prosecution of accused witches. Second, conflicts within the Puritan colonies distracted their inhabitants from witchhunting. By the mid-1650s, Connecticut found itself in the midst of a bitter ecclesiastical dispute known as the Hartford Controversy. Although the exact nature of the disagreements that led to the conflict have been lost to time, factional conflict in the town eventually embroiled Connecticut's government as well as civil and ecclesiastical officials throughout New England. In addition, arguments over standards of church membership that resulted in the promulgation of the Half-Way Covenant in 1662 surfaced in the late 1650s and contributed to the turmoil. Massachusetts faced an additional religious challenge in the form of Quaker missionaries who started to arrive in the colony in the mid-1650s. Thus, Massachusetts authorities did not have to ferret out witches in order to stamp out heresy and focused their attention on the Quaker threat. Finally, anxieties that had helped to stoke witch fears in the late 1640s and early 1650s dissipated in the years that followed. Military conflict between England and Holland ended in 1654, removing apprehensions of an attack by New Netherland. Across the Atlantic, the English

Civil War came to a close in 1651 with a Parliamentarian victory, and by 1653 Oliver Cromwell took charge of the nation as its Lord Protector. With peace restored and the reins of power in the hands of the Protectorate's pro-Puritan regime, New Englanders could rest easy.[49]

Panic, 1662–64

This drought of witchcraft convictions was only temporary, and from 1662 to 1664 the pendulum swung in the other direction, largely as a result of the Hartford witch panic. Of the seventeen witchcraft cases during these years, only three were not related to events in Hartford. In 1664 rumors of black magic emerged against Mary Hall of Setauket, Long Island, and it is possible that a formal complaint was entered against her though she never went to trial. In addition, John Godfrey (who was then living in Haverhill, Massachusetts) avoided conviction after being tried for witchcraft in 1662, and in the same year a woman from Portsmouth by the name of Evans suffered accusation. All told, this brief timespan produced eight trials, five convictions, and four executions related to witchcraft; and these numbers would have probably been higher if not for the fact that several of those accused during the Hartford panic fled in order to escape judgment. The Hartford episode also featured something that had not happened since the early 1650s: a suspect admitted to being a witch, providing one of only a handful of such confessions in New England before the Salem witch hunt.[50]

The Hartford crisis began when eight-year-old Elizabeth Kelly suddenly fell ill in March 1662 and died within a few days. During her rapid decline, Elizabeth complained that a near neighbor, Judith Ayers, had bewitched her. The girl's claim raised suspicions against Goody Ayres, and they grew when an autopsy found evidence that the child's death was supernatural. Sometime thereafter, a young woman by the name of Anne Cole began to suffer from a strange affliction. Hartford residents came to believe that she was a victim of witchcraft, and in the midst of her fits, Cole started to name her alleged tormentors. Soon the list of suspects grew and a mass witch hunt was in the making. Arrests, trials, and hangings began in the wake of Elizabeth Kelly's death and Anne Cole's diagnosis of bewitchment. One of the accused, Rebecca Greensmith, helped to stoke the panic when she confessed and identified her husband and others as fellow witches. In the end, four people went to the gallows, and three other suspects (Judith Ayers, her husband, and James Wakeley) fled Connecticut rather than risk a similar fate. The other individuals caught up in the panic were either acquitted or never came to trial.[51]

Though the Hartford witch panic came to a halt in 1663, the episode's aftershocks continued to be felt, and several people implicated during the crisis came before the courts for witchcraft in the years that followed. James Wakeley, who had returned to Connecticut after the dust had settled from the Hartford hunt, faced another complaint for witchcraft in 1665 and again fled the colony. In the same year, those who believed that Elizabeth Seager was a witch made another attempt at bringing her to justice. She stood trial and the jury came back with a guilty verdict, but to her accusers' disappointment Seager again escaped execution when Connecticut officials overturned her conviction.[52]

The years marked by the Hartford panic stand in contrast to the period of witch-hunting restraint that preceded them and have more in common with the aggressive prosecution of occult crime that characterized the late 1640s and early 1650s. About half of the witchcraft complaints made between 1662 and 1665 led to trials, more than half of these proceedings ended in convictions, and all but one guilty verdict resulted in an execution. In contrast, the dozen complaints entered between 1656 and 1661 failed to produce a conviction. There are also differences in the two peaks of prosecution. The first was more intense in terms of the proportion of the accused who were tried, convicted, and executed. In addition, witch-hunting between 1662 and 1665 was far more concentrated in time and space than was the case between 1647 and 1656. Indeed, Massachusetts and the other New England colonies did not experience any upsurge in witch-hunting in the 1660s—it was a phenomenon limited to Connecticut.[53]

Once again, fully understanding this phase of witch-hunting requires a look at events across the Puritan colonies and the larger English Atlantic. Why witch prosecutions returned with a vengeance in Connecticut likely has much to do with the fact that the Hartford Controversy, which had consumed local attention in the late 1650s, came to an end by 1660. The subsequent quiet provided an opportunity for folk to turn their attention to witchcraft. Moreover, the guilt and anger that doubtlessly lingered in the dispute's wake provided an atmosphere conducive to witch prosecutions. Hartford residents may have turned to witch-hunting as a form of catharsis and community building—as a project over which neighbors could join together to visibly expel evil from their midst.[54]

Events back in England also served to reignite anxieties among Puritan colonists that found release in witch-hunting. The stability that had settled over the English Atlantic under the Protectorate began to unravel at the end of the 1650s. Oliver Cromwell died in 1658, sparking a period of political instability brought to a close by the restoration of the Stuart monarchy under Charles II in 1660. Doubtlessly most Puritans believed that this cure was worse than the disease, for the son of Charles I—the king who Puritan-aligned Parliamentarians had executed—sat on the throne. When news of the Restoration reached New England in the summer of 1660, many feared that the new political order would spell their doom. The wave of Puritan refugees who fled England after the resumption of monarchical rule did little to allay such concerns. As it turned out, the prospect of renewed Stuart rule was worse than the reality. Charles II never seriously cracked down on New England, and some of its colonies came out quite well under the new regime. In 1661 Connecticut governor John Winthrop Jr. traveled to England in order to lobby for a new charter for the colony and by 1662 had succeeded in obtaining one that exceeded all expectations. The big loser in Restoration-era New England was the New Haven colony, which lost its political independence when Connecticut, armed with its new charger, absorbed it the mid-1660s.[55]

The dissolution of the Protectorate and restoration of the monarchy brought plenty of worry to New England but never resulted (with the exception of the feud that erupted between Connecticut and New Haven officials over the former colony's takeover of the latter) in the sorts of conflict that would have served to divert the colonists from prosecuting witches. Moreover, like a providential sign of God's displeasure, the return of the Stuart dynasty triggered widespread social unease conducive to witch fears and helped set the stage for the Hartford panic.

Decline, 1665–70

The final phase of witch-hunting in New England before 1670 started in the mid-1660s. Its most defining traits were a sharp decline in convictions and the absence of executions. During this period eleven complaints were filed, between five and seven trials (the records are unclear) occurred, resulting in only one conviction. Katherine Harrison of Wethersfield, who stood trial in 1668, was the only defendant found guilty. However, upon a review of her case that dragged into 1670, Connecticut suspended Harrison's death sentence and banished her from the colony. An unwillingness to condemn the accused, so clearly on display during the proceedings against Harrison, increasingly characterized court officials' attitudes toward witch-hunting.[56]

The case of John Brown further illustrates magistrates' growing caution when it came to cases of occult crime. Born to a respectable family in the town of New Haven (now under Connecticut's jurisdiction), as a young man Brown engaged in disrespectable behavior and had repeated run-ins with the law. Things took a more serious turn in January 1665 when several witnesses accused Brown of trying to raise the Devil, and Brown should have found himself on a fast track to trial. Yet the justices who conducted Brown's initial examination accepted his explanation that he had acted in jest and put off a decision on whether he should go before a grand jury till a future session. The court's response to Brown's case was hardly one of vigorous action; indeed, the magistrates eventually dropped their investigation altogether. In sum, while his father's reputation may have helped to shield Brown from legal jeopardy, his treatment was also indicative of a broader change in attitude toward witch prosecutions.[57]

Other witchcraft cases between 1665 and 1669 demonstrate this same pattern of judicial restraint. In 1665 a woman from Cambridge by the name of Gleason became the target of a witchcraft complaint, but legal proceedings ended when a grand jury failed to endorse the charge. The other five Massachusetts cases from these years followed a similar path. During the winter of 1665–66 that perennial witchcraft suspect John Godfrey went through another round of arrest, indictment, trial, and acquittal. Furthermore, Thomas Welles, Jane Walford, Robert Williams, and Susannah Martin faced charges of occult crime in 1669. The case against Welles never got past his initial examination and such may also have been the case for Walford. Williams ended up going before a grand jury and facing trial but was acquitted. Susannah Martin also faced a grand jury, but what happened after this point is not certain. If she went to trial, then the court almost certainly acquitted her, for she was again arrested for witchcraft during the Salem crisis of 1692. Unfortunately for Martin, her luck then ran out and she ended up going to the gallows.[58]

Besides John Brown and Katherine Harrison, Connecticut only initiated legal action against one other witch suspect in the second half of the 1660s, and the case never went to trial. In 1667 William Graves of Stamford fell under suspicion after being accused of murdering his married daughter, Abigail Dibble, through occult means. Local authorities arrested Graves and collected testimony against him but eventually dropped the charge.[59] An action for slander brought forward in 1667 also highlights the colony's turn away from witch-hunting. Matthew Griswold sued John Tilleston for defaming his wife, Hannah, claiming that Tilleston had used "expressions tending to lay the said Matthews wife under the suspicion of witchcraft." The court seemed to exhibit little interest in finding out if Tilleston's accusation was true and ruled in the plaintiff's favor. Rather, its biggest concern was that Tilleston was too poor to provide Griswold with appropriate compensation.[60]

On one level, this decline in witch-hunting can be attributed to the same dynamics that inhibited prosecutions between 1656 and 1662. Conflicts emerged that consumed the time and effort New Englanders would have otherwise been able to devote to finding witches. The return of religious controversy to Hartford, Wethersfield, and other towns so recently engaged in rooting out occult criminals was one reason Connecticut saw levels of legal action related to witchcraft drop precipitously by mid-decade. After a brief pause from discord in the early 1660s, the colony fell once again into the abyss of ecclesiastical conflict. The trouble started when two Hartford ministers, the Reverends John Whiting and Joseph Haynes, fell out over the merits of a Congregational versus a Presbyterian church polity. This dispute was not limited to the town, and the Congregational-Presbyterian rivalry roiled congregations throughout New England. Conflict also returned in the form of the Second Anglo-Dutch War. Fought between 1665 and 1667, it preoccupied the Puritan colonies and, unlike the first round of conflict in the early 1650s, actually resulted in fighting that culminated in the English conquest of Dutch New Netherland. Finally, tensions between the colonists and the restored English monarchy finally took on concrete form in 1664 when Charles II sent a team of royal commissioners to New England to formulate recommendations for promoting royal authority over the region. In the presence of these imperial interlopers, the colonists had to mind their manners. This included avoiding the excesses of witch-hunting.[61]

Legal reforms that first took shape in England and then made their way across the Atlantic also dampened witch-hunting in the Puritan colonies. In the wake of the East Anglian witch panic of 1645–47 and Kent's Maidstone hunt of 1652, English jurists began to take a stand against what they saw as the dangerously flawed process by which courts determined innocence or guilt in cases of occult crime. For example, in 1653 Sir Robert Filmer published *An Advertisement to the Jurymen of England, Touching Witches*, in direct response to the deadly Maidstone trials. Filmer discredited many of the standing methods for detecting witches and set a high bar in terms of the evidence needed to achieve a conviction. In response to this rising tide of judicial skepticism, witch prosecutions declined in England. For instance, after dealing with more than 130 witchcraft cases in the 1640s and 1650s, the Home Circuit Assizes only encountered fifty during the remaining four decades of the seventeenth century. By the mid-1660s many of these legal reforms had filtered into New England and a new generation of colonial leaders applied them in the courtroom.[62]

Witch fears and prosecutions came to the surface in New England by 1640 and waxed and waned in intensity over the three decades that followed. After a couple of isolated cases in the late 1630s, the Puritan colonies' campaign against black magic intensified between the late 1640s and early 1650s when legal actions against witch suspects dramatically increased and a high proportion ended in convictions and executions. After a brief downturn in the momentum of prosecutions starting in the mid-1650s, the course of witch-hunting again took a turn in 1662 with the outbreak of the Hartford witch panic, which produced a wave of arrests, trials, and executions. After the mid-1660s witch prosecutions again slowed down and largely came to a halt by decade's end. Importantly, these ups and downs in New England's history of witch-hunting were not only shaped by local conditions within the Puritan colonies but by events that reverberated across the English empire during the middle decades of the seventeenth century.

While establishing this periodization is an essential first step to understanding the history of occult crime in the Puritan colonies and its ties to the broader English Atlantic, it is important to look beyond a chronology of events and gain a deeper understanding of the social dynamics of witchcraft. One critical issue is how New Englanders understood occult crime and if their views on the matter were unified.

CHAPTER 2

"Being Instigated by the Devil"

The Crime of Witchcraft

In the spring of 1658, Elizabeth Garlick traveled from her home in Easthampton, Long Island (which was under Connecticut's jurisdiction at the time), to stand trial in Hartford for witchcraft. After hearing testimony, the jury reached a verdict of not guilty, and the court duly released her from custody. Her husband, however, had to enter a bond of thirty pounds to ensure that he and his wife would "carry good behavior to all the members of this jurisdiction" and appear before the next court held at Easthampton, so it could confirm that Goody Garlick had not been a source of disorder. Eight years later in March 1666, John Godfrey was prosecuted for occult crime in Massachusetts, it being the third time he faced the charge. The court found him "suspiciously guilty of witchcraft but not legally guilty according to the law" and, as with his previous cases, he went free.[1]

These two events illustrate New Englanders' understandings of witchcraft. The one thing all the colonists agreed on was that it was a crime, a view rooted in English law and culture. Just as important to the Puritans, the Bible condemned the sin of witchcraft. Among other passages, "Thou shalt not suffer a witch to live" (Exodus 22:18) indicated that it was a serious infraction. Beyond this point, however, consensus was more elusive and two perspectives on occult crime competed in peoples' minds. The first focused on witchcraft as *maleficium*, a Latin term referring to injury or harm committed through magical means. This outlook dominated the views of ordinary folk who tended to be most concerned with the immediate threat that witches posed to their lives and livelihood. The second emphasized not what witches did with their powers but where they got them from in the first place. This diabolical construct of the witch held that they obtained their malevolent abilities from the Devil and that all magic was ultimately demonic in nature. New England's clergy and the civil officials who enforced its biblically inspired laws promoted this view. Under this formulation, witchcraft was not just an offense against humankind but a betrayal of God, and the witch was both a criminal and a heretic.[2]

The trials of Elizabeth Garlick and John Godfrey reflect both the malefic and diabolical concepts of witchcraft. Evoking diabolism's religiously charged view of the crime, Connecticut authorities accused Garlick of "familiarity with Satan the great enemy of God & mankind," while Massachusetts officials prosecuted Godfrey for communing with a demonic "familiar spirit." Drawing on the view of the witch as an agent of magical misdeeds, Godfrey's indictment states that he had "done much hurt & mischief by several acts of witchcraft to the bodies and goods of several persons" and Garlick's accused her of performing "works above the course of nature to the loss of lives of several persons."[3] This blending of views also appears in witness testimony. Several of Goody Garlick's accusers claimed that she employed black magic to harm people and livestock. Likewise, John Remington Sr. deposed that John Godfrey used his malefic powers to seriously injure his son.[4] Mixed in with these allegations of magical mayhem are references to diabolical witchcraft. Samuel Parsons and others recalled that Elizabeth Howell, one of Goody Garlick's supposed victims, saw a demonic creature at the foot of her bed. Moreover, Charles Brown testified that Godfrey once said that if witches were not "kindly entertained the devil will appear unto them and ask them if they were grieved or vexed with anybody."[5]

These and other witchcraft episodes in early New England show that its inhabitants blended together the two understandings of occult crime. While the diabolical concept of witchcraft was very much the preserve of the educated elite and common folk tended to focus their attention on the magical harm at the center of its malefic conception, this does not mean that these outlooks were incompatible or that one social class rejected the beliefs of the other. Rather, both views coexisted in the minds of New Englanders of all ranks.[6]

The Malefic Witch

The act of harm lies at the heart of the malefic construct of witchcraft. Accordingly, witches were not just evil persons but *evildoers* spewing out injury to those around them. The notion that someone could cause injury to others through occult means has deep roots in Western culture. In Roman law, the term *maleficium,* which literally means "an evil deed" or "wickedness," originally referred to ordinary criminal mischief. However, it eventually changed into a reference for harmful magic, and by the high Middle Ages this newer meaning held sway across Europe. England fully shared in these developments, and by the early modern era this idea of the witch was second nature to its inhabitants.[7] When Puritan colonists came to the New World, they brought the image of the malefic witch along with them, and in blaming misfortunes large and small on black magic, they kept company with most early modern Europeans.

Illness and death, the meat and drink of maleficium, were the most common harms attributed to witchcraft. Out of the witch prosecutions that took place in New England before 1670, it is possible to identify the sorts of injury blamed on the accused in twenty-eight of them. The vast majority of these cases (twenty-four) saw defendants charged with having used black magic to sicken or kill someone. Maladies attributed to harmful magic were sometimes indistinguishable from more run-of-the-mill illnesses, and learned treatises on witchcraft frequently discussed ways to distinguish between natural and supernatural ailments.[8] Elizabeth Howell's alleged bewitchment started out innocently enough, and at first she just suffered from a headache. Likewise, a supposed magical assault on eight-year-old Elizabeth Kelly began with her simply complaining of a stomachache. Nothing seemed alarming about the girl's condition, and her parents thought her well enough to attend church that afternoon.[9]

More often, ailments attributed to witchcraft exhibited clearer indications of occult origin. A letter from New Haven physician Nicholas Auger concerning witchcraft accusations made against Elizabeth Godman in 1653 provides insight into the types of situations that led people to see an illness as a product of a supernatural attack. In it he recounted the cases of three women who blamed their maladies on the suspect, writing "the disease which with these women were taken to me was and still is very dubious, not so much in respect of the fit and manner of taking them as . . . in their cure, which to me is as strange and more strange than the fits themselves." The doctor explained that all of his attempts to treat the women's sufferings failed; but when the authorities took Godman into custody, "their fits left them, and they never were troubled with them since." To Auger, this indicated that Godman had caused the illness and that her apprehension brought it to a close.[10]

Like Doctor Augur, English folk commonly associated unusual "fits" with occult ailments. A piece of testimony concerning the alleged bewitchment of a Mrs. Bishop characterized her as suffering a "sore fit," while reports concerning two other supposed victims of black magic described them as experiencing "raging" and "strange" fits. The physician Philip Reed also drew a connection between Sara Townsend's "unnatural fits" and witchcraft. Sometimes New Englanders provided more details concerning the extraordinary symptoms attributed to supernatural illness. Ann Smith attended Abigail Dibble at the time of her strange affliction and death and recounted how the deceased complained of being "so bitten" on her back and elsewhere that "she could not lie still." Another witness, Mary Schofield, was horrified to see Dibble's "lips turning black and her eyes staring out in a ghastly manner," while Thomas Steadwell recalled that the dying woman's tongue flared "out of her mouth near a handful long and about as thick as his wrist and as black as possible might be." Likewise, during the illness that led to Elizabeth Howell's death, one of attendants allegedly pulled a pin from her mouth while she was in the midst of a fit. All those present agreed that the sick woman's mouth had previously been empty and concluded that the pin's sudden appearance pointed to witchcraft.[11]

Illnesses that came on suddenly or involved the sick describing attacks by invisible specters also drew suspicion. Rebecca Smith complained of "being suddenly taken her thigh and leg being stiff like a stick, and dreadful sick, having strange fits in so much that . . . she thought or doubted that some evil person had bewitched her." A vision of three spectral snakes marked Jonathan Taylor's unusual affliction and contributed to a diagnosis of witchcraft. Likewise, John Stebbing testified that his wife saw Hugh Parsons's specter sitting on a pole in the chimney corner during "one of her fits"; and before her death, Elizabeth Howell claimed that Elizabeth Garlick stood by "the bed side ready to pull me in pieces." In both cases, witnesses could not see the figures of which the two women spoke and took it as a sign that dark forces were at play.[12]

The physical harm supposedly inflicted by witches frequently led to a victim's death. When Nicholas and Margaret Jennings stood trial for witchcraft in 1661, they faced the charge of having caused the "loss of ye lives of several persons and in particular ye wife of Reynold Marvin with the child of Balthazar de Wolfe." Likewise, people attributed the deaths of the aforementioned Elizabeth Howell and Abigail Dibble to occult attacks.[13] Maybe the strangest allegation of death by witchcraft came in Windsor in 1654. In that year authorities arrested Lydia Gilbert for using malefic magic to kill Henry Stiles. He had died three years earlier on a militia training day when Thomas Allyn accidentally shot him. By the time Gilbert came to trial, the view of who was responsible for Stiles's death had changed, and she was charged with having used witchcraft to cause the shooting.[14]

New Englanders believed that witches' efforts to spread illness and death commonly targeted the young. Springfield residents held Hugh Parsons responsible for the sufferings of Reverend George Moxon's children, while residents of New Haven blamed Elizabeth Godman for causing a number of young people to sicken and suffer. Reverend William Hooke testified that when his son fell ill "in a very strange manner," he looked on Godman "as a malicious one." Elizabeth Garlick was another witch suspect associated with harm to the young. Goodwives Edwards and Davis blamed Garlick for causing their children to fall ill, while additional witnesses attributed the death of two other children to her malignant power. Similarly, in 1662 folk from Hartford became convinced that black magic took the life of eight-year-old Elizabeth Kelly, and Ralph and Mary Hall faced charges of occult crime a few years later for, among other things, allegedly causing the death of an infant.[15]

Allegations of malefic assaults on livestock were another common feature of witchcraft cases in the Puritan colonies. For instance, Elizabeth Godman's neighbors suspected her of occult attacks on their animals. Goodwife Thorp complained that the accused had bewitched one of her chickens to death. Having heard that animals killed by witchcraft "would consume within," Thorpe opened up the dead bird and found that "it was consumed in the gizzard to water and worms," confirming her fears that occult forces were at play. She also claimed that several of her cows were victims of Godman's malevolence, citing the strange nature of their illness as proof that "there was something more than ordinary in it." Allen Ball also came to believe that he was one of Godman's victims after several of his pigs died under suspicious circumstances. People similarly associated John Godfrey with magical attacks on livestock, perhaps because his vocation as a cowherd kept him in constant contact with them. In the mid-1650s, Henry Palmer blamed the mysterious disappearance of several cattle on Godfrey, while Elizabeth Whitaker told of "strange losses in our swine and cows and calves" which she attributed to his malicious power. Likewise, Elizabeth Ayres recounted that soon after Godfrey called one of her calves a "poor rascal" it died, even though it had previously shown no sign of illness.[16]

New Englanders also periodically blamed witches for setbacks in domestic production. In testimony she presented against Elizabeth Seager, Margaret Garrett spoke of how she had "made a cheese better than ordinary," but when she fetched it she discovered that one "side of the cheese [was] full of maggots." Seeing no natural explanation for it, Garrett blamed the uncanny spoilage on black magic. Likewise, Joan Francis recalled how a barrel of beer she had brewed suddenly exploded, and its "head and hoops flew to the end of the hall, and gave such a report [noise] as scared or feared the children." As with Goody Garrett, Francis considered the strange mishap an act of witch-craft. The family of Reverend William Hooke also told a story involving bewitched beer. One evening the Hookes refused to draw some fresh ale for Elizabeth Godman, and the next morning they found that it was "hot, sour, and ill tasted" though it was "good and fresh" just the night before. Stranger still, the barrel holding the beer was hot, "and when they opened the bung it steamed forth."[17]

In addition, the colonists believed that witches interfered with people's ability to perform ordinary tasks. In his testimony against witch suspect James Wakeley, tailor Thomas Bracy recalled that he attempted to make a jacket and pair of breeches following an argument with the accused. Bracy described how he "labored to his best understandings to set on the sleeves aright on the jacket and seven times he placed the sleeves wrong," and that when he went "to cut out the breeches, having two pieces of cloth of dif-ferent colors, he was so bemoidered [confused] in that matter, that he cut the breeches one of one color, and other of another color." To Bracy, only occult forces could account for such incompetence. Similarly, when Goody Hannum discovered that yarn she had spun for Mary (Bliss) Parsons was defective, she agreed to spin more to replace it. However, no matter how she tried, she could not spin good yarn for Goody Parsons and concluded that the woman had hexed her. Sometimes this brand of maleficium manifested itself as a temporary loss of the ability to move or speak. For instance, John Welles related that once when he went out looking for his family's cows, he walked "half way across the street and could go no further my legs were bound to me." He then saw Katherine Harrison "rise up from a cow that was none of her own with a pail in her hand and made haste home." Once she was gone, Welles claimed that he "was loosed," implying that Harrison had caused his paralysis in order to make good her escape after stealing milk.[18]

Popular lore also held that witches used their powers to trespass on peo-ple's private thoughts and conversations. Governor John Winthrop's sum-mary of the case against Margaret Jones mentions that she could tell of "secret speeches" that "she had no ordinary means to come to the knowl-edge of." Likewise, Mary Parsons claimed that her husband, Hugh, was a witch because when she said "anything to anybody, never so secretly, to such friends as I am sure would not speak of it, yet he would come to know it, by what means I cannot tell." Suspicions against Eunice Cole partially rested on the belief that she could eavesdrop on people's conversations through occult means. Goodwife Mary Coleman testified that Cole knew "of some words that were spoke betwixt this deponent and her husband in their own house in private and Goody Cole did repeat the words to this deponent that she and her husband spoke together." Coleman asserted that there was no normal explanation for Cole's knowledge, seeing that she and her husband had not mentioned the conversation to anyone.[19]

According to her many accusers, Elizabeth Godman specialized in this sort of malevolent divination. They wondered how Godman knew that Mr. Stephen Goodyear had fallen "into a swooning fit" after he had spoken against her, even though she was not present when it happened. Similarly, Jane Hooke claimed that Godman, despite that she rarely attended services, "could tell sundry things that was done at the church meeting before meeting was done," and Mary Atwater testified that the accused knew that she had some figs even though they were hidden in her pocket.[20]

New Englanders sometimes saw random accidents and injuries as products of malefic magic. When John Remington Jr's horse fell on him, injuring his leg, he blamed it on that perennial witch suspect, John Godfrey. In a similar episode, after Sarah Bridgeman's eleven-year-old son fell while out looking for their cattle and "put his knee out of joint," she linked the mishap to black magic. Sometimes the misfortune laid at the feet of witchcraft was not so personal in nature. For instance, Massachusetts governor John Winthrop recalled that a ship laying at anchor off Charlestown in calm weather "fell a rolling, and continued so about twelve hours, so as . . . they feared her foundering [sinking]." The ship's troubles started after the authorities barred the witchcraft suspect Thomas Jones from leaving the colony aboard the vessel, and the craft righted itself as soon as he was jailed. The implication was that the strange episode was a product of Jones's anger over being denied a means of escape and his supernatural power to act on it.[21]

On occasion, malefic witchcraft fell short of harm to persons or property and merely resulted in weird and disturbing phenomenon. A woman included the "strong lights" she saw one night in a meadow among other acts of witchcraft allegedly committed by the widow of Thomas Marshfield. More startlingly, a Mrs. Yale related how after she had an angry exchange with Elizabeth Godman, her "things were thrown about the house in a strange manner." Testimony gathered against Katherine Harrison for her 1668 witchcraft trial contained several stories of this ilk. Philip Smith told how early one morning he heard the accused calling out "'Hoccanum, Hoccanum, come Hoccanum,'" and with an unnatural suddenness her cows came running "with great violence tail on end homewards." Harrison's alleged preternatural control over creatures extended beyond her cattle. Richard Montague reported that when "a swarm of her bees flew away over her neighbor Boreman's lot and into the great meadow and thence over the great [Connecticut] River" Harrison was quickly able to fetch them back again, concluding that she could not have used "lawful means" to retrieve them over so great a distance. In another bizarre occurrence, Thomas Bracy claimed that he saw a cart coming toward him full of hay on which "he saw perfectly a full calf's head, the ears standing pert up." A moment later, however, the head disappeared and was replaced by Katherine Harrison.[22]

According to testimony brought against him, Hugh Parsons was a sort of trickster witch who plagued his victims with minor mishaps. Anthony Dorchester recalled that he and Parsons had equal shares in a butchered cow and that Parsons desired the "root of the tongue" even though it fell to Dorchester's share. One Sabbath day the Dorchesters cooked the tongue, but when the family sat down to eat, it had mysteriously vanished. Goodman Dorchester attributed the disappearance to Hugh Parson's maleficence. Likewise, Griffin Jones told how once he could not find a knife, but after briefly attending to one of his pigs, returned to find his "three knives together on the table." Jones wondered how they suddenly appeared since he was the only one at home, and eventually pinned it on Parsons. In a similar episode, John Lombard put a trowel down just outside his door, and when he went back to retrieve it, the tool had vanished. He made a careful search, but it could not be found. Two days later, while Hugh Parsons was visiting, Lombard told him about the trowel's mysterious disappearance, upon which Parsons said, "Look, here it is." Lombard turned and saw that the tool had reappeared in the place that he had left it and concluded that "it came there by witchcraft." In a more harmful instance of supposed supernatural mischief, Thomas Cooper recalled how he, Hugh Parsons, Thomas Miller, and several other men were working together one day when Miller shared his suspicions that Parsons was a witch. Cooper said he was "much troubled in his mind because Thomas Miller spoke so plainly" and feared "some ill event should follow" at Parson's bidding. Shortly thereafter Miller suffered a cut on his leg.[23]

The harms of witchcraft in New England generally matched those reported in the Old World and elsewhere in the English Atlantic. For example, the inhabitants of Bermuda held witches responsible for making an infant fall "into strange fits," afflicting a fifty-year-old Scottish servant, causing a person to fail in their attempts to churn butter, killing pigs, and tormenting turkeys.[24] However, two sorts of witchery seen elsewhere did not generally make an appearance in the English-speaking world. Charges that witches caused crop-destroying storms or droughts were relatively common in continental Europe as was the belief that they interfered with couples' ability to conceive children. This was not true for the English Atlantic. The reason for this probably lies in the fact that England's culture of witchcraft, which powerfully shaped those of its New World colonies, rarely featured weather magic or occult attacks on sexual reproduction. Why this was the case remains a largely open question.[25]

New Englanders described what witches did but provided few clues as to how they did it. For instance, while John Gibson insisted that Winifred Holman bewitched his chickens to death, he had nothing to say about the occult techniques she used to kill them. Early modern Europeans' perception of black magic as a largely invisible crime helps explain this dearth of detail. One English legal guide noted that "the secrecy of the grounds of witchcraft" made it "one of the greatest works of darkness committed this day under the sun." While another stated that justices "may not always expect direct evidence, seeing all their [witches'] works are the works of darkness." In other words, unlike other sorts of criminal activity like murder or theft, unseen forces supposedly caused the baleful effects of witchcraft. Moreover, conventional wisdom held that occult power enabled witches to mount their attacks from an anonymous distance, meaning people could see the effects of witchcraft but not the methods used to bring them about.[26]

In spite of these silences, court testimony and learned treatises make it clear that early modern Europeans believed that witches inflicted harm though a number of specific techniques. Richard Bernard, a seventeenth-century English authority on witchcraft and witch-hunting, summarized them in *A Guide to Grand Jury Men* (1627). He wrote that witches brought about injury through their "cursing and banning, and bitter imprecations" (words), "by their looks" (gaze), and "with the hand or finger" (touch). Bernard also mentions that they employed malevolent technologies to accomplish their evil ends, explaining that witches made "pictures of wax or clay of those which they would bewitch, and either roast them, or bury them, that as they consume, so will the parties." Much akin to poisoning, he additionally spoke of witches causing harm by introducing "enchanted powder, ointment, herbs" or food into a victim's body.[27]

Curses and maledictions, or what the demonologist John Gaule referred to as "hollow muttering or mumbling," was the most common way New England's witches caused injury. Like Gaule, Puritan colonists associated low-spoken utterances with witchcraft, and several of those who stood witness against Elizabeth Godman noted her habit of "talking and muttering to herself." For instance, Reverend William Hooke claimed that Godman "went away in a muttering discontented manner" shortly before she allegedly bewitched his beer.[28] Sometimes witnesses gave a better sense of the words that passed suspects' lips. Susannah Trimmings recalled that when she refused to lend an object to Jane Walford, the accused witch retorted

"That my sorrow was great already, and it should be greater." Not long after, Susannah felt a burning pain in her back. According to Thomas Philbrick, Eunice Cole raged that if his calves "did eat any of her grass she wished it might poison them or choke them." One of his calves later disappeared and a second sickened and died. As these examples make clear, the distinction between a malefic curse and the sorts of threatening words people spoke when angry was a fine one, and the determining factor in whether folk perceived an utterance as an actual malediction was not the words themselves, but if some misfortune followed in their wake or the person who spoke them was a reputed witch.[29]

New Englanders were not alone in associating words with witchcraft, and people throughout the English Atlantic commonly connected the two. This was certainly the case in Bermuda. Jean Gardiner went to the gallows after the colony found her guilty of witchcraft for saying "that she would cramp Tomasin a mulatto woman" and using "many other threatening words tending to the hurt and injury of the said mulatto woman." Another accused witch, Elizabeth Middleton, came before a Bermuda court for having used "many cursed speeches against a young child age 9 months" who then fell into fits. Likewise, Martha Franklin stood trial there in 1672 after "speaking dangerous words which causes her to be suspected of witchcraft."[30]

According to both learned authorities and common folk, witches also worked their dark magic by looking at or touching their victims. John Gaule asserted that purveyors of black magic could inflict injury "by inspecting, or looking on, but to glare, or squint, or peep at with an envious and evil eye." Evoking popular wisdom on the subject, John Puddington's testimony against Jane Walford makes clear the association between misfortune and a witch's gaze. At one point he stated that the accused "did overlook the cattle, which is as much as to say in our country, *bewitching*." People also feared a witch's touch, believing that physical contact was another means by which they caused harm. Governor John Winthrop reported that Margaret Jones went to the gallows after "she was found to have such a malignant touch, as many persons (men, women, and children,) who she stroked or touched with any affection or displeasure . . . were taken with deafness, or vomiting, or other violent pains or sickness." Similarly, a woman recalled that one of her calves died after John Godfrey had "stroked" the animal. Goody Davis likewise tied the death of one of her children to Elizabeth Garlick's touch.[31]

The threat posed by a witch's touch or glance explains why an individual's unwarranted appearance in other people's homes could arouse suspicion. Many English witch-hunting guides counted a habit of intruding into others' dwellings among the signs that a person was a witch. For instance, Richard

Bernard wrote that someone's "over-inquisitiveness" about another person's well-being or their "coming to visit him or her unsent for, especially after they be forbidden the house" were grounds for investigation. This line of thinking lay behind Mr. John Robbins's belief that Katherine Palmer had bewitched his wife, for he reported that he had "2 or 3 times forewarned the said Palmer not to come to his house, yet nevertheless the said Palmer would thrust herself into the company." In light of this, one of the preventative measures a person could take against witches was simply to keep them at a distance. Thus, when Goody Simmons suffered from a mysterious illness, she declared that "she would not have Goody Garlick or Goody Edwards come near her" out of fear they were witches.[32]

New Englanders also sought to keep witches at arms-length so that they could protect themselves from the insertion of bewitched items or substances into their homes and bodies. John Gaule addressed this method of occult attack, warning that evildoers "work their bewitchings. . . . by leaving something of theirs in your house." Thus, not only did Goody Simmons refuse to have Elizabeth Garlick enter her home, she burned some dockweed that the suspected witch had sent to treat her illness. Similarly, suspicion grew against Winifred Holman after she offered some herbs to help Rebecca Stearns's "strange fits." Not only did the latter woman's condition worsen, but her child grew ill. Edibles could also become suspect under the right conditions. Around the time that suspicions of witchcraft first cast their shadow over Elizabeth Seager, she sent her daughter with a "mess of parsnips" to the Hosmer family. Goodman Hosmer refused the gift and "bid the child carry the parsnips home again" for fear that "he should be brought in her craft." Folk also believed that witches employed everyday objects to spread their afflictions. Jonathan Gilbert's wife, for example, complained of pain after wearing a black cap that she had previously lent to Katherine Harrison, a woman with a reputation for occult powers.[33]

In addition, folk throughout the English Atlantic believed that witches created images of those they wished to target or obtained objects belonging to them in order to inflict injury. John Gaule wrote that witches carried out their evil intentions "by getting something of yours into their house," while Michael Dalton's legal guide, *The Country Justice* (1618), states that witches fashioned "pictures of clay or wax . . . made of such as they would bewitch." The belief was that those skilled in the occult could transform a representation of a person or one of their possessions into a magical conduit through which they could deliver harm. Such tools of witchcraft were rarely if ever found, for as with every aspect of black magic, people believed that its practitioners kept them secret. Moreover, this type of magic was easy to hide.

Whereas causing mischief through a look, touch, or the introduction of malevolent substances required close physical proximity, image magic was difficult to detect since it could operate from afar. Nevertheless, references to this method do periodically come to the surface. In his testimony against Winifred and Mary Holman, John Gibson observed that:

> when my daughter was not very well my wife went out and saw Mary Holman sitting on her knees at a hole of water. She took up the water in a dish and held it up a pretty hight and drained [it] into another thing. My wife went presently to her daughter and found her crying so immoderately that the tears fell so fast from her eyes that my wife was fain to stand and wipe them off her face with her apron and her mother asked her wherefore she cried and she said she could not tell but she said she could not forebear.

Here Gibson implied that Mary Holman's actions with the water and dish were directly responsible for the girl's fit of weeping.[34]

The Diabolical Witch

Diabolism also cast its shadow over early New England. This concept focused, not on witches' power to harm but the source of that power, asserting that they obtained their malevolent abilities through a pact with the Devil. According to this outlook, witchcraft was both a civil and religious crime, for its practitioners not only posed a threat to their neighbors' well-being but committed apostasy by renouncing God and casting their lot with Satan.[35]

The roots of the diabolical witch do not go as deep as the malefic version, and this view only fully came into focus in Europe in the fifteenth century. At this time, Catholic clergymen published a number of works that promoted a demonic view of occult crime, including Johannes Nider's *Formicarius* (1438) and the infamous *Malleus Maleficarum* (1486), which translates to "hammer of the witches," by Heinrich Kramer and Jacob Sprenger. Treatises followed in the sixteenth and seventeenth centuries that elaborated on the idea of demonic witchcraft. With the use of judicial torture, officials in continental Europe were able to illicit confessions that bore out their diabolical vision of black magic. The most sensational accounts described black Masses in grotesque detail, including the ritual murder and consumption of infants as well as wild orgies involving witches and demons.[36] For Europe's common folk maleficium remained their primary concern, but they increasingly became aware of the diabolical view of witchcraft due to the efforts of the church and state.

Though diabolism became the official view of witchcraft across much of mainland Europe by the sixteenth century, it emerged more slowly in England. There, theologians and jurists only introduced the concept to their countrymen in the late 1500s, and it did not make much headway among the populace until the seventeenth. England's witchcraft laws reflect this process. The acts of 1542 and 1563 focused on maleficium and contain no references to a pact with Satan or other aspects of diabolism. Only the statute of 1604 broached a demonic view of the crime when it made it a punishable offense to "covenant, or entertain, employ, feed, or reward any evil and wicked spirit." At no point, however, did the law directly mention Satan as the force behind occult power. Moreover, English courts did not generally have access to torture as a means to pry out confessions that could serve to corroborate and publicize the demonic view of witchcraft. This being said, during the seventeenth century the satanic pact and other features of diabolism seeped into popular consciousness and came to the surface during legal proceedings. Witch trials at Lancaster in 1612, for example, produced testimony that featured demonic imps as well as descriptions of an event that could pass as a witches' Sabbath. By midcentury diabolical references appeared with increasingly frequency in cases of occult crime.[37]

In terms of its embrace of diabolism, New England fell somewhere between England and continental Europe. As with the mother country, witchcraft episodes in the Puritan colonies rarely featured stories of satanic pacts or witches' Sabbaths, and the few that did lacked the hair-raising descriptions of demonic orgies, baby killing, and cannibalism that characterized witch trials in mainland Europe. Nevertheless, the concept of the diabolical witch had gained some traction in England by the time that its Puritan dissidents set sail for the New World, and the concept crossed the Atlantic with them. Moreover, the Puritans' intellectual elite were invested in a demonic view of the occult. On one level they were simply in step with English writers who promoted this outlook. On another, Puritan clergy who drew heavily on continental theologians like John Calvin when formulating their religious views were more aware of ideas about witchcraft circulating around Europe than other English folk.

The Puritan colonies' legal codes reflect the influence that diabolism had on their conception of occult crime. Massachusetts's 1641 "Body of Liberties" included a law against witchcraft that Connecticut and eventually Plymouth copied: "If any man or woman be a WITCH, that is, hath or consulteth with a familiar spirit, they shall be put to death." The statute focused on the single diabolical element found in England's 1604 witchcraft act—the witch's relationship to a demonic "familiar spirit"—and made no reference to sorts

FIGURE 2.1 In an image that combines the themes of image magic and diabolism, witches bring wax dolls of their intended victims to be "baptized" by the Devil. From *The History of Witches and Wizards* (London, 1720). Courtesy of the Wellcome Collection.

of malefic harms that dominated the motherland's laws against magical mischief. In a similar vein, witchcraft indictments in New England habitually framed the offense in diabolical terms. For example, in 1651 Connecticut officials charged John and Joan Carrington with having "entertained familiarity with Satan the great enemy of God and mankind and by his help has done works above the course of nature." This evokes the core concept of diabolism: that a witch gave themselves to the Devil in exchange for supernatural power. It is also noteworthy that the Carringtons' indictments, like many in the Puritan colonies, contain no mention of specific acts of maleficium.[38]

Diabolical motifs also appear in accounts of several New England witchcraft cases. For instance, when Mary Johnson faced prosecution as a witch, she admitted to being "guilty of familiarity with the Devil." Indeed, her confession (which admittedly may have been shaped by her confessor, the Reverend Samuel Stone) hit on many of the central themes of diabolism. Mary, who was a servant, related how dissatisfaction with her lot in life led to her to covenant with Satan who, in return, provided help with her chores as well as the dark power of witchcraft. Moreover, evoking some of the more salacious testimony seen in European witch trials, Mary admitted to engaging in carnal relations with devils.[39]

There were several elements of diabolical lore that first emerged in continental Europe, passed to the British Isles, and then made their way to New England.[40] The idea that a person became a witch on entering into a pact with the Devil was one aspect of diabolism that clearly crossed the Atlantic to New England. This is not surprising seeing that it was a regular feature of learned English treatises on witchcraft. In *A Discourse of the Damned Art of Witchcraft* (1618), William Perkins wrote that "the ground of all the practices of witchcraft is a league or covenant made between the witch and the Devil wherein they do mutually bind themselves each to other." References to the satanic pact were not incidental and frequently formed a major focus of such works. For instance, the Reverends Alexander Roberts and Thomas Cooper each devoted a full chapter to it. A few of these works, including

FIGURE 2.2   Illustrating the central concept of diabolical witchcraft, the satanic pact, this image depicts the Devil cutting a woman's finger so she can sign a covenant with him in her blood. From *The History of Witches and Wizards* (London, 1720). Courtesy of the Wellcome Collection.

John Stearne's *A Confirmation and Discovery of Witchcraft* (1648), include lurid details concerning this bond with Satan—such as the assertion that witches had sex with the Devil—commonly found in continental demonologies.[41]

Scattered throughout records and accounts of New England's witchcraft cases are allusions to satanic covenants. William Osgood related a conversation he had with John Godfrey in 1640 in which the latter stated "that he had gotten a new master against the time he had done keeping cows." When Osgood asked his new master's name and where he lived, Godfrey answered that he did not know. Osgood then inquired, "How then will thou go to him when thy time is out," and Godfrey replied, "The man will come and fetch me." Next, he asked if Godfrey had "made an absolute bargain," upon which the cowherd stated that "a covenant was made and he had set his hand to it." Alarmed by his strange responses, Osgood told Godfrey that he was "persuaded thou hast made a covenant with the devil."[42] Likewise, when Rebecca Greensmith's interrogators demanded to know if "she had made an express covenant with him [Satan]," she "owned that the Devil had frequent use of her body." Reverend John Whiting of Hartford passed on this story to the leading New England minister Increase Mather who published it in 1689, and so it possibly reveals more about clerical perspectives than common folks' views. However, Goody Greensmith gave details on her interactions with Satan that appear to be the product of her imagination, such as that "the devil first appeared to her in the form of a deer or faun, skipping about her." Although the clergymen who concerned themselves with Greensmith's case may have encouraged her to give such an account because it reinforced their diabolical view of witchcraft, it is unlikely that they would have chosen such words to describe her encounters with the Devil.[43]

Later accounts of the witchcraft cases of Alice Lake and Mary (Lewis) Parsons describe how Satan turned people to his service. The Devil allegedly drew Goody Lake into a pact by appearing to her "in the likeness, & acting the part of a child of hers then lately dead." Similarly, Parsons "had lost a child and was exceedingly discontented at it." The Devil appeared to her in the "likeness of her child [and] came to her bed side and talked with her, and asked to come into the bed to her, and she received it into the bed to her that night and several nights after, and so entered into covenant with Satan and became a witch." Both stories relate how the Devil's skills as a deceiver enabled him to prey on the weak as he sought to add people to his ranks.[44]

A second theme of diabolism, the witches' Sabbath, only rarely appeared in New England and, when it did, was a mere shadow of the elaborate descriptions of black Masses found in Europe. This makes sense in light of the fact that Protestant demonologists deemphasized this aspect of diabolical witchcraft.[45] Before 1670 there was only one witchcraft episode in the Puritan colonies that featured a clear reference to a witch meeting: the Hartford witch panic of 1662. During this scare, allegations came forward that groups of witches had engaged in demonic rituals. Rebecca Greensmith confessed to attending a witch meeting where she and her fellow servants of Satan "danced & had a bottle of sack [fortified wine]." In a rare New England reference to the witch's supposed ability to shape-shift, Greensmith also stated that "some of the company came in one shape, and some in another, and one in particular in the shape of a crow." Corroborating her story, Robert Stern testified that he saw Greensmith, Elizabeth Seager, and a couple of other women in the forest at night dancing around a kettle over a fire with "two black creatures like two Indians but taller." Here Stern touched on several classic features of the black mass: a clandestine, nocturnal gathering where witches cavorted with demons while potions simmered in a cauldron.[46]

In contrast to the near silence on the matter of the witches' Sabbath, references to animal familiars in the Puritan colonies were relatively frequent. Again, this was in keeping with the occult traditions of the mother country, for unlike the satanic pact, familiars were a regular feature of English witchcraft testimony and treatises.[47] Indeed, the concept of the witch's familiar was unique to England and its New World colonies. This supernatural being could take the form of any ordinary animal or insect and more rarely appeared as outlandish creatures not found in nature. No matter what shape they took, they aided a witch in carrying out acts of magical mischief. By the mid-seventeenth century, familiars had acquired a diabolical connotation, as the English came to view them as a gift the Devil bestowed on a witch and, thus, as a clear sign of their satanic allegiance. Among the suspicions the Gibson family held against Winifred and Mary Holman, was that a strange white bird was the pair's familiar spirit. Goody Gibson stated that it once appeared to her as a cat and then took the shape of a bird, while her son called it "the devilishest bird that ever I saw in my life." Likewise, in his testimony against Mary (Bliss) Parsons, James Bridgeman claimed that his sick child saw the suspect being followed by a familiar spirt in the form of a black mouse. Rebecca Greensmith implicated her husband as a witch when she reported that he possessed "two creatures like gods one a little blacker than the other." In a similar vein, sisters Hannah and Elizabeth Lamberton related how they once went up in the garret above Elizabeth Godman's room (who was then living with them) and looked down on her in bed and saw that she lay "as if somebody was sucking her." The girls' mother claimed that when she listened at the door to Godman's chamber, she heard her say, "Will you fetch me some beer, will you go, will you go, and the like." Since Mrs.

Godman was alone, the woman concluded that she must have been conversing with her familiar.[48]

Closely related to New Englanders' belief in animal familiars was their frequent reports concerning witch marks and teats. European demonologists first spoke of witch marks: a blemish that the Devil placed on a person's body to indicate his dominion over them, and English folk merged this belief with another observable sign of a person's compact with Satan, the witch's teat. This was literally a preternatural nipple through which the Devil or, more commonly, a familiar fed on a witch's blood. The first English pamphlet on a witch trial published in 1566 stressed the importance of the witch mark in establishing a suspect's guilt, and from this point it became a regular feature of English writings on witchcraft.[49] References to witches' teats also appear in some of the earliest prosecutions of occult crime in the Puritan colonies. Governor John Winthrop's summary of factors that led to Margaret Jones's execution as a witch in 1648 includes that "she had (upon search)

FIGURE 2.3 In keeping with the standard motifs of diabolism, this woodcut depicts witches dancing with devils at a black Sabbath. From *The History of Witches and Wizards* (London, 1720). Courtesy of the Wellcome Collection.

FIGURE 2.4   A witch feeds her animal familiars. From *A Rehearsall both Staung and True, of Hainous and Horrible Actes Committed by Elizabeth Stile* (London, 1579). Division of Rare and Manuscript Collections, Cornell University Library.

an apparent teat in her secret parts as fresh as if it had been newly sucked." Likewise, Goody Knapp hanged in the early 1650s after an examination of her body turned up such marks; and Eunice Cole faced trial as a witch later in the decade after constable Richard Ormsby, who was preparing to whip her naked back in punishment for another crime, saw "a blue thing like unto a teat hanging downward about three quarters of an inch long [and] not very thick." Ormsby recalled that he had "a great suspicion in my mind about it (she being suspected for a witch)" and wanted the court to appoint some women to look at the mark. However, Cole "pulled or scratched it off in a violent manner" before any search could be made. Similarly, Charles Brown deposed that once when John Godfrey yawned he saw "a small teat under his tongue," and Zachary Dibble's suspicions that his wife was a witch largely rested on his belief that "she had a teat in the secret part of her body that was sometimes bigger and sometimes lesser."[50]

The assertion that witches could fly was also tied to diabolism, and early modern Europeans believed that this power enabled them to quickly cross vast distances in order to attend their nocturnal Sabbats. If its near absence in court testimony is any indicator, this notion was not a commonly held belief among New Englanders. In the only direct reference to witch flight outside of the Salem crisis of 1692, a witness who spoke out against Elizabeth Seager in the 1660s reported that "she did fly." More common, but still rare, was testimony claiming that witches had the ability to cross distances with preternatural quickness. In his testimony against John Godfrey, John Griffing stated that seven years earlier he had met the accused as he traveled:

> Godfrey on foot and this deponent on horseback . . . and when I was at Goodman Gage's field I saw John Godfrey in the same field a little before me . . . but when I had ridden a little further not seeing Godfrey nor any track at all and it was at a time when there had fallen a middling snow overnight, and not seeing him nor his steps I ran my horse all the way to Andover; and the first house I came into at Andover was Goodman Rust's house and when I came in I saw John Godfrey sitting in the corner, and Goody Rust told me that he had been there so long as that a maid that was in the house had made clean a kettle and hung on peas and pork to boil for Godfrey and the peas and pork was ready to boil.

FIGURE 2.5 This image of two witches flying on broomsticks with the Devil reflects how the idea of magical flight was closely tied to the diabolical concept of witchcraft. From *The History of Witches and Wizards* (London, 1720). Courtesy of the Wellcome Collection.

As is the case with this story, such accounts do not specify how suspects managed to accomplish such feats of rapid movement; nevertheless, the claim that Godfrey left no footprints in the snow certainly gives the impression that he flew through the air.[51]

The paucity of testimony concerning witch flight is not surprising in light of the origins of New Englanders' witchcraft beliefs. Many European demonologists reacted to the idea that witches could fly with deep skepticism or outright disbelief. Even the authors of the *Malleus Malificarum* (1486), who gave voice to some of the most outrageous notions concerning witchcraft, admitted that witches' claims of flight may have been products of Devil-induced delusion. Hesitation to give the idea the stamp of legitimacy was even more pronounced among English writers. Thus, while James I's *Daemonologie* (1597), which tended to toe the line of more credulous continental writers, includes an entire chapter on witch flight, many English authors ignored the phenomenon or denied its reality. Their response was the product of a larger Protestant brand of demonology that rejected the more sensational aspects of diabolism.[52] It follows then that the Puritans, who were well attuned to both English and continental sources of Protestant thought, imbibed this more conservative stance.

Besides a belief in satanic pacts and witches' Sabbaths, diabolism involved theological concepts that distinguished it from the malefic outlook on witchcraft. Like Protestant clergymen who promoted the diabolical construct of witchcraft in Europe, New England's ministers and like-minded lay people arrived at a different set of answers concerning the causes of misfortune and the proper response to it than folk preoccupied with maleficium. According to Protestant thinkers, while Satan may have been the source of a witch's power, God was the ultimate author of occult harm since it was only by His will that the Devil and witches were able to inflict injury. In line with their emphasis on an all-powerful, all-knowing Creator and articulation of a providential worldview in which everything that happened was an expression of divine will, God brought harm to people to punish their sins or, as was the case with the biblical Job, test their faith. This perspective deemphasized witches and the Devil as agents of loss and called on believers to look to their own deeds when seeking the source of ill fortune.[53]

This focus on God, rather than the witch, as the ultimate source of misfortune is a constant theme in the writings of English demonologists, and these works were one of the vehicles through which this view made its way to New England. For example, in *The Mystery of Witch-craft* (1617), Thomas Cooper submits that God allowed witchcraft to exist in order to punish the wicked and that even Satan was ultimately an instrument of

God's providence. Richard Bernard's *A Guide to Grand Jury Men* (1627) echoes Cooper's observations when it's opening chapter states, "God's hand is first to be considered in all crosses [misfortunes], whatsoever the means be, and whosoever the instruments: for he rules over all." Likewise, in his *Select Cases of Conscience Touching Witches and Witchcrafts* (1646), John Gaule highlights the biblical story of Job to prove that God caused bad things to happen in order to take the measure of people's faith and asserts that witchcraft was one of the means through which such a test might come.[54]

Taken to its logical end, this line of thinking could actually inhibit witch-hunting. If God was the fountainhead of all injury and periodically employed witches and the Devil to deliver it, then to aggressively root out witches was, in a sense, to battle against divine providence. Moreover, according to Protestant theologians, focusing on a witch as the source of injury diverted sufferers from the path they need to follow in order to experience relief: putting themselves right with the Lord by avoiding sin and repenting for those already committed. Thus, instead of blaming black magic for their troubles, a person needed to cast their eye inward and consider what behaviors had triggered God's rebuke. In sum, Protestant thinkers stressed that the true mother of misfortune was not external (a witch) but internal (sin) and that witch-hunting was, at best, a distraction from the believer's task of spiritual reformation and, at worst, a denial of personal culpability. New England clergymen did not interpret this view as a censure against witch-hunting and, referencing biblical passages that enjoined the faithful to punish occult criminals, supported the fight against magical mischief. However, like many Protestant pastors, they warned their congregants not to forget the role that God and sin played in ill fortune or turn to witch-hunting as a substitute for introspection and repentance.[55]

Another corollary of diabolism was its stance on so-called white magic. The malefic view of witchcraft, which defined the crime as the use of occult forces to do harm, kept the door open to the existence of good and helpful magic. In contrast, the diabolical outlook rested on the belief that *all* magical power emanated from Satan and was therefore innately evil, and those who cleaved to this view saw no distinction between black and white magic.[56] As Richard Bernard wrote, "All witches, in truth, are bad witches, and none good" and that "those therefore which go to these [white] wizards, seek help of the Devil." Similarly, the Puritan theologian William Perkins expressed his belief that "good" witches were more dangerous than "bad" ones, because the former ensnared the innocent in sin and made the Devil's instrument, magic, appear beneficial. He concluded his diatribe against white witches by saying that if death was the punishment meted out to witches by God's law, then "a thousand deaths of right belong to the good witch." John Gaule also argued that the distinction between good and bad witches was a false one and that of the two, white witches were the worst because they shrouded the Devil's malice in the guise of good deeds, or as he put it, "For as Satan, being a fiend of darkness, is then worst when he transforms himself into an angel of light, so likewise are his ministers." Another English demonologist, Reverend Alexander Roberts, confirmed the demonic origins of white witches' power, adding that they only had the ability to cure illnesses that they had caused.[57]

These views on misfortune and magic made their way to New England. The ultimate power of God and the need to take personal responsibility for sin were bedrock Puritan principles that shaped its inhabitants' understanding of the occult. Likewise, the region's ministers took their cue from Protestant demonologies and periodically issued warnings against the use of white magic, asserting that all occult power was demonic.[58] However, not all of New England's learned folk embraced this line of thinking. For instance, John Winthrop Jr. was not only a political leader but also a physician and scientist (he became a member of England's premier scientific association, the Royal Society, in 1662) with an interest in alchemy. He did not see all magic as evil but drew distinctions between illicit, harmful witchcraft and legitimate, "natural" forms of magic. Nevertheless, it appears that Winthrop and any like-minded intellectuals represented a small minority among a regional elite who held more orthodox views.[59]

Glimpses of this uncompromising attitude toward magic in New England periodically came to the surface during witchcraft episodes. In 1669 a group of ministers gave their views on the case of Katherine Harrison, reiterating the connection between seemingly benign acts of white magic and the Devil. Asked if having the ability to tell the future was a sign of diabolical compact, the clergymen replied that things that could not "be known by human skill in arts, or strength of reason arguing from the course of nature, or are made known by divine revelation . . . must needs be known (if at all) by information from the Devil." Thus, while they did not completely close the door to less damning explanations for the power of divination, they argued that it was a strong indication of "familiarity" with Satan. Testimony gathered in 1679 for Elizabeth Morse's witch trial reveals that members of the laity held similar views. Esther Wilson deposed that her mother, a purported victim of Morse's occult power, had nailed an iron horseshoe above the entrance to her home. This was a common piece of folk magic used to keep out evil persons and spirits. However, a neighbor, William Moody, "said [it was] a piece of witchery and knocked it off." Clearly he believed that all magic, even when used for protection against witchcraft, was ungodly, and when another neighbor put the horseshoe back up, Moody returned and "carried it away." Wilson noted that while the horseshoe was above the door, Goody Morse stayed away, but when it was removed, the suspected witch freely entered her mother's house. So, whatever the theological implications of this act of countermagic, Wilson believed that it worked.[60]

Confluences

While in theory there were distinct malefic and diabolical conceptions of witchcraft, in the day-to-day experience of early New Englanders they blended together. Ministers who promoted the demonic view of occult crime and civil authorities who prosecuted it under such terms also accepted

FIGURE 2.6 Reflecting how malefic and diabolical conceptions of witchcraft often overlapped, this image depicts the Devil helping a witch to forge a hexed nail with which the latter intends to inflict magical harm on a victim. From *The History of Witches and Wizards* (London, 1720). Courtesy of the Wellcome Collection.

the idea of maleficium. Indeed, from their perspective, the acts of misfortune caused by witches were clear signs of Satan's power. Similarly, ordinary folk who focused on the harm caused by witchcraft were not oblivious to the diabolical perspective. Though they may not have dwelled on the matter, they would have doubtlessly assented to the notion that black magic had a dark and demonic origin.[61]

This confluence of popular and learned views first took shape in England when the malefic and diabolical concepts of witchcraft intermingled in the decades preceding Puritan migration to the New World. England's witchcraft act of 1604 blended together concerns over maleficium and diabolism, and the image of the diabolical witch clearly made inroads into popular consciousness. Bringing together long-standing folk beliefs about witchcraft and newer, clerical understandings of it, witness testimony from as far back as 1566 featured stories of animal familiars as emissaries of the Devil. The Lancashire witch trials of 1612 produced some of the earliest accounts concerning the witches' Sabbath, and by midcentury, testimony featuring references to demonic witchcraft became increasingly frequent. Unlike the situation in continental Europe where the practice of judicial torture enabled authorities to squeeze out testimony that suited their religiously informed understanding of occult crime, it does not appear that English authorities simply imposed their views on the masses. Instead, what unfolded was a process whereby elites added popular ideas about witchcraft to their store of knowledge, and common people incorporated learned elements into their understanding of the crime.[62] Of course, there were limits to this meeting of the minds. No matter how much they bought into the concept of diabolical witchcraft, many commoners eschewed one of its core principles: that all magic was demonic and the distinction between white and black magic was a false one. As a consequence, they also rejected the clergy's categorical hostility to white witches.[63]

New England came even closer to developing a unified culture of witchcraft. In contrast to England, which harbored a good deal of popular anticlericalism, the colonies attracted a large number of devout Puritans whose outlook more closely matched those of their religious leaders. Moreover, life in the New World brought together clergy and laity in ways that undercut the social and economic separation that fed popular discontent with the church in the motherland. While the Puritans believed hierarchy was part of God's order, the system of church governance they created reduced barriers between ministers and their parishioners: each congregation generally ran its own affairs without interference from larger ecclesiastical institutions and, thus, pastors and parishioners dealt with each other on relatively equal terms. The "middle-class" background of many of New England's early Puritan migrants also promoted the region's social and cultural homogeneity. Additionally, in contrast to the yawning gulf of literacy that separated elites from commoners in the Old World, early New England maintained some of the highest literacy levels in the Western world, further shrinking the distance between rank-and-file colonists and their social betters.[64] Thus English popular culture, which contravened elite understandings of witchcraft through its permissive attitudes toward white magic and focus on maleficium, arrived in New England truncated by the self-selecting process of migration.

This is not to say that the clergy, civic leaders, and common people in the Puritan colonies always saw eye to eye on matters related to the occult. There were most certainly differences of opinion and degrees of belief. White magic was one area where there was disagreement. While the clergy condemned the use of occult power in any form, at least some among the laity saw nothing wrong with using magic to serve good ends. But even here, the distance that separated ministers from their congregants was not nearly as great as in England. In the old country there was a class of white witches, or "cunning folk" in the parlance of the time, who made a living off of their supposed supernatural ability to heal injuries, tell the future, and detect black magic. No similar group seems to have taken root in New England. Several of its inhabitants gained a reputation for occult skill and many more may have dabbled in magic, but it appears that few if any primarily lived off of the magical trade.[65]

Evidence that at least some New Englanders periodically resorted to white magic appears in relation in several witchcraft episodes. Namely, they employed countermagic, or what Richard Bernard condescendingly referred to as the "charms and other detestable remedies used by vain people" to identify or punish witches. Common methods included burning a hexed object, scratching a witch so they bled, or boiling a witchcraft victim's urine.[66] In 1650 Hannah Lancton described such practices when she recalled how a neighbor threw what they believed was a bewitched pudding into the fire. An hour later, Lancton "heard one mutter and mumble at the door" and found Hugh Parsons standing outside. The upshot of all this is that the burning of the hexed item had drawn the responsible party to the Lanctons' door. In his account of the witchcraft trial of Margaret Jones, Reverend John Hale alluded to the same means of magical detection, writing that Jones became a suspect because "some things supposed to be bewitched, or have a charm upon them, being burned, she came to the fire and seemed concerned." Mention of this folk practice again emerged in a 1657 slander suit brought by William Meaker against Thomas Mullenner after the defendant called the plaintiff a witch. The trouble started when several of Mullenner's pigs died "in a strange way" and, in order to confirm his suspicion that Meaker had bewitched them, he "cut off the tail and ear of one and threw [it] into the fire."[67]

Depositions generated by New England's witchcraft cases betray other slippages between ministers' and ordinary folks' views of occult crime. In particular, references to diabolism found in court testimony are frequently vague and imprecise. For instance, when asked if her husband had ever done "anything beyond the power of nature," Mary (Lewis) Parsons replied that one night as she was returning home she saw "a thing like a great nasty dog by the path side." It is unclear whether she thought that it was Goodman Parson's familiar spirit or if she believed he had shape-shifted into the animal—Mary only stated that the mysterious dog's appearance was "done by witchcraft from my husband." Likewise, Agnes Puddington's testimony against Jane Walford includes obscure references to cats. She recalled that Goody Evens "was followed by a cat wherever she went" and claimed that when her husband tried to shoot it, his gun inexplicably malfunctioned. Soon after, Puddington saw three cats, one of which "vanished away on the plain ground." Though she does not spell it out, Puddington implies that the cats were animal familiars. In a similar vein, several people made mention of "a black thing" during the witchcraft trial of Elizabeth Garlick, but at no point did they clearly establish its identity. They may have thought that the creature was Garlick's familiar, but it just as easily could have been the Devil or a demon.[68] These sorts of stories did not provide the clarity New England courts sought as they faced the task of proving witch suspects' complicity with Satan. Nevertheless, this sort of vagueness also characterized statements concerning acts of maleficium. Thus, no matter if witnesses' stories featured malefic or diabolical witchcraft, they often let inferences stand in for clear accusations and left it to judges and juries to fill in the blanks.

Regardless of its lack of clarity, New Englanders' testimony reflects a high degree of cultural consensus. Though Puritan colonists often focused on the misfortunes they blamed on witchcraft, they also frequently spoke of the crime in the diabolical terms advanced by the clergy. By the time of the English settlement of the New World, the mother country had already witnessed a merging of the malefic and diabolical views of occult mischief, and so it is not surprising that a similar blending of traditions took hold throughout the English-speaking world—especially in areas populated by Puritans who were more predisposed to accept their ministers' demonic portrayal of the witch.[69] This confluence of belief can be seen in the fact that of the sixty-odd people formally accused of witchcraft in New England before 1670, nineteen had testimony featuring familiar spirits, satanic rituals, or other diabolical content leveled against them. These cases only include instances where demonic references appear in witness depositions and not just official indictments, which invariably described witchcraft in terms of diabolism, or published accounts penned by clergymen who may have introduced diabolical elements after the fact.[70]

The malefic and diabolical views of black magic were not separate ideologies but flip sides of the same coin of the occult. Regardless of their conceptual differences, the two outlooks came together in communities and courtrooms across New England and the rest of the English Atlantic. That much of the testimony generated by witchcraft prosecutions in the Puritan colonies failed to produce clear references to diabolism does not mean that it embodied a purely malefic view of the crime. Rather, New Englanders assumed that malefic acts had diabolical origins. It is clear that the clergy held this view. To them, all magic emanated from the Devil, and they believed that even seemingly harmless occult acts such as predicting the future could be evidence of a diabolical compact. Colonists who adhered to even the most basic tenants of Puritanism would have seen things the same way, and the notion that witches obtained their powers from Satan informed even their most maleficium-focused testimony.[71]

Like many Europeans during the early modern era, New England's colonists supported two intermeshed understandings of witchcraft. First there was the age-old image of the malefic witch as an agent of occult injury. Next to this stood the diabolical concept of black magic that came into focus in the fifteenth century and posited that what made witches so deserving of punishment was not the harm they wrought, but that they obtained their powers by renouncing God and embracing the Devil. Each of these outlooks resonated with some segments of New England society more than others. Nevertheless, while clergymen may have primarily thought of witches as servants of Satan, they were also quite concerned with the injury occult criminals inflicted on their communities. Likewise, although the laity devoted much of their attention to the misfortunes they attributed to black magic, they had no trouble believing that the Devil underwrote them. A level of cultural consensus largely unknown in Europe—where the gulf between rich and poor, educated and illiterate, church and unchurched was far greater—reinforced a shared view of occult crime in the Puritan colonies.

But if this was how New Englanders understood the crime of witchcraft, the next question is what sorts of people did they think were its most likely perpetrators. Not everyone was equally vulnerable to accusations of occult mischief, and there was a general profile of those who fell under the shadow of suspicion that had much in common with witch stereotypes in Europe and across the English-speaking world. Exploring the components of this profile provides a good starting point for understanding the social dynamics of witchcraft accusations.

Chapter 3

"A Forward, Discontented Frame of Spirit"

The New England Witch

By pure chance, a pair of witch suspects who came to the attention of New England authorities in the 1650s, Mary Parsons (née Lewis) and Mary Parsons (née Bliss), had the same name. The coincidence deepens in that each resided in Massachusetts towns along the Connecticut River (Springfield and Northampton respectively), married entrepreneurial husbands with whom they had children, and were relatively young (probably in their late twenties or thirties) when they faced suspicion for witchcraft.[1] A number of differences also separated the two women. Both were wives and mothers, but Goody Parsons of Northampton was a far more prolific bearer of children than her Springfield counterpart. Mary Lewis Parsons had three offspring, but only one was alive when she went on trial for witchcraft. In comparison, Mary Bliss Parsons had five children, of whom four were still living, by the time she became a focus of witch fears and went on to bear eight more. Their husbands were also different sorts of men. Mary Bliss Parsons's husband, Joseph, was a fur trader destined to become one of the wealthiest men in the Connecticut Valley, while Mary Lewis Parsons's spouse, Hugh, was a brick maker and sawyer and not nearly as rich or respectable. The second man's name was so black among his neighbors that they also accused him of witchcraft.[2]

What happened to them after they fell under suspicion further distinguishes the two Mary Parsons. The authorities imprisoned, indicted, and tried Mary Lewis Parsons. Although it acquitted her of witchcraft, the Court of Assistants convicted her for the murder of her infant son, but it appears that she died in prison and so was spared the hangman's noose. Mary Bliss Parsons, in contrast, was never even formally charged with witchcraft (although she did eventually stand trial for the crime in the mid-1670s). Instead, her husband took the legal offensive and successfully sued her accusers for slander.[3] Why witch suspects like these experienced such different fates and why some people managed to escape suspicion while others fell under its shadow are vital questions.

Although there were no theological or legal stipulations limiting who could be accused of witchcraft, people in New England and across the English Atlantic did not equally share the risk of denunciation. Additionally, once in the hands of the law, some suspects fared better than others. The challenge is in teasing out why certain individuals were more vulnerable to suspicion and, once accused, more apt to suffer arrest, trial, and conviction. What complicates things is that New Englanders rarely spoke of these matters. One of the few who did was Reverend John Davenport of New Haven. In the early 1650s he gave a sermon during which he stated that a person with "a forward discontented frame of spirit was a subject fit for the Devil." In other words, Davenport believed that those who were dissatisfied with their lot in life were more likely to turn to Satan's service.[4]

Taking a close look at the accused in New England furnishes a better picture of the sorts of people who fell victim to witch fears than scattered references on the subject found in Davenport's and other colonists' writing. In particular, an assessment of their personality traits, demographic profile (sex, age, and marital status), socioeconomic standing, and personal history provides insights into why they came under suspicion. Nevertheless, the minister's words signal that one of the more important variables in determining who became a target of accusation was the community's perception of a person's character. In particular, those suspected of witchcraft tended to be people with unsavory reputations. Moreover, they were women more often than men, from the lower ranks of society rather than its upper echelons, and older married folk rather than young and single. They were also periodically associated with the healing arts or occult practices such as fortune telling.[5]

Of all the facets of the witch profile, behavior was the most salient; and if others perceived a person's actions as immoral or un-neighborly, it could go a long way toward bringing them under suspicion. Nevertheless, while factors such as sex, age, and social status may not have been instrumental to witchcraft accusations, they were hardly irrelevant. Those at the top—

namely wealthy, powerful men—could often get away with forms of behavior that placed those at the bottom—women and the poor—in the crosshairs of suspicion. In addition, women and the economically disadvantaged lacked the money, influence, and access to the judicial system needed to successfully fend off witchcraft accusations.

"Her Carriage Doth Justly Render Her Suspicious of Witchcraft"

Behaviors deemed as antisocial and deviant anchored witch stereotypes. The association of an individual with such traits was, however, as likely a product of an accuser's imagination as a suspect's actual deportment. Whether a person's actions were blameless or indicative of a black heart was in the eye of the beholder, and those who stood witness against the accused were not impartial observers. Thus their testimony, while it provides a rich source of information about otherwise anonymous suspects, cannot be taken at face value.[6]

English demonologists asserted that a number of negative personality traits characterized those who turned to black magic. Richard Bernard wrote that individuals with "malicious spirits, impatient people, and full of revenge, having hearts swollen with rancor" were apt to become witches. Thomas Cooper came to a similar conclusion when he drew a line between witchcraft and the emotions of wrath, discontent, revenge, and greed. Likewise, when enumerating the "sins that more eminently dispose [people] to witchcraft," John Gaule included "envy, hatred, malice, [and] desire of revenge" as well as "covetousness," "inordinate, vagrant lusts," and "curiosity." Allegations of such behavior thread their way through New England's witch trials. For instance, the justices of New Haven's Court of Magistrates drew a link between Mrs. Elizabeth Godman's actions and her reputation for black magic when they stated that "her carriage doth justly render her suspicious of witchcraft."[7]

The Puritan colonists viewed discontent, pride, and envy as invitations to witchcraft. To them, pride was an emotion that could easily overrun the banks of pious humility and lead to sin. They saw it as the parent of discontent, for the latter resulted when a person's overblown sense of self came up against a reality of more humble circumstances. Discontent fueled challenges to authority, the social order, and God's providence. To Puritans, for whom all things were an expression of divine will, to express discontent with one's lot in life was to challenge His rightful rule. It followed that folk who felt dissatisfied were vulnerable to Satan's guile and more prone to join his ranks as witches. From discontent came the equally troublesome emotion of envy. Those who lacked prosperity and happiness were apt to look jealously on those who possessed them, and early modern folk believed that such feelings lay at the root of witchcraft.[8]

The theme of discontent threads its way through many of New England's witchcraft episodes. In his account of Mary Johnson's case, Reverend Cotton Mather states that her "familiarity with the devils came by discontent." According to Mather, she was displeased with her work as a servant, and Satan took advantage of this when he appeared to the women "tending her the best service he could do for her." Reverend John Hale told a similar tale about Mary Lewis Parsons, explaining that she was "discontented" at the death of one of her children, and this sense of loss became the wedge the Devil used to insert himself into her life. The theme of dissatisfaction also enters into Eunice Cole's 1656 witch trial. Witnesses testified that Cole once interrupted a meeting of Hampton's selectmen and "demand[ed] help" from them "for wood or other things." When the town's leaders responded that she "had an estate of her own and needed no help," Cole retorted that they treated her unfairly.[9]

New Englanders likewise associated envy and greed with occult misdeeds. Eunice Cole not only complained that her community failed to give her what was her due, but enviously observed that the town "could help Goodman Robe being a lusty [healthy] man and she Cole have none." Before she stood trial for witchcraft, Mary Lewis Parsons accused Thomas Marshfield's widow of the same crime, claiming that the woman had caused the death of one of her children because she "envied every woman's child." The colonists also attached these negative traits to male suspects. Greed supposedly characterized Goody Parsons's husband, and by the time he stood trial for occult crime, he had gained a reputation as a hard-bargaining, grasping man. Likewise, John Godfrey's reputation as a greedy, money-grubber fed suspicions that he was a witch.[10]

If pride, discontent, envy, and greed were invitations to witchcraft, then aggression, hostility, and malice were incitements to acts of magical harm. Though never formally accused, Anne Edwards of Easthampton aroused suspicions, and her purportedly bad temper was probably one of the factors that contributed to rumors that she was a witch. Edwards once threatened a constable who came to serve a warrant and then proceeded to assault the man and his assistant. When her husband told her to quietly submit, she "bid him let her alone or else she would kill him." From this it appears that Anne Edwards hardly fit the mold of a meek and mild goodwife. A reputation for anger also followed John Godfrey. For instance, Haverhill selectman

Henry Palmer reported that Godfrey badgered him about being hired as the town's cowherd and that when he refused, Godfrey "showed himself much displeased."[11] Hugh Parsons was another suspect noted for his wrath. John Lombard deposed that he "often heard him [Parsons] say, when he hath been displeased with anybody, that he would be even with them for it." Likewise, Blanch Bedortha recalled that when she intervened in an argument between her husband and Parsons, the latter responded with the veiled threat, "Gammer, you needed not have said anything, I spoke not to you, but I shall remember you when you little think on it." Hugh's wife agreed that he was a man driven by malice and revenge, stating that if her husband "had fallen out with anybody, he would say that he would be even with them."[12] Early modern Europeans believed that just such a combination of anger and vengefulness drove witches to translate their dark power into actual acts of harm.

New Englanders also commonly accused witch suspects of committing physical acts of aggression. Indeed, it appears that they saw malefic magic as a supernatural extension of more ordinary acts of violence. Thus, New Haven's Court of Magistrates warned Elizabeth Godman "not to go in an offensive way to folks' houses in a railing manner as it seems she hath done, but that she keep her place and meddle with her own business." Margaret Jones of Charlestown also earned a reputation for hostility that intersected with suspicions of witchcraft, and Governor John Winthrop claimed that "her behavior at her trial was very intemperate, lying notoriously, and railing upon the jury and witnesses, etc., and in the like distemper she died." Hugh Parsons also reportedly translated a malicious spirit into acts of aggression, including abusive behavior toward his wife. In the same vein, witnesses portrayed John Godfrey as a man prone to violent words and deeds, and Abigail Remington recalled how he spoke with "great rage and passion" during an argument.[13]

The pugnaciousness associated with witch suspects extended to a perceived over-eagerness to take their neighbors to court. Katherine Harrison initiated a number of lawsuits against people she held responsible for damages to her crops and livestock. It is not clear if the vandalism was in retaliation for her supposed acts of witchcraft; but regardless of what precipitated it, the widow's efforts to punish the alleged perpetrators added to the impression that she was a spiteful, aggressive woman. Harrison, however, appears a mere amateur when compared to the campaign of litigation John Godfrey waged over the course of his life. He was involved in at least 132 court cases (including many related to debt and defamation) and in just over two-thirds of them appeared as a plaintiff. Another suspected witch, James Wakeley, accrued a similar record of activity. As a Wethersfield merchant, he habitually sued others over unpaid debts or unfulfilled contracts. In just the two decades from 1643 to 1664, he went to court on at least thirty-seven occasions, including twenty-one times as a plaintiff.[14]

Writing years later about the witchcraft case of Anne Hibbins, Reverend William Hubbard and Massachusetts governor Thomas Hutchinson reflected on the line the colonists drew between anger and witchcraft. Hubbard observed that "many times persons of hard favor and turbulent passions are apt to be condemned by the common people for witches"; and Hutchinson drew the same conclusion, stating that Hibbins's "natural crabbedness" and "her turbulent and quarrelsome" spirit "rendered her so odious to her neighbors as to cause some of them to accuse her of witchcraft." These authors penned their accounts long after witch-hunting had been discredited in New England and imply that charges of occult crime provided a convenient excuse for Boston's inhabitants to rid themselves of an unpleasant woman. But regardless of their views on the colonists' motives, the pair indicate that a reputation for malice often crossed paths with suspicions of witchcraft.[15]

New Englanders regularly portrayed witch suspects as challenging social norms in both word and deed. This includes their alleged habit of issuing shocking statements. During her run-in with suspicions of witchcraft, New Haven's magistrates took Goodwife Bayley to task for making "filthy & unclean speeches," recounting that when John Moses advised her husband to kill a dog that had tried to copulate with a sow, she retorted, "What would you have the poor creature do, if he had not a bitch, he must have something." Likewise, when the claim that George Larremore had "miscarried with many persons in a filthy way" (an allusion to fornication) came up in conversation, Goody Bayley said, "Alas, what would you have the man do, if his own wife was weak, he must have somebody." Puritans, who placed a premium on sexual propriety, did not take such scurrilous talk lightly.[16]

In a number of cases, words attributed to the accused involved disturbing references to witches and the Devil. When a bird got into Job Tyler's house and he wondered aloud "wherefore it came," John Godfrey, who happened to be present, replied, "It came to suck your wife," impudently jesting that Goody Tyler was a witch and the bird her animal familiar. Judith Ayers reportedly told a shocking tale about having met the Devil in London in the shape of "a fine young gentleman." Though she claimed that she saw through his disguise and rebuffed his overtures, the story may have made others question why Satan saw her as a fit target for his advances in the first place. Similarly, Mr. William Hooke testified that Mrs. Elizabeth Godman "would be often speaking about witches and rather justify them than condemn them." When

Mrs. Goodyear stated that she "never knew a witch die in their bed," and Godman replied, "You mistake, for a great many die and go to the grave in an orderly way," it confirmed that the latter knew more about witches than any decent person should.[17]

Sometimes the accused purportedly compounded indiscreet words with bizarre, off-putting behavior. Goodwife Thorpe reported that when she encountered Elizabeth Godman "in ye street," the suspected witch took her to task for testifying against her and "gnashed and grinned with her teeth in a strange manner." Hugh Parsons's reputation as a witch only deepened when, on receiving word that one of his children had died, he flatly stated, "I hear my child is dead: but I will cut a pipe of tobacco first before I go home." Afterwards, those who witnessed the episode "did much wonder at the lightness of his carriage, because he showed no affection or sorrow for the death of his child."[18]

FIGURE 3.1 The story about Judith Ayers's encounter with the Devil parallels a much larger body of lore in which Satan appeared to those he attempted to recruit as witches in the guise of a finely dressed gentleman. From *The History of Witches and Wizards* (London, 1720). Courtesy of the Wellcome Collection.

The link between occult crime and antisocial activities was even more tightly drawn when it came to disrespect for authority. Shortly before they came under suspicion for witchcraft, John Bradstreet spent an hour in the stocks "for affronting the court with words," and John Blackleach found himself in front of Connecticut's General Court facing judgment for "his contemptuous expressions against several persons in authority." John Brown was another witch suspect with a history of disruptive and disrespectful behavior. He landed in a New Haven Colony court for drunkenness in 1661 and, a year later, stood before the magistrates "to answer for some contemptuous carriages to authority." Eunice Cole was doubly damned in the eyes of her neighbors, for she not only had a reputation for discontent and aggression but also disrespect for those in position of power. As previously mentioned, on one occasion she insolently interrupted a meeting of Hampton's selectmen to air her complaints against them. On another, Cole and her husband insulted and assaulted a constable. Likewise, Easthampton officials ordered Goody Edwards to pay a fine "or have her tongue in a cleft stick" to punish her "for the contempt of a warrant" issued against her by the town after she refused to obey the summons and threatened "that she might burn it."[19]

Following in the footsteps of English demonologists, the Puritan colonists saw contempt for religious institutions as a sign of witchcraft. Thomas Cooper listed disregard for God's ordinances, "gross and open profaneness," and "desperate impenitence" as clear indications that a person had turned to Satan and become a witch. John Gaule agreed, identifying idolatry, superstition, and blasphemy as sins tied to black magic.[20] The link between irreverence and occult crime was clear in New England. One of the reasons that folk thought Hugh Parsons was a witch was his dismal record of church attendance. John Brown had a similar reputation for avoiding religious services and disrespecting the clergy. One witness reported that he left Sabbath-day worship early so he could go outside and smoke with some sailors, while another claimed that "when Mr. Davenport was speaking of the power of sin in a natural man, that John Brown laughed." Likewise, Elizabeth Smith accused Katherine Harrison of being a "sabbath breaker"—a person who did not observe the religious injunction against unnecessary activities on Sundays. The association between religious delinquency and occult mischief was so strong that proving that a person was a devout Christian could go a long way to countering suspicions of witchcraft. Thus a petition entered in support of Winifred Holman during her 1660 witchcraft trial states that she "frequents public preaching, and gives diligent attention thereunto."[21]

New Englanders also included dishonesty among the traits they bundled with witchcraft. Seeing that the Bible characterized Satan as the father of lies (John 8:44), it is not surprising that Puritans associated this trait with his supposed servants. A New Haven court berated Goody Bayley for her "impudent and notorious lying" and laid bare the diabolical dimensions of dishonesty when they observed that for this and other sorts of bad behavior, she "acted as one possessed with the very devil, who is a malicious, lying, unclear spirit." Thomas Waples testified that Katherine Harrison "was a noted liar," and another witness described her as "a great or notorious liar."[22] His alleged lack of honesty was also a prominent feature of the case built against Hugh Parsons. Witnesses testified to his penchant for telling untruths, and the court repeatedly caught him in what they asserted were outright lies.[23]

Of Goodmen and Goodwives, Gaffers and Gammers

While the alleged character traits and behaviors of the accused come through loud and clear in New Englanders' testimony, suspects' sex, age, and marital status did not illicit much attention. Moreover, the references that do appear are often brief, matter-of-fact statements with no commentary on how they contributed to an individual's reputation as a witch. Nevertheless, this triumvirate of demographic traits was foundational to identity in early modern Europe and its New World colonies. Whether a person was male or female had a profound impact on their life and level of power they achieved. Age also determined a person's status. Once a boy passed from youth to full adulthood (and marriage) he earned the status of a "Goodman," while a girl who came of age and entered into wedlock gained the respectable title of "Goodwife." English folk likewise used the terms *gaffer* and *gammer* (contractions of "godfather" and "godmother") to label men and women who slid past the prime of life and into the greater levels of dependency that came with old age. Similarly, marriage framed a person's social standing, and that adult women went by the title of Goodwife shows how closely bound the institution was to female identity. Seeing that this trio of factors so powerfully shaped a person's life, it is not surprising that they had a bearing on witchcraft suspicions.

Women ran a much greater risk of being prosecuted for witchcraft than men. Of the fifty-nine New Englanders who faced legal action for occult crime before 1670, just over two-thirds were female. What makes this sex imbalance even more noteworthy is that during the first decades of English settlement men outnumbered women and continued to do so in many communities well into the seventeenth century.[24] Even so, this association between women and witchcraft was not as strong as it would later become. Excluding cases related to the Salem witch panic, 90 percent of those formally accused of witchcraft in the last three decades of the seventeenth century were women. Even during the Salem crisis, when witch fears reached epidemic proportions and touched people normally safe from suspicion, women still made up three-quarters of the accused. Moreover, at midcentury women in the Puritan colonies did not bear the same risk as those in the mother country. Of thirty-two accused witches who faced trial in Kent between 1625 and 1636, only one was a man, and in Essex County over 90 percent of witch suspects in the sixteenth and seventeenth centuries were women.[25]

Age was another element of the witch profile. How old the accused were when they became a focus of witch fears is often difficult to determine, making it a challenge to draw firm conclusions about which age groups were most prone to accusation. Nevertheless, the ages of forty-four of New England's pre-1670 witch suspects are known or can be estimated, revealing that most were between forty and fifty-nine years old, a small number were sixty or older, and the balance were under forty. In comparison, out of fifteen individuals who came before England's Essex Assizes for witchcraft in 1645 whose ages are known, two were in their forties, three in their fifties, seven in their sixties, and three in their eighties. While this sample is admittedly meager, it indicates that English witch suspects at midcentury were, on average, older than their New England counterparts. If true, this may reflect that somewhat different social dynamics drove witch accusations on each side of the Atlantic. For instance, it is possible that in the mother country, where land and resources were in short supply relative to the Puritan colonies, the tensions that led to witchcraft suspicions may have centered more on elderly folk who required support yet were unable to fully contribute to the households and communities to which they belonged. Nevertheless, as the Puritan colonies matured so too did their witch suspects, and the proportion of the accused who were sixty or older grew during the late-seventeenth century.[26]

Though a good number of New England's midcentury witch suspects were under forty, they were not the prime focus of its campaign against occult crime. It appears that the colonists did not formally accuse any children or teenagers before 1670; and except for a handful in their twenties, all of the individuals in this group were in their thirties when they came under suspicion.

Table 3.1   Sex of accused witches in New England

	BEFORE 1670	NON-SALEM CASES 1671–99	SALEM CRISIS
Male	18 (31%)	3 (10%)	41 (26%)
Female	41 (69%)	28 (90%)	115 (74%)

FIGURE 3.2   As depicted in this image, during the early modern era the witch was commonly stereotyped as an old woman. From John Hammond, *A Most Certain, Strange, and true Discovery of a Witch* (1643). Division of Rare and Manuscript Collections, Cornell University Library.

Table 3.2   Ages of witch suspects in New England before 1670 (two suspects are counted twice since they were accused on multiple occasions and fit under more than one age category. In light of this, N = 46 for the purposes of calculating percentages)

Aged 15–39	20 (43%)
Aged 40–59	22 (48%)
Aged 60+	4 (9%)

Placed in context with the age structure of early New England, it becomes clear that twenty- and thirty-year-olds were not inordinately subject to suspicions of witchcraft, for their proportion among the accused was about the same as among the general population.[27] Another indicator that the under-forty crowd was not the prime target of witch-hunting is that young suspects tended to fare better in court than older ones. Just over a third of the accused from this age cohort never even came to trial, while only a fifth of older witch suspects avoided facing judge and jury. No matter what their age, however, New Englanders who went to trial faced roughly the same rate of conviction and execution, with about one out of every four going to the gallows.[28]

People between forty and fifty-nine bore the brunt of witch-hunting. They constituted almost half of those accused before 1670, which is signifi-

Table 3.3 Ages of witch suspects in New England compared to the general population

	PRE-1670 WITCH SUSPECTS	SEVENTEENTH-CENTURY WINDSOR	NEW ENGLAND 1650–1700
Aged under 20	0%	38%	44%
Aged 20–39	43%	46%	38%
Aged 40–59	48%	12%	13%
Aged 60+	9%	4%	5%

cant considering that the middle-aged constituted a far smaller portion of the general population. For instance, in seventeenth-century Windsor, only about 12 percent of the town's residents were between forty and fifty-nine. This closely matches estimates concerning the age structure of New England in the decades after 1650, which indicate that about 13 percent of the region's population fell into this category. In sum, the proportion of witch suspects who were in their forties and fifties was *four times higher* than their proportion among the population as a whole.[29]

That only a small fraction (9 percent) of the accused from before 1670 were sixty or older appears to fly in the face of the popular stereotype of the witch as an elderly person. However, it is important to again place this figure in context with early New England's age distribution. The population of the fledgling Puritan colonies—where the hard work of settlement called for strong backs and hardy constitutions—was relatively young. As late as 1686, those sixty or older represented only about 4 percent of the population in Windsor—a figure that matches the proportion of seventeenth-century New Englanders who reached the sixty year mark. This indicates that older folk disproportionately drew their neighbors' suspicions and fell victim to accusation at about twice the expected rate relative to their numbers in the general population.[30]

New Englanders never reflected on why those middle-aged and older were prime targets of accusation, but one explanation is that it often took time for an individual to develop a reputation as a witch. Decades could go by before suspicions deepened to the point that a person became the subject of legal action. This means that the older a person was, the greater the chance that feelings against them would reach the critical mass needed to trigger a formal complaint. It is also possible that those over sixty drew more than their fair share of denunciations because they were frequently incapable of carrying out socially proscribed roles: women could no longer bear or even care for children, and as men aged they relinquished heavy labor, militia service, and even dominion over a household. Their inability to do many of the things expected of Puritan men and women may have marked them as deviant and made them a magnet for the sorts of negative feelings that sometimes led to suspicions of witchcraft. Finally, that older folk often held on to land and resources that younger generations required in order to prosper may have generated resentment against the elderly that periodically manifested itself as witchcraft accusations.[31] Meanwhile, the concept of power likely stands at the center of why middle-aged colonists drew the lion's share of attention for witchcraft. This period of life commonly represented the apex of a man's and woman's influence during the early modern era. Seen in its most elemental form, witchcraft was the misuse of power, and it follows that New Englanders may have looked to their powerful middle-aged neighbors when seeking out persons who engaged in black magic. Suspicious may have been especially pronounced when middle-aged folk lacked the prestige normally associated with that stage in life, for others may have perceived them as being prone to discontent, envy, and malice and apt to act on them through witchcraft.[32]

The profile of the New England witch also intersected with marital status. Roughly four-fifths of the people who faced the charge of witchcraft before 1670 were wed at the time they came before the courts, a tenth were widowed, and a tenth had never married. That the vast majority of the accused were wed is not surprising considering that Puritans saw marriage as an essential part of God's order and as natural a part of life as birth, aging, and death.[33] As for the much smaller number of witch suspects who were widowed or single, they were slightly overrepresented among the accused when compared to society at large. Colonists who never married probably hovered somewhere around 5 percent of the population before 1670, and at any given time widows and widowers constituted just under 10 percent.[34]

For those widowed and single people who did became targets of accusation, their marital status probably contributed to their plight. Because wedlock was such an elemental part of life to the Puritans, being a single adult could potentially contribute to a reputation for deviance. To the Puritan way

Table 3.4   Marital status of witch suspects in New England before 1670 (the marital status of three of the accused is unknown; one witch suspect, Jane Walford, is counted twice since she was both married and widowed when she came under suspicion)

MARITAL STATUS	NUMBER	PERCENTAGE
Married	45	79%
Single	6	10.5%
Widowed	6	10.5%

of thinking, a man without a wife or a woman without a husband did not live in accordance with God's will and were perhaps more apt to disregard the Lord in other respects, such as turning to witchcraft. His status as a life-long bachelor surely marked one of New England's most notorious witch suspects, John Godfrey, as outside the norm. Likewise, when she fell under suspicion, Mary Holman was single and around thirty years old—an age by which most women had already found a husband. A similar stigma may have shadowed widows. Though she faced trial for occult crime before her husband's death, accusations against Eunice Cole intensified after she became a widow. In the same vein, accusations of witchcraft followed after Katherine Harrison, Winifred Holman, Ann Burt, William Graves, and Anne Hibbins lost their spouses.[35]

A look at the New Englanders who came before the courts for occult crime reveals an association between low levels of childbearing and witch accusations. Early modern Europeans closely linked marriage to childbirth and assumed that the former would regularly lead to the latter.[36] Therefore, a married man or woman who lacked offspring was suspect, for people could assume that those who did not have children were jealous of those who did, and this emotion stood among the constellation of negative character traits associated with witchcraft. Gaps in the historical record often make it difficult to nail down how many children witch suspects had at the time of their denunciation. Moreover, it is important to ascertain not only how many children were born to the accused before they became a target of legal action but also how many may have died; for like the failure to have children, losing them could stand as a black mark on a person's reputation. Further complicating matters is that some of the accused died before their years of childbearing were over, thus limiting their number of offspring. Neverthe-less, it appears that only a small number of witch suspects had large numbers of children, and most had relatively few or none at all. Taken as a group, married women accused of witchcraft before 1670 bore an average of four children. In contrast, couples in early Andover, Massachusetts, produced an average of just over eight offspring.[37] Thus, if this town is any indication, witch suspects averaged only about half the number of children as other New Englanders.

Another basic element of an individual's identity, ethnicity, was not a significant feature of the witch profile in New England. Only a couple of suspects from before 1670 stood out in terms of their ethnic background. Judith Varlett, who fell under suspicion in 1662, was Dutch. Her father, Captain Casper Varlett, was one of a small number of traders who occupied a post established near Hartford by the Dutch colony of New Netherland in the 1630s and which remained in operation into the 1650s. In addition, Anne Edwards came to New England from Kent but was possibly of Irish extraction.[38] This lack of ethnic diversity is not surprising considering that colonial settlements in early New England were highly homogenous with many of their inhabitants hailing from communities in southeastern England. Of course, the colonists' Native American neighbors served to temper this ethnic uniformity. Nevertheless, while the English almost invariably assumed that Native peoples were under Satan's sway, they did not envision them as witches. Indeed, there is not a single case in New England before 1670 in which colonists brought a Native to book for occult crime. They reserved such charges for people who were like themselves, for New Englanders envisioned witchcraft as a crime most likely to be perpetrated by a close neighbor or someone the victim knew quite well. Because of their alien culture and exclusion from Puritan communities, Natives did not generally fall into these categories.[39] This pattern generally also held true through the rest of New England's history of witch-hunting, although a Goody Glover who hanged as a witch in Boston in 1688 was an Irish Catholic, and at least two African-Americans and a Native American, Tituba, were arrested for witchcraft during the Salem crisis of 1692.[40]

Likewise, few witch suspects stood out in terms of their religious affiliation. Jane Hawkins's association with Massachusetts's Antinomian dissidents likely sparked the attention she received as an alleged witch. Similarly, Mary Lewis Parsons's first husband was reportedly "a papist [Roman Catholic]," a damning charge among Puritans who saw the Catholic Church as the antichrist.[41] Another group of religious dissenters who emerged in England in the 1640s, the Society of Friends or Quakers, also largely escaped prosecution as occult criminals in New England. At first glance this is somewhat surprising considering the strong associations between Quakerism and witchcraft that took root in the mother country and since Quaker missionaries first landed on New England's shores in the 1650s during a major upswing in witchcraft prosecutions. However, there were factors that mitigated the persecution of Quakers as witches. First, these religious dissidents remained relatively few in number in New England until well into the second half of the seventeenth century, and by that time witch prosecutions and convictions had lost some of their earlier momentum. More important, several New England colonies put laws on the books that made it possible for the authorities to punish, banish, and even execute Quakers because of their religious views. Thus, if the colonists wanted to target members of the Society of Friends, there was no need to go through the difficult process of proving they were witches.[42]

Wealth and Status

Property and social rank had a bearing on witchcraft prosecutions. In both the Old World and the New, the accused were frequently folk of low social standing. However, there were numerous episodes in New England when middle-class inhabitants fell victim to witch fears and even a few where members of the elite became a target of accusation. Of twenty-eight witch suspects from before 1670 whose economic standing can be determined with some confidence, about two-thirds came from among the poor and lowest ranks of the middle class, just over a fifth were solidly middle class, and the remainder came from the upper echelons of property holders. This breakdown likely understates the lower-class origins of the accused since the poor had a greater chance of not leaving a trace in the historical record. Therefore, of the roughly thirty suspects from this period for whom no clear indicators of wealth exist, a high proportion were likely drawn from New England's underprivileged.[43]

The poor were most vulnerable to accusation and conviction, and several of New England's witch suspects had few if any financial resources when they came to the attention of authorities. That Mary Johnson was a servant when she hanged for witchcraft almost certainly means that she was poor and propertyless; and upon his death in 1663, Eunice Cole's husband left her a paltry £8, 10 shillings, and 2 pence. Similarly, in the wake of his execution for witchcraft, assessors valued the estate of John Carrington at a mere £10 and 9 shillings after subtracting debts. Additional suspects had meager estates that also landed them among the ranks of the poor. For instance, Peter Grant, whose wife suffered accusation during the Hartford witch panic of 1662, died in 1681 holding property worth about £51. Though it is possible that he suffered economic setbacks in the years following the Hartford episode, in all likelihood Goodman Grant and his wife were poor at the time of her arrest. Likewise, Thomas Gilbert, the husband of the convicted witch Lydia Gilbert, held an estate valued at just over £189 when he died just a few years after his wife's execution. However, this figure masks the fact that the couple was living largely on credit, and after debts only £19, 8 shillings, and 7 pence was left for his heirs.[44]

Table 3.5   Socioeconomic status of New England's pre-1670 witch suspects (N = 28)

Lower class	18 (64.3%)
Middle class	6 (21.4%)
Upper class	4 (14.3%)

Even in cases where no estate evaluations are available, other evidence points to the limited economic means of many witch suspects. Nicholas Bayley and his wife were repeatedly called before New Haven's town court because they were unable to raise £90 to cover several bonds the justices had laid against them to guarantee their good behavior, indicating that the couple lacked any substantial property or collateral. Likewise, in his will, Thomas Pell forgave four "poor" men their debts to him. Among them were the husbands of Goodies Knapp and Bassett, two women hanged for witchcraft in the early 1650s. Again, unless the two men suffered a reversal of fortune between their wives' executions and Pell's death, it appears that both of the condemned woman belonged to cash-strapped households. The itinerant cowherd John Godfrey was likely a poor man through much of his life, though he did have the wherewithal to act as a money lender from time to time in his later years. William and Judith Ayers also appear to fit into this mold: a Hartford tax assessment taken just six years before they stood accused of witchcraft shows that Goodman Ayers held a small freehold worth around £56.[45]

People of middling means were by no means immune to accusation. A number of witch suspects possessed estates worth from £100 to £200, placing them beyond outright poverty but still below the greater material security enjoyed by those of solid middle-class standing. John Bradstreet appears to have fallen into this category. He died eight years after his run-in with the law over witchcraft, leaving behind property valued at £103. Likewise, Elizabeth Seager's husband, Richard, had holdings worth about £100.[46] Other accused witches stood more firmly in the ranks of the middle class. At the time of his and his wife's execution, Nathaniel Greensmith held an estate worth about £182, placing the couple on the cusp of middle-class prosperity. William Brown, who became a target of witch fears in 1657, died five years later with property worth over £223, and several women who stood trial also belonged to middle-class households. Mary Barnes's husband, Thomas, was one of the original proprietors of Farmington, Connecticut, and a prominent landholder in the town. Judith Varlett also came from a financially secure background and her father, who died around the same time she fell under suspicion as a witch, left an estate behind valued at just over £205.[47]

Only a handful of suspects caught up in New England's midcentury witch prosecutions were wealthy. Four of them were merchants or the wives of merchants residing in Wethersfield, Connecticut, including John Blackleach and his wife. When Mr. Blackleach died in 1683 his estate was worth a little over £374, and he had in all likelihood previously distributed portions of his property to grown children in the form of marriage portions or other endowments. Likewise, Katherine Harrison married a rich trader who left her an estate valued at just over £900 upon his death in 1666. The exact size of James Wakeley's holdings at the time of his accusation is unknown, but all indications are that he was a man of some means. Anne Hibbins of Boston was another accused witch who came from a privileged background and her husband, William, was a successful merchant.[48] It is not too surprising that wealthy witch suspects were few and far between. On the one hand, their small numbers simply reflect the fact that the rich only constituted only a small proportion of New England society. On the other, having money and the power and influence that came with it helped shield the rich from charges of occult crime. If nothing else, their ability to afford costly litigation must have made potential accusers think twice before tangling with them in court.

Money was only one measure of status in early New England, and the possession of civil or military positions, personal reputation, and church membership rounded out a person's standing in the community. Exploring these indicators of rank as they relate to New England's witch suspects buttresses the conclusion that many of them came from the lower ranks of society. Several of the accused were servants or former servants who stood on the lowest rungs of the social ladder. Mary Johnson was bound to a master at the time of her execution as a witch, and Nicholas and Margaret Jennings had been servants previous to their accusation.[49] Likewise, the middling status of a number of witch suspects is confirmed by their, or their husband's, low- or mid-level positions in local government. For instance, Andrew Sanford served as one of Hartford's chimney viewers (they were responsible for inspecting house chimneys in order to limit the danger of fire) about a decade before he and his wife faced trial for witchcraft, while Hugh Parsons won appointment as a fence viewer (an official tasked with making sure that the barriers that kept livestock out of gardens and fields were in good repair). In addition, several of the accused occupied the position of town constable. James Wakeley held this post in 1656, as did William Brown after his brush with suspicions of witchcraft. In a similar vein, Mary Barnes's husband, Thomas, won appointment as sergeant of Farmington's militia in 1651.[50] Another item that points to the middling rank of several witch suspects is that they or their husbands obtained the title of freeman. Andrew Sanford, Ralph Hall, and the husbands of Mary Barnes and Katherine Palmer, among others, achieved this status. This designation, which gave men the right to vote in elections, required them to be a property holder in good standing with their community.[51]

Only a few witch suspects or their spouses possessed the public office, rank, or reputation that marked them as members of New England's upper crust. Among them was Anne Hibbins. Her husband served as a deputy to the

Massachusetts General Court in 1641–42 and obtained the higher office of assistant in 1643, which he held to his death. Mary Bliss Parson's husband, Joseph, worked his way up from fence viewer and surveyor of highways to become a selectman, and later went on to serve as an officer in Hampton County's prestigious cavalry troop. In addition, he won appointment to a committee to build Northampton's first meetinghouse and was a signatory to the founding covenant of the town's church.[52] Another well-heeled witch suspect, John Blackleach, served as a constable for Hartford's "north side;" and Katherine Harrison's wealthy husband held the posts of constable, town crier, fence viewer, and surveyor in Wethersfield. While none of these positions was especially noteworthy, they were in line with the sorts of responsibilities held by the Puritan colonies' leading inhabitants.[53]

Whether or not a person moved up or down the social ladder is also pertinent to the witch profile. New Englanders could entertain the idea that those whose fortunes rose rapidly may have achieved their success through an unholy alliance with the Devil. Likewise, if a person experienced a sudden drop in wealth and status, their neighbors might fear that such ill fortune could easily turn them to discontent, envy, and witchcraft.[54] Social mobility marked the lives of several New England witch suspects. Joseph and Elizabeth Garlick saw their economic standing substantially increase in the years leading up to the latter's arrest for witchcraft. Although they were poor when they arrived in New England, by the mid-1650s Joseph was a landholder in Easthampton. By the third quarter of the seventeenth century, Goodman Garlick possessed more than eighty-two acres of land, an estate that placed him in the middle ranks of the town's property holders. Another couple touched by witchcraft allegations who also experienced upward social mobility was Joseph and Mary Parsons. They started out as folk of middling rank, progressively improved their fortunes after moving to Northampton in the 1650s, and had amassed a fortune by the time of Joseph's death in the 1680s. Katherine Harrison presents an even more dramatic rags-to-riches story. When she first came to Connecticut, she worked as a servant, but in 1653 she became the wife of the wealthy merchant John Harrison. Upon his death, Katherine found herself in the rare position of being a financially independent woman.[55] Meanwhile, Anne Hibbins's story illustrates how a persons' ill fortune could also stoke suspicions of occult mischief. She enjoyed the material comforts and social status that came with her husband's wealth and position but later in life suffered a series of reversals. She was excommunicated from her church, felt the impact of financial setbacks suffered by her husband, and lost the prestige that came with his high political office when he died in 1654. Two years later, she was tried and executed as a witch.[56]

Personal Background

The personal histories of the accused reveal several recurring themes that served to identify them as deviant and even dangerous. First, it did not pay to know a witch in seventeenth-century New England, and suspects were commonly tied to other alleged occult criminals. For instance, two women who testified against Eunice Cole reported that she had said "she was sure there was a witch in the town, and she knew where he dwelt and who they are." They saw Cole's words in an incriminating light, believing that her knowing a witch meant that she was likely one herself. Those who possessed close ties to a person accused of occult crime ran the risk of falling under suspicion themselves. The reasons for this are not difficult to fathom. Though early modern folk believed that witches carefully hid their true nature, they found it difficult to believe that one could practice the dark arts without those close to them knowing and abetting it. Moreover, the malefic and diabolical views of witchcraft held that witches sought to pass on their knowledge and spread their apostasy to those around them.[57]

Witch suspects were frequently tied to other suspects by bonds of blood and marriage. Out of the almost sixty people formally charged with witchcraft in the Puritan colonies before 1670, twenty faced the charge alongside a spouse.[58] In contrast, parent-child ties among the accused were relatively rare during the first three-quarters of the seventeenth century. The only episode involving charges of occult mischief leveled against a parent and their offspring was that of the mother and daughter Winifred and Mary Holman. In light of the numerous witchcraft prosecutions involving parent-child suspects that took place in Europe, why there was a dearth of such cases in the Puritan colonies at midcentury remains an open question.[59] The only thing that can be said for certain is that first- and second-generation New Englanders did not generally pin the blame for occult crime on children or young adults. However, intergenerational witchcraft suspicions did emerge by the late-seventeenth and early eighteenth centuries. Alice Young Beamon, a Springfield woman accused of occult misdeeds in 1678, was in all likelihood the daughter of Alice Young, who was executed for witchcraft thirty years earlier. Jane Walford had run-ins with the law over accusations of black magic in the 1650s and 1660s and passed on these suspicions to her daughter, Hannah Walford Jones, who faced the charge in 1682. In addition, Mary Bliss Parson's reputation as a witch rubbed off on her eldest daughter, Hannah, who came under suspicion in 1702.[60]

Witchcraft suspicions also spread through ties of friendship and neighborhood. Some of the suspicions against Mary Bliss Parsons rested on her association with the accused witches Hugh and Mary Lewis Parsons. Like-wise, a number of people accused of witchcraft during the Hartford witch panic of 1662 were well acquainted with each other. Several deals involving the sale and purchase of land tied together Andrew and Mary Sanford, Nathaniel and Rebecca Greensmith, and William and Judith Ayres. Besides these more formal sorts of interaction, it is easy to imagine that the couples, who were all near neighbors, developed a close familiarity as they worked and socialized together.[61]

A criminal background was another frequent feature of the accused, and out of the individuals who came before the courts for witchcraft before 1670, just over half of them (thirty) had been previously brought to book on other charges including slander, theft, and sexual and religious crimes. Seeing that only an estimated 10 to 20 percent of seventeenth-century New Englanders faced criminal prosecution, this is a striking statistic.[62] Simply put, witch suspects appear to have been especially prone to criminal behavior and thus stood out as troublesome neighbors at best or, at worst, dangerous deviants who needed to be purged from society.

The most common crime committed by New England's witch suspects were verbal offenses such as slander or "unclean speeches"—a catch-all phrase used to describe foul and indecent language. About half of the accused with documented criminal histories had previously come before the magistrates for this sort of activity. New Haven's town court admonished Goodwife Bayley for her "filthy corrupting words," while John Blackleach and John Bradstreet faced charges for disrespectful words aimed at those in positions of authority.[63] However, the vast majority of those prosecuted for offensive utterances ended up in court for defamation. Katherine Harrison, Ralph and Mary Hall, Elizabeth Garlick, William Ayres, James Wakeley, Eunice Cole, Mary Lewis Parsons, and Susannah Martin all came before the

Table 3.6   Criminal charges brought against New England's pre-1670 witch suspects (N = 30).

Verbal crimes (slander, etc.)	14 (47%)
Theft/fraud	7 (23%)
Sexual crimes (fornication, adultery, etc.)	6 (20%)
Religious crimes (blasphemy, etc.)	3 (10%)
Assault	3 (10%)
Other misdemeanors (drunkenness, etc.)	10 (30%)

Note: The percentages in this table add up to more than a hundred because various individuals committed crimes under multiple categories.

bar—sometimes on multiple occasions—to answer for slander. Seeing that early modern Europeans believed witches used maledictions in order to perform acts of magical harm, it makes sense that other forms of illicit speech could contribute to a person's reputation as a witch.[64]

Tied for second place in terms of frequency, acts of theft and sexual crimes also marked the criminal histories of witch suspects. Five of the accused—Mary Johnson, Margaret Jennings, Margaret Jones, William Ayres, and Nathaniel Greensmith—sported previous convictions for stealing. Mary Johnson and Margaret Jennings were servants when they committed the crime. Like other members of this low-ranking group, the former may have turned to larceny in order to acquire comforts her otherwise Spartan existence would not allow, while the latter did so in order to help finance her escape from servitude. Greensmith's career as a thief involved him absconding with some wheat, a hoe, and a canoe, while Ayres's crime spree included the theft of a cow, a hog, and an iron bar. Katherine Harrison and Andrew Sanford also faced charges, not for outright theft, but for robbing others of their rightful belongings or time. Sanford's apprentice, Gabriel Lynch, sued him "for fraudulent dealing about the time of his apprenticeship," and Harrison came before the magistrates for wrongfully "detaining a kettle" a Native American had purchased from her.[65]

Five of the accused had also faced charges for crimes of a sexual nature. Nicholas and Margaret Jennings got married after a New Haven colony court ordered the two to wed on convicting them of fornication. Though not as well documented, Alice Lake allegedly engaged in the same crime while she was a young woman. More seriously in the minds of the Puritans, three witch suspects were accused or convicted of adultery. This was a far more troubling sexual crime because it entailed having illicit sex with another person's husband or wife and thus constituted a threat to the vital institution of marriage. Adulterous women also undermined their husbands' exclusive right to their bodies and, if they bore a child from the illegal union, could rob his rightful heirs of their inheritance. In light of this and following biblical precedents, adultery was a capital offense throughout Puritan New England. Connecticut appears to have issued an arrest warrant against Mary Barnes for "that foul sin of adultery" in 1649, but the results of the case are unknown. In addition, Elizabeth Seager was arrested, tried, and convicted of adultery in 1663. However, as invariably became the case with the prosecution of this crime by midcentury, the court substituted other punishments for the death penalty.[66]

Religious infractions, acts of violence, and various other offenses made up the balance of criminal activity among New England's pre-1670 witch suspects. Surviving records indicate that only three of the accused faced charges for religious offenses. Elizabeth Bailey of Maine and Martha Batchelor of Ipswich both had to pay fines for the relatively minor transgression of failing to attend Sabbath services, while Elizabeth Seager stood before the bar for the more serious charge of blasphemy. There were other suspects who earned a reputation for irreverence, but whose behavior fell short of triggering legal action.[67] The accused favored verbal over physical violence, and only four of them went to court for assault. Eunice Cole found herself facing a judge after attacking a constable as did Nicholas Jennings for beating another man's cow, and courts found Nathaniel Greensmith and Thomas Welles guilty of battery.[68] In addition, authorities punished John Godfrey and John Bradstreet for lying and John Brown for drunkenness. Several of the accused also suffered punishment for misdemeanors that compromised their neighbors' security. James Wakeley and Nicholas Jennings both paid fines for failing to take part in the town watch and attend militia training, while John Carrington had a £10 fine levied against him for "bartering a gun with an Indian"—a serious offense at a time when attacks by Native Americans were still a threat.[69]

Though not as common as a criminal past, the lives of a number of witch suspects featured domestic discord. The Puritans put a heavy premium on household harmony, believing that without well-functioning families all other social institutions would ultimately fail. Thus conflict between spouses, parents, and children carried negative connotations, and the New England colonies mobilized the coercive power of the law in order to maintain the integrity of family life. For example, under a 1646 Massachusetts act, a child over the age of sixteen "and of sufficient understanding" who cursed or struck their parents could be put to death by stoning. Though the colony never imposed this punishment, the very fact that it was on the books points to the premium its leaders placed on family order. In light of this, it is easy to understand how a history of household conflict could single a person out as ungodly and a fit vessel for witchcraft.[70]

Domestic contention among the accused most frequently took the form of conflict between husbands and wives. Testimony gathered for the trials of Hugh and Mary Lewis Parsons paints a picture of a deeply troubled marriage. She accused her husband of various sorts of abuse and was herself was no model Puritan spouse, but "spoke very harsh things against him [her husband] before his face." Mary Bliss Parsons also lived a life marred by domestic strife. William Hannum reported that he once saw her husband, Joseph, "beating one of his little children for losing its shoe"; and when Mary tried to intervene, he violently "thrust her away." Though Puritan fathers had the right to inflict corporal punishment, Hannum felt that Goodman Parsons went beyond what was acceptable and had beat his child "unmercifully." John Matthews likewise testified that Joseph punished his wife by "locking her into the cellar." Even though the husband appears to be the driving force behind this contention, Mary's association with such familial dysfunction likely contributed to the witchcraft suspicions that emerged against her. Finally, in an episode that involved conflict between spouses as well as parents and children, a Massachusetts's court presented Susannah Martin and her son, Richard, for "abusing his father and throwing him down, taking away his clothes and holding an axe against him." Richard was found guilty and whipped. This took place in 1669—the same year that Susannah went on trial as a witch.[71]

Perhaps the best example of the connection between domestic conflict and a reputation for witchcraft comes from somewhat later in the seventeenth century. In 1680 Bridget Oliver came before a jury for witchcraft but managed to avoid conviction. She again faced the charge twelve years later during the Salem crisis after she had remarried and went by the name Bridget Bishop. She was not so lucky on this occasion and became the first victim of the witch hunt that would take so many lives. Before any of these events unfolded, Bridget had accrued a reputation-damaging record of marital conflict. In 1670 she was punished for trading blows with her husband, Thomas Oliver. Eight years later the couple again came before the magistrates for verbal violence—Bridget allegedly called Thomas an "old rogue and old devil"—and the court ordered them to stand back-to-back and gaged in Salem's public market for an hour "with a paper fastened to each of their foreheads upon which their offence should be fairly written."[72]

Sometimes domestic deviance took forms other than outright conflict between family members. Three years before he was accused of invoking the Devil, John Brown faced trial for holding "disorderly and unseasonable night meetings" at his home. According to the charges laid against him, instead of promoting order, sobriety, and godliness as was expected of a household head, Brown made his dwelling a site of sin where servants and young people danced, sang, and played cards. Brown was not an ideal Puritan patriarch, and his wife later sought to divorce him on the grounds that he had "broken his matrimonial bond by unlawful company with another woman" and for "totally forsaking & deserting" her.[73] Likewise, shortly before Nicholas and Margaret Jennings went on trial for witchcraft, a court-appointed panel of midwives examined their unmarried daughter, Martha, and found that she was not pregnant. The implication here is that there was some suspicion that she had conceived a child out of wedlock—a charge that hardly put the parenting skills of Nicholas and Margaret in a good light. James Wakeley's courtship of the widow Alice Boosy provides perhaps the oddest example of how concerns over domestic impropriety shadowed the accused. Widow Boosy agreed to marry Wakeley in the early 1650s but then tried to renege on her promise. Instead of accepting her change of heart, Wakeley sued her for breach of contract. The widow relented and went through with the nuptials. Wakeley did nothing illegal, yet his decision to coerce a woman into marrying him hardly fell in line with the mutual support and respect Puritans believed were at the core of a good marriage.[74]

Clear ties between witchcraft suspicions and occupation are infrequent because those of the accused are generally unremarkable and do little to distinguish them from other New Englanders. The men who fell under scrutiny were mostly farmers, while the overwhelming proportion of female suspects carried out the various labors of a housewife. For several women, however, activity as a healer played a role in their denunciation for occult crime.[75] The idea that midwives were particularly vulnerable to accusation—that their association with matters of life and death and the competition they posed to professional, male physicians made them a target—is not born out by New England's witchcraft cases. Indeed, before 1670 there was only one witch suspect, Jane Hawkins, who was clearly a midwife. Moreover, midwives served as agents of witch prosecution far more often than they became its victim. In both Europe and the Puritan colonies, they functioned as officers of the court when they examined female suspects for witches' teats or Devil's marks. For instance, during Goody Knapp's witchcraft trial in 1651, a panel of women examined her and found incriminating marks on the defendant's body that helped to cement her conviction.[76]

While it does not appear that midwives were especially prone to accusations of occult misdeeds, there was a more general link between witchcraft and the healing arts. That Katherine Harrison dabbled in medicine came up during her trial. The same was true for Winifred Holman. Likewise, the various medical activities of Margaret Jones formed a major plank of her prosecution.[77] In the early modern era there was no clear line between medicine and magic, and healing techniques often combined ordinary remedies with magical charms and incantations. In light of this collapsing of natural and supernatural cures, people assumed that those who could cure also had the power to inflict magical harm.[78]

Like a vocation in the healing arts, engaging in supernatural activities such as countermagic or fortune telling could nurture suspicions of witchcraft. In early modern Europe, people variously known as white witches or "cunning folk" used occult methods to heal the sick, foretell the future, or combat witchcraft. These village-level magic users frequently found themselves condemned as witches by theologians who considered their activities blasphemous. Though a vibrant class of folk magicians does not seem to have emerged in New England, concerns over their activities still periodically came to the surface there. One piece of evidence against John Godfrey was that he had "come to places where some cattle where bewitched . . . and said, 'I will unwitch them,' and presently they were well"—a clear reference to countermagic. Likewise, that things Margaret Jones "foretold came to pass accordingly" sealed her reputation as a fortune-teller and a witch.[79] Similarly, as a young servant woman in Hartford, Katherine Harrison found time to predict the future, and her alleged activities as a fortune-teller featured in the testimony presented during her witchcraft trial. According to several witnesses, she engaged in divination and did "often speak and boast of her great familiarity with Mr. Lilly," a reference to the English astrologer William Lilly. Moreover, they asserted that Harrison's predictions were accurate and reported that she once told fellow-servant Elizabeth Bateman, who was then being courted by William Chapman, that she would marry a man named Simon. This came true when she later wed Simon Smith.[80]

It is not always easy to judge how elements of an individual's personal history figured in the process whereby New Englanders identified witches. Many colonists had close ties with purported witches, committed crimes, engaged in conflict with family members, and worked as healers but never became targets of suspicion. Except for their criminal behavior, it is also unclear whether the accused featured these traits more frequently or with a greater intensity than others. What this points to is that witch suspects' personal backgrounds were not a driving force behind their accusations. Rather, they helped support and validate witchcraft suspicions born of their perceived antisocial behavior and negative character traits.

Witchcraft denunciations in New England were not random, and suspicion gravitated toward certain kinds of individuals. First and foremost, the accused were, or were at least perceived as, individuals ruled by discontent, anger, and malice. In terms of their demographic and socioeconomic profile, they tended to be women, middle-aged or older, married but with fewer children than the norm, and of humble rank. Finally, many had ties to other witch suspects and histories featuring previous run-ins with the law, domestic discord, or activity as a healer or fortune-teller. In sum, the New Englanders who were most likely to come under suspicion were those seen as having failed to live up to Puritan religious and social strictures.

The reality and perception of a person's behavior had the greatest bearing on whether they faced accusation, for early modern Europeans on both sides of the Atlantic primarily identified someone as a witch based on their actions. Whether an individual was male or female, young or old, wealthy or destitute contributed to witchcraft suspicions in a secondary but significant way because these characteristics helped determine if society judged their behavior as acceptable or deviant. Subordinate groups such as women and the poor disproportionally suffered from witch fears because they enjoyed less latitude in meeting (or breaking) social norms. Moreover, when their failures to fall in line with social expectations transmuted into suspicions of witchcraft, they possessed fewer means to deter or defend against accusation.

Of all the traits of the early modern witch, that they were commonly women has drawn the most attention. Understanding why this was the case is the next step in this analysis and pushes the discussion well beyond who was accused of witchcraft in New England to why they became targets of suspicion in the first place.

CHAPTER 4

"The More Women, the More Witches"

Gender and Witchcraft

John Bradstreet came before a Massachusetts court in 1652 on "suspicion of hav[ing] familiarity with the devil" after stating before several witnesses that he had consulted "a book of magic" in order to invoke a demonic spirit. Two years later, Lydia Gilbert faced trial in Connecticut for having "killed the body of Henry Stiles" and committing "other witchcrafts." Bradstreet's alleged crime may appear trivial compared to Gilbert's, but in the Puritan colonies where witchcraft was legally defined as a compact with the Devil, the charge laid against him was just as serious as murder and should have led to a thorough investigation and possibly a trial. Nevertheless, the authorities gave little credence to Bradstreet's self-incriminating words and released him. In contrast, Goody Gilbert faced trial and was convicted, and there is no indication that the justices had any qualms about sending her to the gallows. Likewise, both Margaret and Thomas Jones stood accused of occult crime in 1648, but only the wife hanged for it; and when Andrew and Mary Sanford went on trial for witchcraft over a decade later, Goody Sanford ended up with a rope around her neck while her husband went free in spite of their close association and the identical charges they faced.[1]

As these cases illustrate, the treatment of witch suspects in the Puritan colonies often varied according to sex, and women bore a greater risk of accusation, trial, and execution. Before 1670 female suspects outnumbered male ones by more than two to one; and of the fifteen people sent to the gallows for witchcraft, thirteen were women. What makes this all the more striking is that males outnumbered females in the first decades of New England's colonial settlement and maintained a numerical edge in many of its communities well past midcentury.[2] This gender imbalance in witch-hunting is consistent with patterns in England and across much of continental Europe. The English jurist Richard Bernard recognized this, and in his book *A Guide to Grand Jury Men*, wrote that "of witches there be commonly more women than men: this is evident." William Perkins put it even more bluntly when he evoked what he claimed was an ancient Hebrew proverb: "The more women, the more witches."[3]

These observations raise the question of how central gender—the cultural construction of what it is to be a man or a woman and the power dynamics associated with it—was to witchcraft and witch-hunting in Puritan New England. One point of view contends that it was at the core of witch prosecutions across early modern Europe and its New World colonies. According to this outlook, witch-hunting served to maintain male dominance and undermine female power, and men who fell victim to accusation were simply collateral damage of what was essentially a war against women.[4] Another perspective holds that gender, while important, was but one of a constellation of factors that shaped patterns of accusation. In the words of historian Christina Larner, witch-hunting, "while sex-related, was not sex specific." It also asserts that men were often witch suspects in their own right rather than secondary figures.[5] A close look at the Puritan colonies' campaign against black magic supports this latter view. While New Englanders' assumptions concerning womanhood and manhood were a critical component of witch fears and prosecutions, gender dynamics were not the only variable. Moreover, like their cousins across the Atlantic, the colonists did not think that witchcraft was a crime unique to women.[6]

Patterns

An analysis of sex-related patterns of prosecution indicates that women were the primary victims of witch-hunting. Across New England's entire history of witch prosecution from the mid-seventeenth to early eighteenth centuries, roughly four out of every five people accused of occult crime were women.[7] Before 1670 the various New England colonies all featured a similar sex imbalance among witch suspects. Connecticut prosecuted two women for every man, and removing the unusually gender-balanced cases related to the Hartford witch panic leaves the colony with a ratio of three female suspects to every male. Massachusetts followed suit, and of its witch suspects almost three-quarters were women. Similarly, two of the three people accused of occult crime in New Haven were women.

A comparison of the legal fates of male and female suspects confirms women's greater vulnerability to witchcraft fears. Just over two-fifths of the men avoided trial, never proceeding beyond the stage of an initial examination or grand jury presentment. Moreover, of those who did go before a jury, less than a quarter went to the gallows. Accused women had a different collective experience. Only about a third of them managed to escape trial, and of the remainder, half of their cases ended with an execution. Put a different way, while less than one in four men who faced trial for witchcraft hanged, the figure for women was one out of every two.[8]

Once denounced for witchcraft, women were also more likely to be subsequently accused of the crime than men. Of the eleven suspects from before 1670 who had multiple encounters with charges of occult mischief, nine were women. The two male repeat offenders were James Wakeley, who faced accusation twice, and John Godfrey, who went to trial for witchcraft three times. Six of the women came under suspicion twice and the rest were accused three times. These multiple run-ins with witchcraft could be concentrated within a few years or spread across a much longer time span. For instance, Winifred Holman and Elizabeth Seager faced several witchcraft accusations over the course of just two or three years, while Eunice Cole's and Katherine Palmer's histories as witch suspects stretched over several decades.[9]

Table 4.1   Witchcraft prosecution in New England before 1670 by sex

	CONNECTICUT (INCLUDING THE HARTFORD HUNT)	CONNECTICUT (W/OUT THE HARTFORD HUNT)	MASSACHU-SETTS	NEW HAVEN
Women	19 (69%)	11 (73%)	18 (72%)	2 (67%)
Men	9 (31%)	4 (27%)	7 (28%)	1 (33%)

Table 4.2   Trial and conviction rates for male and female witch suspects before 1670 (cases involving suspects who fled before being able to go to trial are not included)

	CASES NOT LEADING TO TRIALS	CASES LEADING TO TRIALS	CASES LEADING TO EXECUTIONS	EXECUTION RATE OF THOSE TRIED
Women (N = 38)	12 (32%)	26 (68%)	13 (34%)	50%
Men (N = 16)	7 (43%)	9 (56%)	2 (13%)	22%

Moreover, the descendants of women accused of witchcraft occasionally came under scrutiny for the crime, while male suspects do not appear to have passed on this dark mark to their children. For example, Winifred Holman faced trial as a witch in 1659 alongside her daughter Mary, and it is highly likely that witch fears against Winifred—a widow who dabbled in the healing arts—eventually transferred to her offspring. Likewise, as previously mentioned, the daughter and grandson of Alice Young, who was hanged for occult crime in 1647, were dealing with the taint of witchcraft thirty years later. Events that unfolded in Massachusetts in 1702 present another example of how suspicions of occult mischief against a woman could cast a shadow over generations to come. In that year Peletiah Glover of Northampton lodged a complaint against "Betty Negro" for defaming his spouse and mother-in-law as witches. Goodman Glover's wife's maiden name was Parsons, and her mother was none other than Mary Bliss Parsons, a woman who had faced down accusations of witchcraft in the 1650s and 1670s.[10]

Sex also intersected with other features of the witch profile. For instance, the relationship between age and suspicions of occult crime differed depending on whether the accused were male or female. Middle-aged men in the prime of their life were overrepresented among witch suspects, and the same was true for women over sixty. Among the latter, it is possible that their inability to bear children may have marked them as deviant and more vulnerable to the lure of occult power. As for the men, they may have drawn undue attention since Puritan colonists associated witchcraft with power and its abuse, and this period of a man's life commonly witnessed the apex of his wealth and influence.[11]

In terms of marital status, male and female witch suspects had much in common. For both sexes, a large majority of the accused (about four out of every five) were married, and around a tenth had never entered into wed-

Table 4.3   Ages of male and female witch suspects before 1670

	UNDER 40 YEARS OLD	40–59 YEARS OLD	60+ YEARS OLD
Women (N = 32)	15 (47%)	13 (41%)	4 (12%)
Men (N = 14)	5 (36%)	9 (64%)	0

Table 4.4   Marital status of male and female witch suspects before 1670

	MARRIED	SINGLE	WIDOWED
Women (N = 40)	31 (77%)	3 (8%)	6 (15%)
Men (N = 17)	14 (82%)	2 (12%)	1 (6%)

lock. However, the proportion of female suspects who were widowed was two and a half times higher than among men. This gives the impression that losing a spouse had much more of a bearing on women's likelihood of coming before the courts for witchcraft than was the case for men. Indeed, the denunciations of women like Katherine Harrison and Anne Hibbins for occult mischief came in the wake of their husbands' deaths. The explanation may partially lie in widows' and widowers' different relationship to the law. In a society where only men had full access to the courts, the death of a husband meant the loss of a male protector who could fend off accusations through legal means. Meanwhile, a man who lost his wife suffered no such disadvantage.[12]

Gender also colored associations between witchcraft and certain occupations. Following the general pattern of sex-specific jobs, most male suspects were farmers, wage laborers, and artisans. For instance, John Brown of New Haven at least periodically worked as a sailor when he fell under suspicion, for he stated that he could not guarantee his attendance of a hearing because "he was to go to sea & knew not whether he should be at home."[13] Likewise, most accused women were hard-working housewives. None of this set them apart from the general population. However, a more specialized female employment did have a bearing on allegations of witchcraft. Although women generally cared for family members and neighbors during times of sickness, a smaller subset of female "doctoresses" practiced medicine more regularly, and they crop up in a number of witchcraft cases. Margaret Jones's work as a healer contributed to her conviction for witchcraft, and Ann Burt's medical activities were at the center of her accusation. Since folk commonly believed that those who could cure could also harm, such work made women more vulnerable to charges of occult crime. Interestingly, although there were male physicians, none of them seemed to have aroused suspicion before 1670. That they were men and associated with more formal, learned medical practice perhaps gave their activities an air of legitimacy that shielded them from accusation.[14]

To a large degree witchcraft is an act of the imagination, and early modern Europeans imagined male and female witches somewhat differently. In particular, the motifs of diabolical witchcraft as well as the harms attributed to malefic magic varied according to the sex of the alleged offender.[15] The image of a witch as a servant of Satan was not exclusive to either sex, and there is some consistency in the sort of demonic imagery attached to male and female suspects. For instance, animal familiars—the magical beings provided by the Devil to aid witches in their evil deeds—appear in about a quarter of cases for both men and women. Despite this, the texture of diabolism did differ between the sexes. Testimony concerning the preternatural teats witches supposedly used to feed their familiar spirits appears twice as often among women as men, and it makes sense that people more strongly associated them with women since they nursed infants in everyday life. Nevertheless, in the upside-down world of witchcraft, New Englanders also believed that men could engage in the act of nursing, albeit of a dark, malevolent kind. For instance, Mary Lewis Parsons accused her husband of possessing a witch's teat, saying that the "Devil came to him in the night, at the bed, and sucked him." The only thing separating this from standard testimony concerning these diabolical appendages is that Hugh Parson allegedly fed Satan himself and not one of his diabolical underlings. Such distinctions speak to how English folk constructed male and female witches differently. Befitting their role as the subordinate sex, people imagined female witches nourishing the Devil's lesser minions but, in line with notions of masculine dominance, envisioned male witches occupying a space higher up on the demonic food chain.[16]

As the allegation against Goodman Parsons illustrates, the most striking difference in the gendered construction of diabolical witchcraft was how New Englanders envisioned male and female suspects' relationship to the Devil. They tended to portray men as having a very direct relationship with Satan; and out the six men who had diabolical testimony presented against them, half included descriptions of them invoking the Devil or demons. Connecticut authorities accused John Brown of such behavior and gathered testimony from a number of witnesses who saw him use "some art to raise the Devil." According to Eliakin Hitchcock, Brown came to his home late one night and asked for ink, a quill, and paper. He then proceeded to make "a round circle, & made figures in it" such as Hitchcock "never saw the like" and then asked his host, "Will you see the Devil raised?" Brown then led Hitchcock outside "and told him the names of the stars & the planets . . . and said the Devil may be there, do you not see him?" Similarly, John Bradstreet and Thomas Welles stood accused of knowing how to "set spells & raise the Devil."[17]

It is also noteworthy that charges of witchcraft aimed at men often involved some form of magical text, while those directed against women did not. For example, John Brown wrote a series of astrological symbols to allegedly raise the Devil, while John Bradstreet supposedly "read in a book of magic" to invoke a demonic spirit. The closest a female suspect came to such allegations was when Katherine Harrison was accused of being familiar with the works of the English astrologer William Lilly. This fits a view common across much of early modern Europe that associated bookish and learned forms of magic with men. In contrast, people on both sides of the Atlantic saw female witches as the Devil's servants and supplicants rather than as magic users who commanded diabolical powers. This distinction reflected the widespread belief that women were innately subordinate beings who rightfully lived under the rule of husbands, fathers, or even the masculine figure of the Devil.[18]

Likewise, there was both common ground and subtle distinctions when it came to gender-specific constructs of the malefic witch. The majority of charges laid against male and female suspects involved illness and death among people and livestock. Of the men for whom information is available on their purported offenses, half stood accused of afflicting or killing adults, a third for the injury or murder of children, and a quarter for damaging or destroying livestock. For female suspects whose supposed misdeeds are documented, two-thirds were blamed for harm to adults, about half for attacks on children, and just over a quarter for the magical abuse of farm animals. Early modern Europeans were more apt to believe that female witches spent their time inflicting illness and death on the young and old because caring for children and the sick fell into their sphere of activity. Likewise, allegations of magical attacks against livestock were leveled equally at male and female suspects because the sexes more evenly shared responsibility for domesticated animals. In a similar vein, colonists blamed female suspects for domestic mishaps far more often than they accused men of such crimes. Once again, considering their daily management of domestic tasks, it makes sense that folks attributed this variety of occult mischief to women. These were trends, not hard and fast rules, and sometimes witch suspects were charged with crimes commonly associated with the opposite sex. For instance, people believed that Hugh Parsons "had bewitched his child to death" and also blamed him for a mysterious illness that struck the children of Springfield's minister, Reverend George Moxon.[19]

Table 4.5   Male and female witch suspects' alleged malefic acts before 1670

	ATTACKS ON ADULTS	ATTACKS ON CHILDREN	ATTACKS ON LIVESTOCK
Female (N = 21)	14 (67%)	11 (52%)	6 (29%)
Male (N = 12)	6 (50%)	4 (33%)	3 (25%)

Note: Since suspects could be accused of more than one type of malefic attack, the percentages in this table do not add up to a hundred.

Women

The connection between women and witchcraft suspicions operated on several levels. Learned opinion and popular lore stereotyped them as being more likely to turn to the dark arts than men. Moreover, their day-to-day responsibilities placed them at the center of aspects of life such as illness, childbirth, and death that commonly formed the backdrop to allegations of magical mischief. Also, women who were unable or unwilling to live within narrow social expectations fell under the shadow of suspicion as perceptions of social deviance bled into fears of occult crime. Of course, these stereotypes, roles, and expectations were a product of gender norms. Thus, while women's vulnerability to charges of witchcraft was not simply the outcome of some innate misogyny or blunt efforts to impose male dominance, gender did play an important part in their association with the crime.

The consensus among English demonologists was that women were more apt to be witches than men, and the Puritan colonists inherited this view.[20] When James I asked "What can be the cause that there are twenty women given to that craft, where there is one man?" in his *Daemonology* (1597), he readily answered, "The reason is easy, for as that sex is frailer than man is, so is it easier to be entrapped in these gross snares of the Devil." William Perkins supported this outlook, saying "that the woman being the weaker sex, is sooner entangled by the Devil's illusions." Similarly, Richard Bernard wrote that women were easily drawn to witchcraft since they were "more superstitious, and being displeased, more malicious . . . and so herein more fit instruments for the Devil." Thomas Cooper, John Gaule, and Alexander Roberts hit on the same theme. Gaule described women as "a feeble sex" and "the fittest subject" of Satan's efforts to turn people to witchcraft, while Cooper explained that they more frequently embraced witchcraft because of their ignorance and ambition. Noting that "more women in a far different proportion prove witches than men, by a hundred to one," Roberts suggested this was due to their "credulous" nature, dangerous curiosity, proclivity to sin, "slippery" tongues, and "insatiable desire for revenge."[21]

These writers also strengthened the association of witchcraft with female sexuality. Richard Bernard listed a number of places where the Devil's mark or witch's teat might be found but stressed that they were most often located near suspects' "secret parts" (genitals), and he specifically mentioned the case of a condemned witch, Margaret Flowers, who had a Devil's mark located there. Likewise, Michael Dalton advised that these signifiers of satanic allegiance were frequently located on peoples' "secretest parts" and that discovering them required "diligent and careful search." Building on these learned views, people increasingly associated witch marks not just with sex organs, but particularly those of women. For instance, twenty suspects came before the bar during a series of witch trials held in Lancaster in 1634; and of the sixteen women among them, thirteen were found to have Devil's marks on or near their genitals. It is not clear if the remaining four men were subjected to such a search, but there is no report of incriminating marks being discovered on their bodies. Keep in mind, people across the English Atlantic did not exclusively connect witch marks with women. For instance, Mary Lewis Parsons suspected her husband had a witch's teat and searched him "when he hath been asleep in bed, and could not find anything about him unless it be in his secret parts."[22]

Ideas about women's bodies and concerns over female sexuality further contributed to the notion that they were more likely to turn to witchcraft. Early modern Europeans believed women's physical frames were weaker than men's, making them more vulnerable to Satan's advances. Moreover, in both theory and practice, Puritans drew a straight line between illicit female sexuality and witchcraft. Again, with one exception, all of New England's early witch suspects convicted of sex crimes were women. In addition, sexuality intertwined with diabolical witchcraft in the cases of several female

FIGURE 4.1   This image of three female witches reflects how across most of early modern Europe and its Atlantic World colonies, women were accused of occult crimes far more often than men. From *The Wonderful Discoverie of the Witchcrafts of Margaret and Philip Flower* (London, 1619). Division of Rare and Manuscript Collections, Cornell University Library.

suspects. When Mary Johnson confessed to being a witch, she reportedly admitted to engaging in sexual indiscretions with "men and devils." Similarly, according to accounts of her confession, Rebecca Greensmith let it be known that "the devil had frequent use of her body." Notably, no such sexually charged stories emerge in connection with witchcraft cases in New England involving male suspects.[23]

The roles that women played in everyday life served to reinforce their links to witchcraft. Care for the sick and the dead were female responsibilities that drew them into a vortex of witch fears, for matters of life and death were often at the root of witchcraft episodes.[24] Women were also at the center of childbirth, and the occasion (when the death of the mother or child was a real possibility) was another stressful situation with potential to spark witch fears. Indeed, the case of Jane Hawkins grew out of events that took place in the birthing room, and Winifred Holman drew suspicion after caring for a new mother and her child. Abigail Dibble's tumultuous labor best illustrates how childbirth drew women together in what could be very difficult circumstances. Midwife Sarah Bates, along with Mary Holmes, Ann Smith, and Mary Scholfield aided Goody Dibble as she gave birth, and they described how the young woman's lips and tongue turned black during a "ghastly" ordeal that ended with her death. Rumors of black magic spread in the wake of this bizarre tragedy.[25]

Women's involvement in local social and economic networks also exposed them to suspicions of occult misdeeds, for such activities frequently generated the sorts of interpersonal conflict that sparked witchcraft suspicions. Goody Bayley's accusation was anchored in neighborhood-level frictions, and among other things, she became a target of suspicion after allegedly fostering "discord among neighbors." Likewise, neighborhood squabbles contributed to witchcraft allegations aimed at Elizabeth Garlick, and about half-a-dozen women who had a history of negative encounters with the accused testified against her.[26] Female-on-female conflict also reared its head when Mary Staples came under suspicion as a witch. Right after Goody Knapp of Fairfield was hanged for witchcraft in 1653, Staples examined the corpse, looking for the witch's teats that had been discovered on her body by a panel of court-appointed female searchers. One witness recalled that Staples declared that "these were no witches teats, but such as she herself had, and other women might have the same." With their judgment called into question, the women who had conducted the search turned on Staples. They cried her down, stating that "no honest women had such, and then all the women rebuking her and said they were witches' teats." Several of these women recalled this event when Staples came under scrutiny for occult crime the following year, citing it as evidence of her sympathy for witches and opposition to those who sought to root them out.[27]

Concerns over female deviance was a third factor that tied women to witchcraft. Puritan society provided women opportunities to achieve social acceptance, prestige, and self-worth, but the path they had to follow was a narrow one. They did not enjoy a broad scope of options beyond the accepted roles of wife and mother, and there was little tolerance for those who trespassed on the boundaries of female subordination. When society deemed that a woman had fallen from the straight and narrow, she ran the risk of being identified with aberrant behaviors associated with witchcraft.

Puritans saw the roles of wife and mother as sanctified duties and believed that a woman who fell short in fulfilling them committed, as with witchcraft, an offense against God and society. That Mary Holman was a single woman on the verge of becoming an old maid may have contributed to her neighbors' suspicions that she was a witch. Upholding God's ordinance to "be fruitful and multiply" (Genesis 1:28), Puritan colonists expected that wives would have large numbers of offspring. However, female witch suspects on average only bore about half the number of children produced by other New England mothers during the first generation of settlement. Katherine Harrison, Goody Knapp, and Alice Stratton each had three living children at the time of their prosecutions; Ann Burt, Elizabeth Garlick, Rebecca Greensmith, and Margaret Jennings had two; and Mary Lewis Parsons only had one. All of these individuals (except for Harrison and Parsons) were at least in their forties when they were accused and could have been expected to have had more children than they did.[28] Not only did these women stand out as deviant in this respect, but their neighbors may have assumed that their frustration over not having a large brood of offspring motivated them to lash out against those more fortunate than them through occult means.

To the Puritans, the model wife was meek, good natured, kind, nurturing, and obedient. As the Puritan writer Richard Baxter put it, such a woman lived in "a voluntary subjection and obedience" to her husband, maintained a "humble, peaceable temper," and was "careful in the government" of her speech.[29] In short, she was the opposite of a witch. Accordingly, women could come under suspicion when the engaged in behavior perceived as insubordinate, aggressive, or otherwise at odds with the image of the good wife.[30] When Elizabeth Garlick stood before the bar in 1654 for allegedly uttering "scandalous speeches" against the wife of William Mulford, she faced prosecution for a crime that involved both aggression and insubordination in the sense that a social inferior (a woman) attacked a superior (a man) by impugning his wife's reputation. Anne Hibbins was another witch suspect who people perceived as angry and prone to challenge male authority. Among other strikes against her, Hibbins suffered "censures" at the hands of her Boston congregation after she accused a carpenter of overcharging for work done for her husband and, in so doing, transgressed "the rule of the Apostle in usurping authority over him whom God hath made her head and husband." In other words, by inserting herself in the dispute with the workman, Hibbins had offended God and society by taking on a role that rightfully belonged to her spouse.[31]

A woman's financial independence could also generate suspicions. This helps to explain why witchcraft fears fastened on widows, especially when they inherited a valuable estate upon their husband's death. By challenging men's monopoly on property, such women may have drawn unwanted attention. More critical still were cases where rich widows did not quickly remarry or had no male heirs to whom they could pass on their property. Anne Hibbins was one witch suspect who fit the profile of a wealthy widow with no male heirs. She did have three sons, but all were from a previous marriage and thus had no claim on her second husband's property.[32]

Katherine Harrison's story best illustrates how female economic autonomy crossed paths with witchcraft. She came to New England as a lowly servant and went on to marry the up-and-coming Wethersfield merchant John Harrison in 1654. He died in 1666, leaving an estate valued at nearly a thousand pounds to his wife and children. It is pertinent that all three of the Harrisons' offspring were daughters, meaning that none of his wealth would end up in the hands of men unless his heirs wed. After setting aside her daughters' portions, Katherine ended up inheriting property worth £300 which she held in her own name since she did not remarry.[33] Evidence that the issue of female independence may have been on the minds of Wethersfield residents comes in the form of a series of attacks on widow Harrison's property in 1668. She claimed that several of her neighbors injured or killed her cattle and "spoiled" her crops. There is no indication that the courts took any action to address the widow's complaints. They did, however, adjudicate several slander cases in which Harrison stood as a defendant and punished her with a fine of £40—an excessive sum when compared to fines levied in similar cases. Taken together, these events paint a picture of a campaign against Harrison and her property and give the impression that financial independence may have been among the factors that aimed the finger of suspicion at her.[34]

Men

While learned authorities agreed that the majority of those who turned to witchcraft were women, they also made it abundantly clear that men were not free from this sin. As William Perkins wrote, "I comprehend both sexes or kinds of persons, men and women, excluding neither from being witches." After reviewing why women were more likely to embrace Satan and practice the dark arts, John Gaule similarly stated, "But let not the male be boasting, or secure of their sex's exemption" and followed up by listing several male witches mentioned in the Bible. These and other English demonologists stressed that there was no basis for believing that men could not be witches. Ordinary folk apparently agreed, and men faced accusations of occult crime. Indeed, one of the most infamous witch suspects in the Puritan colonies was John Godfrey who gained notoriety from his many run-ins with the law over allegations of black magic.[35]

Scholars have long held that men were mostly secondary figures in New England's witch scares and only came under scrutiny as a result of their association with female suspects. In some instances this was clearly the case. For example, Nathaniel Greensmith's spouse clearly triggered his prosecution for witchcraft when she implicated him in her confession to the crime. It also appears that William Ayres and Andrew Sanford became suspects as a result of allegations made against their wives.[36] Nevertheless, these men were "secondary" suspects in the sense that their accusation came after that of their spouses, not because their cases were marginal in importance or impact. Indeed, it is doubtful that Goodman Greensmith or his contemporaries would have seen his case as being somehow second rate, seeing that it resulted in his execution.

Though accusations against some male suspects stemmed from suspicions against female associates, many who came before the courts for occult crime ended up there on their own accord. Among the eighteen men charged with witchcraft in the Puritan colonies before 1670, only six can be confidently labeled as secondary suspects who faced legal action as a result of ties to an accused woman. Three more—John Carrington, Nicholas Jennings, and John Blackleach—came under scrutiny alongside their wives and not enough evidence remains to judge whether they or their spouses were the initial focus of suspicion. The remaining nine were clearly the primary targets of prosecution. John Godfrey and John Bradstreet were unmarried and William Graves was a widower when they came before the courts, and thus they had no wife through whom they might have attracted attention as a witch. The rest were married men whose reputations as witches started and ended with them. Hugh Parsons and Nicholas Jennings were part of this group, and their spouses also became targets of prosecution, but even here the husbands were the primary focus of suspicion.[37] Goodman Parsons was undoubtedly the leading suspect, and just about all witness testimony focused on him rather than his wife. And in the case of Nicholas and Margaret Jennings, the jury harbored more suspicions against him than his wife: a "major part" of them believed him guilty of witchcraft, while only "some" held this conviction about her.[38]

There was one variety of witch suspect in New England that was nearly monopolized by men. They were a set of young braggarts whose loose behavior and swaggering claims to supernatural power brought them before the law. For instance, John Bradstreet was a single man in his early twenties who had already been punished for lying, giving false testimony, and insubordination when Massachusetts officials investigated him for allegedly invoking a demon.[39] In his younger years, John Godfrey also fell into this category. One witness recalled a disturbing conversation with a twenty-year-old Godfrey during which he playfully implied that he had made a covenant with the Devil.[40] This pattern carried on into the latter part of the century. Caleb Powell came under suspicion in 1679 after he bragged of his occult expertise. Four years later James Fuller found himself standing trial before a Massachusetts court after he supposedly admitted that he prayed to the Devil, and in 1693 Hugh Crotia of Fairfield drew attention after he stated that he signed a pact with Satan. The only female who matches this profile is Abigail Hobbs who was arrested during the Salem witch hunt. By all accounts she was an irreverent teenager who, among her other "wicked carriages," repeatedly claimed to have "sold herself body and soul" to the Devil.[41]

Suspicions against these male suspects grew out of broader efforts to police the activities of young men who threatened to upend Puritan standards of order and decorum. John Brown of New Haven was about twenty-four and only recently married when he had his run-in with the law over witchcraft, and the episode was part of a broader pattern of misbehavior. He repeatedly came before magistrates for drunkenness, carousing in the streets (again while drunk), and hosting sin-laden revels at his home. To this he added several instances of disrespectful behavior—or what officials described as "contemptuous carriages"—in church and at court. Seen in this context, Brown's 1665 presentment for using occult rituals to invoke the Devil was in keeping with the bad-boy behavior that marked his life. Like most of his encounters with the law, it featured irreverent acts and involved a circle of male friends, and depositions gathered by the court give the impression that his experiment with occult power was just another instance of Brown's attempts to impress his peers with a bold disregard for social conventions. This is how the magistrates interpreted it, and like other young men suspected of black magic, they let him off with a stern warning.[42]

While close, the construction of the male witch in New England did not exactly match that of the female—they spoke the same language but in different dialects. Like their feminine counterparts, men accused of witch-craft came from a variety of social backgrounds but tended to cluster in the lower and middle ranks of society, were married, had histories of crime and domestic discord, and possessed reputations for antisocial behavior. Folk also accused male witches of a similar range of malefic injuries. Moreover, in keeping with patterns of accusation among women, people associated a few male suspects with fortunetelling and magical healing, such as when John Godfrey purportedly healed cattle that he claimed were bewitched or, during the Salem crisis, when several people asserted that Samuel Wardwell used occult means to tell the future.[43]

Just as women increased their chances of accusation when they failed to meet social expectations as wives and mothers, so too did men if they fell short of their duties as husbands and fathers. Puritan men were supposed to be firm but fair heads of households who imposed godly discipline on them-selves and their dependents. Those who ignored their patriarchal respon-sibilities stood contrary to God and appeared as likely recruits for Satan's ranks. Self-control was one quality of the godly man that several male witch suspects lacked. When John Brown appeared in court for excessive drinking and keeping a disorderly house, Thomas Wells for striking another man, or Nicholas Jennings for beating a neighbor's cow and committing fornication, they advertised that they were not in control of their own passions let alone capable of promoting order in their households.[44] Adding to perceptions of a dearth of self-discipline, almost half of male suspects from before 1670 had at some point come before the courts for intemperate speech. In addition, reports of domestic discord against several male suspects further fed their reputations as dysfunctional husbands and fathers.[45]

Several male suspects also contravened standards of behavior concerning commerce and business. More often than not, their economic misbehavior was not explicitly illegal, and several men who fell victim to witchcraft accu-sations were known for sharp dealing. Such was the case for the merchants John Blackleach and James Wakeley, who appeared as a plaintiffs in many court cases related to unpaid debts. Some folk felt Blackleach's pursuit of money strayed beyond the bounds of acceptable behavior, and in 1655 he faced a Connecticut court "to answer several complaints against him for oppression," or his overly aggressive attempts to obtain repayment. James Wakeley presents a similar profile. There was nothing about his penchant for litigation that placed him outside the bounds of the law, and New Englanders could not prosecute him simply for being hard-driving businessmen. Lack-ing other means to censure men like these, people may have subconsciously turned to allegations of witchcraft.[46]

Of all the cases of occult crime in early New England involving men, those of John Godfrey and Hugh Parsons are the best documented and provide a rich source of insight into how their domestic and economic lives engendered suspicions of witchcraft. John Godfrey stood in opposition to just about everything New Englanders thought a good Christian man should be. He never became a husband or a father—two things the Puritans placed at the center of their vision of godly masculinity. As a young man his lack of a spouse or children may not have raised many eyebrows. However, when he first faced charges of witchcraft in 1659 he was in his late thirties, and during his final run-in with the law for the crime in 1665 he was in his mid-forties. Thus by the time Godfrey fell under the shadow of suspicion, he was well past the point when a respectable man would have become a husband and a father. He also failed to live up to Puritan expectations concerning manly self-control. Court testimony paints a picture of Godfrey as a person ruled by his passions. According to Elizabeth Whitaker, when Godfrey got into an argument with her father over money, he "rose up in a great rage," issued several threats, and in a fury "knocked his head against the manteltree [fireplace lintel]." On top of all this, he never stayed in one place for very long and so failed to develop the network of relationships or record of community service expected of respectable men who set down roots.[47]

Godfrey also flouted norms of economic conduct. He may have come to New England as a poor servant, but by the late 1650s he had enough financial resources to dabble in money lending. Far from being generous or forgiving, Godfrey came off as a greedy, grasping man who aggressively dunned his debtors. Another sign of Godfrey's cutthroat approach to life was his appetite for litigation. Between 1660 and 1669 (a period that roughly coincides with his prosecutions for witchcraft), he appeared in court about eighty times, more often than not as a plaintiff. By then Godfrey's reputation for sharp dealing was so well established that others invoked his name as a synonym for dishonesty. During court proceedings in 1668, a witness testified that Thomas White "said that he could have as good dealing from a Turk or pagan or Indian as from Mr. Newman, yea, said he, from Godfrey himself." A short time later Thomas Welles had to defend himself against the charge that he had defamed a county judge by saying that the magistrate "was a worse useror [one who charged excessive interest on a loan] than Godfrey." Thus Godfrey appeared to many as an avaricious and malicious man—like Ebenezer Scrooge with an air of diabolical menace. One of his many accusers, John Singletary, summed it up when he told Godfrey, "Your nature is nothing but envy and malice which you will vent through to your own loss and you seek peace with no man."[48]

Like Godfrey, Hugh Parsons's behavior marked him as deviant. Although he was married, had children, and held property, Parsons was hardly a paragon of paternal virtues. Hugh's wife repeatedly complained of his abusive behavior, and by all accounts he was also a cold, uncaring father. Several people witnessed what they took as his lack of feeling over the death of one of his children, including Anthony Dorchester who noted that Parsons "expressed no kind of sorrow for his child . . . but carried himself as at other times without any regard of it." Hugh's irreverent, anger-driven behavior also widely missed the mark of the ideal Puritan patriarch. He preferred to stand outside the meetinghouse on Sabbath day smoking a pipe than attend the services within. Worse yet, his wife complained that if she did not threaten to complain to the magistrates, "he would not let her go [to meeting] once in the year." So instead of promoting religion in his household, Parsons appeared to oppose it. Those who testified against him also brought up his quick temper, including one woman who spoke of his "threatening speeches he uttered with much anger." Goodman Parsons admitted to this failing, explaining that "in his anger he is impatient, and doth speak what he should not."[49]

Hugh Parsons's offenses against masculine norms also applied to economic life, and stories concerning conflicts related to his work as a brick maker thread their way through testimony gathered for his witch trial. For example, several people linked the bewitchment of Reverend George Moxon's children to an argument the minister had with Goodman Parsons over the delivery of some bricks. The theme of avarice also cropped up when Anthony Dorchester recalled that he had some words with Parsons over a choice cut of meat during which the latter forcefully declared, "I will have it." One sort of malefic charge laid against Parsons takes on new meaning in light of his reputation for breaching norms of commercial conduct. Several men complained that Parsons used magical means to steal objects such as a knife and a trowel. These witnesses extended Parsons's predatory economic behavior into the realm of the occult, and the malefic acts they described mirrored the sort of ordinary material losses people suffered as a result of his disreputable business practices.[50]

According to those around him, Hugh Parsons's greed and unrestrained pursuit of self-interest also loomed over his relationship with his wife and children. When Goody Ashley asked Mary Parsons why her husband wanted her to serve as a wet nurse to Mrs. Smith, she replied "for luker [money] and gain; one may well know his reason." Goody Parsons also complained that Hugh put the pursuit of profit before the welfare of his children, complaining that even though she was busy taking care of a newborn baby, he kept at her "to help him about his corn." After the infant died, Mary Parsons blamed her husband, saying that he bewitched the child to death so "that she might be at liberty to help him in his Indian [corn] harvest."[51] Whether these allegations have a shred of truth to them or not, they reflect the public perception of Hugh Parsons as a man driven by money.

Husbands and Wives

Of the fifty-nine people prosecuted for witchcraft in New England before 1670, twenty of them (a third of the group) stood accused alongside their spouse. These alleged witch couples include Margaret and Thomas Jones, Joan and John Carrington, Hugh and Mary Parsons, Nicholas Bayley and his wife, Nicholas and Margaret Jennings, Judith and William Ayers, Rebecca and Nathaniel Greensmith, Andrew and Mary Sanford, John and Elizabeth Blackleach, and Mary and Ralph Hall. While the Ayers, Sanfords, Greensmiths, and Blackleaches were accused during the Hartford witch hunt of 1662, the remaining couples came under suspicion during more run-of-the-mill witchcraft episodes. Thus, the joint prosecution of spouses was not simply a byproduct of extraordinary witch panics but a regular feature of witch-hunting in New England. Moreover, although not unique to the Puritan colonies, allegations of black magic against married couples appear to have been more pronounced there than elsewhere in the English Atlantic during the middle decades of the seventeenth century.

If events had gone in a slightly different direction, New England's midcentury witch hunts may have produced even more allegations against spouses. Joseph Parsons, the husband of the suspected witch Mary Bliss Parsons, possessed traits commonly attributed to witches and for this reason, as well as his close association with his wife, was vulnerable to accusation. He was a shrewd, hard-dealing merchant whose aggressive business tactics echoed the sort of avariciousness New Englanders associated with male witches. Like many of the accused, Parsons also had a criminal history. In 1664 he appeared in court to answer for his "lascivious carriage to some women of Northampton," faced charges for assaulting a constable not long after, and in 1665 he had to pay a fine for his "contemptuous behavior" toward the selectmen of the town. Goodman Parsons's reportedly abusive behavior against his wife and children also fell into line with the profile of the male witch. On top of all this, his life featured the sort of pronounced social mobility that sometimes raised fears of witchcraft. Parsons started out as an ordinary fur trader, but by the time of his death in 1683 he was a powerful man who held one of the largest estates in Hampshire County, Massachusetts.[52] In spite of all this and the witchcraft accusations leveled against his wife, any suspicions that emerged against Goodman Parsons remained latent. It is likely that his wealth and influence shielded him from legal action just as it helped his wife get the better of her accusers.

The husband of accused witch Katherine Harrison may have also been perilously close to prosecution. As with Joseph Parsons, dramatic upward social mobility marked John Harrison's life. He started out plying the relatively low-paying trade of shoemaker, but at some point was able to make the lucrative leap to merchant. By the time he married Katherine in 1653, he was already experiencing economic success; and at his death in 1666, he had held a valuable estate. It appears that Goodman Harrison may have been suspected as a witch but died before his neighbors' fears coalesced into a formal complaint. During his widow's witchcraft trial, Mary Kercum gave testimony implicating him. Although she was somewhat imprecise on the point, Kercum claimed that a Mrs. Wickam "had seen Goodwife Harrison & her husband" in a spectral vision. Witnesses periodically brought forward these supernatural sightings of a person's disembodied spirit as evidence that they were in Satan's service. Thus, it appears that at least one person believed that John Harrison was a witch.[53] Thus, if he had lived a couple of years longer, it is possible that the charges of witchcraft against his wife may have also touched him.

Compared to New England, witchcraft prosecutions that ensnared both husbands and wives appear to have been much less common in the rest of the English Atlantic. Of the 474 people indicted for occult crimes by England's Home Circuit Assizes between 1559 and 1736, only twenty-eight of them (about 6 percent) came before the court as pairs of husbands and wives. There were times in the mother country when such accusations emerged with greater frequency. For instance, out of thirty people who came before the bar for witchcraft in Yorkshire in the 1640s, four (or 13 percent) were joined by marriage.[54] Nevertheless, there is no indication that the proportion of husband-and-wife suspects ever approach the level seen in New England during the mid-seventeenth century. Witch couples were even scarcer in other parts of the empire. In Bermuda, only a single pair of accused witches were married to one another, and in this case legal action against them was not simultaneous. No other English colony ever prosecuted—either concurrently or at different times—a husband and wife for witchcraft.[55]

The higher frequency of accusations against husbands and wives in New England can be partially explained by the fact that a larger proportion of its witch suspects were married than elsewhere in the English Atlantic and, through a process of guilt by association, ensnared more of their spouses in allegations of occult mischief. As previously mentioned, about four-fifths of those accused of witchcraft in New England before 1670 were married when they came under suspicion. In comparison, the accused witches who came before England's Home Circuit Assize between 1625 and 1701 present a different profile. Out of 140 female suspects whose marital status is mentioned in their indictments (those of male suspects, who were a small minority of the accused, do not generally indicate if they were single or wed), two-fifths were identified as being married and the rest as widows and spinsters. This proportion should be taken as a minimum: England's record keepers did not always use the term *spinster* as a synonym for a single woman, meaning that several suspects labeled as such may have been married or widowed. Similarly, out of the thirty people prosecuted for witchcraft in Yorkshire in the 1640s, thirteen were married, two were widows, and one was single. The marital status of the remaining suspects is unclear, but since there is no mention of spouses during their trials, they were most likely single or widowed. Thus, as with those who came before the Home Circuit Assize, about two-fifths of the Yorkshire suspects were probably married at the time of their prosecution. It appears then that at midcentury the proportion of married folk among the accused in New England was two times higher than in Old England. While this difference helps explain the higher rate of allegations against spouses in the Puritan colonies, it is unlikely that it fully accounts for it. Before 1670 a third of those arrested for witchcraft in New England faced prosecution alongside their husband or wife, while the proportion of accused spouses among the witch suspects who came before England's Home Circuit Assize during roughly the same period was *over five times lower*.[56] Moreover, the greater number of married witch suspects in New England does not explain why joint denunciations of husbands and wives occurred in some periods and disappeared during others. Married people were accused of witchcraft in the Puritan colonies throughout the seventeenth and early eighteenth centuries, but only during certain times did suspicions extend to their spouses.

At first glance, there is little about New England's witch spouses that sets them apart from other suspects or explains why they so regularly became targets of accusation. They obviously maintained a gender balance not seen among the larger body of the accused, for as with most of early modern Europe, female witch suspects greatly outnumbered male ones in the Puritan colonies. Besides this, in terms of age, marital status, social standing, and personal background, witch spouses were nearly indistinguishable from other suspects.[57] Like the rest of the accused, husbands and wives who purportedly partnered in magical crimes tended to be middle-aged; came from

a range of socioeconomic backgrounds; were often characterized as possessing negative personality traits such as malice, greed, and vengefulness; and
commonly had personal histories marked by criminal behavior.[58]

However, one aspect of New England's witch couples does perhaps stand
out: their relative lack of children. This trait was by no means unique to
them, and a lack of offspring characterized a good number of the accused.
Nevertheless, many witch couples had especially lackluster records when it
came to producing children and raising them to adulthood. Of the ten pairs
of husbands and wives accused of witchcraft in New England before 1670
only one—John and Elizabeth Blackleach—was especially fertile (they had
eleven children), and perhaps their success as parents helps explain why the
case against them never gained any momentum. Three more couples—the
Jones, Sanfords, and Greensmiths—approached more average-sized comple-
ments of children. The first had six children and the latter two five each;
however, it is worth noting that two of the Joneses' children and all of the
Greensmiths' were from previous marriages. The remaining six pairs had
between one and three children. For example, Nicholas and Goodwife Bayley
only had two or three children when they faced charges of occult crime in
1655, even though the couple had been married for more than a decade. John
and Joan Carrington seem to have had two children, and one of them was
a son born to Goodman Carrington's previous wife. Moreover, of the three
children Hugh and Mary Parsons bore, only one was living by the time they
came before the courts for witchcraft.[59] All told, these witch spouses produced an average of about four children; and if the Blackleaches are removed
from the equation as an outlier, the figure drops down to under three. In contrast, married couples in New England's pioneering generations produced an
average of seven or eight offspring.[60]

The Puritans' views on marriage have much to do with why the joint
accusations of husbands and wives became a frequent feature of witch-
hunting in New England. Marriage was an essential social institution to
early modern Europeans. It framed relations between men and women, regulated sexual reproduction by marking the boundaries between legitimate
and illegitimate births, and determined lines of lineage and inheritance.[61]
The Puritans attached an even greater importance to wedlock. Having
experienced decades of persecution by civil and ecclesiastical authorities in
England, they developed a comparatively dim view of the ability of man-
made institutions to bring about God's kingdom on earth. They searched for
better instruments to forge a godly society and found what they were looking for in marriage and the family. The Puritans saw the bond between husband and wife as a divinely sanctioned instrument of social order that was

far more dependable than worldly hierarchies rooted in wealth and class. As Daniel Rogers put it in his book *Matrimoniall Honour* (1642), the institution of marriage "not only fashion the family relations, the children and servants, much the more orderly; but also extended itself to the Church and Commonwealth." To them, marriage was the fountainhead of godly families that would raise the next generation of pious Christians and assure harmony in every aspect of life.[62]

Since marriage was so central to the Puritan colonists, they may have also reasoned that it would be a prime target of the Devil's malevolence. Early modern Europeans envisioned witchcraft as a sort of diabolical inversion of the natural, God-given order of things. For instance, they conceptualized the female witch as the opposite of a good mother.[63] In a similar vein, New Englanders sometimes imagined witchcraft as a dark alter-ego of nuptial relations. Accusers periodically portrayed witch spouses as failing to live up to expectations concerning marriage as a harmonious relationship resting on male self-restraint and female subordination. For example, Rebecca Greensmith appears more as a double-crossing accomplice than a loyal partner in crime, and she gave damning testimony against her husband stating that he possessed dark powers and kept company with familiar spirits. In addition, while husbands normally took the lead in family governance, the colonists commonly perceived the lines of power between witch spouses as moving in the opposite direction. In six out of the ten instances where accused witches were married to one another before 1670, it was the wife who was the leading suspect, while the husband appears as a more junior partner in crime.[64] In God's kingdom it was the husband who preceded his wife, while in the Devil's dominion women took the lead. Thus, rather than a Christian union promoting righteousness and social harmony, married witches represented a diabolical partnership designed to overturn divine order.

Such fears were not limited to the Puritan colonies, but drew on concerns first expressed in sixteenth-century European demonologies. These commentaries warned that couples who fell into Satan's clutches passed on knowledge of the dark arts to their offspring; and in keeping with this view, witchcraft cases involving spouses in England saw suspicions extend to their children. In contrast, New Englanders did not generally suspect the young as witches, voice fears of parents turning their progeny toward Satan, or imagine the existence of witch families. Indeed, only during the highly unusual Salem crisis of 1692 did accusations of witchcraft ensnare several sets of mothers, fathers, and children.[65]

Thus, in the Puritan colonies, accusations against married couples at midcentury appear to have rested on concerns that they were not bearing enough offspring rather than worries over whether they were exposing them to black magic. The reason for this distinction may lie in certain challenges that faced New England's pioneering colonists. During the first decades of colonization, settlers and labor were in short supply, and the emphasis Puritans' placed on the duty of parents to "be fruitful and multiply" intersected with real social and economic needs. New Englanders knew that fashioning their "City on a Hill" would require people to build its communities, work its fields, and fill its churches. Unlike planters in the southern colonies who met their demand for workers by purchasing European indentured servants and, eventually, enslaved Africans, most New England farmers did not possess the means to buy bound laborers. Thus, in order to grow the population and meet their labor needs, the early Puritan colonies relied on married couples to produce large numbers of children. In light of this, it makes sense that a failure to produce children, rather than concerns over how they were raised, contributed to suspicions against spouses. Simply put, the concern was not about the *quality* of their parenting but the *quantity* of their offspring. As historian Laurel Thatcher Ulrich explains, parenting in seventeenth-century New England was an "extensive" rather than an "intensive" pursuit. Simply put, the colonists ranked couples' ability to generate and raise offspring over their skills in nurturing them.[66] Suspicions of witchcraft often focused on people who were perceived as deviant, and New England's pioneering Puritans may have seen couples who lacked children as flouting their responsibilities to God and society.

The dynamics of witch-hunting and witch lore also help to explain the prevalence of witch couples in early New England. The fact that such cases increasingly came before the courts at midcentury is not surprising, considering that witchcraft prosecutions peaked in that period. In addition, the frequency with which New Englanders accused spouses of occult crime can be understood in terms of how long-standing traditions and more immediate events shaped the region's culture of witchcraft. The Puritan colonists did not have to create the idea of the husband-wife witch duo out of whole cloth but drew on precedents from England. Although accusation aimed at married couples in the mother country may have been rarer than in New England, such cases did occur, and the colonists doubtlessly brought this witch type with them to the New World. Once in America, the aforementioned social, religious, and demographic factors made the witch couple a more powerful motif that resonated with day-to-day realities. Moreover, once one pair of spouses became a target of accusation, it became easier for folk to imagine others as partners in occult crime. For example, one of the region's opening prosecutions of a husband and wife for witchcraft—that of

John and Joan Carrington of Wethersfield in 1651—cleared a path for more such cases. Just a year later, Hugh and Mary Parsons of Springfield were arrested on the same charge, and testimony gathered for their trials made explicit reference to the Carringtons' case.[67]

The husband-wife witch duo, a frequent target of accusation in the 1650s and early 1660s, disappears from the historical record for almost the next thirty years. Only during New England's most explosive episode of witch-hunting, the Salem crisis of 1692, did married couples once again come under scrutiny.[68] It is difficult to tell why the image of the witch couple came into vogue and fell out of fashion when it did. It is possible that as settlement proceeded and the population grew, concerns over childbearing eased and the emphasis on parenting shifted toward raising godly children and away from simply bearing a lot of them.[69] This, in turn, would have drawn unwanted attention away from couples with few children who had previously been vulnerable to accusations of witchcraft. Such a scenario also helps to explain why when spouses again came under scrutiny for occult crime at century's end, they were frequently accused of raising witch sons and daughters. In other words, falling into line with similar cases in Europe, the concern that underlay denunciations aimed at Salem's witch couples was not how many offspring they had, but whether they were bringing them up to serve God or the Devil.

Gender constructs shaped the contours of witch-hunting in early New England. Namely, they helped determine who was most at risk of being accused, tried, and convicted for occult crime. Deeply rooted stereotypes regarding women, the realities of daily life, and Puritan expectations concerning female behavior all contributed to their greater vulnerability to suspicions of magical mischief. Nevertheless, New Englanders did not see witchcraft as a solely female offense, and there were both male and female witch profiles that lined up with Puritan concepts of masculinity and femininity. Falling in line with their vision of occult crime as an inversion of the natural order, the colonists imagined witches as dark versions of wholesome goodmen and goodwives.

While critical to unlocking its meaning, understanding how personal traits, public perceptions, and the social position of the accused made them targets of suspicion is not the only key to understanding witchcraft. It is equally important to explore the identity and motives of their accusers as well as the social situations that brought them together and generated fears of occult mischief.

CHAPTER 5

"There Was Some Mischief in It"

The Social Context of Witchcraft

In 1657 William Meaker of New Haven initiated a slander suit against his neighbor, Thomas Mullenner, claiming that the defendant had called him a witch. Questioned by the court, Mullenner explained that several of his pigs had died "in a strange way, and he thought them bewitched" by Meaker. The two men had a contentious history, and the witchcraft accusation that put them at odds was but one act of a longer feud. The trouble started the previous year when Meaker provided testimony against Mullenner as he stood trial for stealing swine. Mullenner lost the case and, among other reparations, had to compensate Goodman Meaker for the time he spent at court, which would have hardly improved the former's feelings toward the latter. Later, Meaker accused Mullenner of "breaking open his fence." This confrontation precipitated Mullenner's witchcraft accusation, for he believed that Meaker had hexed his pigs in order to get even with him. The defamation case that followed ended in victory for the plaintiff, and the defendant had to publicly apologize for his intemperate words and post a hefty £50 security for his future good behavior. However, this did not end friction between the two men; and in the years that followed, Meaker again took Mullenner to court for slander and testified against him in a property dispute.[1]

This story illustrates the important link between witchcraft and interpersonal conflict in early New England. For in addition to the accused, the other regular elements of witchcraft episodes were an accuser, a contentious relationship between the two, and an event that transformed this hostility into suspicions of occult mischief. Thus, understanding the social context of witchcraft involves examining the social situations that gave birth to fears of malefic attack as well as the motives that drove one person to accuse another of black magic. The findings that emerge from such an analysis are not unique to the Puritan colonies but closely match dynamics of witch-hunting across the early modern English Atlantic.

Accusers

Broadly speaking, there were two categories of accusers. The first and by far the largest was made up of adults who gave testimony against those who purportedly committed acts of malefic harm against their persons, loved ones, or property. The second and smaller group was people—the vast majority of them children and young women—who complained of being "bewitched," or physically and spiritually tormented by witches and their demonic agents.[2] The first is the focus of this chapter; the second receives attention in the one that follows.

While they had some things in common, early New England's accusers were distinct from the accused in several respects. Of the 181 identified individuals who provided testimony against witch suspects before 1670, a solid majority (nearly two-thirds) were men, whereas women dominated among those accused. Indeed, the sex ratios of the two groups are nearly inverted.[3] The predominance of men among prosecuting witnesses held true for witchcraft cases involving both male and female defendants, but it was most pronounced when men were the sole or primary suspects. In these cases, two-thirds of the accusers were male. This is not surprising considering that men and women were somewhat separated by gender-defined spheres of activity, and witchcraft accusations commonly emerged between people who traveled in the same social circles. In cases of occult crime targeting women, the split was closer to fifty-fifty but still favored male accusers. The predominance of male witnesses was likely a consequence of the fact that only men had full access to the courts and consequently brought suits and testified, not for only themselves, but on behalf of their wives and dependents. For example, during the witchcraft proceedings against Hugh and Mary Parsons, Anthony Dorchester gave testimony about events that he *and his wife* witnessed.[4]

When it comes to age and marital status, differences between accusers and accused are less pronounced and there are even some similarities between the two groups. While a higher proportion of witch suspects were middle-aged or elderly than those who testified against them, the disparity is not striking. Indeed, when compared to the age structure of seventeenth-century New England, the two groups have much in common. The proportion of middle-aged folk in each greatly exceeded that found in the general population, while people under forty were under-represented. This makes sense considering that established, adult householders had greater chance than younger people of possessing the resources needed to initiate the prosecution of someone for a capital crime.[5] Of the hundred-odd accusers whose marital status is known, more than nine out of every ten were married, and the small remainder was evenly split between single folk and those who were widowed. Interestingly, all of the widowed accusers blamed their spouse's death on the witch suspect they testified against. These figures diverge somewhat from those for the accused, among whom eight out of every ten were married, and a tenth each widowed or single.[6] In sum, while more accusers lived within the respectable bonds of matrimony than the accused, there was no dramatic difference between them on this point.

Like those they spoke out against, accusers came from every strata of New England society, although the former collectively held somewhat of an advantage in terms of economic and social standing. John and Bethia Kelly,

Table 5.1   Gendered patterns of accusation before 1670

SEX OF ACCUSER	ACCUSATIONS IN CASES INVOLVING BOTH MALE AND FEMALE SUSPECTS	ACCUSATIONS IN CASES INVOLVING MALE SUSPECTS	ACCUSATIONS IN CASES INVOLVING FEMALE SUSPECTS
Female	39%	33%	45%
Male	61%	67%	55%

Table 5.2   Age of accusers compared to that of accused and the general population

AGE	ACCUSERS (N = 34)	ACCUSED (N = 46)	GENERAL POPULATION
15–39	18 (53%)	20 (43%)	75.2%
40–59	14 (41%)	22 (48%)	20.4%
60+	2 (6%)	4 (9%)	4.4%

Table 5.3   Marital status of accusers compared to that of the accused before 1670

	ACCUSERS (N = 101)	ACCUSED (N = 57)
Married	95 (94%)	45 (79%)
Single	3 (3%)	6 (10.5%)
Widowed	3 (3%)	6 (10.5%)

who played a leading role in stoking suspicions against Judith Ayres and others during the Hartford witch panic, were among many low-status accusers. Indeed, when Goodman Kelly died shortly after the panic subsided, he left behind a threadbare estate valued at just under £15. James and Sarah Bridgeman of Northampton numbered among the numerous accusers of middling status. He possessed about forty-two acres of land in 1648 and eventually held a number of civic posts including that of constable, while she was a full member of Northampton's church.[7]

Compared to those from the middling and lower rungs of society, elites were less frequently found in the ranks of accusers. This is not too shocking considering that those of true wealth and influence were few in number in early New England. Before 1670 only a single clergyman, Reverend George Moxon of Springfield, offered testimony against a witch suspect; and only a few other divines, such as Reverend Samuel Stone of Hartford, facilitated prosecutions by recording evidence against the accused or encouraging them to confess. The participation of secular elites was also limited. One locally prominent man who took a leading role in ferreting out an alleged witch was John Robbins, who issued a complaint against Katherine Palmer in 1648. An early settler in Wethersfield, he accrued a large estate, served as a selectman and representative to Connecticut's General Court, and eventually earned the title of "Gentleman." Probably the highest-ranking person to take part in a witch denunciation was Mrs. Mary Gardiner, the wife of the powerful Mr. Lion Gardiner, when she testified against Elizabeth Garlick of Easthampton.[8]

Testimony presented during witch trials gives the impression of a black-and-white situation that pitted good (the accusers) against evil (the accused), but in reality the lines between sinner and saint were not so clear. It was in the interest of accusers to portray defendants as bad people and themselves as innocent, upstanding victims of malefic attacks. A number of them, however, led lives marked by contentiousness and crime. For instance, Thomas Bracy and Samuel Hurlbut, two of the people who spoke out against Katherine Harrison, had checkered pasts. A Hartford County court once fined Bracy £1 for his "night walking & overturning the carts & stocks." In other words, he was out of doors, vandalizing the instruments of local law enforcement, past the time when any decent person should have been in bed. For his part, Hurlbut faced a fine of ten shillings and an hour in the stocks as a consequence of his night walking. In addition, he and his wife each had to pay a fine of £3 "for committing fornication" (which likely means that they had premarital sex), and later on Hurlbut paid a further thirty-shilling fine for "notorious drunkenness."[9] Thomas Mullenner was another shady character who issued accusations of witchcraft. Besides coming before the bar for theft, slander, and other infractions, he faced New Haven's magistrates after he ordered his servants "to gather oysters on the Sabbath day," breaking the rule banning labor on Sundays. In addition, the court noted that he and his wife did "not attend the ordinances [worship] duly as they ought." Mullenner also had to answer for the un-neighborly act of placing one of his fences so close to the sea that during high tide other men's livestock were "in hazard to be drowned."[10]

As with Goodman Mullenner, the accuser John Tilleston exhibited a pattern of disruptive behavior commonly associated with witch suspects. Ten years before he cast suspicions of witchcraft on Hannah Griswold in 1667, he faced the magistrates "for scandalous and reproachful speeches cast upon the elders and others in a public church meeting on the Lord's day." Tilleston also later faced prosecution "for abusing his wife on Sabbath day . . . and chaining her leg to the bed post with a plow chain, to keep her within doors," and on another occasion was fined for giving a false oath. This misbehavior extended beyond Tilleston to his first wife, and she was charged with "not believing in infant baptism, and speaking contemptuously of it," which likely indicates that Goody Tilleston and her husband were dissenting Baptists. New Englanders generally associated such faults—insubordination, irreverence, domestic discord, and religious deviance—with witchcraft.[11]

William Edwards and his wife, Anne, also illustrate the fine line that sometimes separated accusers from the accused. Goody Edwards was one of several women who denounced Elizabeth Garlick for witchcraft, but she and her husband engaged in antisocial activities commonly attributed to occult criminals. The record of their bad behavior starts in 1641 when they lived in Lynn, Massachusetts. In that year the authorities fined Goodman Edwards twenty shillings "for untrue & false dealing about bees," and not long after presented Anne "for striking a man and scoffing at his [church] membership." In 1649 William also faced two separate slander suits. Things continued on this way once the couple moved to Easthampton, Long Island, and in 1651 Anne Edwards was punished for assaulting a constable. This sort of violence, dishonesty, and disrespect for authority were traits frequently ascribed to the accused; and, indeed, Goody Edwards was a target of witchcraft suspicions, though they never resulted in formal legal action.[12] Thus, in some cases the behavior of witch suspects and those who denounced them was not all that different, and in a few instances it is not difficult to believe that if events had taken a slightly different turn, the shoe could have easily been on the other foot.

Relationships

Accusers and the accused usually knew each other well, and only in more extraordinary episodes such as the Salem witch crisis did people cast suspicion on strangers. Three types of connection between plaintiffs and defendants—kinship ties, contractual relationships, and interactions as neighbors—merit attention.

Generally speaking, early modern Europeans infrequently accused fellow family members of witchcraft. An obvious reason for this is that such charges could easily rebound on the accuser. Since people believed that knowledge of black magic often passed between close associates, suspicions against one family member could easily spread to others. Before 1670 there are only four cases in New England of intrafamily accusations, and all of them involved kin ties based on marriage, not blood.[13] Three feature one spouse denouncing another. One of Hugh Parsons's most persistent accusers was his wife; and in her confession, Rebecca Greensmith identified her husband as a fellow witch. Likewise, Zachary Dibble cast suspicion on his wife. While he never translated his claims into a formal legal complaint, Goodman Dibble said that his wife had a demonic "teat in her secret part" which he described as "half a finger long." The remaining episode involved people affiliated by marriage who were not husband and wife. After Abigail Dibble (who was the sister-in-law of Zachary Dibble) died a horrible death during childbirth, her husband gave testimony against his father-in-law, William Graves, implying that he had murdered his daughter through occult means.[14]

There is not a single clear case in the Puritan colonies where formally structured ties (such as between a landlord and tenant) played a leading role in accusations of occult crime. That said, witch suspicions had the potential to insert themselves into these kinds of relationships. For example, in early modern Germany, accusations periodically grew out of tensions between lying-in-maids (women hired to help a mother care for newborn babies in the weeks following delivery) and the families who employed them.[15] Only a glimmer of such patterns can be discerned in New England. Mary Johnson was a servant when she faced trial for witchcraft in 1648, but the episode is largely undocumented, and it is not known if there was any connection between her master and the accusation. Likewise, Elizabeth Garlick's husband Joseph had once worked for Lion Gardiner and the couple also rented land from this powerful gentleman before they obtained a freehold in Easthampton. During this time there arose "some difference between Mr. Gardiner or some of his family & Goodman Garlick," and Joseph made "some threatening speeches." Folks recalled this years later when Goody Garlick stood accused of bewitching Mr. Gardiner's daughter to death. Eunice Cole was clearly receiving poor relief during some of her later run-ins with the law over witchcraft, and her need for charity even figured in some of the testimony gathered against her. However, this appears to be a singular case, and there is no body of evidence demonstrating that recipients of poor relief were especially prone to accusation in the Puritan colonies.[16]

Relationships fostered by close physical proximity had the most bearing on witchcraft episodes, and accusers and accused were frequently neighbors. For early modern Europeans, living next to someone entailed a host of daily interactions from swapping tools and labor to sharing gossip and a cup of cider. It also produced frictions such as arguments over property lines or damages caused by wayward livestock. Neighborliness, and the avoidance of neighborly conflict, was especially important to New England's Puritan colonists; for they were intent, not just on individual salvation, but on creating strong Christian communities. To them, this meant living in close-knit settlements where the faithful could support and watch over each other as they struggled to carve settlements out of the wilderness and follow the narrow path toward God's grace. Thus, while the religious connotations Puritans attached to community were somewhat novel, the realities of village life were not, and as in many parts of Europe, they provided fertile ground for the sorts of everyday conflicts that nurtured witch fears.[17]

Some of New England's earliest witchcraft cases illustrate the connection between face-to-face social ties and accusations of occult crime. In 1648 Goodwife Katherine Palmer suffered arrest on suspicion of practicing malefic magic. The author of the complaint was Mr. John Robbins, who resided on an adjoining home lot. Likewise, testimony gathered during the 1659 witch trial of Winifred and Mary Holman reveals that their primary accusers, the Gibson family, lived next door. Witchcraft episodes did not just pit immediate neighbors against one another, but also involved larger neighborhood networks. Time and again, those who came out against or in support of witch suspects were people who lived close to them. For instance, everyone involved in Elizabeth Garlick's witchcraft trial occupied home lots on either side of Easthampton's single thoroughfare. One of the witnesses for the prosecution lived next door to the accused, and four more resided just across the street. All five would have likely seen and interacted with Goody Garlick and her family on a daily basis. Similarly, those who spoke out against Hugh and Mary Parsons lived in the same Springfield neighborhood as the accused, a narrow area between the town's main street and the Connecticut River. Measured by the number of depositions they entered against the Parsons, those who played the largest role in the couple's prosecution lived closest to them. This same pattern emerged when Joseph Parsons of Northampton brought a defamation suit against Sarah Bridgeman for calling his wife a witch. All of the town's residents who gave testimony in the case lived within a quarter mile of each other and nearly all of them resided on just two streets.[18]

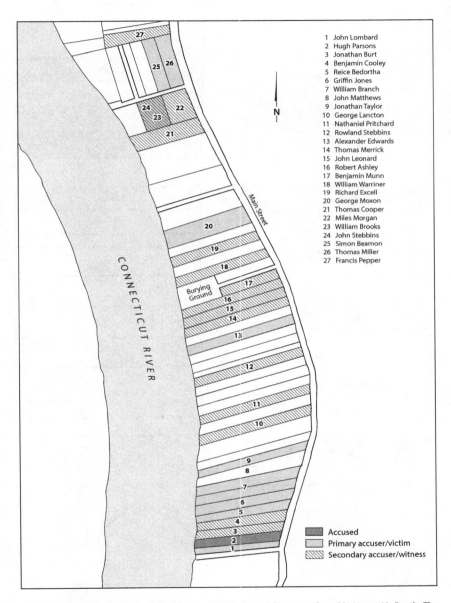

MAP 4. House lots in Springfield, MA, ca. 1650 (adapted from map found in Henry M. Burt's *The First Century of the History of Springfield*, vol. 1, and inspired by a map found in John Demos's *Entertaining Satan*)

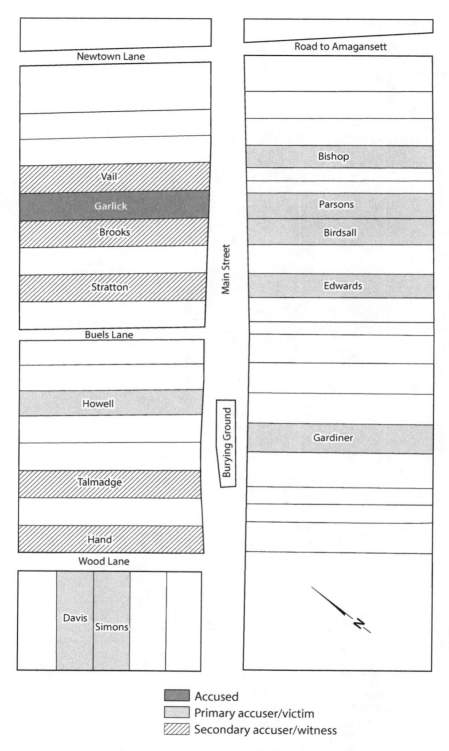

MAP 5. House lots in Easthampton, Long Island, ca. 1658 (adapted from map found in Henry Parsons Hedges's *Records of the Town of East Hampton*, vol. 1, and inspired by a map found in John Demos's *Entertaining Satan*)

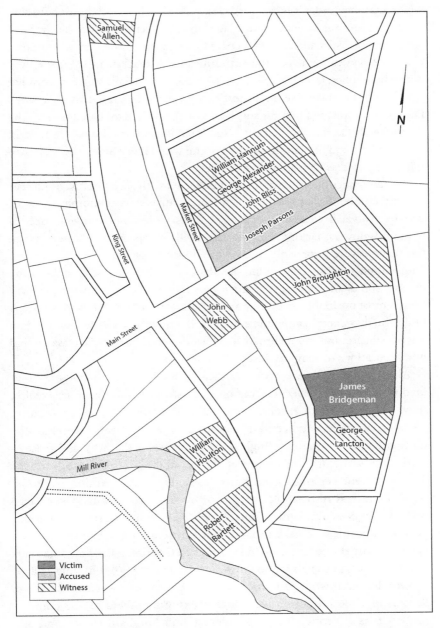

MAP 6. House lots in Northampton, MA, ca. 1656 (adapted from map found in James Russell Trumbull's *History of Northampton, Massachusetts from its Settlement in 1654*, vol. 1)

Sometimes ties between accusers and accused were even more intimate, as when husbands and wives cast suspicion on each other. Such household connections were not limited to marriage, and the accused sometimes resided with their accusers and alleged victims as a servant or boarder. When Elizabeth Godman came before the authorities for witchcraft in 1655, she lived with Mr. Stephen Goodyear's family who claimed to have suffered from her malefic powers. Likewise, in his testimony against Hugh Parsons, Anthony Dorchester explained that his suspicions of the defendant dated back to the time when his family dwelled with Goodman Parsons and his wife. Similarly, Lydia Gilbert and her family shared a home with Henry Stiles, the man who reportedly died as a result of her witchery.[19]

The dynamics of accusation also intersected with social status. A number of obstacles hinder an assessment of the relative socioeconomic status of people involved in cases of occult crime. In many instances evidence needed to pin this down is lacking. For instance, while it appears that John and Joan Carrington were poor when they came under suspicion for witchcraft, no information survives concerning the identity of their accusers, making any comparison of their social standing impossible. Additionally, witch prosecutions almost invariably involved multiple accusers drawn from various social ranks, further complicating the situation. Bearing these challenges in mind, it is possible to draw some broad conclusions about how social class figured into accusations of magical mischief.

Although there were witchcraft cases in the Puritan colonies that involved destitute suspects facing off against those with far more wealth, they appear to be an exception rather than a rule. The social disparity between accusers and accused may have generally been greater in the mother country, or at least English folk perceived it that way, and as Reginald Scott wrote in *The Discovery of Witchcraft* (1584), "Poor [and] sullen" folk who went begging "from house to house, and from door to door" were often held responsible for acts of occult crime against their social betters.[20] In New England, Eunice Cole's case comes close to fitting this portrait, and she and her husband were desperately poor when she first became a target of accusation in 1656. When Goodman Cole died six years later, Hampton officials valued his estate at around £40, but only half of this modest sum went to Eunice, and she ended up a ward of the town. Several of Cole's accusers were high-ranking members of the community, such as selectmen Thomas Coleman and Abraham Drake, and others appear to have occupied its middling ranks. The witchcraft case of Mary Johnson also probably fits the profile of a low-status defendant who faced charges at the hands of higher-ranking individuals. Johnson was a servant when she stood trial, and though the identities of her accusers are unknown, at least some of them must have had the financial resources it took to pursue charges for a capital crime.[21]

The other situation where plaintiffs and defendants were unequally matched in terms of status was when the accused ranked higher than their accusers. Like those that pitted the poor against people with far more wealth and influence, such cases were rare, and legal activity related to them most often took the form of a defamation suit where an imputed witch took their accusers to court. For example, Matthew Griswold, a prominent resident of Saybrook, successfully sued John Tilleston, a man below him in social stature and wealth, for slander after the latter spread rumors that Griswold's wife was a witch. Those with money and power had the resources to mount effective legal counterattacks, and this was a significant deterrent to accusers, especially those who did not possess the same level of financial and social clout. During the Hartford panic of 1662, for instance, the well-heeled merchant John Blackleach and his wife came under suspicion. However, none of the witnesses against them came close to matching the couple in terms of social standing, and Mr. Blackleach sued them for slander, stopping the case against them in its tracks. This fits a broader pattern of criminal prosecution in early New England where courts regularly acquitted high-status defendants who went up against low-ranking plaintiffs.[22]

A 1656 slander case initiated by Joseph Parsons against James and Sarah Bridgeman presents the best documented instance of a witch suspect going up against accusers of a lower socioeconomic rank and illustrates the usual results. The Bridgemans were respectable middle-class farmers, while the Parsons were several cuts above them and moving steadily up the social ladder. Joseph Parsons made his fortune as a fur trader and accrued a substantial estate worth £2,000. Not only did the Parsons exceed the Bridgemans in terms of wealth and influence, but many of those who testified in support of the former outranked those who spoke on behalf of the latter. Indeed, the Parsons were able to bring the richest and most powerful man in Massachusetts's Connective Valley, John Pynchon, to their side. Not surprisingly, a court ruled in the Parsons's favor.[23]

Witch accusations most often played out between people of parallel rank, and accusers and the accused usually came from the same social strata or the next one up or down. Thus, witnesses against lower-class suspects most frequently occupied positions on the lower or middle rungs of the social ladder, while an accused person of middling status might have opponents from a lower-, middle-, or upper-class background. That accusers and those they accused were of similar social standing makes sense since suspicions of occult mischief commonly emerged out of intimate relationships, and it is more likely that people who traveled in the same social circles would develop this sort of connection. This pattern was not just true for New England, but played out in the mother country and across the English Atlantic. For example, in 1586 Joan Cason was arrested, tried, and executed for witchcraft in Kent, England, after a number of witnesses of similar rank accused her of various acts of maleficium. Likewise, Nicholas Stockdale, well-off yeoman farmer from Norfolk squared off against several other men in his community, including a local constable and justice of the peace, when they accused him of witchcraft.[24]

The witchcraft case of Hugh and Mary Parsons was one of many that pitted people of approximately equal social rank against one another. A property assessment made shortly before his trial shows that Goodman Parsons held 37.5 acres in Springfield and paid 10 shillings and 9 pence in tax. The men who gave testimony against him and who appear on the tax role possessed an average of about 34 acres. More tellingly, the land holdings of just over half of them fell within 10 acres of Parsons's. Likewise, the accusers' average tax assessment of 9 shillings and 6 pence was very close to that paid by Parsons, and a little more than half had tax bills within 3 shillings of his assessment. Also, like Goodman Parsons, his male adversaries tended to hold low-level positions in local government. All of this indicates that many who stood against Hugh Parsons occupied a similar socioeconomic position.[25]

Tension among social equals also undergirded witchcraft allegations against Elizabeth Garlick of Easthampton. The accused and her husband stood in rough economic parity with most of her adversaries. A tax assessment from Easthampton drawn up four years before Elizabeth's witch trial shows that she and her husband occupied a place at the top of the town's lower social strata or at the bottom of its middling ranks. Many who stood witness against Goody Garlick fit a similar profile: they were people of low status and limited means who had long associations with the accused. For example, Samuel Parsons and the husbands of Goody Simmons and Goody Brooks appear alongside of Joseph Garlick on Easthampton's assessment roll as holding thirteen acres of land. Two other prosecuting witnesses, Goodies Birdsall and Bishop, were also wives of humble farmers.[26]

Regardless of how accusers and accused stacked up to each other in terms of social class, whenever high-status plaintiffs got involved in witchcraft cases, they tended to play an oversized role in turning inchoate suspicions into legal action. While it was relatively rare for the high and mighty to weigh in on accusations of occult mischief, their participation had significant consequences.[27] Rumors that Elizabeth Garlick was a witch appear to have existed well before her 1658 trial, but what translated these latent fears into judicial proceedings was the intervention of powerful individuals after the untimely death of Elizabeth Howell. She was the young wife of a prominent resident of Easthampton, Arthur Howell, and daughter of one of the Puritan colonies' leading figures, Mr. Lion Gardiner. When folk blamed Goody Garlick for Mrs. Howell's demise and Mr. Howell and Mrs. Gardiner took up the cry, it quickly bloomed into a full-scale witch trial. In a similar turn of events, suspicions against Eunice Cole coalesced into a witchcraft trial after she had an angry encounter with selectmen Thomas Coleman and Abraham Drake, and they blamed her for various misfortunes they suffered soon after. The same dynamic played out in England in 1582 when the Essex County gentleman Brian Darcy took up the role of witch finder and helped promote the prosecutions of two long-suspected witches, Anne Heard and Joan Robinson.[28]

The involvement of high-status accusers also fueled the Hartford witch hunt and the witchcraft prosecution of Katherine Harrison. The Hartford episode started when the young daughter of a poor couple suddenly took ill and died, triggering fears of witchcraft. However, the situation escalated into a witch panic when more socially prominent individuals became involved. Specifically, when a young woman from a pious and respectable family came down with a strange affliction many attributed to witchcraft, named her tormentors, and high-ranking members of the community like Reverend Samuel Stone supported the accusations, the witch hunt gained momentum. The participation of high-status accusers also helped push forward suspicions against Katherine Harrison of Wethersfield. A wealthy widow, she outgunned her initial accusers in terms of wealth, and if this situation had continued to hold true, then her case may not have gotten very far. However, two powerful men, Michael Griswold and John Blackleach, took up the cause against Harrison and propelled her case to trial. Although the pair did not provide testimony against the accused, they helped orchestrate her prosecution. Blackleach went as far as soliciting depositions from former Wethersfield residents who had moved to Hadley, Massachusetts, many miles up the Connecticut River.[29]

Tensions and Triggers

No matter how they were connected, long-standing disputes that nurtured fears of occult attack commonly marked relations between accusers and accused, and there was frequently an emotionally charged confrontation or tragedy that tipped suspicions toward legal action.[30] One witch suspect, William Graves, had a contentious relationship with his son-in-law, Samuel Dibble, who later bore witness against him. Conflict simmered between the two after Dibble asked Goodman Graves to turn over property he had promised him upon his marriage to his daughter. Graves refused, saying that the younger man should "carry [behave] better to him." When the son-in-law initiated legal action to obtain his wife's portion, Graves menacingly responded that Dibble would "repent" the decision for as long as he lived. When his wife later died during childbirth, Dibble connected the tragedy to his father-in-law's threat and concluded that he had bewitched her.[31]

The case of Hugh Parsons exemplifies the ties between interpersonal conflict and witchcraft. He had a history of contention with several people who later accused him of black magic. Reverend George Moxon had previously argued with Parsons over the delivery of some bricks. Likewise, Samuel Marshfield successfully sued Hugh and his wife in 1649 for slandering his widowed mother as a witch, and soon thereafter Parsons retaliated by accusing Marshfield of perjury. Another prosecuting witness, John Matthews, had already earned Parsons's enmity when he testified in favor of Samuel Marshfield during the aforementioned defamation suit. A similar legacy of conflict marked Parsons's relationship with another accuser, Blanche Bedortha, who recalled a confrontation between her husband and the accused that predated Parsons's witch trial. In addition, Simon Beamon spoke of several past encounters he had with Parsons that left the accused "offended."[32]

If there was not already antipathy between accusers and accused, then the former's denunciation of the latter as a witch brought them into conflict. Goody Thorpe was one of many people who provided testimony against Elizabeth Godman, and while it is unclear how the two got along before that, Thorpe's actions certainly did nothing to improve their relationship. Thorpe recalled how Mrs. Godman confronted her in the street and in words dripping with sarcasm said, "How doth Goody Thorpe? I am beholden to Goody Thorpe above all the women in the town: she would have had me to the gallows for a few chickens." Similarly, Godman came into conflict with Mr. Stephen Goodyear as a result of her accusation. When she asked to join a private prayer meeting he held "upon occasion of God's afflicting hand upon the plantation [colony] by sickness," Goodyear rebuffed her, saying that "she was under suspicion [for witchcraft], and it would be offensive" for her to attend. This set off further rounds of contention between Mrs. Godman and her neighbors, and she later took several of them to court for giving "out speeches that made folks think she was a witch."[33] Godman was one of several suspects who struck back by bringing defamation suits against their accusers. Joseph Garlick sued the wife of Faulk Davis after she stated that his spouse was as witch, and Winifred Holman did the same to those who denounced her. John Godfrey, living by the dictum that the best defense was a good offense, took his accusers to court on two occasions. Jane Walford of Portsmouth matched his record, and she or her husband brought would-be witch hunters before the magistrates in 1648 and again in 1669.[34]

Events that transformed witchcraft suspicions into prosecutions in the English-speaking world commonly involved the exchange of goods and services. Specifically, formal complaints often grew out of situations where one person denied an object or favor to another. The person who initiated the failed exchange usually became the target of accusation, while the rejecter tended to become a persecutor. Simply put, the refused became the accused and the refuser became the accuser.[35] For instance, in 1582 in Essex County, England, Bennet Lane accused Agnes Heard of magically interfering with her spinning after the former sought the return of a dish she had lent to the latter. Seventy-four years later and an ocean away, Susannah Trimmings of Portsmouth complained of malefic misfortunes after she refused Jane Walford's request for a pound of cotton. The same pattern held true in Bermuda, and in 1653 Thomas Murrill testified that the accused witch Goody Christian Stevenson "came unto his house . . . with her a croseleth wrought with gold, & would have him purchase it, but he refused it &. . . . she went away very much discontented."[36] This dynamic helps explain why witchcraft cases commonly pitted folk of roughly equal status against one another, for the events that triggered accusations of occult mischief often revolved around the favors, borrowing, and exchange that characterized relations between people of similar rank.

Some early modern Europeans recognized the link between neighborly disputes and allegations of occult crime. In *A Candle in the Dark* (1656), the witchcraft skeptic Thomas Ady observed that people mistakenly ascribed personal loss to black magic:

> Seldom hath a man the hand of God against him in his estate, or health of body, or any way, but presently he cries out of some poor innocent neighbor, that he, or she hath bewitched him; for saith he, such on old man or woman came lately to my door, and desire some relief, and I denied it . . . my mind gave me she looked like a witch, and presently my child, my wife, myself, my horse, my cow, my sheep, my sow, my hog, my dog, my cat or somewhat was thus and thus handled, in such a strange manner, as I dare swear she is a witch, or else how should those things be, or come to pass?

Outlining the psychological process by which folk translated misfortune into witch trials, Ady starts with one neighbor's desire to obtain something from another and the latter's decision not to fulfill the request. Next, some ill fortune strikes the person who denied their neighbor, and they make the intellectual leap that it was not a result of bad luck or God's providence, but of black magic wielded by the party they so recently offended. This thought process was evident when Goody Thorpe rebuffed Elizabeth Godman's offer to buy some of her chickens. After the encounter, Thorpe thought that if Godman was as "naught [bad] as folks suspect, maybe she will smite my chickens," and when some of her chickens died soon after, she concluded that Godman was a witch. The same mental process was at work on Bermuda when John Burt testified against Alice Moore in 1653. He told the court that the accused's husband came to his house in order to buy one of his pigs, but they could not agree on a price. When the same pig died six weeks later, Burt became convinced that Goody Moore had used black magic to kill the animal.[37]

Accusations of occult crime did not spring forth every time one person snubbed another, but such events shed light on the social and psychological contexts of witchcraft. While one neighbor's denial of another's requests contravened Puritan ideals of charity and Christian fellowship, they did not break any laws, and the hostility engendered by such encounters had no institutional means of resolution. Thus, negative emotions born of minor disputes could fester and transmute into suspicions of witchcraft. When a person who denied a neighbor suffered a loss or setback, they could easily look to the person they rejected, and logically believed was angry with them, as the source of their trouble. This outcome only required the belief—readily at hand for early modern Europeans—that people could harness supernatural power to take their revenge. Guilt suffused this process, for the alleged victims of witchcraft implicitly believed that they had brought it down on themselves by mistreating someone.[38]

This confluence of neighborly conflicts and suspicions of black magic was a regular feature of New England's witchcraft episodes. Allen Ball recalled that when Elizabeth Godman came to his house "and asked his wife for some butter-milk," she refused and "bid her be gone." The widow allegedly replied, "What, you will save it for your pigs, but it will do them no good," and when nearly all of the couple's pigs subsequently died, the Balls blamed Godman. Likewise, Reverend William Hooke and his wife testified that Godman came to their home "to beg some beer," and they eventually offered her some "which stood ready drawn, but she refused it and would have some newly drawn, which she had." Even though Godman got what she came for, the couple reported that she went away in a "discontented manner." When the Hooke's beer went sour soon after and the next four of five batches they brewed mysteriously suffered the same fate, they concluded that Godman had taken her revenge on them through supernatural means. In a similar vein, Joan Francis reported that one of Katherine Harrison's daughters came to her house "for some emptyings" (possibly a reference to materials left over from the brewing process), but the goodwife told her that she had none. Not long after Frances suffered a mishap when a barrel of ale she had recently brewed exploded, and she attributed it Harrison's malefic meddling. Sarah Edwards told the same story, recounting how Hugh Parsons came to her home to buy some milk and left dissatisfied after she told him that she could only give him a "half-penny worth." Afterward, when her cow gave far less milk than it previously had and what it did produce was of a "strange, odd color," she attributed it to Parsons's occult powers.[39]

Thus New Englanders believed that denying a purported witch something they desired could elicit their malice. Thomas Bracy thought he became a victim of James Wakeley's maleficence after refusing to lend the suspect his saddle. Similarly, Henry Palmer testified that the inhabitants of Haverhill, Massachusetts, suffered from John Godfrey's occult aggression after he and his fellow selectmen declined to hire him as the town's cowherd. Simon Beamon followed the same logic when he concluded that Hugh Parsons bewitched him because the accused was "offended at his refusal" to give him a piece of leather or carry home a bag of meal for him. Another of Goodman Parsons's alleged victims, William Branch, stated that he was "troubled that he [Parsons] had made so many errands to my house for several things, and yet I could not tell how to deny him what he desired." Like most early modern Europeans, Branch feared that failing to act as an open-handed neighbor could incite occult retaliation.[40]

Not every witchcraft episode followed the accuser as refuser, accused as refused model. Economic conflicts among men who later ended up on opposite sides of a witch prosecution did not always see the injured party become the focus of suspicion, and in many cases the alleged witch was clearly the victimizer rather than the victim. By the time he reached middle age, the money-lending John Godfrey initiated disputes with several future accusers when he aggressively demanded repayment. Hugh Parsons was cut from the same cloth. He possessed a well-earned reputation for dishonesty, and several men who later testified against him were victims of his shady business practices.[41]

There were also witchcraft cases involving women that did not fit into the standard pattern. For example, the interpersonal tensions that formed the backdrop of the witchcraft case involving Mary Bliss Parsons and Sarah Bridgeman did not feature a suspect who asked the aid of a neighbor and suffered rejection. Rather, it appears that Bridgeman, driven by grief over the recent loss of an infant and jealous of Goody Parson's large number of healthy offspring, came to believe that Parsons had caused the child's death through black magic. Likewise, Rebecca Gibson's suspicion that Winifred Holman was a witch took root after she failed to cure Gibson's sick daughter. This was not a case where an accuser refused to give something to the accused, but where a suspect failed to deliver a service to someone who later denounced them.[42]

As the above examples illustrate, events that triggered witchcraft accusations were also tied to emotionally charged moments involving matters of life and death. Such occasions were well suited to generating the personal anguish that fueled fears of the occult and, like more pedestrian conflicts, often involved neighbors. Indeed, during the early modern era, when women gave birth and sickness and death struck, people called in those who lived close to them for help and support.

The loss of a mother or baby during childbirth was not unusual in the early modern era, giving people ample opportunity to turn to occult explanations when such misfortune befell. The ones who usually became targets of accusation in these situations were neighbors or acquaintances who supposedly held a grudge against the mother or her family or had already developed a reputation as a witch. As previously mentioned, Winifred Holman came under scrutiny after the daughter of a near neighbor gave birth and the new mother and child became ill. It is unclear if Holman attended the birth, but it seems probable, seeing that she lived next door and had some sort of reputation has a healer. The most startling witchcraft episode related to childbirth in early New England is the aforementioned case of Abigail Dibble. According to witnesses, around the time she went into labor, her father William Graves predicted that she would die. As it turned out, Goody Dibble did die in a shocking manner while giving birth to a daughter (who lived). Soon thereafter, suspicions of occult mischief grew against Graves. Likewise, the misfortunes of childbirth also lay behind the imputations of witchcraft aimed at Mary Bliss Parsons.[43]

A mysterious illness or person's sudden demise were other occasions that triggered anxiety, sorrow, and accusations of witchcraft. Such was the case with the Robbins family of Wethersfield. In late 1659 and early 1660, Mr. and Mrs. Robbins and a newborn all sickened and died within months of one another. Before her death, Mrs. Robbins accused Katherine Palmer of bewitching her. Although her husband allegedly drew up a document in which he laid out the case against Palmer, he did not enter a formal complaint. This, however, was not the end of the connections between the Robbins family, death, and witchcraft. One of Mr. and Mrs. Robbinses' surviving children, Mary, grew up and wed Eleazer Kimberly but passed away shortly thereafter. The widowed husband attributed his wife's death to occult forces and pinned the blame on Katherine Harrison. Death also triggered the witchcraft case of Hugh and Mary Parsons. Goody Parsons gave birth to a son in October 1650, but he passed away six months later. This event provided the catalyst for Goodman Parsons's arrest as a witch when his wife accused him of killing the boy with black magic. Similarly, while not much is known about the events that led to the witchcraft trial of Ralph and Mary Hall, it is clear that the demise of George Wood and his child precipitated the couple's arrest.[44]

Motives

Beneath the conflict-ridden relationships and emotion-laden events that rippled across the surface of households and communities in the English Atlantic fostering fears of witchcraft, were deeper social and psychological dynamics that motivated people to translate personal disputes and loss into accusations of occult crime. At the individual level, the belief in black magic provided a way to explain misfortune, take action against its alleged agents, and avoid feelings of guilt or culpability. Collectively, witch prosecutions brought neighbors together in cathartic, community-building efforts to cast out evil and set boundaries of socially acceptable behavior.

In an era before the comprehensive development and dissemination of scientific knowledge, early modern Europeans looked to occult explanations for all sorts of odd and distressing phenomenon. Thus when a child suddenly sickened and died, a cow inexplicably stopped giving milk, or fresh butter went rancid, people sometimes blamed witchcraft.[45] Indeed, attributing injury to the supernaturally charged malice of others was a central feature of testimony gathered for witch prosecutions on both sides of the Atlantic. In Essex County, England, Grace Thurlow testified that her newborn "fell out of the cradle and broke its neck and died," claiming that the tragedy was no accident but the result of an act of witchcraft perpetrated by Ursula Kemp after Thurlow refused to let her nurse the child. While in Easthampton, Long Island, the wife of Faulk Davis recounted how her "child died strangely at the Island [Gardiner's Island] & she thought it was bewitched & she said she did not know of any one on the Island that could do it unless it were Goody Garlick."[46] Pinning the blame for these events on occult forces did not diminish victims' grief but it at least made the tragedies comprehensible.

Knowing why bad things happen may offer some comfort, but being able to take action against a perceived foe is even more empowering. Early modern Europeans believed that a person at the sharp end of an occult attack could fight back. Thus, identifying black magic as the cause of misfortune was only a step toward finding out who authored the injury and taking action against them. Those suffering reversals or loss could take satisfaction at being able to put the blame on a witch and punish them for their evil deeds. The course people took against suspected occult criminals fell into two categories. First, there was the option of fighting fire with fire. Europeans on both sides of the Atlantic harnessed supernatural forces to identify and inflict punishment on a witch. Even in New England, where acts of magical vigilantism earned official condemnation, there are glimpses of occult counterattacks. Goodwife Margaret Garrett recalled how she cut a maggoty chuck off a round of cheese, "flung it into the fire," and soon after "Goodwife Seager came into the house, [and] cried out she was full of pain and sat wringing of her body and crying out what do I ail, what do I ail." Here Garrett described a classic piece of countermagic in which a person burned a hexed object, transferring the damage back to the offending witch. The second and officially sanctioned method for acting against witches was to take them to court. By 1670 dozens of New Englanders had been charged with witchcraft; and from the perspective of the plaintiffs, fifteen of these cases concluded successfully with the execution of the accused. In one sense, these episodes were part of government-sponsored efforts to enforce law and order. On a more personal level, however, legal action fulfilled the same promise of personal revenge offered by countermagic.[47]

Witchcraft also served as an excuse for incompetence or failure, and when things went wrong, some cast blame on black magic rather than take personal responsibility. For instance, after Thomas Bracy found himself unable to properly fit a sleeve to a jacket or cut cloth for a pair of breeches, he attributed it to occult forces. Likewise, when Simon Beamon fell from a cart and repeatedly toppled from his horse, he put forward witchcraft as the cause of his clumsiness, concluding that "there was some mischief in it from Hugh Parsons." Looking to magical mischief as an explanation for personal failings sometimes involved more tragic events. Such was the case when Sarah and James Bridgeman blamed the loss of their infant son on witchcraft. Not everyone, however, reached the same conclusion. Anne Bartlett stated that the Bridgemans' newborn gave signs that he was sick from birth "insomuch that it did groan something much" and suffered from a "great looseness." Hannah Broughton and Hannah Lancton supported this view, and both agreed that the Bridgemans' infant "was ill as soon as it was born." These witnesses described a sickly baby who died of natural causes, which begs the question of why the Bridgemans turned to a supernatural explanation for the infant's death. In the wake of the loss of a child, parents might be left asking themselves if their actions somehow contributed to the tragedy, and James and Sarah Bridgeman may have blunted such murmurs of guilt by placing the blame, not on themselves, but on a witch. That the couple had lost several other children soon after birth would have only increased the desire to externalize their anguish.[48]

In a few instances it appears that blaming a witch for personal failings may have been a self-conscious effort to avoid culpability. Such may have been the case when Goody Davis blamed Elizabeth Garlick for the death of one of her children. Jeremiah and Katherine Vaile challenged her assertion, reporting that they heard the respected Mr. Lion Gardiner say that "Goody Davis had taken an Indian child to nurse & for lucre [profit] of a little wampum [valuable shell beads] had merely starved her own child." In other words, Davis's greed was the cause of her child's untimely end, not witchcraft. A similar dynamic may have underlain the prosecution of Lydia Gilbert for the occult murder of Henry Stiles. He died in 1651 after being accidentally shot by Thomas Allyn, the scion of one of Windsor's leading families. Allyn was found guilty of homicide by misadventure, fined, and banned from militia service. Three years later, however, a court decided that Lydia Gilbert had used supernatural means to cause Allyn's gun to fire and was therefore responsible for Stiles's death. It is unclear if the Allyn family played a direct role in bringing about this turn of events; but whether they did or not, the court's verdict was certainly good news for them. Thomas had his fines remitted, his name cleared, and returned to the militia where he eventually became an officer.[49]

The belief in witchcraft also helped people cope with guilt by enabling them to transfer their sense of wrongdoing to another. In Puritan New England, the situations that triggered this process of psychological displacement often revolved around norms that framed what it was to be a good Christian. The colonists' religious and social outlook placed a premium on compassion and charity, fair-dealing and forgiveness, and mutual support. When they failed to live up to these expectations, the result could be a deep-seated sense of shame. Besides feeling that they had contravened social and religious strictures, New Englanders who mistreated others saw themselves as legitimate targets of enmity. Therefore, if misfortune befell the person holding these feelings, they might conclude that the source of their ill luck was malefic magic aimed at them by the person they had wronged. This is why it was commonly those guilty of breaches in neighborly conduct who initiated witch accusations and the victims of such uncharitableness who came under suspicion. Indeed, out of roughly one-hundred documented witchcraft episodes in seventeenth-century Massachusetts that involved the denial of a request, the accused were clearly the injured party in 90 percent of them.[50]

In light of this, even seemingly mundane interpersonal disputes could become a source of witch fears. As already mentioned, Allen Ball pointed to his wife's refusal to comply with Elizabeth Godman's request for some buttermilk as the cause of the widow's malefic assaults against them. What appears to be a relatively minor lapse in generosity clearly became a psychologically charged event that played a central role in the Balls' identification of Godman as a witch. This dynamic may also have been behind Mary Coleman's denunciation of Eunice Cole. She testified that Cole had used black magic to gain knowledge of words "spoke betwixt this deponent and her husband in their own house in private." Significantly, Coleman admitted that the conversation featured "words of discontent" about the accused, an act that was hardly in line with notions of godly deportment and neighborliness. Thus, it is possible that the couple felt guilty over their behavior and that this contributed to their belief that Goody Cole was a witch.[51]

Considering the Puritans' emphasis on an omnipotent God who punished the wicked, the idea of witchcraft had other emotional benefits. Focusing on black magic as a cause of misfortune avoided the more distressing explanation that it was a chastisement administered by God in response to sin and faithlessness. This uneasy connection between injury, God's providence, and witchcraft came to the surface in testimony presented against Mary Bliss Parsons. After describing occult attacks he allegedly suffered at her hands, William Hannum stated that "these things do sometimes run in my mind . . . that if she be not right this way she may be a cause of these things, though I desire to look at the overruling hand of God in it all." Hannum's words reflect how New Englanders' witchcraft beliefs and providential faith pulled them in opposite directions when it came to answering the question of why bad things happened.[52] Of course, even when folk like Goodman Hannum came down on the side of witchcraft, it did not totally free them from culpability. According to Puritan orthodoxy, even if a witch was to blame for misfortune, it was still an act of God's will. This meant that a victim of black magic still had to shoulder part of the blame, because their sins had opened them up to Heaven's rebuke in the first place.

Additionally, witchcraft accusations provided individuals, families, and factions a means to lash out at their foes. Far from being the peaceable Christian enclaves imagined by later generations, disputes often divided early New England's communities. Such was certainly the case in Massachusetts's

Connecticut River Valley towns. These settlements were not primarily products of a communitarian impulse but an individual striving after wealth. The
result was places where contention sometimes overwhelmed Christian fellowship. Thus the witchcraft accusations that pitted Hugh and Mary Parsons against their Springfield neighbors or the ones in Northampton that
brought Joseph and Mary Bliss Parsons, James and Sarah Bridgeman, and
each couples' supporters into conflict were part of a wider array of face-to-
face struggles and factionalism that roiled the colony's western frontier.[53]

The slander suit Joseph Parsons initiated against the Bridgemans presents
a clear-cut instance of witchcraft suspicions intersecting with feuds between
families and neighbors. This confrontation did not come out of the blue but
was the product of growing tensions between the two couples, and once
the legal battle was joined, they set about enlisting their neighbors' support.
Eleven people backed the Parsons and thirteen sided with the Bridgemans,
but four of the latter eventually switched sides. One of these turncoats was
John Matthews. He alluded to the pressure that the Bridgemans put on him to
testify on their behalf when he deposed that "he hath at present no grounds
of jealousy for himself, of Mary Parsons the wife of Joseph Parsons, to be
a witch, and that what he testified yesterday on oath was upon the earnest
importuning of James Bridgeman and his brother." William Hannum and
his wife mirrored this testimony, stating that "James Bridgeman hired them
to [go] down to Springfield to give in their testimony or else they would not
have gone." The Parsons likely undertook similar efforts to rally support.[54]

Community conflict also fueled witchcraft accusations in Connecticut.
Bitter disputes over church polity and governance that plagued Wethersfield
in the mid-seventeenth century set the stage for charges of occult crime.
The contention split the town in two factions: one rallied around its minister, Reverend John Russell, while the other sided with Lieutenant John Hollister. Katherine Harrison's husband was among Hollister's supporters and
attached his name to one of the petitions they sent to Connecticut authorities decrying Reverend Russell. After years of infighting, Russell and many of
his followers left Wethersfield and moved to Hadley, Massachusetts. When
Katherine Harrison fell under suspicion as a witch in 1667, many of those
who offered up testimony against her were from among the pro-Russell folk
who had relocated upriver, which raises the prospect that her prosecution
may have been connected to her deceased husband's association with Hollister and his followers. This pattern emerges elsewhere in the English Atlantic,
and the 1645 witchcraft trial of Joan Cariden of Faversham, England, appears
to have been linked to feuds over the distribution of political power in the
town.[55]

Disputes between individuals and factions as well as simple opportunism created the potential for false accusations. Decades after Elizabeth Kendall hanged for allegedly bewitching a child to death, Reverend John Hale reported that that the infant's nurse was herself responsible for the child's demise by neglectfully leaving "it abroad in the cold a long time" and that she pinned the blame on Kendall in order to avoid her own culpability.[56] Such miscarriages of justice were more numerous (or at least better documented) in the motherland. Over the course of the sixteenth and seventeenth centuries, English courts uncovered several bogus witch accusations. In 1574, for instance, teenagers Agnes Briggs and Rachel Pinder admitted to faking signs of bewitchment and wrongly accusing a woman named Joan Thornton. Thirty years later, an investigation revealed that witchcraft charges leveled against three women by the teenager Anne Gunter had no merit and were a product of her father's malice toward the accused.[57]

In the vast majority of New England's witchcraft cases, it appears that complaints of occult crime were not self-conscious efforts to blacken an enemy's name but a largely unconscious process whereby people transfigured their opponents into enemies of God and humankind. Except for Reverend Hale's after-the-fact claims of deception during Elizabeth Kendall's witch trial, there is no other evidence of malicious accusations in New England before 1670. Thus it appears that the line between the sorts of aggressive acts that normally marked rivalries and occult attacks became blurred in the minds of accusers, and they truly believed that those they accused had employed black magic against them. Of course, New England's full history of witch-hunting is not as free from implications of fraud, and there is good evidence that at least some of the people who helped to drive forward the Salem witch crisis of 1692 gave false testimony.[58]

Witchcraft prosecutions also periodically functioned as a sort of collective catharsis in which communities came together to expel evil.[59] For instance, the witch trial of Elizabeth Garlick was an enterprise pushed forward by the inhabitants of Easthampton. Her accusers and those who supported them ranged from the town's poorer denizens to its leading inhabitants, and there appears to have been no major pushback against her denunciation. Either by contributing to her prosecution or doing nothing to stop it, Easthampton's residents largely came together to battle against occult crime. This pattern of neighbors closing ranks against witch suspects also characterized the prosecution of Hugh and Mary Parsons. Out of the twenty-six people who testified, none had anything good to say about the couple.[60]

In communities fractured by discord, witch-hunting could revive a sense of collective purpose. Efforts to recover from communal conflict intertwined with witchcraft in Wethersfield, Connecticut. Unlike other first-generation New England towns, a unified group of pioneers did not establish the community. Instead, competing factions developed the settlement, and from the start it lacked a strong collective identity. Internal disputes led to a high rate of turnover among its inhabitants and hindered the formation of a church. Out of this environment emerged a series of witch accusations that followed major bouts of conflict in the town, including those against Mary Johnson in 1648, John and Joan Carrington in 1651, John and Elizabeth Blackleach in 1662, and Katherine Palmer and Katherine Harrison in 1667–68. While it enjoyed more peaceable beginnings than Wethersfield, Hartford eventually suffered similar divisions. In the 1650s the town became mired in ecclesiastical disputes that centered on issues of church governance and standards of membership. The battle ground on for about a decade and in its wake came the Hartford witch hunt.[61]

It appears that both Hartford and Wethersfield sought to heal their wounds through the collective project of exorcising witches from their midst. In the aftermath of bitter internal conflict, the towns' inhabitants may have turned to witch-hunting as a way to reknit the bonds of community and demonstrate their commitment to godly harmony and purity. Thus hunting down supernatural malefactors became a way to right what was wrong and restore God's divine favor. That there were often few clear ties between accusers, the accused, and village factions does not undermine this interpretation. Individuals such as Mary Johnson or John and Joan Carrington became targets of suspicion, not as a result of one group's settling a score with another, but because they symbolized the disorder and malice that people living in towns battered by controversy wanted so desperately to purge from their communities. Put another way, witch-hunting was not so much an instrument of community conflict as a method of overcoming its divisive effects. Such a process may also have been at work in Bermuda in the 1650s when, after a decade of political and religious infighting sparked by the English Civil War, the colony's leadership came together as they prosecuted a dozen people for witchcraft and put five of them to death.[62]

Restraining illicit behavior was another collective function of witchcraft. At their most elemental level, witch suspects served as a moral boundary marker. Whether or not the accused were actually guilty of antisocial activities, witchcraft denunciations branded them as deviant and dangerous, and the prosecutions that often followed provided object lessons of what happened to folk who did not fit in. At a minimum, people who ran afoul of witchcraft fears faced the negative consequences of their neighbors' suspicions. At worst, they suffered imprisonment, expensive court fees, and even death. In sum, cases of occult crime made clear the costs of, and so acted to deter, bad behavior.[63]

Having a suspected witch in the neighborhood had other uses. For one, they served as a convenient explanation for ill fortune and a target of blame. So, when tragedy struck, people could readily point fingers at known male-factors and channel negative emotions toward them instead of letting their destructive force have play in the wider community. Even when misfortune did not show its face or witch prosecutions failed to materialize, having a reputed witch in town provided a visible counterpoint to the model Christian. Three perennial witch suspects—Eunice Cole, John Godfrey, and Elizabeth Seager—may have served this role. Besides being suspected of witchcraft, all three faced charges for other crimes. Seager stood trial for adultery and blasphemy; Godfrey came before the bar for slander, lying, and even suborning a witness; and Cole faced charges for defamation and other offenses. In short, Cole, Godfrey, and Seager furnished living reminders of how not to behave.[64]

The accused were just one set of figures in the witchcraft dramas that played out in communities and courtrooms across early New England. Their accusers and alleged victims were also key players, for without them there would have been no complaints that set prosecutions for occult crime in motion. Accusers and the accused were usually familiar with one another—most frequently through the close interactions that came with being neighbors—and their relationships were generally marked by conflict. Suspicions of witchcraft sometimes grew out of these tense situations when emotionally charged misfortunes such as the death of a loved one transformed interpersonal friction into fears of supernatural attack.

Regardless of what triggered witch prosecutions, a belief in black magic helped individuals and communities understand and respond to misfortune. On a personal level, the concept of witchcraft served as a means to explain failures, externalize guilt, and battle foes. Collectively speaking, it provided a sense of communal catharsis and a means to define and enforce appropriate behavior.

Witch hunts and those who instigated them did not always fit into the dynamics of accusation outlined above. Periodically, New England experienced witch panics whose scale and intensity contrasted with the single-suspect cases that generally emerged out of interpersonal tensions. These more expansive hunts also commonly featured "bewitched" accusers whose social position and dramatic claims of supernatural affliction distinguished them from more run-of-the-mill complainants. The task now turns to understanding these more exceptional features of witch-hunting.

CHAPTER 6

"Very Awful and Amazing"

Witch Panics and the Bewitched

Elizabeth Kelly died on Wednesday, March 26, 1662, at the tender age of eight. While child mortality was a regular part of life in seventeenth-century New England, there was nothing ordinary about this death. The illness that took Elizabeth's life was strange and sudden. The girl's parents, John and Bethia Kelly, recalled that she was "in good health" on the morning of March 23 but screaming in pain by evening. Even more alarming, she complained of being pinched, pricked, and choked by an assailant only she could see and who she identified as a near neighbor, Judith Ayers. The girl suffered for three days before dying. According to her mother and father, Elizabeth's last words were "Goodwife Ayres chokes me."[1]

The grief and suspicion that took hold of the Kellys after their daughter's untimely passing broke to the surface when they had her body readied for burial. Among the women who performed the task was none other than Goody Ayers, the leading suspect in the child's death. As if this were not awkward enough, Goodman Kelly ratcheted up tensions when he called Ayers to "come up to it [the body] and to handle it," whereupon she approached Elizabeth's corpse and, it "having purged a little at the mouth," wiped the child's lips with a cloth. Next, he told her to turn up his daughter's sleeves so as to reveal her arms. Ayers attempted to comply, "but the sleeve being somewhat straight [tight], she could not well do it." Anger boiling up within him, John Kelly pushed forward and violently "ripped up both the sleeves" revealing that the backs of the girl's arms "were black and blue, as if they had been bruised or beaten," which he and others present saw as evidence of the supernatural assaults that had led to her demise.[2]

Not all witchcraft cases were alike, and Elizabeth Kelly's death helped trigger an epidemic of fear and suspicion that led to the largest witch hunt in New England before the Salem crisis of 1692. During what has become known as the Hartford witch hunt, fourteen men and women faced accusation for occult crime and four of them hanged for it. The execution count would likely have been higher if not for the fact that several suspects fled before they could come to trial. This witch hunt stands out for its size and intensity and crosses the line between more ordinary prosecutions for magical misdeeds and what can better be described as witch panics. In keeping with this sort of event, the Hartford hunt was a product of explosive social tensions that found an outlet in witch fears. A close look at what happened in 1662 highlights how witch panics diverged from more regular instances of occult crime in terms of their scale, high conviction rates, and emphasis on diabolism. Moreover, it puts the broader features of witchcraft prosecution into motion, illustrating how accusers, the accused, local social dynamics, and elite and popular understandings of occult crime all came together to produce a witch hunt.

The Hartford episode also sheds light on the critical role that a distinct category of participants played in sparking witch panics. Elizabeth Kelly was one of several "afflicted" or "bewitched" accusers who dot the annals of witch prosecutions on both sides of the Atlantic. They are most famous for the role they played in fueling the Salem witch trials but also featured much earlier in New England's battle against occult crime. Like the Kelly girl, most were young, female, and socially subordinate—a set of traits that set them apart from most other accusers. In addition, unlike more run-of-the-mill witnesses who commonly blamed witches for illness and death among loved ones or domestic mishaps, the afflicted complained of being victims of a systematic assault by demonic forces. Another distinguishing feature of this group is that they claimed to be able to see the invisible world of the occult as a result of their supernatural affliction and denounced people as witches using this "spectral sight."

The Hartford Witch Hunt

The Hartford witch hunt started in the home of John and Bethia Kelly with a bowl of hot broth and a bellyache.[3] Their daughter, Elizabeth, was well when she left to attend Sabbath-day services on March 23. After spending the morning at worship, she came back home in the company of Judith Ayers. While visiting with the Kellys, Goody Ayers helped herself to some "broth hot out of the boiling pot" and, according to the girl's parents, "required our said child to eat with her of the same." John and Bethia, believing "it was too hot for her," told their daughter not to eat the broth, but she did not heed their words and "did eat with her [Ayers] out of the same vessel." Soon after, the girl complained of "pain at her stomach," and Bethia gave her something to ease her discomfort before Elizabeth headed back to church (the colonists spent a good part of their Sundays at meeting and took a mid-day break between morning and afternoon sessions). The Kellys later remarked, "We did at that present wonder [why] the child should eat broth so hot having never used so to do," but did not suspect that she was in any danger. They could not have been more wrong.[4]

Elizabeth Kelly seemed fine when she returned home that afternoon, but in the night she awoke, crying, "Father, father help me help me, Goody Ayers is upon me, she chokes me, she kneels on my belly, she will break my bowels, she pinches me, she will make me black and blue." Astonished by his daughter's outburst, Goodman Kelly told her to lie down and be quiet, but Elizabeth only "cried out with greater violence than before." He then put the girl into bed with his wife, but Bethia had no better luck calming the child, who was in a "great extremity of misery." The girl's strange affliction continued into the following days, and at one point she shouted, "Goody Ayres torments me, she pricks me with pins, she will kill me, Oh! father set on the great furnace and scald her, get the broad axe and cut off her head." John and Bethia did what they could for their daughter, and several of their neighbors helped them care for her, including Rebecca Greensmith and the wife of Thomas Whaples. Judith Ayres also offered her aid, and when she entered the house Elizabeth Kelly asked, "Why do you torment me and prick me." Goody Whaples told the child not to say such things, and Elizabeth settled down and fell asleep. This respite was not to last, and after midnight the girl "broke out fresh as before." On Tuesday Elizabeth asked her father to go to the magistrates and enter a complaint against Ayers, adding that "if I could go myself I would complain to them of her how she misuses me." The child's ordeal finally ended when she died the following day.[5]

Witchcraft fears grew in the wake of Elizabeth Kelly's death. As previously mentioned, Judith Ayres, who was a focus of suspicion, helped prepare the girl's corpse for burial. She may have been there to show her support as a loving neighbor or, seeing how eager he was to have her touch his child's body, Goodman Kelly may have demanded her attendance. Either way, those present kept an eye out for evidence of the occult. Nathaniel Willett testified

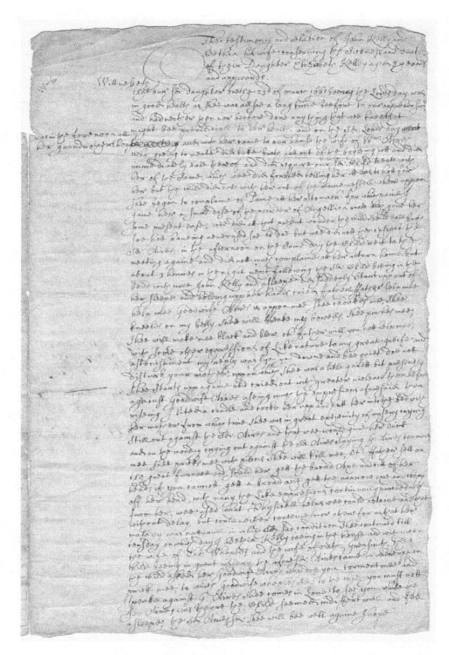

FIGURE 6.1 A part of the deposition John and Bethia Kelly gave against Judith Ayers that helped spark the Hartford witch hunt of 1662–63. From the Samuel Wyllys Papers, 1638–1737, MS. 342, W-6. Courtesy of the John Hay Library, Brown University.

that the Kelly girl's body was strangely bruised, and when it was turned over "there came such a scent from the corpse, as that it caused some to depart the room," giving the impression that it gave off an abnormal stench. Witnesses also noted that instead of being stiff with rigor mortis, the body "did appear to be very limber." Most ominously, John Kelly told those in the room to look at his child's face, and they saw "a reddish tawny great spot, which covered a great part of the cheek, it being on the side next to Goodwife Ayers where she stood." Several of those present concurred that the mark was not there before, implying that it was the result of the woman's close proximity to the deceased. They came to this conclusion in light of the belief that a murder victim's corpse would bleed when their killer came near, a piece of lore known as the "blood cry."[6]

Things took an even darker turn when Hartford magistrate Samuel Wyllys ordered an autopsy of the Kelly girl, the first and only time in New England that a person allegedly murdered by witchcraft underwent this procedure. There was a shortage of trained physicians in the Puritan colonies, and so Wyllys called in Dr. Bryan Rossiter who lived in Guilford in the neighboring colony of New Haven to undertake the macabre task. Exactly when the doctor carried out the autopsy is unknown, but he had certainly completed it by March 31 when he made his report.[7] If Samuel Wyllys hoped that the autopsy would nip rumors of witchcraft in the bud, then he was badly disappointed.

Dr. Rossiter concluded that the unusual condition of Elizabeth Kelly's corpse indicated that the girl died as a result of supernatural forces. He observed that "the whole body, the muscles, nerves, & joints were all pliable, without any stiffness, or contraction," noting that "experience of dead bodies rendered such symptoms unusual." It appears that the doctor was unfamiliar with the physical effects of death, because he did not seem to know that rigor mortis usually abates two to three days after death. Elizabeth died on March 26 and as many as five days passed before Rossiter performed the autopsy. In addition, rigor mortis is often difficult to discern in children due to their lack of muscle mass. The doctor also expressed surprise over the "deep blue tincture" he found in some of the body's tissues as well as "the appearance of pure fresh blood in the backside of the arm." Though it is impossible to say for certain what the physician saw, he may have misconstrued the effects of decomposition as evidence of witchcraft.[8] Regardless, the results of his postmortem examination placed the weight of professional medical opinion behind an occult explanation for the child's death.

After Elizabeth Kelly's burial, the wheels of justice started turning. The authorities ordered an investigation into the girl's death and convened a court of inquest on May 13 during which several people presented testimony supporting the idea that Judith Ayers had killed the child through occult means. Joseph Martin, who witnessed Elizabeth Kelly's illness, corroborated her parents' testimony and confirmed that the girl had accused Goody Ayers of bewitching her. In addition, Anne Barr and her son deposed that Ayers had a history of contact with the Devil. They recalled that the suspect had once told them that "when she lived at London in England, that there came a fine young gentleman [who] made her promise to meet him at that place another time," but "she perceived it was the Devil" and decided not to keep her promise. Ayers allegedly ended her account by saying that when Satan returned and found that she had stood him up, he tore off some iron bars from a nearby fence and carried them off in a rage.[9] No one appeared to wonder how she would have known this if she did not keep her rendezvous, and whether Ayers told this story or not, it has all the appearance of a tall tale.

While Judith Ayers was the main focus of attention at this stage, others fell under the shadow of suspicion. On the same day that the court of inquiry met, Nathaniel Greensmith initiated a defamation suit on behalf of his wife against Goody Ayer's husband, William. Records do not specify what Goodman Ayers said, but it almost certainly related to witchcraft. Rebecca Greensmith had aided the Kellys during their daughter's illness, and William Ayers may have pinned the blame for the girl's death on the woman in an attempt to shift attention away from his wife. In addition, Elizabeth Seager was present at the inquest and did some things that attracted attention. According to witnesses, when Goody Ayers heard the depositions against her read before the court, she exclaimed, "This will take away my life," upon which Seager motioned her to be silent and hissed through clenched teeth, "hold your tongue"—actions that struck many as the behavior of a co-conspirator.[10]

The Hartford witch hunt may not have reached a critical mass if Elizabeth Kelly had been the only supposed victim of black magic in the community. The girl's parents lacked the wealth and influence generally needed to bring a suspect to trial. Indeed, they were so badly off that when Goodman Kelly died soon after the witch panic ended, the town had to provide poor relief to his widow. Besides being poor, the couple hardly possessed a spotless reputation and were an unlikely lightening-rod for community mobilization. For instance, in 1661 John sat in the stocks for two hours in punishment for drunkenness. In addition, except for the accusations of a traumatized child, the Kellys did not present any solid evidence against Goody Ayers or offer up a motive for her alleged supernatural assault.[11]

However, Elizabeth Kelly and her parents were not alone in raising the alarm of witchcraft. A young woman by the name of Anne Cole also began to exhibit symptoms of bewitchment but differed from the Kelly girl in several important respects. She came from a highly respected family who were members of Hartford's church. Goodman Cole, who Hartford minister Reverend John Whiting described as "a godly man," held several posts in the town including chimney viewer, surveyor, and constable. Another reason Anne Cole's words carried more weight was that she was no mere child but a pious young woman in her early twenties. She was also a far more prolific accuser. Anne's affliction was long and drawn out (but not fatal), giving her the opportunity to point the finger of suspicion at a number of people.[12]

While it is not clear when Anne Cole began to exhibit symptoms of bewitchment, it probably happened in the weeks following Elizabeth Kelly's death.[13] Several influential people who observed the young woman's strange condition concluded that its causes were supernatural. One witness, Reverend John Whiting, wrote a letter about twenty years later to the leading Puritan divine Increase Mather, in which he described how, "taken with strange fits," Cole related that "a company of familiars of the evil one [the Devil] . . . were contriving how to carry on their mischievous designs, against some and especially against her, mentioning sundry ways they would take to that end." Whiting also recalled that the young woman's diabolical ramblings sometimes "passed into a Dutch tone. . . . which was very awful and amazing to the hearers." Besides strange speech, she exhibited other signs of bewitchment such as "extremely violent bodily motions . . . even to the hazard of her life in the apprehension of those that saw them."[14]

Anne Cole was not the only Hartford resident exhibiting disturbing signs of occult affliction, and two other women developed similar symptoms. With concerns over witchcraft on the rise, Samuel Wyllys held a special day of prayer at his home attended by the bewitched and a number of concerned townspeople, but instead of bringing peace and healing, "the motion and noise of the afflicted was so terrible, that a godly person fainted under the appearance of it." Although not alone in her suffering, Cole remained the focus of attention because of her willingness to name her supernatural assailants.[15]

With Anne Cole's aid, witch suspects began to pile up. She named Judith and William Ayers, Rebecca Greensmith, and Andrew and Mary Sanford as her tormentors and publicly denounced Elizabeth Seager as a witch during the prayer meeting held at Mr. Wyllys's home. In keeping with general patterns of accusation, it appears that the young woman had some level of acquaintance with those on whom she cast suspicion. The Coles were the Greensmith's next-door neighbors, and the other suspects all lived close to the afflicted young woman. For their part, the accused were near neighbors and well acquainted with one another. Goodmen Ayers, Sanford, and Greensmith had all bought and sold land from one another. In addition, Andrew Sanford successfully sued William Ayers for slander in 1654—an episode that speaks to familiarity, though of a negative sort, between the two households.[16]

Judith Varlett, a young, unmarried woman who belonged to a Dutch family living in Hartford, also became caught up in what was fast becoming a witch dragnet. Observers noted that Anne Cole sometimes spoke in a Dutch accent during her diabolical trances and suspicion may have fallen on Varlett as a result. Moreover, an incident took place just prior to the witch panic that may have contributed to her accusation. In December 1661, someone entered a complaint against Judith's father, Casper Varlett, "for bringing in a Dutch man named Baltus & his wife into the town . . . in such a manner as the town is not secured." Hartford officials ruled that his actions were "prejudicial & offensive" and decided that if he could not satisfactorily explain them, he had to leave the town within a year, pay a staggering £100 fine, or suffer criminal prosecution. Hartford's inhabitants never spelled out why they were so bent out of shape over a Dutch couple surreptitiously entering the town. Their reaction may have been a product of anti-Dutch sentiment stoked by rumors of war between Holland and England that circulated in the Puritan colonies during the 1650s and early 1660s. Casper Varlett likely became a surrogate for Hartford residents' fears of the Dutch; and when he died just before the outbreak of the witch hunt, this stigma may have passed to his daughter.[17]

The Hartford panic got another boost after one of the accused confessed. According to Reverend Whiting, when he and Reverend Joseph Haynes confronted Rebecca Greensmith with Cole's testimony against her, the suspect "forthwith and freely confessed those things to be true, that she (and other persons named in the discourse) had familiarity with the devil." Upon "being asked whether she had made an express covenant" with Satan, Greensmith replied that she had not, but added "that the Devil told her that at Christmas they would have a merry meeting, and then the covenant should be drawn and subscribed." When pressed as to why she admitted to her misdeeds after having previously denied any wrongdoing, Rebecca declared that "when Mr. Haynes began to read, she could have torn him in pieces, and was as much resolved as might be to deny her guilt . . . yet after he had read a while, she was as if her flesh had been pulled from her bones . . . and so she could not deny any longer."[18] A less dramatic explanation is that the physical and psychological effects of intense interrogations and imprisonment in a cold, comfortless jail brought Greensmith to the breaking point and prompted her admission of guilt.

Rebecca Greensmith followed up her initial confession by providing information about a larger diabolical conspiracy that implicated several others. Among those she identified as fellow servants of Satan were people who had already been denounced as witches—Judith Ayers, Elizabeth Seager, Judith Varlett, and Mary Sanford—as well as several new suspects. The latter group included Goody Greensmith's husband. Describing him as "a man of little body and weak," she claimed that he employed several familiar spirits to help him with both his farm work and malefic deeds. It also included the wife of Peter Grant, Wethersfield residents James Wakeley, and the long-time witch suspect Katherine Palmer. Greensmith mentioned witch meetings where "some of the company came in one shape, and some in another, and one in particular in the shape of a crow" and hinted at their depravity when she "owned that the devil had frequent use of her body with much seeming (but indeed horrible, hellish) delight to her."[19]

Even before Goody Greensmith made her shocking confession, several of the accused faced trial. A Connecticut court presented Andrew Sanford for witchcraft on June 6 and his wife exactly a week later. Both stood charged of having "entertained familiarity with Satan" in order to commit acts of malefic harm. It is unclear how Andrew came to the attention of authorities. Anne Cole may have named him as one of her tormentors, or he might have fallen under suspicion as a result of his close association with his accused wife. No testimony related to the Sanfords' trials survives and little is known about them other than their outcome. The court acquitted Andrew Sanford after the jury could not reach unanimous agreement that he was guilty but convicted his wife. Mary Sanford eventually went to the gallows, and the Hartford witch hunt claimed its first victim.[20]

Instead of taking their chances before a jury, several suspects decided that discretion was the better part of valor and, as Reverend Whiting recalled, "made their escape into another part of the country." Judith and William Ayers, the couple who first came under suspicion for witchcraft, were the first to flee and took refuge in Rhode Island. In their haste to escape the pair left much behind, including their nine-year old son, John. Connecticut officials eventually confiscated Goodman Ayers's abandoned property in order to satisfy his debts and apprenticed his son to a local cooper. Reverend Increase Mather's *An Essay for the Recording of Remarkable Providences* includes a story about the Hartford panic that may explain the couple's hasty exit. It recounts how several inhabitants of the town "had a mind to try whither the stories of witches not being able to sink under water, were true; and accordingly a man and woman mentioned in Anne Cole's Dutch-toned discourse, had their hands and feet tied, and so were cast into the water, and they both apparently swam after the manner of a buoy," indicating their guilt. Mather concludes by saying that the pair feared that a "halter [hangman's noose] would choke them, though the water would not, [and] they very fairly took their flight."[21] If the man and women featured in the Reverend's account were husband and wife, then the tale is undoubtedly about the Ayers, for they were the only accused couple who fled the witch hunt.

Two other individuals also managed to evade prosecution. It never hurts to have friends in high places, and such was the case for Judith Varlett. Sometime after her arrest, a letter arrived from the woman's brother-in-law, who was none other than governor of the Dutch colony of New Netherland, Peter Stuyvesant. He vouched for his relative's good character and assured that she was "innocent of such a horrible crime." Not wanting to further roil their already tense relationship with the Dutch, Connecticut authorities released her. Like the Ayers, James Wakeley fled, leaving behind his wife and much of his property, and made for the relative safety of Rhode Island. He came back to Connecticut in 1665, but finding that suspicions toward him still ran high, he escaped to Rhode Island once again, forfeiting a £150 bond that he and two associates had posted to guarantee his appearance in court. Having gotten away a second time, Wakeley never returned and lived out the rest of his life in Providence.[22]

The Hartford witch panic reached its deadly peak as 1662 ended and 1663 began. In January 1663, William Goffe—one of the Regicides responsible for the execution of Charles I in 1649 who was then hiding in New Haven after the restoration of the English monarchy made life too dangerous for him in the mother country—wrote in his diary that "three witches were condemned at Hartford." The entry makes reference to the final executions related to the witch hunt: the hangings of Rebecca and Nathaniel Greensmith and Mary Barnes. Connecticut authorities indicted the couple on December 30 for having "entertained familiarity with Satan the grand enemy of God and mankind." Goody Greensmith confirmed her confession during their trial in early January, and a jury dutifully found the pair guilty. The Greensmiths went to the gallows later that month.[23] The final casualty of the Hartford panic was Mary Barnes of Farmington. Anne Cole had first identified her as a witch and Goody Greensmith's confession corroborated the accusation. Not much is known about her case other than that it was quick. A grand jury indicted Barnes just a week after sending the Greensmiths to trial, and she faced judgment during the same court session as the couple and with the same result. Her prison fees (people in early New England had to pay for their own incarceration) indicate that her arrest, trial, and execution took place in the span of three weeks.[24]

Although no one knew it at the time, these executions were the final ones associated with the Hartford hunt and, as it turned out, the last for witchcraft in Connecticut. The panic had subsided, and the remaining suspects avoided trial. Suspicions against Wethersfield merchant John Blackleach and his wife, Elizabeth, first came out into the open during the trial of Rebecca and Nathaniel Greensmith. Maria Skreech stated that she and Mrs. Blackleach went to see a dead sow, recalling that "I did look upon the sow and it was my girl's sow" and that "afterwards Goodwife Stedman came to my house and was troubled and said she saw this sow a day or two before in Mr. Blackleach's lot and did believe that they had hurt the sow." While at least some people suspected the Blackleaches of using black magic to harm the animal, the case against the couple was pretty flimsy (there is no evidence that they were even taken into custody), and Mr. Blackleach put a stop to further rumors of witchcraft by suing their accusers for slander. Likewise, Goody Grant's case never got very far, and there is no indication that it came before a grand jury.[25]

The Hartford hunt also dredged up witchcraft suspicions that had remained dormant for decades. Katherine Palmer, whom Goody Greensmith identified as a diabolic co-conspirator, had been previously arrested for witchcraft in 1648, but the authorities let her off with a warning. Suspicions against her were raised again in the early 1650s but did not result in legal action. So when witch fears threatened to ensnare Goody Palmer a third time in 1662, her husband sold off his property in Wethersfield, and they moved to that premiere refuge for witch suspects, Rhode Island. The couples' troubles with allegations of occult crime did not end there. In 1667 Connecticut officials received an official complaint against Goody Palmer, but the fact that she no longer lived in the colony shielded her from prosecution. Suspicions lingered into the following decade, and in 1672 Stephen Sebeere of Rhode Island had to "acknowledge unto Henry Palmer" that he had "done wrong unto him and his wife in saying that his wife is a witch."[26]

Elizabeth Seager was a final figure who got caught up in the Hartford witch hunt. She first emerged as a suspect when Anne Cole named her as one of her tormentors; and Seager did not help her situation when she disrespectfully declared that Reverend Joseph Haynes, who recorded the young woman's accusations, had written "a great deal of hodgepodge." Goody Seager was arrested and indicted alongside Mary Barnes and stood trial in late January. Lucky for her, the jury considered the evidence insufficient and returned a verdict of not guilty. Although Seager escaped the hangman's noose, it would not be the last time she faced the charge of witchcraft.[27]

Anatomy of a Witch Panic

The Hartford witch hunt of 1662 was not unique and illuminates a larger story of witch panics in the early modern English Atlantic. It was the first of three such episodes that took place in New England. The other two occurred thirty years later when Massachusetts experienced the massive Salem witch crisis and Connecticut the far smaller Fairfield witch hunt.[28] The mother country was also no stranger to witch scares. The largest struck East Anglia between 1645 and 1647 and led to several hundred arrests and more than a hundred executions. Witch panics in Lancashire in 1612 and 1634 involved scores of accusations, a couple of dozen convictions, and at least ten executions. A mass hunt in Northumberland in 1649–50 led to thirty arrests and eighteen hangings, and another in Kent in 1652 resulted in eighteen arrests and six executions. Scotland was even more prone to witch panics and experienced several between the late-sixteenth and mid-seventeenth centuries. Parts of continental Europe, such as Germany, also saw endemic, large-scale witch hunts in the early modern era; and even countries with more restrained histories of prosecution suffered panics, like the waves of witch trials that marked Sweden between 1668 and 1676.[29]

No matter where they took place, witch scares grew out of pervasive anxiety and conflict. The Salem crisis, for instance, took root amid religious disputes within Salem Village, colonywide fears stoked by bloody warfare with Native Americans, and the political disorder surrounding Massachusetts's acquisition of a new charter. The upheavals of the English Civil War likewise helped to lay the foundations for the massive East Anglian witch hunt, and religious disputes set the stage for an intensive bout of witch prosecutions in Bermuda in the 1650s. The story was much the same across much of Europe, as the Protestant Reformation and the cycles of warfare, social unrest, and political instability it triggered created an environment conducive to witch panics.[30]

New England was also a host to contention and apprehension in the early 1660s. The decade opened with the collapse of the English Commonwealth and the return of the Stuart dynasty under Charles II, a political transformation which reverberated across the empire. The shift was especially worrisome for New England, as it had thrown in its lot with Parliament and for that reason did not expect to fare well under the restored Crown.[31] Besides the threat emanating from a resurgent monarchy, the Puritan colonies had to deal with disputes between one another. Each worried that its neighbors would seek to advance their position at its expense as they jockeyed for position in the new political order. Such concerns were not unfounded. When

Connecticut renegotiated its charter with the king, it obtained surprisingly good terms, including control over what had up till that point been the independent jurisdiction of New Haven. When the latter colony's officials got wind of this, they were outraged at what they considered Connecticut's betrayal. The bitter contention that ensued reached a climax just as the Hartford witch hunt took shape. Added to these woes, disease stalked New England in the early 1660s, and communities throughout the region experienced sickness and death.[32]

Hartford was especially ripe for a major witch hunt. Besides the regional and imperial disturbances its inhabitants experienced alongside other New Englanders, the community faced its own problems. The death of its pastor, Thomas Hooker, in 1647 marked the start of trouble. His passing left Hartford with Hooker's assistant, Reverend Samuel Stone, to carry the weight of its spiritual needs. Unfortunately, he did not possess the prestige or personality needed to maintain harmony. Inflexible and stubborn, Stone promoted an expansive view of clerical authority and more liberal terms for joining the church, thoroughly upsetting congregants who preferred the lay authority and restrictive membership policies that were hallmarks of New England Congregationalism. The conflict came out into the open in 1655 when Hartford's church sought a replacement for Reverend Hooker. In an effort to impose his more potent view of pastoral power, Stone vetoed the congregation's decision to invite a prospective pastor to preach before them. Outraged at what they saw as ministerial overreach, a group of dissidents led by Elder William Goodwin challenged Stone, while others in the church remained loyal to their pastor. The dispute continued into 1659, and on more than one occasion, Connecticut's government and church synods made failed attempts to settle the conflict. In the end, the controversy only came to a close when William Goodwin and many other dissidents left Hartford.[33]

Another Connecticut town touched by the witch panic of 1662, Wethersfield experienced a pattern of contention very similar to Hartford's. Indeed, disputes in the two communities became intertwined. Founded in 1634, by 1641 Wethersfield had seen three ministers come and go due to disagreements over religious authority and belief. After this the town experienced a period of relative peace before ecclesiastical conflict returned in the mid-1650s. The roots of this renewed contention lay in Reverend John Russell's arrival in Wethersfield as its new minister in 1649. Like Samuel Stone in Hartford, he elicited opposition by attempting to expand his authority at the expense of the congregation's power and proposing a more open path to church membership.[34] The conflict became an open breach when Russell excommunicated the dissident John Hollister in 1656 without consulting the congregation. While the reverend maintained the support of most church members, Hollister enjoyed the backing of a large majority of the town's residents, who promptly elected him as their representative to the General Court and petitioned it for their Russell's removal. The reverend and many of his followers eventually came to the conclusion that the only way to end the feud was to leave, and in 1658 Russell and those loyal to him went north to Hadley, Massachusetts.[35]

Although witch panics commonly followed major episodes of conflict, it is not always easy to connect one to the other, and such is the case with the Hartford Controversy and the witch hunt of 1662. Few Hartford church records from before 1685 survive, making it difficult to determine whether patterns of accusation in the town paralleled the community's factional divides. However, there is evidence pointing to such a correlation in Wethersfield. Four years before he fell under suspicion for witchcraft, James Wakeley signed a petition against Reverend John Russell, and the husband of the accused witch Katherine Harrison added his name to the same document. This may indicate that those who supported Reverend Russell promoted the witch hunt, while those who opposed him became its targets. That several of the individuals who later provided testimony against Katherine Harrison came from Hadley, Massachusetts—the town where Russell and his followers settled after leaving Wethersfield—supports this hypothesis.[36]

While large witch hunts tended to emerge out of unusually fraught circumstances, the profile of the accused was similar to that of more ordinary cases of occult crime. With regard to their age, marital status, and sex, the fourteen people accused during the Hartford panic had much in common with New England's other witch suspects. With the possible exception of Judith Varlett, who was probably in her twenties and single, those who fell under suspicion in 1662 matched the standard profile of the accused in that they were between thirty and sixty years of age and married. This continuity extends to sex, and during the witch hunt of 1662 nine (around two-thirds) of the fourteen suspects were female and the remainder of those accused were male. This closely follows the general sex ratio of witch suspects in Puritan colonies before 1670. Thus the heightened fears that marked the Hartford panic did not overturn the general profile of the New England witch.[37]

The people who came under scrutiny during the Hartford hunt also matched other witch suspects in terms of their personal background and reputation. Most of them had checkered pasts and criminal histories, and even those who avoided previous run-ins with the law acted in ways that put them at odds with expected norms of behavior. There is no evidence that Judith Varlett or Goody Grant were subject to any reputation-ruining criminal prosecutions, although their character may have been impugned in less visible ways. Similarly, as a full member of Hartford's church, Judith Ayers must have maintained some semblance of respectability. Nevertheless, every other person who faced accusation during the Hartford panic possessed a criminal record or a proclivity for disreputable behavior. William Ayers had previously been found guilty of or charged with theft, slander, and other misdemeanors. Goody Ayers was also not without blemish, and in 1655 her husband had to post a £20 bond in order to assure that she would "carry good behavior to all the members of this commonwealth." While there is no record of a trial, there are indications that Mary Barnes was charged with the scandalous crime of adultery in 1649, and the Sanfords, Palmers, and Greensmiths also had various run-ins with the law. In particular, Nathaniel Greensmith stood out as a quarrelsome, unsavory figure who had been convicted of theft, assault, and lying.[38]

The Hartford suspects also generally fell in line with New England's other accused witches when it came to social status. Like the larger group, they hailed from a variety of socioeconomic backgrounds but with most coming from the lower and middling ranks. At one end of the spectrum was Goody Grant, whose husband only held an estate worth £50 at the time of his death in 1681. At the other stood John Blackleach and James Wakeley who were among the economic elite of their community. The rest fell somewhere in between. The Ayers, Seagers, and Palmers were all of humble means. Meanwhile, the Greensmiths were among the town's middling property holders; and indications are that the Sanfords, who held nearly forty acres of land in Hartford, fell into the same category. Likewise, Mary Barnes's husband had built up a comfortable estate and held public offices that reflected his solid standing by the time she fell under suspicion. Judith Varlett, whose father held property worth about £200 when he died in 1662, also appears to have come from a financially secure background.[39]

In sum, witch panics were not accusatory free-for-alls, and they often paralleled more ordinary episodes of witch-hunting with respect to the type of people who came under scrutiny. For instance, although the East Anglian witch panic of the 1640s netted hundreds of suspects and led to scores of executions, the extraordinary nature of the event did not extend to the profile of those who faced trial. Of course, unusual suspects such as John Lowes, whose sex and position as a parish minister would have most likely shielded him from conviction under more normal circumstances, fell victim to the panic. Nevertheless, the vast majority of the accused during the witch hunt were the sorts of people who regularly ended up before English courts on charges of occult crime. Similarly, while the Salem witch crisis saw the arrest, trial, and execution of unusual suspects such as the respectable church member Rebecca Nurse, such instances do not erase the fact that most of those ensnared during the panic fit the profile of the typical New England witch. Indeed, except for Salem Village and Andover where witch fears reached epidemic levels, most towns involved in the crisis experienced it in ways that closely paralleled ordinary witchcraft episodes.[40]

While the types of people arrested during the Hartford panic do not sharply distinguish it from run-of-the-mill witchcraft episodes, what does is the high proportion of suspects who faced trial, conviction, and execution. Of the half-a-dozen culprits who went before a grand jury during the witch hunt, all of them were indicted and sent to trial, and four (two-thirds) ended up going to the gallows. In contrast, New England's other pre-1670 witch prosecutions saw just under three-quarters of presentments lead to trials, and only about a third of these court appearances resulted in guilty verdicts. The upshot is that during witch panics like the one that struck Connecticut in 1662, the accused had a significantly higher chance of being tried, convicted, and executed than those denounced under more ordinary circumstances.

Witch panics also stand out because of the amount of testimony concerning diabolism they produced. Lurid stories concerning the Devil and witches' demonic activities did pop up in more ordinary prosecutions of occult crime but not with the frequency or depth that characterized witch panics. For example, the depositions and confessions generated by the Salem witch hunt went well beyond descriptions of magical harm and included numerous accounts of witches attending black Sabbaths and signing the Devil's book, promoting the idea that Massachusetts was the target of a vast diabolical conspiracy. In England, the Lancashire panic of 1612 and the East Anglian witch hunt of 1645–47 likewise produced copious amounts of testimony concerning satanic meetings, sexual encounters with devils, and demonic covenants.[41]

Table 6.1   Witchcraft cases during the Hartford panic compared to others before 1670

	INDICTMENTS LEADING TO TRIALS	TRIALS RESULTING IN CONVICTIONS
Hartford cases	100%	66.6%
Non-Hartford cases before 1670	72.5%	36.3%

Note: The Hartford suspects William and Judith Ayers and James Wakeley who fled before they could come to trial are excluded from this calculation, leaving eleven accused who were available for indictment, trial, and conviction. The figures for nonpanic cases are drawn from my own research and John Demos, *Entertaining Satan*, 401–9.

The Devil was also on everyone's lips during the Hartford panic. Diabolical concerns came to the forefront when those who witnessed Anne Cole's strange illness judged it a case of demonic affliction. Though previously unknown in New England, Devil worship and witches' Sabbaths featured in testimony generated by the witch hunt of 1662. In his deposition, Robert Stern described the sort of witch meetings imagined by European demonologists when he claimed that he saw Rebecca Greensmith, Elizabeth Seager, and several other women in the woods dancing around a simmering cauldron in the company of demonic creatures.

Goody Greensmith provided an even more elaborate description of such gatherings and introduced the satanic pact, the central motif of diabolical

FIGURE 6.2 This image of witches dancing with devils evokes the testimony Robert Stern presented during the Hartford witch panic in which he claimed to have seen witches frolicking in the woods with demons. From Nathaniel Crouch, *The Kingdom of Darkness* (London, 1688). Division of Rare and Manuscript Collections, Cornell University Library.

FIGURE 6.3 Witches feasting with devils at a black Sabbath. From *The History of Witches and Wizards* (London, 1720). Courtesy of the Wellcome Collection.

witchcraft. She confessed to meeting the Devil several times in the woods near her home where she joined with other witches to dance and drink "sack" (fortified wine). Greensmith also tapped into the dark, carnal fantasies of diabolical witchcraft when she admitted to having sex with the Devil. In addition, Margaret Garrett claimed that Goody Seager could fly, a power closely associated with demonic witchcraft during the early modern era.[42]

Furthermore, the scale of witch panics distinguished them from other cases of occult crime. While every other instance of witch prosecution in the Puritan colonies before 1670 involved only one or two suspects, the Hartford panic led to legal action against fourteen people. Put another way, just under a quarter of all those formally charged with witchcraft in New England during this period were implicated during this single episode. Witch scares also tended to have a greater geographical reach. Except for the Hartford hunt, during the first three-quarters of the seventeenth century witchcraft cases in the Puritan colonies involved suspects drawn from a single town. In contrast, the panic of 1662 ended up ensnaring victims from three communities

(Hartford, Wethersfield, and Farmington). While this is not a stunning departure from the norm, it does put it in a class of its own. The Salem crisis that struck Massachusetts thirty years later provides an even better illustration of witch panics' expansive nature, and by the time it was all over, it had touched dozens of communities stretching from Maine to Boston. This pattern was also characteristic of panics in Europe. The East Anglian hunt of 1656–47 involved dozens of communities in counties across Southeast England, while many of Scotland's major witch hunts affected wide swaths of its lowland region.[43]

Several dynamics account for the size and intensity of witch panics. They commonly erupted in the midst of widespread unease, producing an environment conducive to chain-reaction hunts where one accusation led to another. This was certainly the situation in Hartford. Elizabeth Kelly's shocking affliction and death sparked witch fears and formed the backdrop to Anne Cole's bewitchment and career as an accuser, which in turn paved the way for Rebecca Greensmith's confession, which implicated additional suspects. As was the case with both Cole and Greensmith in 1662, witch panics on both sides of the Atlantic commonly got a boost from high-yield accusers who denounced multiple suspects. Confessions were another signature feature of large-scale witch hunts, especially in those parts of the Old World (such as Scotland) where authorities could employ judicial torture to pry them from the accused. Admissions of guilt like Goody Greensmith's commonly served to implicate others, stoke popular fears, and give credibility to the authorities' prosecutorial efforts.[44]

Another distinguishing feature of many witch panics was the involvement of witch finders. These individuals came in many guises, from people who pursued occult criminals as a full-time vocation, to those who briefly took it up in response to circumstance. In terms of their background and social standing, witch finders ranged from educated elites in positions of authority to the peasants who served on early modern Germany's village-level witch-hunting committees. The most infamous witch hunters in the English Atlantic were two men who pushed forward the East Anglian witch hunt of 1645–47, the "Witch finder General" Matthew Hopkins and his partner, John Stearne. In Scotland, witch finders were a bit more prolific and, because of their practice of using long needles to detect witch marks, became known as "pricks." One of these individuals made his way south into England and helped to spark a witch hunt in Northumberland in 1649.[45]

Witch finders also made an appearance during the Hartford panic in the form of a clutch of local clergymen. Anne Cole's strange affliction drew the attention of Hartford ministers Samuel Stone and John Whiting, Reverend

Samuel Hooker of Farmington, and Reverend Joseph Haynes, who was without a church and living in his hometown of Hartford. Haynes was the son of Connecticut's first governor, John Haynes, a hardline Puritan who led the colony during a deadly phase of witch-hunting a decade earlier. These men helped move the Hartford hunt forward by documenting Anne Cole's affliction, diagnosing it as bewitchment, and interrogating the suspects she named. The aged and ill Samuel Stone held that Cole's "Dutch-toned discourse" was evidence that diabolical forces were at work, judging it "impossible that one not familiarly acquainted with the Dutch . . . should so exactly imitate the Dutch tone in the pronunciation of English." This assessment drew on the belief that a person's ability to speak in an unknown foreign tongue indicated that demonic forces were at play. Be this as it may, no one claimed that the young woman was speaking Dutch, only that she spoke English with a convincing Dutch accent. That Cole lived in a town which contained at least one Dutch family (the Varletts) and thus could have been exposed to the sound of Dutch-accented English seems to have escaped the clergymen's notice, making it appear that they were eager to attribute the young woman's behavior to occult forces. This situation was not unique to Hartford but characteristic of other witch panics such as the Salem crisis during which several local clergymen took an active role in the witch hunt.[46]

Haynes, Stone, Hooker, and Whiting also elicited Rebecca Greensmith's admission of guilt. Samuel Stone was an old hand at pressing confessions out of the accused, having helped obtain one from Mary Johnson that paved the way for her execution in 1648.[47] The ministers may have also shaped Greensmith's confession, and it contains several features that indicate that she may have responded to cues from her interrogators. Her declaration that the Devil intended her to sign a covenant with him at Christmas would have been music to the ears of Puritan ministers who considered the holiday a repository of pagan traditions and popular excess. Indeed, after she made the admission, Reverend Stone "solemnly took notice . . . of the Devil's loving Christmas." Likewise, her accounts of witch meetings and having sex with the Devil were in line with notions of diabolical witchcraft familiar to Puritan clergymen.[48]

Bewitched Accusers

The presence of individuals like Anne Cole also separate New England's major witch hunts from other episodes of prosecution. Besides clergymen and demonologists who dabbled in detecting the occult, such alleged victims of bewitchment served as witch finders in their own right and played an oversized role in witch panics. Cole joins the afflicted persons who pushed forward the Salem witch crisis and Katherine Branch who triggered the much smaller Fairfield witch hunt among the Puritan colonies' most prolific accusers.[49]

The bewitched differed from other accusers by virtue of their suffering. Most prosecuting witnesses complained about acts of maleficium that caused illness, accident, or death and were often only indirect victims of witchcraft in that it was their property or loved ones who bore the brunt of an occult attack. In contrast, afflicted accusers directly felt the power of the witch through painful physical torments and frightening spectral visions. In his account of Anne Cole's ordeal, Increase Mather states that she was "amazingly handled" and "taken with very strange fits, wherein her tongue was improved [controlled] by a demon to express things which she herself knew nothing of." Not only did they suffer more intensely, but their ordeal commonly unfolded over a period of days, weeks, or even months. Both Elizabeth Kelly's and Anne Cole's suffering extended beyond a single magical assault; and although Kelly's affliction was much briefer than Cole's, it could have stretched longer if it had not been cut short by her death.[50] Likewise, the alleged bewitchments of Katherine Branch and the accusers involved in the Salem witch crisis lasted for months.[51]

In addition, afflicted accusers stood apart from other witnesses in terms of their age, sex, and status in that they were commonly young, female, and of low social rank. Just about everyone who experienced bewitchment in the Puritan colonies before 1670 was female. The exceptions were perhaps some of the children of Reverend George Moxon allegedly targeted by Hugh Parsons and the son of Thomas and Elizabeth Farrar who supposedly suffered at the hands of Ann Burt.[52] This pattern held true for New England's entire history of witch-hunting, and out of the dozens of victims of bewitchment, only about one in ten was male.[53] The afflicted were also distinguished by their youth. Elizabeth Kelly was a child when she underwent her torments. Similarly, the children of James Bishop, Thomas Farrar, and Reverend Moxon were in all likelihood still quite young when they experienced their purported supernatural torments. Elizabeth Howell was in her late teens and Anne Cole her early twenties when they fell victim to occult forces. This fits a broader pattern. Over half of the bewitched in New England were nineteen or younger, while another fifth were between twenty and twenty-nine.[54] In light of this, it is not surprising that almost two-thirds of New Englanders who suffered bewitchment were unmarried.[55] Furthermore, low social status characterized this group, as most were females in a society dominated by men and young in an era when wealth, position, and power came with age.

In some cases, such as that of Elizabeth Kelly, the poverty of a bewitched person's family only added to their lack of standing. Moreover, many of the afflicted from later in the century were servants, including Katherine Branch, Elizabeth Knapp, and several of those involved in the Salem crisis. Nevertheless, that Anne Cole and the children of Reverend Moxon were from prominent families shows that the afflicted sometimes had more privileged backgrounds.[56]

Another characteristic shared by a number of afflicted accusers in the Old World and the New was their or their families' reputation for piety. That Reverend Moxon's children stood among the ranks of the bewitched is certainly congruent with the idea that they were frequently members of devout households. Anne Cole also fits this profile. Increase Mather described her as "a person of real Piety and Integrity," while Reverend John Whiting referred to the young woman as "a person esteemed pious, behaving herself with a pleasant mixture of humility and faith." That Cole's father was among the men Hartford appointed in 1667 "to correct any disorders that they shall discover in the time of public worship" appears to confirm that she came from a family known for its uncompromising godliness.[57]

Finally, the bewitched distinguished themselves by the nature of their testimony. Instead of stories about a strange illness, a cow suddenly going lame, or some domestic mishap, they spoke of spectral forms (which only they could see) that tortured them. The tone of their complaints also differed from those of ordinary accusers. Whereas most witness testimony presents rather matter-of-fact descriptions of malefic harm, a near hysterical incoherence often characterizes the utterances of the afflicted. They did not calmly recount their run-ins with witches but struggled to make sense of terrifying, and ongoing, occult attacks. Elizabeth Kelly, for instance, denounced Judith Ayers in the midst of physical torments that left her screaming and writhing in pain. Likewise, Anne Cole issued her accusations while in the midst of "awful and amazing" suffering. In the decades following the Hartford panic, the afflicted accuser Katherine Branch as well as those active during the Salem crisis presented similarly breathless accounts of assaulting specters.[58]

Cases of bewitchment were not self-diagnosed, and people who observed the afflicted—especially those in positions of authority such as physicians and clergymen—introduced and legitimized an occult explanation for their torments. As they puzzled over the strange symptoms exhibited by Elizabeth Kelly, Anne Cole, and other alleged victims of malefic assault, early modern Europeans first had to decide if they were caused by natural or supernatural maladies. Demonologies and judicial manuals provided guidelines for separating ordinary illnesses from those brought on by diabolical agents. For instance, Michael Dalton's *The Country Justice* (1655) identified several indicators of bewitchment, including sudden illness; the ability of an afflicted person to tell what a suspected witch was doing or wearing at a distance; a sufferer's unusual strength "as that a strong men or two shall not be able to keep down a Child or weak persons upon a bed"; and their vomiting "up crooked pins, needles, nails, coals, lead, straw, hair, or the like."[59]

The diagnostic process was not over once authorities identified an illness as having occult origins, and determining the specific nature of the affliction was a second and equally difficult task. Writers agreed there were two basic types of supernatural aliment—"obsession" and "possession"—and that telling one from the other was not easy. In the case of obsession, the Devil or a demonic entity gained power over victims' bodies in order to torment them. Students of the occult held that this condition could occur through

FIGURE 6.4 Depicting one of the symptoms that early modern Europeans interpreted as a supernatural sign of bewitchment, this woodcut shows a young girl vomiting up nails and pins. From *The History of Witches and Wizards* (London, 1720). Courtesy of the Wellcome Collection.

the agency of a witch and, under these circumstances, be more accurately described as bewitchment. The idea was that witches invited demons to assault a person in order to coerce them into betraying God and joining Satan's ranks. For instance, Katherine Branch claimed to be tormented by spectral cats that spoke to her and promised "fine things and that she should go where there were fine folks" if she would submit to them and serve the Devil. Possession, in contrast, entailed that demonic forces had gained control over a person's body *and* soul. This spiritual malady was far more serious and, in the view of learned authorities, was the consequence of significant moral failings. Since a victim of possession was under Satan's sway, they came perilously close to becoming a witch. The only thing separating the two was that the latter consented to their enslavement by the Devil, while the former did not.[60]

Parsing out whether a person was suffering from obsession or possession was not just an academic exercise but could have a significant impact on the process of witch-hunting. On the one hand, authorities held that an obsessed person was a largely innocent victim of demonic forces whose testimony could help identify occult criminals. On the other, if they labeled someone as possessed, the sufferer had to accept some responsibility for the condition, seeing that their sinful nature led to their plight. Moreover, because they were under Satan's thumb, a possessed person's testimony held no legal merit.[61] English folk on both sides of the Atlantic struggled to establish a clear distinction between possession and obsession, but there was no simple procedure for determining whether a person suffered from one or the other. The only way to reach a diagnosis was to observe the victim. Even then, because the symptoms associated with the two conditions were very similar, it was difficult to reach a definitive conclusion. In the 1680s Increase Mather identified the ability to speak unfamiliar languages, knowing secrets that were beyond one's knowledge, unusual strength, and speaking without moving the mouth as signs of possession. Although he provided some guidance, Mather's list came too late to help New Englanders who faced the problem of diagnosis at midcentury.[62]

Uncertainty over whether sufferers were possessed or obsessed framed New England's best-documented cases of occult affliction. One took place in Groton, Massachusetts, in 1671, when a servant by the name of Elizabeth Knapp began to suffer from fits and broke into unseemly speeches during which she accused others of bewitching her. She came under the care of Reverend Samuel Willard who later became a critic of the Salem witch trials. After months of observation and study (during which he suppressed Knapp's witch denunciations) Willard concluded that the young woman suffered from demonic possession, meaning that the main agent in Knapp's supernatural illness was the Devil or a demon, not a witch. Likewise, during the Salem panic, the status of the afflicted accusers was ambiguous. Over time, however, views moved away from the idea that they were innocent victims of bewitchment and toward the conclusion that they were possessed, and this shift helped to bring the crisis to a close by calling the accusers' credibility into question.[63]

The Hartford witch hunt of 1662 appears to have avoided any serious struggle over the diagnosis of the afflicted. When observers asserted that a demonic entity took control of Anne Cole's voice, the symptom fit the bill for possession. However, there is no evidence that anyone characterized her as such, and people (or at least those who recorded their views) saw the young woman as being obsessed. Cole was devout and from a pious family, and this may have shielded her from the prognosis of possession. In addition, for anyone wishing to see witch prosecutions move forward, avoiding this conclusion was essential since the testimony of the possessed was not considered trustworthy. Whatever the reason, the decision to view Cole as a victim of bewitchment legitimized her as a witness and fueled the witch panic.[64]

A close look at the striking behaviors exhibited by the afflicted opens up a window onto the deeper psychological and cultural aspects of bewitchment. Those supposedly suffering from supernatural torments acted in ways that were shockingly deviant—especially for the female adolescents and young women who constituted the overwhelming majority of such victims. As the afflicted screamed, shouted, and fought, they hardly adhered to notions of female subservience or the sort of deferential respect the young were supposed to have for their elders. Perhaps even more transgressive was their tendency to mock the clergy or disrupt meetings of worship. In his account of Anne Cole's bewitchment, Reverend Whiting noted that "very often great disturbance was given in the public worship of God by her and two other women who had also strange fits." Elizabeth Knapp had a similarly tense relationship with Reverend Samuel Willard, careening back and forth between expressions of contempt for the clergyman while in the depths of a diabolical episode and those of gratitude when she regained control of her faculties. Likewise, during the early phases of the Salem crisis, several of the afflicted disrupted church services and even taunted a minister as he preached.[65]

The acts of physical and verbal aggression committed by the bewitched may represent an effort by individuals who were commonly young, female, and otherwise subordinate to exert some sort of power. Such behavior also likely reflected inner turmoil as the bewitched lashed out against internalized social norms that enforced their inferior position. In some cases this rebelliousness took the form of a struggle between the afflicted and authorities over whether they suffered from possession brought on by their own moral failings or obsession involving one or more witches. For instance, there was a considerable amount of sparring between Elizabeth Knapp and Katherine Branch and the clergymen and civil officials who evaluated the young women's claims of occult torment. Indeed, one of the things that made the Salem crisis stand out was the lack of such conflicts as the magistrates uncritically accepted of the accusers' claims that they were innocent victims of bewitchment. For her part, there is no indication that Anne Cole ever challenged the clergymen who interpreted her case. Anyway, seeing that they came to the conclusion that Cole was bewitched rather than imposing the more morally dubious idea of possession, there was little reason for her to contest their authority. That Anne was no lowly servant like Knapp or Branch but the member of a prominent Hartford family may have helped bring about this mutually satisfactory diagnosis.[66]

No matter how transgressive their behavior, the afflicted ultimately acted within the bounds of their culture and reinforced social norms even as their behavior challenged them. Possession and bewitchment were not only culturally accepted, but rested on assumptions vital to maintaining the social order. That the afflicted were often young and female served to confirm social hierarchies based on age and gender. Additionally, the idea of diabolical affliction presupposed the existence of demonic forces and, by extension, God. This served the purposes of clergymen who wished to focus society's attention on spiritual rather than worldly concerns. Supernatural explanations for the behavior of the afflicted also worked to channel inquiries away from more socially uncomfortable conclusions. If a person was possessed, then their moral failings were the root cause of the problem—if they were bewitched, then the job turned to discovering and punishing the person or persons responsible for the occult attack. Either explanation forestalled any consideration of how social and cultural structures contributed to these unusual episodes of personal trauma.[67] The belief in supernatural affliction also allowed its alleged victims to sidestep whatever discontent they felt by interpreting it as something imposed on them by an external force. To admit that such emotions emanated from within would have risked shattering their self-perception as good and godly people. This helps to explain why devout individuals were especially prone to this sort of psychological condition, for such feelings would have been especially difficult for them to face in light of their pious upbringing.[68]

Most of New England's bewitched accusers quickly faded from view. The vast majority of them were young women who did not leave behind many traces before or after their moment of fame, and they rapidly returned to a state of relative anonymity. With only one exception, all of the young women who formed the core group of accusers during the Salem crisis quickly drop from the historical record. The same is true of Katherine Branch and Elizabeth Knapp.[69]

Anne Cole is a different matter. She came from a respectable family and remained in Hartford long after her alleged bewitchment, making it possible to trace her life after 1662. By some accounts, Cole recovered from her affliction following the triple hanging of Rebecca and Nathaniel Greensmith and Mary Barnes in January 1663. William Goffe noted that after the executions "the maid was well," and Reverend Increase Mather reported that "after the suspected witches were either executed or fled, Anne Cole was restored to health." However, there is at least one indication that Cole's encounter with the occult may have lasted somewhat longer. According to a story passed down by Reverend Mather, at the exact moment Anne's brother Matthew "was struck stone dead" by lightning at Northampton, Massachusetts, a demon "which disturbed his sister Ann Cole (forty miles distant) in Hartford spoke of it, intimating their concurrence [involvement] in that terrible accident." Mather stated that this event took place on April 28, 1664, which means that either he got his dates wrong, or Anne Cole's trouble with demonic forces lingered long after the Hartford witch hunt had subsided. No matter what the case, by the late 1660s her life appears to have returned to a regular course. She became a member of Hartford's church, married, bore four children, and proved "herself truly godly to the charity of all observers." In a strange twist of fate, Anne ended up living in the house that had previously belonged to Nathaniel and Rebecca Greensmith after her husband purchased it in 1668. Thus she spent her days in a dwelling that had once been occupied by a couple who became casualties of a witch panic she had helped to ignite.[70]

Explosive episodes of witch-hunting marked New England and Europe during the early modern era. These scares ensnared more suspects, produced higher levels of diabolical testimony, and saw a greater proportion of the accused face trial and execution than in more pedestrian witch prosecutions. Nevertheless, the differences between ordinary and extraordinary witchcraft cases were ones of degree rather than kind. In particular, the people who came under scrutiny during witch panics sometimes pressed up against the margins of the standard profile of suspected occult criminals but did not overturn it.

Another feature that separated witch panics from regular cases of supernatural crime in New England was the presence of bewitched accusers. Their age, gender, and social position distinguished alleged victims of diabolical assault from other witnesses. Moreover, they claimed to be able to see the invisible world of the occult and often became witch finders who played an important role in sparking witchcraft prosecutions.

But this group does not deserve all the limelight when it comes to explaining why witch panics took shape, for the support of the authorities was also essential to their emergence and growth. Without the participation of government officials, widespread witch fears could not translate into a wave of legal action against the accused. Thus, in order to understand the ebb and flow of witchcraft prosecutions, it is vitally important to explore the judicial dimension of witch-hunting, including the debates over evidence and due process that shaped it.

CHAPTER 7

"According to God's Law"

Witch-Hunting as a Judicial Process

When Connecticut authorities arrested Elizabeth Seager for witchcraft in 1662, no one could have predicted the ensuing twists and turns of her case. One of several suspects who fell under suspicion during the Hartford witch panic, she came before a grand jury on January 6, 1663. Seager's indictment declared that she had "entertained familiarity with Satan the grand enemy of God and mankind and by his help has acted things in a preternatural way beyond the ordinary course of nature for which according to God's law and the laws of this colony thou deserves to die." The jurors endorsed the charge, to which Seager pleaded not guilty. Much to the disappointment of her accusers, the trial ended with an acquittal.[1]

Goody Seager was not out of the woods yet, and six months later she was arrested and indicted for the capital crimes of blasphemy, witchcraft, and adultery. A jury cleared the defendant of the first two charges but convicted her for the third. However, Connecticut had never imposed the death penalty for adultery but substituted other forms of punishment. Such was the outcome of Seager's case, and she lived to see another day. Accusations of witchcraft caught up with her again in 1665. Once more she was indicted and pled her innocence, but this time her trial resulted in a guilty verdict. Before Seager's accusers had the satisfaction of seeing her hang, Connecticut's governor declared his "desire that the matter might be respited to a further consideration for advice in those matters that were to him so obscure and ambiguous" and suspended her execution until the case could be reviewed. This delay turned into a reprieve when a panel of judges decided that the jury's verdict did "not legally answer the indictment" and set Goody Seager free. Having weathered the storm of accusation a third time, she and her husband left Connecticut and moved to that well-known refuge for witch suspects, Rhode Island.[2]

Elizabeth Seager's experience is a reminder that court proceedings were a critical component of witch-hunting. Her odyssey through the legal system, although longer and more complex than that of most witch suspects, involved the arrest warrants, indictments, and trials familiar to any criminal prosecution. As William Perkins remarked in *A Discourse on the Damned Art of Witchcraft* (1618), "The discovery of a witch is a matter judicial."[3] In keeping with other aspects of witch-hunting, events in the courtroom placed New England in dialogue with the mother country, for the Puritan colonists drew heavily on English jurisprudence when it came to occult crime. Witch prosecutions also involved the encounter of popular and elite culture, for it was before the bar of justice that folk views on black magic came into contact and sometimes clashed with more learned understandings. In addition, jurists and demonologists disagreed among themselves over what constituted legitimate grounds for conviction, and this debate shaped the fate of witch suspects across the English-speaking world.[4]

The Law and Witchcraft

The process by which New Englanders brought suspected witches to justice had its roots in the Old World. During the Middle Ages, Europe supported an accusatorial legal system in which cases came to court on the initiative of an individual accuser rather than the state, hence the "accusatorial" label. Under this model, judges were essentially impartial arbiters of judicial contests between plaintiffs and defendants who both faced risks. The accused could be found guilty of the crime laid against them, while the accuser, under the concept of *lex talionis* (law of retaliation), could be punished for entering a false charge. In its most antiquated form, accusatorial law did not involve the investigation of crimes or the collection of evidence—judicial officials' relatively limited role in court proceedings largely precluded this—but relied on trial by ordeal or comparing how many supporting witnesses a plaintiff or defendant had lined up in order to come to a verdict.[5] In light of these features, this legal system was not an apt instrument for battling occult crime. Accusers needed to initiate prosecutions that could be time-consuming and costly. In addition, if their case failed, they faced the real possibility of pun-ishment, including death. None of this encouraged would-be witch hunters.

The move toward inquisitorial judicial procedures that marked much of Europe in the late medieval and early modern periods provided a more effec-tive tool for witch-hunting. Inquisitorial legal systems differed from accusato-rial ones in several respects. First, the authorities could initiate prosecutions and did not rely on plaintiffs to bring forward complaints. Second, accusers were not generally held liable for advancing charges that did not stick, and often defendants never even discovered who had denounced them. Third, judges took on new and expanded roles. No mere impartial umpires, they managed prosecutions and had broad investigative powers. Finally, inquisi-torial law promoted a greater emphasis on the need for definitive proof in order to reach a guilty verdict.[6]

While its more rationalized standards of evidence could have theoreti-cally put the brakes on runaway witch prosecutions, the acceptance of anonymous accusations and involvement of the state in promoting pros-ecutions helped to make inquisitorial procedure a more powerful means for hunting witches. So did the enactment of coercive means to gather proof in response to inquisitorial law's more robust evidentiary standards. Specifi-cally, it encouraged the revival of judicial torture: the practice of inflicting pain on culprits in order to pry testimony and confessions from their lips. This had been a regular feature of Roman and Germanic law, but the Church largely banned it during the Middle Ages. Ironically, such coercive measures reemerged as a consequence of ostensibly more enlightened legal practices that took root during the Renaissance.[7]

Unlike much of continental Europe, England did not adopt inquisitorial law. There, venerable aspects of accusatorial procedure—such as trial by ordeal—were long gone by the seventeenth century and had been replaced by more modern practices including trial by jury and rational standards of evidence. Nevertheless, England's legal system remained accusatorial since initiating prosecutions still rested primarily on individual subjects. Equally important, it did not embrace torture as a regular feature of criminal justice, largely reserving it for cases of treason. This is not to say that English witch suspects avoided physical torment, as witch hunters did periodically turn to coercive techniques to force confessions from the accused, such as during the East Anglian witch panic of 1645–47. But this represents an exception rather than the rule, and these abuses were more often perpetrated by locals than the courts.[8] Thus, England sustained legal traditions that, at least in the abstract, were not especially conducive to witch-hunting.

The levels of centralization and professionalization that characterized a polity's judicial system also had a bearing on if it became a home to aggressive witch hunts, since they influenced whether or not its courts came under the sway of popular pressures that could undermine due process. At one end of the spectrum stood states that allowed local tribunals—frequently staffed by judges with little formal training—to prosecute capital crimes such as witchcraft with minimal oversight. Such conditions created a situation where the public's fear of witches could exert a pernicious influence on courts' treatment of the accused. Thus it is not surprising that Scotland, the Holy Roman Empire, and other parts of early modern Europe with low levels of judicial centralization and professionalism saw high levels of witch prosecutions and convictions.[9] At the other end were more tightly controlled legal systems staffed by professionally trained justices who enforced judicial procedures or at least provided systematic review of lower-court rulings. Such places generally avoided runaway witch hunts because their judiciaries were better insulated against popular prejudice. For example, France maintained a good degree of centralized oversight of its judicial system through its provincial appellate courts, or *parlements*. Operated by trained magistrates, they enforced rules of evidence, restricted the use of torture, and contributed to France's relatively restrained history of witch-hunting. Likewise, through its centrally run circuit courts staffed by professional jurists, the English state regulated the prosecution of capital crimes such as witchcraft.[10]

The Puritan colonies retained many of England's accusatorial practices but also added some inquisitorial procedures. They largely relied on complaints from ordinary inhabitants to initiate criminal proceedings and eschewed torture as a means for acquiring evidence. Nevertheless, New England leaned more toward an inquisitorial approach to law enforcement than the mother country. Puritan justices saw themselves as godly magistrates who were duty-bound to ferret out and punish sin and, in keeping with inquisitorial law, periodically took an active role in bringing forth criminal prosecutions. This impulse was most pronounced in New Haven, which dissolved distinctions between judges' prosecutorial and adjudicative functions and where magistrates routinely initiated proceedings against wrongdoers. Only Rhode Island avoided this inquisitional impulse by creating the posts of attorney and solicitor general in 1650, allowing judges to shed any duties related to managing criminal prosecutions and take a more neutral position in cases that came before them.[11]

New England also diverged from the mother country in terms of its top-to-bottom lack of judicial professionalism. This was a product of both happenstance and design. In the early decades of settlement, not enough experienced judges migrated to New England to staff its courts. The Puritans were also suspicious of professional lawyers, believing that they instigated legal disputes in order to line their pockets, and so before midcentury several New England colonies either banned them or heavily regulated their activities. Thus their courts were often manned by amateurs who were less likely to fully understand or respect legal procedure. Among Connecticut's early leaders, only Roger Ludlow had any formal legal education; and it was not until 1659 that the colony saw the arrival of its first experienced attorney, William Pitkin. Although the Puritan colonies each possessed a high court with jurisdiction over serious crimes like witchcraft, this dearth of professionalism combined with the colonies' small populations undermined their ability to insulate judicial proceedings from popular prejudice. As late as 1660 there were only about eight thousand colonists in Connecticut and just over twenty thousand in Massachusetts, making them relatively tight-knit communities where even the highest officials were sensitive to local views.[12]

In sum, New England's judiciaries had some features that inhibited aggressive witch-hunting and others that tended to promote it. Specifically, their embrace of inquisitorial procedures and lack of professionalism theoretically increased the potential for witch prosecutions, while the retention of many of England's accusatorial practices worked in the opposite direction. The way things worked out in practice was complicated, and gauging how each of the colonies' legal systems approached witch-hunting is not simply a matter of determining their balance of accusatorial and inquisitorial features. For instance, New Haven, which leaned the furthest toward inquisitional law, had the lowest rate of witchcraft prosecutions and no executions for the crime. The colony could have been an efficient witch killer, for its courts sported an overall criminal conviction rate of over 90 percent. Nevertheless, its rejection of torture and the scrupulousness of its judges kept witch prosecutions under control.[13]

The Puritan colonies' witchcraft laws also differed from those of the mother country. England's statues focused on the harmful effects of black magic, and only the act of 1604 included a brief nod to diabolism. This displeased Puritan thinkers who believed that the crime of witchcraft rested on a pact with the Devil. As one of their number, Richard Bernard, wrote: "All the strange fits, apparitions, naming of the suspected in trances, sudden falling down at the sight of the suspected . . . be no good grounds for to judge them guilty of Witchcraft" without evidence that they had formed a "league" with Satan. New Englanders took this view to heart and drew up their criminal codes accordingly.[14] Massachusetts's, Connecticut's, and Plymouth's laws against black magic echoed the diabolical reference found in England's 1604 witchcraft act when they made reference to consulting with a "familiar spirit," but they wholly ignored the statute's lengthy discussion of maleficium. In doing so, the colonies made it clear that the essence of witchcraft was a person's association with the Devil rather than the evil acts they committed.[15]

New England generally possessed uniform procedures for handling occult crime that closely paralleled those for any criminal prosecution. While lower, town- or county-level courts could initiate legal action against suspected witches, only a colony's high court could try and condemn them. New England also followed the English tradition of trial by jury. The exception was New Haven, and this may help explain why it saw so few legal actions (and no convictions) against suspected witches. Without a jury bringing popular fears into the courtroom, the colony's magistrates could impose their narrower diabolical definition of witchcraft, protect due process, and provide suspects with a more impartial hearing. As for the other colonies, they only stipulated the use of juries in civil trials and serious criminal cases, including witchcraft. In keeping with English practice, the colonies' courts also forbade sworn testimony from the accused. Early modern folk believed that allowing a suspect to speak on their own behalf opened the door to perjury, which was bad for both the court's efforts to find the truth as well as the defendant's immortal soul. Even more unjust to modern sensibilities was the borrowed English practice of withholding legal counsel from people accused of felonies like witchcraft.[16]

Whereas the mother country allowed for various punishments in cases of occult mischief—including imprisonment, corporal punishment, and execution—the New England colonies' legal codes prescribed death. Their harshness toward witches was balanced out by a more restrained approach to other sorts of crime; and while people in England went to the gallows for a host of offenses against persons and property, the Puritan colonies took their cue from the Bible and reserved execution for the most serious of infractions such as murder, blasphemy, incest, adultery, bestiality, and witchcraft. They did not necessarily administer the law with Old Testament severity, however, and courts frequently downgraded charges or simply did not impose the death penalty. It was this sort of leniency that spared Elizabeth Seager's life when she was convicted of adultery in 1663. Unfortunately for New England's witch suspects, such moderation did not generally extend to occult crime. Nevertheless, there were some instances where judicial officials stopped short of imposing the death penalty. In cases where there was strong evidence of a person's guilt but not enough to justify a death sentence, they could banish a defendant. Such was Katherine Harrison's fate after she faced an extended period of litigation over witchcraft in the late 1660s.[17]

Of Judges and the Judicial Process

New Englanders who came to the attention of the courts for witchcraft started down a path that began with a formal accusation and could end in execution. The length of their journey depended on the strength of the case against them, judicial procedures which varied from colony to colony, and judges' idiosyncratic approaches to the prosecution of occult mischief.[18]

As with any crime, witch prosecutions in the Puritan colonies commenced with a complaint against a suspect, their arrest, and examination by local magistrates. For example, John Godfrey's first trial for witchcraft came after four men and a woman accused him of magical misdeeds before a court in Ipswich in 1659. Similarly, when Winifred and Mary Holman were accused of black magic, a justice ordered the constable of Cambridge to arrest the pair and "immediately bring them before the County Court now sitting at Charlestown, to be examined on several accusations presented." As the warrant makes clear, judicial officials questioned the accused (as well as their accusers) to determine if there was enough evidence to justify further legal action.[19]

If a preliminary inquiry indicated that a complaint had merit, the accused remained in custody while the authorities gathered more evidence to present before a grand jury. In keeping with English precedent, the New England colonies (except for New Haven) required the body to review all felony charges. Consisting of a dozen men chosen from prominent members of the community, grand juries decided if the case should go to trial. An official document known as an indictment, which laid out specific allegations against a defendant, came into play at this stage. If the grand jury determined there was not enough evidence to support the charge, it returned a report of *ignoramus* (meaning "we do not know"), and the accused went free. If, however, they concluded there was enough to sustain the indictment, the jurors endorsed it *billa vera*, or "true bill," and the case went to trial. In principle, the wording of an indictment was critical, and once confirmed by a grand jury, a defendant could only be tried for the specific offenses it identified.[20]

Witchcraft indictments in New England generally followed a consistent formula. The one brought against Joan and John Carrington accused the couple of "not having the fear of God before thine eyes," having "familiarity with Satan the great enemy of God and mankind," and for committing "works above the course of nature." A Massachusetts court similarly presented Hugh Parsons for "not having the fear of God before his eyes," engaging in "familiar and wicked converse with the devil," and employing "devilish practices, or witchcrafts, to the hurt of many persons." In keeping with the general pattern, these examples feature a culprit's having "entertained" Satan as the leading charge followed up with some mention of malefic harm. This was in line with the Puritans' demonic understanding of witchcraft, and allegations of magical harm always played second fiddle to accusations of diabolical compact with the Devil.[21]

In charging witch suspects, New England's judicial officials generally followed the advice of English jurist Michael Dalton. In *The Country Justice* (1618), he wrote that "there must good care be had . . . in the drawing of their indictments" and specified that they had to include such "material points" as invoking, employing, and covenanting with a spirit and having "killed, or lamed" a person. By including references to diabolism and maleficium in their indictments, the Puritan colonists carried out Dalton's recommendations.[22] New England courts did, however, frequently break with his model by including only vague allusions to acts of magical harm. For example, Hugh Parsons's indictment accused him of using witchcraft "to the hurt of many persons," while one of those drawn up against John Godfrey only stated that he had "done much hurt and mischief by several acts of witchcraft to the bodies and goods of several persons." Some indictments even left out any clear reference to maleficium, and Joan and John Carrington were only charged with having "done works above the course of nature." Such broad allegations likely made it easier to convict the accused, because instead of having to show that a culprit committed a specific malefic act against a particular person, proof of nearly any magical misdeed could suffice. Not all indictments were this vague and some contained detailed allegations of occult harm, such as when Elizabeth Garlick stood charged with "the loss of lives of several persons . . . in particular the wife of Arthur Howell," or when Goody and Goodman Jennings were tried for causing the deaths of Reynold Marvin's wife and Balthazar deWolfe's child.[23]

If a grand jury endorsed an indictment, the legal process entered the trial phase. Witchcraft suspects awaited their day in court in prison since the New England colonies rescinded the right to bail for felonies like witchcraft. Moreover, popular opinion and even some learned authorities believed that close confinement robbed witches of their ability to commit harm. Seen in this light, keeping a suspected witch in jail was a matter of public safety. New England's witch trials have left behind few traces. The only information that commonly survives is the charge against the accused, the names of the justices and jurymen who heard the case, and their verdict. In some instances, even these slim records have been lost. Nevertheless, judicial procedures the Puritan colonies used in ordinary criminal prosecutions provide clues as to what happened in the courtroom during witchcraft trials. Keeping with

English practice, witnesses testified in open court so that the accused had the opportunity to cross-examine them. Judges were, at least in principle, responsible for protecting the legal rights of defendants; but without trained attorneys at their side, many of the accused probably had difficulty rebutting the charges laid against them. Defendants could call witnesses to counter the prosecution's claims, but as previously mentioned they were barred from testifying on their own behalf.[24]

Once they had heard all the evidence, a jury rendered a verdict. With the exception of New Haven, the New England colonies mandated the use of juries in all capital cases. As with grand juries, upstanding inhabitants composed these juries of "life and death," but, unlike them, they generally had to reach a unanimous decision in order to render a verdict. If consensus eluded a trial jury, they returned a special verdict in which they reported their findings, explained the basis of their disagreement, and turned over final judgment to the justices of the court. For instance, the jurors at Elizabeth Seager's first witchcraft trial took this step after failing to come to an agreement. The foreman outlined the main points of evidence against Seager and explained that though "half the jury or more" voted to convict her, the others were only "deeply suspicious." On this occasion, the jury's indecision eventually led to the accused's acquittal. In Connecticut, if a jury was hopelessly deadlocked, the verdict was sometimes determined by the vote of the majority, which was "deemed to all intents and purposes a sufficient and full verdict . . . as though all had agreed." This loophole in the rule that jurors had to achieve unanimity in capital cases may help explain why, with the exception of the Salem crisis of 1692, Connecticut sported a much higher conviction rate for cases of occult crime than Massachusetts.[25]

If a trial resulted in a verdict of not guilty, the judicial process came to an end with the defendant's release, but a conviction triggered a final act of sentencing and punishment. In keeping with English legal precedent that treated witchcraft as a civil crime, New Englanders hanged those convicted of black magic. Burning witches was a method of execution (commonly preceded by strangulation) practiced in much of continental Europe. This had been a traditional punishment for heresy and so witches, as servants of Satan, suffered the same fate. Even though the Puritan colonies placed religion at the center of daily life and promoted a diabolical understanding of witchcraft, they stuck with England's method of executing witches. New England courts did not leave much time for the dust to settle after convictions for witchcraft and, as with other capital crimes, swiftly meted out punishment at the gallows. Only in exceptional cases such as those of Hugh

Parsons, Elizabeth Seager, and Katherine Harrison were there postconviction periods of judicial review.[26]

Using this judicial process, Massachusetts, Connecticut, and New Haven all took action against suspected witches, but not necessarily with the same frequency or gusto. The small and short-lived New Haven colony brought just three people before the bar for occult crime—Elizabeth Godman and Nicholas and Goody Bayley—between 1653 and 1655. Only Godman's case reached the trial stage and she escaped conviction. Meanwhile, Massachusetts and Connecticut prosecuted dozens of witch suspects over a period of several decades. Before 1670, the two colonies arrested nearly equal numbers of people for magical misdeeds. Nevertheless, Connecticut emerged as the more aggressive witch hunter: three-quarters of its grand jury presentments led to trials and more than two-thirds of them resulted in convictions. In contrast, Massachusetts sent around two-thirds of suspects to trial, and the colony acquitted almost three-quarters of them.[27]

FIGURE 7.1 English folk throughout the Atlantic World saw the use of black magic as a civil crime and hanged those convicted of witchcraft. From *The History of Witches and Wizards* (London, 1720). Courtesy of the Wellcome Collection.

Table 7.1 Legal action against witch suspects in Connecticut and Massachusetts before 1670

	TOTAL COMPLAINTS	INDICTMENTS LEADING TO TRIALS	TRIALS RESULTING IN CONVICTIONS	CONVICTIONS LEADING TO EXECUTIONS
Connecticut	31	76%	68%	84%
Massachusetts	28	69%	28%	80%

One factor which helps account for Connecticut's less restrained history of witch-hunting is that, unlike Massachusetts, it frequently used grand jury members to staff its trial juries. For example, the grand jurors who indicted Lydia Gilbert for witchcraft in 1654 also later served on the trial jury that convicted her, and as late as the Hartford panic of 1662–63 there was a significant overlap between the two. Thus ten of the dozen grand jurors who indicted Elizabeth Seager for witchcraft in 1663 later served at her trial. A limited pool of qualified jurors probably explains this practice. The Puritan colonies drew jurors for capital cases from the upper ranks of society, and during Connecticut's first decades of existence there were relatively few residents of such stature. Thus, as a matter of practicality, the colony used the same jurors at presentments and subsequent trials.[28] This situation may have led to the colony's higher conviction rate because grand jurors who had already decided that a case had enough merit to go to trial may have been more likely to lean toward a suspect's guilt when they switched to serving on a trial jury. Seeing this potential for prejudgment, England passed a statue in 1352 that allowed defendants to challenge a person's admission to a trial jury on grounds that they had served on the grand jury that indicted them.[29]

The intensity of witch prosecution in New England also varied across time. It spiked in the late 1640s and early 1650s when Connecticut initiated legal action against eight people and executed all but one of them, and Massachusetts arrested a dozen witch suspects, out of whom nine went to trial and five suffered conviction (although the colony eventually reversed the verdict in one of these cases).[30] By the late 1650s, Massachusetts and Connecticut started to turn their backs on the prosecution of occult crime. Between 1657 and 1670, fifteen witchcraft cases came to the attention of Massachusetts authorities and as many as nine went to trial, but none resulted in a guilty verdict. During this same period, twenty-three colonists came before the bar in Connecticut for supernatural misdeeds. A dozen went to trial and six garnered guilty verdicts, but the colony reversed two of the convictions. Thus, although Connecticut exhibited a greater willingness to punish occult criminals during these years, witch-hunting in the colony lost momentum in light of the 100 percent execution rate it maintained before 1658.[31]

Changes in judicial procedure help account for New England's move away from witchcraft convictions and executions. In the 1660s, courts in the Puritan colonies implemented stricter standards of evidence and afforded criminal defendants the right to challenge jurors and withhold information that could incriminate them. Elizabeth Seager took advantage of this last reform at her first witchcraft trial when she refused to speak about her association with other suspected occult criminals. Furthermore, Connecticut's revised legal code of 1672 forbade any overlap in the membership of grand and trial juries, thereby eliminating the prejudicial impact blending the two may have had on earlier witchcraft prosecutions.[32]

The individuals who sat in judgment of the accused also powerfully influenced conviction rates. Several of Connecticut's leaders helped drive forward its deadly witch purge of the late 1640s and early 1650s. One of them was its first governor, John Haynes. He took office in 1639 and held it during alternating years (Connecticut's first frame of government banned a person from serving consecutive terms as governor) till his death. Since the governor or deputy-governor at this time led the colony's Particular Court, which tried all capital crimes, they had a significant impact on the outcome of witchcraft cases. Tribunals led by Haynes condemned at least four of the seven people who went to the gallows as witches in Connecticut before 1654, and he likely oversaw several other trials for occult crime that resulted in executions. Previous to his arrival in the colony, the stern and pious Haynes had been a law-and-order governor of Massachusetts who favored the strict prosecution of wrongdoing, and so it is not surprising that he took a hard line against witchcraft while at the helm in Connecticut.[33] Another of the colony's leading inhabitants, Roger Ludlow, earned a reputation as an energetic witch hunter. As its three-time deputy-governor (he served terms in 1639, 1642, and 1648) and one of the few early Connecticut inhabitants with legal experience, Ludlow habitually sat on the colony's Particular Court. He presided over this body when it the condemned Goody Knapp in 1653 and assisted in several other witch trials that ended in executions. The prominent Connecticut clergyman Reverend Samuel Stone backed these two men's witch-hunting efforts. He took the lead in eliciting a confession of witchcraft from Mary Johnson in 1648 and pursued witches with righteous zeal during the Hartford panic of 1662.[34]

By the 1660s most of these witch hunters were out of public life and a new generation of leaders came into power in Connecticut who were far less strident in the battle against black magic. John Haynes died in 1654,

Roger Ludlow left the colony for England in the same year, and Samuel Stone passed away sometime in 1663.[35] Amid these deaths and departures, John Winthrop Jr. became governor. As the oldest son of Massachusetts's illustrious governor John Winthrop, John Jr. was well-connected, educated (he studied law and medicine), and traveled. After spending many years shuttling back and forth between England, Massachusetts, and Connecticut, he and his family took up residence on an estate at Nameaug (New London) in 1650. Connecticut had granted the land to attract the younger Winthrop

FIGURE 7.2   John Winthrop Jr., portrait, oil on canvas by unidentified artist of the school of Sir Peter Lely or William Dobson, 1634–35. Collection of the Massachusetts Historical Society.

to the colony, for he had acquired a reputation as an excellent physician and its inhabitants were eager to acquire his services. In addition to doctoring, Winthrop became politically active and served as an assistant to Connecticut's General Court from 1651 to 1656, was elected governor from 1657 to 1658, and again continuously from 1659 until his death in 1676. (The colony was so enamored with him that it rescinded the law banning governors from holding consecutive terms.)[36]

Governor Winthrop brought a new attitude to witch prosecutions. Owing to his background in the law, he was likely familiar with English legal works which voiced doubts that the invisible crime of witchcraft could be proven to the satisfaction of judicial standards. As a physician and member of England's premiere scientific organization, the Royal Society, Winthrop looked for natural explanations for phenomenon that others may have attributed to black magic. Finally, his study of alchemy entailed practices that some would have perceived as dabbling in the supernatural, and thus it is not surprising he took a cautious position when it came to convicting people for witchcraft. Indeed, Winthrop's experiments led him to believe that not all magic had demonic origins, putting him at odds with the orthodox view on this subject and furthering the restraint with which he approached the prosecution of occult crime.[37]

John Winthrop Jr. put this outlook into action when he presided at witchcraft trials. He oversaw the 1658 proceedings against Elizabeth Garlick that ended with her acquittal—the first time since Connecticut started prosecuting cases of occult crime that it did not convict and execute the accused. Though Winthrop was absent from the colony during the 1661 trial of Nicholas and Margaret Jennings, he had been present while their case took shape and likely influenced the court's decision to acquit the couple. It is surely no coincidence that the Hartford witch panic broke out while Winthrop was in England negotiating a new charter for the colony and unable to exert his moderating influence over the situation. He returned to the colony at the tail end of the crisis and once back in place worked to restrain the witch hunt. Fortunately for Elizabeth Seager, the governor sat in on her witchcraft trials in July 1663 and June 1665. She was found not guilty during the first, and when a jury convicted her at the second, Winthrop called a special session of the Court of Assistants that overturned the verdict. Several years later the governor played a similar role in confounding attempts to execute Katherine Harrison.[38]

English Witch-Hunting Theory

Supposedly harnessing invisible forces to inflict harm on others, witchcraft was difficult to prove and prosecute. Fortunately for New England officials, they could turn to English legal guides and demonologies that identified how to find and convict occult criminals. These treatises, however, did not speak with one voice but presented conflicting standards for conviction that authorities in the Puritan colonies had to parse out for themselves. Thus, instead of moving forward with a clear set of guidelines for dealing with magical misdeeds, its magistrates and ministers entered into a transatlantic debate over how to apply judicial procedures to the prosecution of supernatural crimes.[39]

English writers identified different types of proof that could identify a witch, including circumstantial evidence of occult activity, supernatural witch-finding tests, physical evidence of black magic, and more conventional indicators of guilt such as confession. Furthermore, they divided them into two broad categories. First there were "presumptions" that served as grounds for suspicion, arrest, and trial; or as John Cotta put it in *The Infallible True and Assured Witch* (1625), this sort of evidence was "alone no sufficient proof, yet do they yield matter and occasion for diligent and judicious inquisition."[40] Next, there was convictive evidence that could send a suspect to the gallows. However, authors sometimes disagreed over which kinds of proofs justified conviction and which were less potent presumptions.

Learned authorities generally agreed that circumstantial evidence could only justify a suspect's arrest and initial examination. In *A Discourse of the Damned Art of Witchcraft* (1608), William Perkins provides a list of such proofs, including the "common report" of the people that a person was a witch, incriminating testimony from "a fellow witch," if harm befell someone soon after they quarreled with a suspect, an individual's close association with a "known and convicted witch," and the accused's "unconstant or contrary" answers to questions. Michael Dalton's *The Country Justice* (1618) contains a similar catalogue of circumstantial evidence, as does Richard Bernard's *Guide to Grand Jury Men* (1629), which adds additional items such as a suspect inquiring too much after a sick person, "especially after they be forbidden [from] the house," and an afflicted person naming a suspect in their fits.[41]

A second category of presumption involved controversial witch-finding techniques rooted in the occult, such as "swimming," the touch test, and spectral evidence. In his *Daemonology* (1597), James I promoted supernatural methods of detection such as the swimming test, which involved binding a suspect and throwing them into a body of water to see if they would float. Those who did not sink were purportedly witches who had "shaken off them the sacred water of baptism" when they gave themselves to Satan. English authorities periodically employed this method, and witch hunters subjected

A DISCOVRSE OF THE DAM-

NED ART OF WITCH-
CRAFT; SO FARRE FORTH
as it is reuealed in the Scriptures, and
manifeſt by true expe-
rience.

FRAMED AND DELIVERED
by M. WILLIAM PERKINS, *in his ordi-*
narie courſe of Preaching, and now publiſhed
by THO. PICKERING *Batchelour of*
Diuinitie, and Miniſter of Fin-
ching field in Eſſex.

WHEREVNTO IS ADIOYNED
a twofold Table ; one of the order and Heades
of the Treatiſe; another of the texts of Scripture
explaned , or vindicated from the cor-
rupt interpretation of the
Aduerſarie.

PRINTED BY CANTREL LEGGE,
Printer to the Vniuerſitie of *Cambridge* .
1 6 0 8.

---

a number of people to the water ordeal during the East Anglian witch hunts of the mid-1640s.[42] In addition, the king endorsed a touch test known as the "blood cry" which posited that if a murderer (including a witch) touched their victim's corpse, it would bleed. Intellectuals such as Reginald Scot and Francis Bacon supported this belief, as did witch-hunting theorists John Gaule and Michael Dalton, although the former did think it a "probable, yet not so certain" sign of wrongdoing. Another version of the touch test held that a suspect's occult power could be confirmed if he or she touched a bewitched person and their afflictions suddenly stopped.[43]

In contrast to the credulous James I, most other English writers' reactions to supernatural proofs ranged from skepticism to outright criticism. Perkins placed the swimming and touch tests on a list of "less sufficient" methods of detection, which also included employing the witch-finding services of a white "wizard." He concluded that "all of these proofs are so far from being sufficient, that some of them, if not all, are after a sort practices of witchcraft." In other words, these forms of evidence were illegitimate since they

FIGURE 7.4 At the center of this image, a woman is "swum" in order to determine if she is a witch. From *Witches Apprehended, Examined, and Executed* (London, 1613). Courtesy of the Wellcome Collection.

depended on the very forces at the heart of occult crime. Likewise, Bernard rejected supernatural witch-finding methods and admonished people who turned to white witches in order to detect black ones, warning that even seemingly helpful acts of magic ultimately had diabolical origins. Following this same line of thinking, John Cotta firmly opposed "erroneous" occult proofs of witchcraft, concluding that it was "unjust that the forenamed miraculous effects by the Devil . . . should be esteemed a sign or infallible mark against any man, as therefore convinced a witch."[44]

Spectral sightings of the accused by their alleged victims constituted another highly disputed sign of witchcraft. The axis of the debate was over whether the Devil could masquerade in the shape of an innocent person; for if he could, then spectral evidence was rendered useless. James I defended this proof, arguing that "God will not permit Satan to use the shapes or similitudes of any innocent persons at such unlawful times." Michael Dalton and Richard Bernard approved spectral sightings as presumptions justifying a person's arrest and examination but did not think that they should serve as grounds for a trial. Countervailing James I's view, Bernard urged justices to approach such evidence with caution since the Devil could "represent a common ordinary person, man or woman unregenerate (though not a witch) to the fantasy of vain persons, to deceive them and others." John Cotta discounted spectral evidence as "the works of the Devil" and asserted that there was "no other way for their [witches] detection by man, but that which is ordinary unto men, and natural and possible unto man." Simply put, he argued that legitimate proof of witchcraft could only come through regular observation and reason—a proviso that certainly took sightings of witches' specters out of the running. Despite such warnings, spectral evidence gained currency in England by the seventeenth century and played a major role in the infamous Bury St. Edmunds witchcraft case of 1662.[45]

Physical evidence of witchcraft constituted a third category of proofs. For instance, Michael Dalton recommended careful inspections of suspects' homes for "pictures of clay, or wax, etc. hair cut, bones, powders, books of witchcrafts," or other tangible instruments of black magic. The attraction of this sort of evidence was that it had the potential to open up the invisible world of the occult to regular judicial procedures and normalize witch prosecutions, even if some of it—such as diabolical spirits in animal form and the preternatural nipples witches supposedly possessed in order to feed them— was anything but normal. The challenge came in determining if observable objects or phenomenon resulted from demonic forces or had explanations rooted in the workings of the natural world or even divine intervention.[46]

In their search for concrete proof of witchcraft, English jurists and demonologists latched onto an idea rooted in their native lore that witches communed with corporeal, animal-shaped spirits, or "familiars." They brought this folk belief in line with the concept of diabolical witchcraft by reenvisioning these imps as envoys of Satan. Michael Dalton wrote that "witches have ordinarily a familiar or spirit, which appears to them; sometimes in one shape, sometimes in another; as in the shape of a men, woman, boy, dog, cat, foal, fowl, hare, rat, toad, etc." Richard Bernard likewise considered these demonic beings as legitimate evidence of witchcraft. The technique used to discover familiars was known as "watching." Although John Gaule was highly critical of this witch-finding method, calling it a "practice of so much folly & superstition," he provides a good description of the process. A suspect was "placed in the middle of a room upon a stool, or table, cross-legged, or some other uneasy posture, to which if she submits not, she is then bound with cords, [and] there is she watched & kept without meat or sleep for the space of 24 hours" or more waiting for "her imp come and suck." Gaule noted that watchers made "a little hole . . . in the door for the imp to come in at; and lest it might come in some less discernable shape, they that watch are taught to be ever & anon sweeping the room, and if they see any spiders or flies, to kill them. And if they cannot kill them, then they may be sure they are her imps."[47] Gaule condemned watching because he saw it for what it was: a form of torture. Whether or not watching resulted in the sighting of an alleged familiar, the sleep deprivation and physical duress associated with the ordeal often led to admissions of guilt. Scottish witch hunters known for their brutal treatment of the accused apparently developed the method, and it spread south to England. Indeed, the self-styled witch finders Matthew Hopkins and John Stearn habitually employed watching during the East Anglian witch hunt, which helps account for the numerous confessions they wrung out of suspects.[48]

English writers upheld the idea born of continental demonologies that every witch bore a bodily mark signifying their covenant with Satan, and advanced the closely aligned folk belief that witches possessed a supernatural teat from which they fed familiars their blood. The concept of the Devil's mark first made its way to England in the sixteenth century. Courts that tried witches 1579 and 1582 searched the accused for it, and James I promoted the mark as one of the primary ways of discovering a witch in his 1597 demonological treatise. By the seventeenth century, the notion of the Devil's mark and witch's teat had won wide acceptance among English intellectuals. William Perkins, William Cooper, John Gaule, and Richard Bernard all gave attention to Devil's marks and witches' teats, citing them as evidence of black magic's diabolical origins.[49]

They also explained how to find and identify these signs of demonic allegiance. Richard Bernard advised officials to "search diligently" for witch marks "in every place" and noted that they were "insensible, and being pricked will not bleed." Furthermore, he asserted that they often appeared as an unobtrusive "blue spot." Michael Dalton closely followed Bernard's lead, observing that Devil's marks could only be found through a careful examination of a suspect's body. He described them as "sometimes like a blue spot, or red spot, like a flea-bite" most likely found near a person's "secretest parts." English courts put these recommendations into practice.[50]

Learned authorities disagreed on how much weight to give familiars, Devil's marks, or witches' teats when trying someone as a witch. Perkins, Cooper, and Gaule considered them presumptions that could justify suspects' apprehension, indictment, and trial, but not their conviction. John Cotta also took this position and urged caution when it came to assessing the meaning of marks on a person's body. He argued there were natural explanations for most bodily blemishes and strongly advised that court officials consult with physicians before assigning occult significance to them. In addition, he proposed that even if a mark had a supernatural provenance it was not necessarily a sign of a pact with Satan, reminding readers that God afflicted Job's body with boils. James I, in contrast, saw the trio of proofs as grounds for conviction. So too did the respected jurists Richard Bernard and Michael Dalton, who considered witch marks a clear indication that a person had "made a league with the Devil" and the "main points to discover and convict" those guilty of witchcraft.[51]

At the apex of witchcraft proofs stood two sorts of convictive evidence that experts agreed were clear indicators of guilt. The first was confession. William Perkins asserted that a suspect's admission of wrongdoing was solid grounds for conviction, providing that it was "voluntary" and not compelled by intimidation or torture. Richard Bernard and Thomas Cooper agreed, as did Michael Dalton who wrote that an open confession "exceeds all other evidence." Nevertheless, some authors recommended caution, even when it came to this seemingly clear-cut proof. John Cotta noted that a confession was only legitimate when given by a person "capable of reason" and stopped short of giving it the stand-alone power to condemn a witch, stressing that other evidence had to corroborate a confession for it to be truly iron clad. In a similar fashion, Sir Robert Filmer's *An Advertisement to the Jurymen of England, Touching Witches* (1653) advised that confessions were invalid if given under duress or by a person who was not of sound mind.[52] A second line of debate opened up around how the courts should proceed when a confessing witch implicated others. While Perkins, Dalton, and Filmer considered such testimony a presumption, Bernard and James I believed it could justify conviction.[53]

There was broad agreement over the second sort of convictive proof: the testimony of two reputable, corroborating witnesses who saw a suspect commit a clear act of witchery. William Perkins wrote that, besides confession, only the testimony of at least a pair of upstanding witnesses confirming that a suspect had "made a league with the Devil, or hath done some known practice of witchcraft" could secure a conviction. The logic of this position was that corroborating witnesses guarded against testimony that was simply mistaken or falsified in order to pursue a personal vendetta. The two-witness rule had biblical origins, which lent it even more legitimacy in the eyes of the Puritans. As John Cotta noted, the Bible "required that no man be judged in matter of weight, or death, but by the testimony of two witnesses, at the least"; and he concluded that witchcraft, "being a matter both of weight and death, cannot according to God's words be judged but by testimony of witnesses."[54]

New England Witch-Hunting in Practice

Early New Englanders scrupulously documented many aspects of their lives but were uncharacteristically tight-lipped when it came to describing their procedures for prosecuting witchcraft. It appears that in certain respects the colonists treated it as an exceptional offense and ignored or bent some of the principles that governed the prosecution of other criminal activity. They initiated judicial proceedings based on suspicion rather than clear evidence of a crime, weakened standards of proof needed to bring about a conviction, and employed types of evidence unique to cases of occult mischief. Therefore, more numerous and better-documented cases of ordinary criminal prosecution do not provide a clear guide to what happened in the courtroom during witch trials.[55] That judicial practice varied between colonies and over time further complicates efforts to make sense of how New Englanders approached witch-hunting.

English legal precedents and judicial guides framed how the Puritan colonies handled witch prosecutions. For instance, Massachusetts officials referred to Dalton's *The Country Justice* when revising the colony's legal code in 1648 and doubtlessly turned to his work for guidance on how to deal with allegations of magical mischief.[56] Indeed, ups and downs in New England's conviction rate for witch suspects can be explained in part by how its judges interpreted demonologies and legal works that addressed the proper methods for identifying and convicting occult criminals.

Following the lead of English jurists, magistrates in the Puritan colonies employed circumstantial evidence as "presumptions" that could justify the arrest, examination, and presentment of a suspected witch before a grand jury. As William Perkins, Richard Bernard, and others recommended, New England courts initiated legal proceedings against those who associated with alleged or convicted witches. Thus, Elizabeth Seager came under scrutiny due to her "intimate familiarity with such as had been witches." Also in keeping with English guidelines, New Englanders took action when misfortune befell a person after a hostile encounter with a suspected witch. For instance, one of the factors behind John Godfrey's first arrest for witchcraft was Elizabeth Whitaker's complaint that several of her father's pigs died soon after he had an argument with the accused. When New Haven authorities decided to investigate Elizabeth Godman after Reverend William Hooke claimed that "when his boy was sick, she would not be kept away from him, nor got away when she was there," they fell in line with Bernard's view that a person's repeated efforts to gain access to the infirm after being warned off were grounds for suspicion of witchcraft.[57]

New England officials also looked to the mother country for guidance on the use of supernatural evidence. In keeping with the general consensus of English writers, they rejected the "swimming" of witches. Although English courts used the procedure on a number of occasions, magistrates in the Puritan colonies followed the lead of skeptics like William Perkins and Richard Bernard who denied the test's efficacy. Despite this official rejection, New Englanders were still familiar with the water ordeal. Increase Mather reported that early in the Hartford witch panic, local residents cast two of the accused "into the water" to see if they were witches, but the authorities did not consider that they allegedly floated as "legal evidence against the suspected persons." Likewise, during one of Elizabeth Seager's witch trials, people spoke to the accused "about trial by swimming," and Katherine Harrison offered to undergo the water ordeal in order to prove her innocence after a Connecticut court found her guilty of witchcraft.[58] This pattern of popular familiarity with and official skepticism toward the swimming test held true after 1670. During the Fairfield witch hunt, Mercy Disborough was "cast into the water," and Elizabeth Clawson was subjected to the same treatment and allegedly would not sink even though a bystander "labored to press her into the water." Once again, judicial officials did not include the results of these episodes in the cases they built against the two women; indeed, they did not even bother to record the outcome of Disborough's dunking. Knowledge of the swimming ordeal also spread to other parts of the English Atlantic, such as Bermuda. Here the test received official approval when the colony held its first witch trial against Jean Gardiner in 1651, for among the evidence that led to her execution was that she was "thrown twice in the sea" and "did swim like a cork." Puritan colonists were also aware of several varieties of the touch test used in witch-finding. In particular, the "blood cry" featured in the Hartford panic and the witchcraft case of William Graves.[59] As with swimming, New England courts generally questioned the validity of such proofs.

Spectral sightings of alleged witches was another sort of supernatural evidence that came before the courts. During Hugh Parsons's trial, John Stebbing recounted that as his wife was "entering into one of her fits, she looked up the chimney" and cried, "O dear! There hangs Hugh Parsons upon the pole . . . Oh! He will fall upon me." In a similar vein, Elizabeth Howell complained that Elizabeth Garlick's specter stood "by the bedside ready to pull me in pieces." In another instance of spectral testimony, Thomas Bracy recalled that he saw Katherine Harrison and James Wakeley standing by his bed "consulting to kill him." According to his testimony, Wakeley "said he would cut his throat, but Katherine counseled to strangle him," and then they pinched and choked Bracy "so as if his flesh had been pulled from his bones."[60]

The witchcraft case of Katherine Harrison provides a window into clerical views on spectral evidence. A Connecticut jury found her guilty of witchcraft in 1669, but Governor John Winthrop Jr. stayed her execution while a committee of minsters considered the soundness of the evidence presented against her.[61] Asked to consider "whether the (preternatural) apparitions of a person, legally proved, be a demonstration of familiarity with the devil," the clergymen answered it was "not in the pleasure of the most high [God] to suffer the wicked one [Satan] to make an undistinguishable representation of any innocent person in a way of doing mischief before a plurality of witnesses." In other words, spectral sightings were a legitimate form of evidence because God would not allow Satan to take the shape of a person who was innocent of witchcraft in circumstances that could lead to their conviction. The committee added that if the Devil did have such power it "would utterly evacuate all human testimony; no man could testify that he saw this person do this or that thing, for it might be said that it was the devil in his shape."[62]

Despite this theoretical endorsement of spectral visions, the clerical committee helped shut the door on them as a credible form of evidence. It asserted that a "legally-proved" spectral sighting could establish a person's guilt, but attached stringent limits on its use in the courtroom by invoking the two-witness rule. By imposing this requirement, the ministers effectively neutered spectral sightings as a definitive proof of witchcraft because they were invariably experienced by individuals and not groups of people who could corroborate one another. On the other hand, the clergymen did undermine the primary criticism of spectral evidence: that Satan could take the shape of a person not guilty of black magic.[63] Thus, while the committee's findings likely contributed to the sharp drop in prosecutions and convictions for witchcraft over the next two decades, they left spectral evidence intact as a proof of occult crime; and it returned with a vengeance during the Salem witchcraft crisis when Massachusetts imprisoned, tried, and executed people on the basis of such testimony.[64]

In keeping with the advice of English writers, officials in the Puritan colonies also strove to collect physical evidence so as to prosecute witch suspects armed with observable facts. For instance, after Massachusetts authorities took Anne Hibbins into custody, they made a thorough search of "her chests and boxes for puppets, images," and other instruments of black magic. When Elizabeth Kelly allegedly died at the hands of a witch, Connecticut officials similarly ordered an autopsy to uncover any clinical evidence of occult activity.[65]

New England officials sought out another physical manifestation of occult crime, animal familiars, and employed the Old World practice of "watching" in order to catch sight of them. The earliest reference to this technique in the Puritan colonies appears in relation to Margaret and Thomas Jones's 1648 witchcraft case when Massachusetts ordered that "the course which has been taken in England for discovery of witches, by watching them a certain time . . . be put in practice" and confined and closely observed the couple. The colony used the same procedure five years later, for Benjamin Cooly, Anthony Dorchester, and Thomas Cooper testified that they had been "charged by the constable to watch Mary Parsons" during the lead-up to her witchcraft trial. Likewise, when Massachusetts prosecuted Eunice Cole for occult misdeeds in 1656, Henry Green received payment "for watching [the accused] one day and one night." Connecticut also employed the technique, and Thomas Lyon recalled that he was "set by authority to watch with Knapp's wife" during her prosecution for witchcraft in the early 1650s. Since all witchcraft proceedings in the colony were under the jurisdiction of a single court, the conduct of Knapp's case was probably not unique.[66] While it appears that New England courts frequently employed watching, it is unclear if it entailed the coercive methods regularly employed in Britain. That there is no mention of such abuses in the Puritan colonies does not mean that they did not happen. It seems unlikely, however, since the brutalities associated with watching in England led to numerous confessions, while only a few New Englanders admitted to being witches before the Salem witch hunt.

New England's magistrates emphasized another sort of tangible evidence of occult crime, the "witch's teat." Whereas English demonologists and jurists divided their attention between the mark that the Devil purportedly inscribed on his followers' bodies and the supernatural nipples though which they fed their familiars, the Puritan colonists focused on the latter. Careful searches for witches' teats were a regular feature of witchcraft prosecutions in Massachusetts and Connecticut. Court-appointed panels of women examined female suspects, and male physicians probably oversaw the job of searching men.[67] For instance, Lucy Pell, wife of Fairfield physician Thomas Pell, identified herself as "one of the women that was required by the court to search the said [Goody] Knapp." Likewise, Margaret Jones went to the gallows partly because "she had (upon search) an apparent teat in her secret parts," and after the arrest of Anne Hibbins, a "search was made upon her body for teats."[68] New England did not contain the only colonies that took up this practice, and in the 1650s Bermuda authorities habitually ordered physical examinations of accused witches. At least ten suspects were subjected to searches on the island colony, and whether or not anything incriminating turned up appears to have played a deciding role in their fate. For instance, John Middleton went to the gallows after his searchers found that he had "teat or dugge about the bigness of a cat's," while Elizabeth Page went free after her's discovered nothing unusual.[69]

The search for witches' teats was not just a feature of officially sanctioned judicial procedures, and ordinary New Englanders also looked for the demonic appendages. Benjamin Cooly reported that Mary Lewis Parsons was so convinced her husband was a witch that she searched him for demonic teats while he slept but came up empty handed. Hugh Parsons returned the favor when he told John Taylor that he "so far suspected his wife to be a witch that he would have searched her" but "she resisted for she told him it was an immodest thing." Along the same lines, Sarah Bridgeman supposedly declared that she had such "suspicions of Mary [Bliss] Parsons [for witchcraft] that she could not be satisfied unless the said Mary were searched by women three times."[70]

The discovery of alleged witch teats contributed to the high conviction and execution rates that characterized the prosecution of occult crime in the Puritan colonies in the late 1640s and early 1650s. As previously noted, English writers to whom New Englanders turned for guidance in battling black magic did not always agree on the weight physical signs of diabolical covenant should carry in the courtroom. Whereas William Perkins, Thomas Cooper, and John Gaule regarded them as presumptions that could not stand alone as the basis of a guilty verdict, Richard Bernard and Michael Dalton saw them as grounds for conviction. The mostly amateur justices of the Puritan colonies probably looked to the practical legal manuals of Bernard and Dalton rather than seeking advice from the more theoretical demonologies of Perkins, Cooper, Cotta, and Gaule and thus were inclined to view witch marks as clear signs of guilt.[71] By treating them as convictive evidence, New England courts turned the prosecution of occult crime into a predictable process whereby successful searches for witches' teats quickly led to hangings. For instance, their purported discovery played a decisive role in the convictions of Margaret Jones and Goodwife Knapp and may have been a factor in less well-documented witch trials.[72]

Before 1670, it appears that New England justices assumed that if a person admitted to being a witch, then they were a witch. There is no indication they followed the advice of English writers who recommended a cautious attitude when it came to confessions—such as only accepting them as valid if they could be backed up by corroborating evidence—and the few people who admitted to witchcraft before the Salem crisis all hanged for the crime. However, an element of caution had entered into Massachusetts' approach to confession by the time Goody Glover admitted to being a witch in 1688. In keeping with John Cotta's recommendation, the judges who heard her case appointed a panel of physicians to confirm that she was of sound mind before they sent her to the gallows.[73] Another point of debate was how to respond when accused witches implicated others in their confessions. While most learned authorities thought such testimony was no better than a presumption, some argued that they could support a conviction. On at least one occasion Connecticut upheld the latter view, for when it sent Nicholas Greensmith to the gallows, his fate was apparently sealed after his wife identified him as a witch in her own confession to the crime.[74]

As with their cousins across the Atlantic, New Englanders saw the corroborating testimony of at least two reputable witnesses concerning an act of diabolical magic as solid grounds for conviction. The Puritan colonists did not need to be trained in the law in order to take this judicial procedure to heart, for it was rooted in the Bible. Deuteronomy 19:15—"One witness shall not rise up against a man for any iniquity . . . at the mouth of two witnesses, or at the mouth of three witnesses, shall the matter be established"—and Numbers 35:30—"one witness shall not testify against any person to cause him to die"—clearly reference the concept, and Puritan colonists eager to align the law with the Bible worked it into the fabric of their judicial systems. A report by the foreman of the jury at Elizabeth Seager's first witch trial makes it clear that the two-witness rule was a key factor in their verdict. He explained that while a pair of deponents said that they saw the accused dance in the woods with several demons—thus satisfying the need for multiple witnesses—the jury rejected the testimony of one, judging that he was too far away from the scene to clearly see such activity. Thus they ruled that that the remaining witness statement could not stand to "to take away life." Likewise, when Hugh Parsons told the magistrates "that one witness was not sufficient" to prove him guilty of witchcraft, he demonstrated that knowledge of this legal principle extended to the general populace.[75]

Unfortunately for the accused, New England officials bent the rules concerning the two-witness requirement when it came to witchcraft. In the mid-1640s, a gathering of clergy and church elders in Massachusetts ruled that a single person's testimony could satisfy the two-witness proviso in cases of occult crime as long as strong circumstantial evidence supported their story. In addition, they concluded that the testimony need not be limited to a single event, but could address occult acts that took place on separate occasions. This watered-down version of the two-witness rule, which the colonies of New Haven and Connecticut also adopted, opened the door to a greater number of guilty verdicts and likely contributed to the spike in witchcraft convictions at midcentury.[76]

The New England colonies only moved to reverse this weakening of the two-witness rule in the late 1660s. The committee of ministers tasked with reviewing Katherine Harrison's witchcraft conviction addressed the question of "whether a plurality of witnesses be necessary, legally to evidence one & the same individual fact?" Backed up by biblical references, they answered that "if the proof of the fact do depend wholly upon testimony, there is then a necessity of a plurality of witnesses, to testify to one & the same individual fact; & without such a plurality, there can be no legal evidence of it." Thus they challenged the notion that circumstantial evidence could substitute for one witness or that deponents did not have to testify about the same event. Connecticut worked this ruling into its revised legal code of 1672, and this helps explain why the colony never again executed someone for witchcraft.[77] Its change in judicial procedure may have also influenced court rulings in neighboring colonies and at least partially accounts for why prosecutions against occult crime lost momentum in New England in the 1670s.

This analysis of witch prosecutions in the Puritan colonies challenges some existing interpretations of how they dealt with occult crime. Specifically, scholars have portrayed New England as being hampered in their battle against witchcraft compared to England and other parts of early modern Europe. They argue that ordinary New Englanders focused on witchcraft as maleficium, while their courts enforced statues that defined the crime in terms of diabolism. Thus, no matter how many stories witnesses brought forward concerning sick children, dying cattle, or sour beer, they did not prove that a culprit was in league with Satan.[78] This view is questionable because New England's earliest decades of witch-hunting demonstrate that its courts did not always fall short in their efforts to convict and execute witches; indeed, Connecticut maintained a nearly 100 percent conviction rate until the late 1650s. Thus, if there was a mismatch between popular and elite views of witchcraft in the New England colonies, it did not necessarily interfere with their ability to achieve guilty verdicts.

In the final calculation, New England courts generated relatively few witchcraft convictions because of the magistrates who oversaw the prosecutions rather than a lack of appropriate evidence. Judges and juries were not dependent on witness testimony and could generate their own proofs of occult mischief. By ordering suspects to be watched for familiars or searched for witch marks, justices could manufacture physical evidence of black magic. Thus, the real determinants of conviction were if the courts discovered these signs of witchcraft and how they interpreted this evidence. If, following the lead of some English writers, they regarded them as proving a person's allegiance to Satan (as they appear to have done in the 1640s and 1650s), then they would have convictions aplenty. If, however, they sided with demonologists like William Perkins, who viewed such proofs as mere presumptions, then acquittals were more likely. The same held true for the courts' approach to the two-witness rule. If they strictly enforced its provisions, then there was a greater chance of suspects going free, but if they interpreted it more loosely, then it opened the door to a greater number of guilty verdicts.

While its social dynamics extended beyond the courtroom, witch-hunting was ultimately a judicial process. The prosecution of occult crime in the Puritan colonies largely followed procedures seen in any criminal proceeding, and these rules helped assure that witch trials upheld due process. Moreover, English legal precedents and guides profoundly influenced what happened when witchcraft cases came before the courts in New England. This is especially true of the standards of evidence the colonists employed when dealing with occult crime. Their efforts to make sense of the various views expressed by English jurists and demonologists on this topic had a significant impact on the fate of individual witch suspects as well as broader patterns of witch prosecution in the Puritan colonies.

Conclusion

The Case of Ann Burt and Witch-Hunting in the English Atlantic

In 1669 a widow residing in Lynn, Massachusetts, by the name of Ann Burt came under suspicion for witchcraft. All that remains of the episode are the depositions of eight people who testified against her. It is safe to surmise that at least one of these witnesses entered a formal complaint against Burt that resulted in her arrest and examination by a magistrate. Beyond this, the widow's progress through the judicial system is less certain. It is possible that the authorities drew up an indictment against Burt that a grand jury declined to endorse, which would explain why there are no records of a trial. If, however, a grand jury did indict her, then Widow Burt likely stood before the colony's Court of Assistants in late 1669 or early 1670. In such an event, her trial must have resulted in an acquittal (or she at least escaped execution) because Burt died of natural causes in 1673.[1]

For all the uncertainties that surround Ann Burt's witchcraft case, the accusations made against her are clear. Witnesses blamed her for afflicting the married daughters of John and Madeleine Pearson, Bethiah Carter and Sara Townsend, as well as three of Thomas and Elizabeth Farrar's children. Having been sent for to treat the Pearsons' daughters, Doctor Philip Reed found that both were "very ill but especially the said Sara Townsend being in a more sadder condition" and "did plainly perceive there was no natural cause for such unnatural fits." During one of his visits, Sarah was able "to give information of her aggrievance and cause of her former fits," claiming that "Burt had afflicted her and told her if ever she did relate it to anyone she would afflict her worse." According to Reed, an hour later the young woman had a "sadder fit than any ever she had before," and when he asked who afflicted her, she "replied with a great screech she had told me already and that she did now suffer for with it." Sarah Townsend's trouble reportedly started after her father brought her to Ann Burt "to be cured of her sore throat." She spent the night at the widow's home where, as Sarah later told her mother, "Goodwife Burt brought the devil to her to torment her." Similarly, Thomas Farrar testified that two of his daughters were "sorely afflicted and in the greatest extremity" and how in the midst of their fits "they would cry out and roar" that Burt tormented them. He added that his son was also in "extreme misery" and that a physician (it is unclear if it was Dr. Reed) had concluded that the boy was "bewitched."[2]

While the malefic affliction of these five victims was the main charge laid against Widow Burt, other witnesses claimed that she could read minds and move with preternatural speed. Jacob Knight testified that he once lodged in the same house as Widow Burt and that on one occasion went into her room to light his pipe and informed her he had a headache. Jacob then went back to his chamber, "which was through five doors," and as he bent over "to lose my shoe" was startled to see Burt standing before him "with a glass bottle in her hand." She said it contained a cure for his headache, but when he drank some of the bottle's contents, the pain worsened. Knight was at a loss to explain how Burt had been able to pass so quickly and quietly through several closed doors and across a floor "that was so loose that it would make such a noise that might in an ordinary way be heard when any passed over it" without some sort of supernatural aid. He also stated that he intended to tell his sister about the strange encounter, but before he could do so, the widow came to him and "said I had a mind to say something to my sister that I would not have her [Burt] hear." From this Jacob concluded that the widow had read his thoughts.[3]

When Ann Burt came under suspicion for witchcraft in 1669, forces operating on a local, regional, and transatlantic level shaped the episode. Widow Burt was undoubtedly familiar with the face-to-face dynamics of witchcraft accusations, for like any other seventeenth-century New Englander she was enmeshed in the day-to-day interactions between family, friends, and neighbors out of which fears of occult attack often emerged. In addition, while Burt almost certainly had at least a passing knowledge of New England witchcraft cases that preceded her own—for they were sensational events whose memory lingered—she was probably only dimly aware of broader regional or transatlantic trends in the prosecution of occult crime. But even if they were beyond her understanding, the forces that shaped witch-hunting across the early modern English-speaking world had a profound impact on Ann Burt's encounter with allegations of occult mischief. How her accusers conceived of the crime and the judicial process that eventually led to the widow's release were all part of a broader dialogue about witchcraft that linked the Puritan colonies to the rest of the English empire and Europe.

Like other prosecutions for occult crime in early New England, the case of Ann Burt did not exist in isolation but was linked to a larger campaign of witch-hunting that stretched across the seventeenth-century English Atlantic. Around the same time that the events described above unfolded in Massachusetts, people from other parts of the English-speaking world faced similar situations. Less than a year before, Bermuda authorities had arrested Christian North for committing acts of malefic harm. In 1668 a Virginia court noted that "Alice Stephens [was] accused as a witch but not cleared," and in the summer of 1669 a court held in Kent, England, indicted Anne Buddle for bewitching a seventeen-year-old girl to death.[4] No matter if they were in Massachusetts, Bermuda, or Virginia, justices faced with occult mischief referred to the works of English demonologists and jurists such as William Perkins, Richard Bernard, and Michael Dalton. Similarly, England's folk culture powerfully shaped understandings of black magic across its Atlantic possessions.

Besides being tied together by a common set of beliefs and doctrines concerning witchcraft, England and its colonies paralleled each other in terms of the ebb and flow of witch-hunting. In particular, a wave of prosecutions that swept over the British Isles in the mid-seventeenth century rippled across the English Atlantic. Bermuda experienced a peak in witch-hunting in the 1650s, when about two-thirds of its witchcraft cases occurred. The New England colonies also saw a significant increase in witch trials and executions at this time.[5] Not all parts of England's empire experienced this surge. For instance, Maryland and Virginia only saw four formal complaints concerning occult crime in the 1650s and 1660s. The reason for this difference may lie in the fact that the Chesapeake colonies, unlike the witch-hunting hot-spots of New England and Bermuda, were not dominated by Puritans and because their Royalist leanings insulated them from the torrent of witch fears that poured out of England during its rejection of monarchical rule in the 1650s.[6]

Ann Burt's encounter with accusations of magical misbehavior similarly illuminates aspects of a culture of witchcraft held by English-speaking people across the Atlantic World, including their habit of blending together malefic and diabolical conceptions of occult criminals. Reflecting the view of the witch as a person who did harm through magical means, Philip Reed, Thomas Farrar, and other witnesses spoke of the injury Burt inflicted on her alleged victims. Testimony against the widow also touched on the image of the witch as a servant of Satan. While English folk generally avoided the more sensational descriptions of Devil worship that often graced accounts of diabolism in continental Europe, they did develop diabolical lore focusing on witch marks and animal familiars. Thus, when Jacob Knight recalled that he saw a strange cat and dog before an encounter with Burt, he was more than likely intimating that these creatures were her familiar spirits.[7]

Likewise, New England's witch suspects fit a profile of occult criminals that broadly held true across the early modern English Atlantic.[8] Ann Burt was no different. She was a woman, as were most suspects across the English-speaking world. The widow also fit the bill in terms of her age. Most witch-craft suspects were middle-aged or older when they faced accusation, and Burt was sixty-seven when she came under suspicion. Finally, building on the commonplace assumption that those with the power to cure also had the power to harm, early modern Europeans associated black magic with the practice of medicine; and as the testimony against her makes clear, Widow Burt's activities as a healer were central to her arrest.[9] Most of the accused did not match every aspect of the witch stereotype and the same was again true for Ann Burt. While many suspects in New England had a history of criminal behavior, it does not seem that Burt possessed any serious penchant for wrongdoing, and she only appears in surviving records in a negative light on two occasions before her arrest for witchcraft. In 1638 Isaac Disbero took her to court for defamation, and five years later Auld Churchman was fined for "having the wife of Hugh Burt locked with him alone in his house." While there is no indication that Goody Burt faced any charges related to this unseemly event, it may have weighed against her reputation.[10] Likewise, Burt seems to have avoided the domestic troubles that commonly marked the lives of the accused. She arrived in Boston in 1635 after sailing from London aboard the *Abigail* alongside her husband Hugh Burt and four children who she had with him and a previous spouse, and she seems to have lived a life consonant with expectations concerning women's duties as wives and mothers. In addition, Ann and her family steered clear of the poverty and social marginalization that characterized some witch suspects. Goodman Burt was one of the original settlers of Lynn and obtained a sixty-acre grant in the town in 1638. He served on grand juries—a duty which marked him as a man of solid standing—and by his death in 1661 possessed an estate worth just over £143 and free from debt.[11]

Ann Burt's case similarly speaks to the social context of witchcraft and how complaints of occult harm regularly emerged out of the tensions that marked early modern village life. Witch suspects and the people who denounced them were frequently members of the same neighborhoods or households, and this was also true for Burt and her accusers. Jacob Knight's deposition makes it clear that he had once lived under the same roof as the accused. Similarly, the Pearsons possessed close ties to the widow, and their daughter Sarah had once worked for her.[12] Burt's experiences also touch on the gendered dimensions of witchcraft and why females fell victim to prosecution more often than males. Women like Ann Burt were pivotal figures in the household and neighborhood networks through which suspicions of occult crime flowed, and they dominated aspects of daily life like child-rearing, domestic production, and medical care that so often crossed paths with witchcraft fears.[13]

In addition, one of Widow Burt's detractors, Dr. Philip Reed, exemplifies how accusers and the accused sometimes had more in common than the former would have cared to admit.[14] As a man and a professional, the doctor may appear to have stood apart from the sorts of people who fell victim to accusations of occult crime; however, Reed was hardly a paragon of virtue and engaged in the same irreverent, antisocial behavior frequently attributed to the accused. Less than two years after he testified against Widow Burt, he came before the magistrates "to answer for some cursed & blasphemous words by him uttered to the reproach of the name of the living God." The authorities gathered several depositions describing how when his wife was very sick and "near death," Dr. Reed said, "The Devil take you & your Christ" and "The Devil take you & your prayers" after his mother-in-law suggested praying to Jesus for her daughter's deliverance. This was no small matter, for blasphemy was a capital offense. Luckily for the doctor, he managed to dodge a guilty verdict.[15] This story about Dr. Reed upends the assumption that accusers were invariably righteous folk who embraced Puritan values, while the accused were deviants who stood out against social norms. From time to time the line between the two disappeared altogether, and people who at one point in their lives denounced others for witchcraft later found themselves on the receiving end of the charge. For instance, Bethia Carter and Thomas Farrar, two of the people who testified against Burt in 1669, ended up being arrested and jailed during the Salem witch crisis twenty-three years later.[16]

The fears of black magic that boiled over in Lynn, Massachusetts, in 1669 also illustrate that not all witchcraft episodes were alike. Generally speaking there were ordinary witch prosecutions characterized by their small number of suspects, limited geographical reach, and garden-variety allegations of maleficium, and more sensational witch panics distinguished by their greater size and tendency to feature diabolical motifs. Ann Burt's case falls into the first category, but it did include several supposed victims of bewitchment, a feature commonly seen in larger hunts. While most witnesses against the widow complained about ordinary acts of malefic harm, the proceedings featured testimony (albeit secondhand) from several afflicted persons who allegedly suffered from demonic torments and, falling in line with learned belief, possessed the ability to see the invisible world of the occult. For instance, a witness testified that during her fits Sarah Townsend experienced spectral sightings of the accused "at her bed's feet and at divers other places in the day and also at night."[17] Thus it is possible that had things been slightly different—if, for instance, the afflicted blamed their torments on more suspects besides Burt—then perhaps the year 1669 and the town of Lynn would hold the same resonance as 1692 and Salem.

Finally, the accusation of Ann Burt shows that witch-hunting in early New England was not a free-for-all of suspicion but a regulated judicial process. While different motives (perhaps some not so honorable) drove those who testified against the accused, they all ended up feeding their stories into a formal legal process. Besides imposing a procedural framework on witch-hunting, the courts also applied standards of proof, and the ultimate test in any episode of occult crime was if the evidence presented against the accused met the requirements for conviction. While those who spoke out against Widow Burt would have doubtlessly been happy to see her hang, the courts decided that the case did not merit a guilty verdict (or perhaps even a trial).

Widow Burt managed to escape conviction, and her case came in the midst of a downturn in witchcraft prosecutions in New England that marked the second half of the 1660s and the decade that followed. Indeed, between 1671 and 1678 only four people came before the bar for witchcraft. Three of them went to trial, and none suffered a guilty verdict.[18] This dearth in legal action related to occult crime was not unique to the region but paralleled a general decline across the English Atlantic.

However, unlike the rest of England's empire, this remission proved temporary in New England and witch-hunting regained momentum there in the 1680s. The events of 1679 put New England out of step with the rest of the English Atlantic. In that year, three witchcraft cases came before the courts in Massachusetts (which nearly equaled the number handled by the colony in the preceding decade), and one ended in the conviction of Elizabeth Morse of Newbury. The authorities ended up overturning the verdict, but despite such judicial restraint, witchcraft prosecutions grew.[19] In the 1680s a dozen witch suspects faced formal proceedings, including a trial that led to the conviction and execution of an Irishwomen named Goody Glover in Boston in 1688.[20] Her hanging was the first for occult crime in New England since 1663. Glover's trip to the gallows ushered in a paroxysm of witch-hunting in the Puritan colonies in 1692 that stood in stark contrast to the decline of prosecutions for occult crime elsewhere in the English-speaking world. That year a half-dozen people were arrested in the Fairfield witch panic, and hundreds of arrests, dozens of trials, and nineteen hangings resulted from the vastly larger Salem crisis.[21] One person who was convicted of witchcraft during the latter episode but escaped the hangman's noose (due to her being pregnant) was Ann Burt's granddaughter, Elizabeth Proctor.[22]

After 1692, witch-hunting—but not the belief in witches and witchcraft—wound down in New England. Only four additional complaints for occult crime issued against three individuals occurred in Connecticut during the final years of the seventeenth century. Hugh Crotia of Fairfield found himself before the magistrates in 1693 after he reportedly claimed to have signed a pact with the Devil. The court was skeptical, Hugh admitted to lying, and a grand jury refused to indict him. In that same year Winifred Benham of Wallingford faced charges of magical mischief, and four years later she and her thirteen-year-old daughter found themselves before a court to answer claims that they bewitched the children of several neighbors. On both occasions the accusations did not gain any traction.[23] Witch trials drew to a close in Connecticut in the eighteenth century. Bethia Taylor of Colchester accused Sarah Clother and a Goodwife Brown of witchcraft in 1713 but later withdrew the charge and publicly apologized for defaming Clother. About a decade later, Elizabeth Ackley claimed that her sister-in-law, Sarah Spencer, had bewitched her. The latter responded with a defamation suit, and the justices ruled in the plaintiff's favor.[24] The situation was much the same across the rest of New England. The excesses of the Salem trials discredited judicial attempts to detect and punish occult crime in Massachusetts, and except for a number of loose accusations that never led to legal action, witch prosecutions in the colony effectively ended. In short, while folk may still have feared witchcraft, it became increasingly clear that the courts would no longer convict anyone for the crime, and so they stopped entering formal accusations.

ABBREVIATIONS

CA   Connecticut Archives, Crimes and Misdemeanors, 1st Series, 1662/63–1789, Vols. 1–3, Connecticut State Library, Hartford, CT.

CCA   Helen Schatvet Ullman, ed. *Colony of Connecticut, Minutes of the Court of Assistants, 1669–1711.* Boston: New England Historical and Genealogical Society, 2009.

CCHS   *Collections of the Connecticut Historical Society.*

CMHS   *Collections of the Massachusetts Historical Society.*

CSL   Connecticut State Library.

HCC   Helen Schatvet Ullman, ed. *Hartford County, Connecticut, County Court Minutes: Volumes 3 and 4, 1663–1689, 1697.* Boston: New England Historical and Genealogical Society, 2005.

IEAHC   Institute of Early American History and Culture.

NEHGR   *New England Historical and Genealogical Register.*

NEQ   *New England Quarterly.*

NHHS   *Collections of the New Hampshire Historical Society.*

NHTR   Franklin Bowditch Dexter, ed. *New Haven Town Records.* Vols. 1 (1649–62) and 2 (1662–84). New Haven, CT: New Haven Colony Historical Society, 1917 and 1919.

OIEAHC   Omohundro Institute of Early American History and Culture.

PRCC   J. Hammond Turnbull, ed. *The Public Records of the Colony of Connecticut.* Vols. 1 (before May 1665) and 2 (1665–78). Hartford, CT: Brown and Parsons, 1850 / F. A. Brown, 1852.

RCA   John Noble and John F. Cronin, eds. *Records of the Court of Assistants of the Colony of the Massachusetts Bay, 1630–1693.* Vol. 3. Boston: Published by the County of Suffolk, 1928.

RCNH, 1   Charles J. Hoadly, ed. *Records of the Colony and Plantation of New Haven, 1639–1649.* Hartford, CT: Case, Tiffany, 1857.

RCNH, 2   Charles J. Hoadly, ed. *Records of the Colony or Jurisdiction of New Haven, 1653–1662.* Hartford, CT: Case, Lockwood, 1858.

REH   Henry Parsons Hedges, ed. *Records of the Town of East Hampton, Long Island, Suffolk County, New York.* Vol. 1. Sag Harbor, NY: John H. Hunt, 1887.

RMB   Nathaniel B. Shurtleff, ed. *Records of the Governor and Company of Massachusetts Bay in New England.* Vols. 3 (1644–57) and 4/1 (1650–1660). Boston: Press of William White, 1854.

RPC   "Records of the Particular Court of Connecticut, 1639–1663." *Collections of the Connecticut Historical Society.* Vol. 22. Hartford, CT: Connecticut Historical Society, 1928.

RQCE   George Francis Dow, ed. *Records and Files of the Quarterly Courts of Essex County*. 9 vols. Salem, MA: Essex Institute, 1911–75.

SWP-CSL   Samuel Wyllys Papers. Connecticut State Library, Hartford, Connecticut.

SWP-JHL   Samuel Wyllys Papers, 1638–1737. John Hay Library, Brown University, Providence, Rhode Island.

WMQ   *William and Mary Quarterly.*

NOTES

Preface

1. There is certainly not enough space here to address all the work on witchcraft in early modern Europe published in the last few decades; however, some of the scholarship that has informed my analysis of the social context of occult crime includes: Éva Pócs, "Why Witches Are Women," *Acta Ethnographica Hungarica* 48 (2003): 367–83; Diane Purkiss, "Women's Stories of Witchcraft in Early Modern England: The House, the Body, the Child," *Gender & History* 7 (1995): 408–32; Lauren Martin, "The Devil and the Domestic: Witchcraft, Quarrels and Women's Work in Scotland," in *The Scottish Witch-Hunt in Context*, ed. Julian Goodare (Manchester University Press, 2002), 73–89; Stuart Clark, "The 'Gendering' of Witchcraft in French Demonology: Misogyny or Polarity?" *French History* 5 (1991): 426–37; James Sharpe, "Witchcraft and Women in 17th-Century England: Some Northern Evidence," *Continuity and Change* 6 (1991): 179–99; Louise Jackson, "Witches, Wives & Mothers: Witchcraft Persecutions and Women's Confessions in 17th-Century England," *Women's History Review* 4 (1995): 63–84; Clive Holmes, "Women: Witnesses and Witches," *Past & Present* 140 (1993): 45–78; E. J. Kent, "Masculinity and Male Witches in Old and New England, 1593–1680," *History Workshop Journal* 60 (autumn 2005): 69–92; Valerie Kivelson, "Male Witches and Gendered Categories in 17th-Century Russia," *Comparative Studies in Society and History* 45 (July 2003): 606–31; Alison Rowlands, ed., *Witchcraft and Masculinities in Early Modern Europe* (London: Palgrave Macmillan, 2009); Kristen Hastrup, "Iceland: Sorcerers & Paganism," in *Early Modern European Witchcraft: Centers and Peripheries,* ed. Bengt Ankarloo and Gustav Henningson (New York: Oxford University Press, 1990), 383–401; and Malcolm Gaskill, "The Devil in the Shape of a Man: Witchcraft, Conflict, and Belief in Jacobean England," *Historical Research* 71 (June 1998): 142–71.

2. Some examples of works that discuss how elite and popular views concerning witchcraft and witch-hunting overlapped in Europe include Michael D. Bailey, *Battling Demons: Witchcraft, Heresy, and Reform in the Late Middle Ages* (University Park: Pennsylvania State University Press, 2003), 29–53; Johannes Dillinger, "The Political Aspects of the German Witch Hunts," *Magic, Ritual, and Witchcraft* (summer 2009): 66–72; Wolfgang Behringer, "Weather, Hunger, and Fear: Origins of the European Witch-Hunts in Climate, Society, and Mentality," *German History* 13 (January 1995): 1–27; and Alison Rowlands, "Witchcraft and Popular Religion in Early Modern Rothenburg od der Tauber," in *Popular Religion in Germany and Central Europe*, ed. Bob Scribner and Trevor Johnson (New York: Palgrave, 1996), 101–17.

3. Examples of scholarship that examine ties between the state and witch-hunting include Brian Levack, "State-building & Witch Hunting in Early Modern Europe,"

in *Witchcraft in Early Modern Europe: Studies in Culture and Belief*, ed. Jonathan Barry et al. (Cambridge: Cambridge University Press, 1996), 96–115; and Dillinger, "Political Aspects of the German Witch Hunts."

4. H. R. Trevor-Roper, "The European Witch-Craze of the Sixteenth and Seventeenth Centuries," in *The Crisis of the Seventeenth-Century: Religion, the Reformation, and Social Change*, ed. Trevor-Roper (Indianapolis, IN: Liberty Fund, 1967), 83–178; Christina Larner, *Enemies of God: The Witch Hunt in Scotland* (Baltimore, MD: Johns Hopkins University Press, 1981); Gary K. Waite, "Irrelevant Interruption or Precipitating Cause? The Sixteenth-Century Reformation(s) and the Revival of the European Witch Hunts," in *Chasses aux Sorcieres et Demonogogie*, eds. Georg Modestin et al. (Firenze: Sismel, 2010), 223–42; Robert Walinski-Kiehl, "Godly States: Confessional Conflicts & Witch-hunting in Germany," *Mentalities* 5 (1988): 13–25. For connections between godly reform movements and witch-hunting, see chapter 4 in Carla Pestana Gardina, *The English Atlantic in an Age of Revolution, 1640–1661* (Cambridge, MA: Harvard University Press, 2004), especially 137–39.

Introduction

1. Benjamin F. Thompson, *History of Long Island* (New York: E. French, 1839), 151–53. As is often the case with long-ago legal proceedings, there are frustrating gaps in the narrative of the Halls' witchcraft case, and all of the testimony related to the trial as well as the names of those who initiated it has been lost.

2. *Records, Town of Brookhaven up to 1800* (Patchogue, NY: 1880), 38; Thompson, *History of Long Island*, 151–53. John Demos indicates that Mary Hall was formally accused of witchcraft in 1664 and presented before a grand jury but apparently avoided an indictment; see *Entertaining Satan: Witchcraft and the Culture of Early New England* (New York: Oxford University Press, 1982), 405. However, I have not been able to uncover any evidence of such an episode, although it may very well be related to the Halls' slander suit against Richard Smith.

3. Thompson, *History of Long Island*, 153–54; Paul Baily, ed. *Long Island: A History of Two Great Counties, Nassau and Suffolk* (New York: Lewis Historical Publishing, 1949), 1:260.

4. Baily, *Long Island*, 1:252–54; RQCE, 1:164, 202; PRCC, 1:428. It is not certain that the Ralph and Mary Hall who appear in Massachusetts records in the late 1640s were the same couple who ended up in Setauket but it seems very likely: among other things, all mention of the couple disappears from Massachusetts records around the time they would have moved to Long Island.

5. RQCE, 1:202.

6. Thompson, *History of Long Island*, 151. In an interesting aside, another member of the grand jury, Jacob Leisler, would later become famous for leading and eventually being hanged for his role in Leisler's Rebellion which roiled the colony of New York from 1689 to 1691. REH, 1:132–33, 139, 140, 152–55.

7. Bertha W. Clark, "Rhode Island Woods on Long Island," *American Genealogist* 39 (July 1963), 129–32; PRCC, 1:338; RPC, 238, 240; Gilman C. Gates, *Saybrook at the Mouth of the Connecticut: The First Hundred Years* (New Haven, CT: Wilson H. Lee, 1935), 141–42. That George Wood did not have the best of relations with the Jennings is borne out by the fact that he brought a suit against the couple and their daughter

for an unnamed complaint in March 1661 just months before the Jenningses were charged with witchcraft: see *RPC*, 227. R. G. Tomlinson, *Witchcraft Prosecution: Chasing the Devil in Connecticut* (Rockland, ME: Picton Press, 2012), 41–43.

8. E. B. O'Callaghan, *The Documentary History of the State of New York* (Albany, NY: Weed, Parsons, 1850), 2:305.

9. Brian P. Levack, *The Witch-Hunt in Early Modern Europe* (New York: Longman, 1995), 24–25; James Sharpe, *Instruments of Darkness: Witchcraft in Early Modern England* (Philadelphia: University of Pennsylvania Press, 1996), 125; Demos, *Entertaining Satan*, 11–12; Carol Karlsen, *The Devil in the Shape of a Woman: Witchcraft in Colonial New England* (1987; reprint New York: W. W. Norton, 1998), 47n1, 288–89— citations refer to the 1998 edition. Figures concerning the number of people accused, tried, or executed for witchcraft represent educated guesses based on incomplete records. John Demos comes up with a figure of 234 witches formally accused in seventeenth-century New England; meanwhile, Carol Karlson, who includes cases in the early eighteenth century and informal accusations that did not necessarily leave any official record, comes up with a total figure of 391 cases of witchcraft concerning 344 individuals.

10. Demos, *Entertaining Satan*, 275–312; Keith Thomas, *Religion and the Decline of Magic* (New York: Charles Scribner's Sons, 1971), 535–69; Alan Macfarlane, *Witchcraft in Tudor and Stuart England: A Regional and Comparative Study* (New York: Harper & Row, 1970), 170–76, 192–97.

11. John Demos explores the connections between various events in New England and the ebb and flow of witch-hunting in the region: see Demos, *Entertaining Satan*, 368–86.

12. David Cressy, *Coming Over: Migration and Communication between England and New England in the Seventeenth Century* (Cambridge: Cambridge University Press, 1987); Francis J. Bremer, *Congregational Communion: Clerical Friendship in the Anglo-American Puritan Community, 1610–1692* (Boston: Northwestern University Press, 1994).

13. Walter W. Woodward, *Prospero's America: John Winthrop, Jr., Alchemy, and the Creation of New England Culture, 1606–1676* (Chapel Hill: University of North Carolina Press for the OIEAHC, 2010), 1.

14. The term *Puritan* actually encompasses a body of English nonconformists who possessed diverse views. One basic split was between Separatists and Nonseparatists. The former believed that the Church of England was so corrupt that the only way to achieve spiritual purity was to fully break from it, while the latter (representing a majority of the Puritan movement) held that they did not have to leave the Church but could work to purify it from within. Another distinction among Puritans was between Independents (or Congregationalists) and Presbyterians. This cleavage revolved around issues of church structure and governance. Independents believed that the formation of independent congregations who appointed their own minister and controlled their own affairs was the only church structure consistent with Scripture. Separatists were almost invariably Independents; however, many Nonseparatists also held this point of view. In opposition were those Puritans who wished to establish some sort of hierarchy and structure that would link together individual churches. Under this model, congregations were not spiritual free agents and clergymen assumed more power within their congregations. Those who held this more

top-down vision of church polity became known as Presbyterians after the church of the same name that grew out of the Protestant Reformation in Scotland and supported the structures of church governance they advocated. For more discussion of these distinctions, see Paul R. Lucas, *Valley of Discord: Church and Society along the Connecticut River, 1636–1725* (Hanover, NH: University Press of New England, 1976) and Philp F. Gura, *A Glimpse of Sion's Glory: Puritan Radicalism in New England, 1620–1660* (Middletown, CT: Wesleyan University Press, 1984).

15. Even though Rhode Island numbered among the New England colonies, I do not consider it as being part of the Puritan Atlantic, for Puritan orthodoxy never monopolized institutional power in the colony or the religious outlook of its inhabitants. Alison Games makes a similar distinction between Puritan colonies and colonies that contained Puritans in *Migration and the Origins of the England Atlantic World* (Cambridge, MA: Harvard University Press), 134–35. For a thorough overview of the extent and depth of Puritanism outside of the New England colonies, see Babette M. Levy, "Early Puritanism in the Southern and Island Colonies," *Proceedings of the American Antiquarian Society* 52 (1960): 69–384.

16. Richard Beale Davis, "The Devil in Virginia in the Seventeenth Century," *Virginia Magazine of History and Biography* 65 (April 1957): 131–49; Francis Neal Parke, "Witchcraft in Maryland," *Maryland Historical Magazine* 31 (December 1936): 271–98. Based on surviving records from seventeenth-century Virginia, the colony saw five or six formal complaints, two trials, and one conviction (which only led to the punishment of whipping and banishment) for witchcraft. In Virginia there were far more cases (eleven) of people suing those who accused them of witchcraft than prosecutions of suspected witches. Similarly, Maryland only saw four formal complaints, three trials, two convictions (one of which was reversed), and one execution.

17. Some recent studies of the Salem witch crisis that highlight its distinctive features include Bernard Rosenthal, *Salem Story: Reading the Witch Trials of 1692* (New York: Cambridge University Press, 1993); Mary Beth Norton, *In the Devil's Snare: The Salem Witchcraft Crisis of 1692* (New York: Vintage Books, 2003); Emerson W. Baker, *A Storm of Witchcraft: The Salem Trials and the American Experience* (New York: Oxford University Press, 2015); and Benjamin C. Ray, *Satan & Salem: The Witch-Hunt Crisis of 1692* (Charlottesville: University of Virginia Press, 2015).

1. "Hanged for a Witch"

1. Matthew Grant Diary, 1637–1654, CSL; James Kendall Hosmer, ed., *Winthrop's Journal* (New York: Charles Scribner's Sons, 1908), 2:323. Lawrance B. Goodheart, *The Solemn Sentence of Death: Capital Punishment in Connecticut* (Amherst: University of Massachusetts Press, 2011), 22, 25–26, 33.

2. John P. Demos, *Entertaining Satan: Witchcraft and the Culture of Early New England* (New York: Oxford University Press, 1982), 505n29—here Demos lays out a compelling case that Alice (Young) Beamon was the daughter of John and Alice Young.

3. The figures presented here and elsewhere in this chapter are based on data gathered by John Demos and presented in his book, *Entertaining Satan*, 402–6, supplemented by my own research. Formal legal action is here defined as an episode that at least resulted in an official complaint being lodged against the accused.

4. David D. Hall, *Witch-Hunting in Seventeenth-Century New England: A Documentary History, 1638–93*, 2nd ed. (Durham, NC: Duke University Press, 1999), 264.

5. Demos, *Entertaining Satan*, 406–9.

6. Demos, *Entertaining Satan*, 368–86 (quote on 369).

7. James Sharpe, *Instruments of Darkness: Witchcraft in Early Modern England* (Philadelphia: University of Pennsylvania Press, 1996), 89–91, 47–48, 81–82, 108–9.

8. Massachusetts's legal code, which first came into focus with its *Body of Liberties* in 1641 and the expanded *The Laws and Liberties of Massachusetts* in 1648, included a witchcraft statue that became a model for the other New England colonies (except for Rhode Island)—see Edgar J. McManus, *Law and Liberty in Early New England: Criminal Justice and Due Process, 1620–1692* (Amherst: University of Massachusetts Press, 1993), 9–10, 16–18, 187–90. For the wording of Massachusetts's, Connecticut's, and New Haven's witchcraft statutes, see Max Farrand, ed., *The Laws and Liberties of Massachusetts, 1648* (Cambridge, MA: Harvard University Press, 1929); *PRCC*, 1:77; and *RCNH*, 2:576.

9. John Demos forwards several of these views: see *Entertaining Satan*, 371. For a work that explores tensions between Native Americans, the Dutch, and early Puritan settlers, see Andrew Charles Lipman, *The Saltwater Frontier: Indians and the Contest for the American Coast* (New Haven, CT: Yale University Press, 2015). For discussions of religious conflict in New England's early decades of settlement, see Stephen Foster, "New England and the Challenge of Heresy, 1630 to 1660: The Puritan Crisis in Transatlantic Perspective," *WMQ* 38 (October 1981): 624–60; and Philip Gura, *A Glimpse of Sion's Glory: Puritan Radicalism in New England, 1630–1660* (Middletown, CT: Wesleyan University Press, 1984); and Michael Paul Winship, *Making Heretics: Militant Protestantism and Free Grace in Massachusetts, 1636–1641* (Princeton, NJ: Princeton University Press, 2002).

10. Carla Gardina Pestana, *The English Atlantic in an Age of Revolution, 1640–1661* (Cambridge, MA: Harvard University Press, 2004), 25–52; David Cressy, *Coming Over: Migration and Communication between England and New England in the Seventeenth Century* (Cambridge: Cambridge University Press, 1987), 192–93.

11. Sharpe, *Instruments of Darkness*, 108–9; Demos, *Entertaining Satan*, 371.

12. For a discussion of the common background of early New England migrants, see Virginia DeJohn Anderson, "Migrants and Motives: Religion and the Settlement of New England, 1630–1640" *NEQ* 58 (September 1985): 339–83.

13. For a more complete recounting of the Antinomian Controversy, see Winship, *Making Heretics*; and David D. Hall, *The Antinomian Controversy, 1636–1638: A Documentary History* (Durham, NC: Duke University Press, 1990).

14. *RMB*, 1:224. It appears that Mary Hawkins had returned from Rhode Island by 1641, for in that year Massachusetts's General Court issued a second order calling for her to leave the colony and "not to return again hither, upon pain of severe whipping & such other punishment as the court shall think meet"—see, *RMB*, 1:329.

15. Carol Karlsen, *The Devil in the Shape of a Woman: Witchcraft in Colonial New England* (1987; reprint New York: W. W. Norton, 1998), 14–19, 120–25, 190–94—citations refer to the 1998 edition. On the female stereotype of the witch, see Éva Pócs, "Why Witches Are Women," *Acta Ethnographica Hungarica* 48 (2003): 367–83; and Stuart Clark, "The 'Gendering' of Witchcraft in French Demonology: Misogyny or Polarity?" *French History* 5 (1991): 426–37.

16. For a comprehensive look at women healers and midwives in early New England, see Rebecca J. Tannenbaum, *The Healer's Calling: Women and Medicine in Early New England* (Ithaca, NY: Cornell University Press, 2002). For a discussion of women, healing, midwives, and witchcraft, see Demos, *Entertaining Satan*, 80–84; Karlsen, *Devil in the Shape of a Woman*, 142–44; Mary R. O'Neil, "Missing Footprints: Maleficium in Modena," *Acta Ethographica Hungerica* 37 (1991–92): 123–42; and David Harley, "Historians as Demonologists: The Myth of the Midwife-witch," *Society for the Social History of Medicine* 3 (April 1990): 1–26.

17. Hosmer, *Winthrop's Journal*, 1:266–69. In his list of known witchcraft cases in New England, John Demos presents Jane Hawkins as being formally accused and presented before a grand jury for indictment; however, I was not able to find evidence of such legal action—Demos, *Entertaining Satan*, 402.

18. Hosmer, *Winthrop's Journal*, 1:268, 2:8; *RMB*, 1:224

19. Hosmer, *Winthrop's Journal*, 2:7–8, 1:277. In *Entertaining Satan* (402), John Demos lists Collins and Hales as being accused of witchcraft; however, a close reading of Winthrop's account does not support this—if anything, the authorities considered Collins and Hales victims of bewitchment.

The case of Anne Hutchinson constitutes one of the few known episodes of witchcraft in Rhode Island. There were no formal complaints, indictments, or trials of witches in the colony. Indeed, Rhode Island became a destination for people from other New England colonies fleeing charges of occult crime. Its immunity to witch-hunting appears to be linked to its greater acceptance of religious diversity and dissent and a legal code that, though it criminalized witchcraft, did not characterize the crime in religious terms.

Massachusetts authorities arrested and executed Mary Dyer in 1660, not for witchcraft, but attempting to spread Quaker beliefs in the colony—see Karlsen, *Devil in the Shape of a Woman*, 123–24.

20. Data on numbers of trials, etc. drawn from Demos, *Entertaining Satan*, 402–4 (his list of witchcraft episodes does not include the 1648 case of Katherine Palmer of Wethersfield), and my own research. For population figures of the New England colonies, see Jack P. Greene, *Pursuits of Happiness: The Social Development of Early Modern British Colonies and the Formation of American Culture* (Chapel Hill: University of North Carolina Press, 1988), 178.

21. John Hale, *A Modest Inquiry into the Nature of Witchcraft* (1702), in *Narratives of the Witchcraft Cases*, ed. George Lincoln Burr (New York: Charles Scribner's Sons, 1914), 409–10; *RMB*, 2:242; and Hosmer, ed. *Winthrop's Journal*, 2:344–46.

22. For documents concerning the trial of Mary and Hugh Parsons, see Samuel G. Drake, ed., *Annals of Witchcraft in New England* (Boston: W. Elliot Woodward, 1869), 219–58; and Hall, *Witch-Hunting*, 29–60. For Alice Lake, see Hale, *A Modest Inquiry into the Nature of Witchcraft*, 408–9; and *CMHS*, 4th Series, 8:58. For Alice Stratton, see Demos, *Entertaining Satan*, 92, 403; and for John Bradstreet, see Hall, *Witch-Hunting*, 87–88.

23. For Jane Collins, see *RQCE*, 1:274, 276, 348. Records relevant to Jane Walford's case can be found in John S. H. Fogg, "Witchcraft in New Hampshire in 1656," *NEHGR* 42 (1889): 182–83; and *NHHS*, 1:255–57. For information on the case of Anne Hibbins, see *RMB*, 4/1:269; Rev. William Hubbard, *A General History of New England from the Discovery to 1680*, 2nd ed. (Boston: Charles C. Little and James Brown, 1848),

574; and Thomas Hutchinson, *The History of the Colony of Massachusetts Bay*, 2nd ed. (London: Mr. Richardson, 1765), 1:187–88.

24. *PRCC*, 1:171; *RPC*, 56; R. G. Tomlinson, *Witchcraft Prosecution: Chasing the Devil in Connecticut* (Rockland, MA: Picton Press, 2012), 34–35. Some earlier historians have confused Mary Johnson with Elizabeth Johnson, who was accused of adultery in Connecticut in 1650: see William K. Holdsworth, "Adultery or Witchcraft?: A New Note on an Old Case in Connecticut," *NEQ* 48 (September 1975): 394–401.

At the same court session during which Connecticut officials convicted Mary Johnson of witchcraft, the justices resolved to free "Henry Palmer from his recognizance for his wife's appearing at the last Particular Court to answer the complaint of Mr. Robins" (*RPC*, 56). In all probability the complaint Robbins lodged against Goody Palmer was for witchcraft (the fact that the Robbins family later charged Katherine Palmer with this crime in 1660 supports this assertion), and it was likely linked to the case brought against Johnson. Two things point to this conclusion: the cases were resolved in the same court session and both women were from Wethersfield. If the Johnson and Palmer cases were connected, then it is possible that Mr. Robbins accused both women or at least was one of several individuals who denounced them.

25. Cotton Mather, *Memorable Providences, Relating to Witchcrafts and Possessions* (1689), in *Narratives of the Witchcraft Cases, 1648–1706*, ed. George Lincoln Burr (New York: Charles Scribner's Sons, 1914), 135–36.

26. Mather, *Memorable Providences,* 136. For a discussion of the links between witchcraft and sexual crimes, see Karlsen, *Devil in the Shape of a Woman,* 134–44, 194–96, 198–202.

27. Tomlinson, *Witchcraft Prosecutions,* 39–47, 53–58. For documents on the Carringtons' case, see *RPC,* 92–93, and the Matthew Grant Diary, CSL. Most of the information concerning the trials of Bassett and Knapp comes through testimony gathered for a defamation suit initiated by Thomas Staples in 1654 on behalf of his wife, Mary, after Roger Ludlow spread rumors that she was a witch. For the case of Goody Bassett, see *PRCC* 1:200 and *RCNH,* 2:81, 84–85; and for that of Goodwife Knapp, see *RCNH,* 2:78–88 (quote from 82). For Lydia Gilbert's prosecution, see *RPC,* 131.

28. For the case of Elizabeth Godman, see *RCNH,* 2:29–36, 151–52; *NHTR,* 1:249–52, 256–57, 264. For the case of Nicholas and Goodwife Bayley, see *NHTR,* 1:245–46, 249, 256–58.

29. Brian P. Levack, *Witch-hunting in Scotland: Law, Politics and Religion* (New York: Routledge, 2008), 55–59, 69–70, 81; Sharpe, *Instruments of Darkness,* 108–12; Malcolm Gaskill, *Witchfinders: a Seventeenth-Century English Tragedy* (Cambridge, MA: Harvard University Press, 2005).

30. Virginia Bernhard, "Religion, Politics, and Witchcraft in Bermuda, 1651–55," *WMQ* 57 (October 2010): 677–708, especially 678, 686–87; Michael J. Jarvis, " 'In the Eye of All Trade': Maritime Revolution and the Transformation of Bermudian Society, 1612–1800" (PhD diss., College of William and Mary, 1998), 232–46.

31. William K. Holdsworth, "Law and Society in Colonial Connecticut, 1636–1672" (PhD diss., Claremont Graduate School, 1974), 398–99; Frederick C. Drake, "Witchcraft in the American Colonies, 1647–62," *American Quarterly* 20 (winter 1968): 712; John M. Murrin, "Coming to Terms with the Salem Witch Trials," *Proceedings of the American Antiquarian Society* 110 (2000): 316; *RMB,* 2: 242.

32. Gaskill, *Witchfinders*, 261, 269, 272; Cressy, *Coming Over*, 209–10, 213–36, 243, 246–47; Bernhard, "Religion, Politics, and Witchcraft in Bermuda," 686.

33. Bernhard, "Religion, Politics, and Witchcraft in Bermuda," 686–87; Babette M. Levy, "Early Puritanism in the Southern and Island Colonies," *Proceedings of the American Antiquarian Society* 52 (April 1960): 214, 310; Louis Dow Scisco, "The First Church in Charles County," *Maryland Historical Magazine* 23 (1925): 155–62; J. Hall Pleasants, ed., *Archives of Maryland: Proceedings of the County Court of Charles County, 1658–1666 and Manor Court of St. Celments Manor, 1659–1672* (Baltimore: Maryland Historical Society, 1936) 53:56, 142–43, 156.

34. Levy, "Early Puritanism in the Southern and Island Colonies," 118; "Witchcraft in Virginia," *WMQ* 1 (January 1893): 127–29.

35. Gaskill, *Witchfinders*, 20; *RMB*, 2:242.

36. Jarvis, "'In the Eye of All Trade,'" 185–86; Gaskill, *Witchfinders*, 121; Tomlinson, *Witchcraft Prosecution*, 16; Bernhard, "Religion, Politics, and Witchcraft in Bermuda," 686–87; Keith Thomas, *Religion and the Decline of Magic* (New York: Charles Scribner's Sons, 1971), 458; Roger Thompson, *Mobility and Migration: East Anglian Founders of New England, 1629–1640* (Amherst: University of Massachusetts Press, 1994), 14–15, 40; Holdsworth, "Law and Society," 399; Francis J. Bremer, *Congregational Communion: Clerical Friendship in the Anglo-American Puritan Community, 1610–1692* (Boston: Northeastern University Press, 1994), 46.

37. David Hackett Fischer contends that about 30 percent of the Puritan colonies' leading men were graduates of Emmanuel College, see *Albion's Seed: Four British Folkways in America* (New York: Oxford University Press, 1989), 39.

38. Fischer, *Albion's Seed*, 31–34; Holdsworth, "Law and Society," 397–99; Charles Edwards Banks, "Scotch Prisoners Deported to New England by Cromwell, 1651–52," *Proceedings of the Massachusetts Historical Society*, 3rd Series, 61 (October 1927–June 1928): 4–29; Christopher Gerrard et al., ed., *Lost Lives, New Voices: Unlocking the Stories of the Scottish Soldiers from the Battle of Dunbar, 1650* (Havertown, PA: Oxbow Books, 2018), 174–206, 245–56; Stephen Innes, *Labor in a New Land: Economy and Society in Seventeenth-Century Springfield* (Princeton, NJ: Princeton University Press, 1983), 9–10, 58, 86, 109, 143; Levy, "Early Puritanism in the Southern and Island Colonies," 120–21; Jarvis, "'In the Eye of All Trade,'" 234–38.

39. Alan Macfarlane, *Witchcraft in Tudor and Stuart England: A Regional and Comparative Study* (New York: Harper & Row, 1970), 142; Frederick Valletta, *Witchcraft, Magic, and Superstition in England, 1640–70* (Burlington, VT: Ashgate, 2000), 1, 25–26, 27–29, 57, 61; Gaskill, *Witchfinders*, 149.

40. Lyle Koehler, *A Search for Power: The "Weaker Sex" in Seventeenth-Century New England* (Urbana: University of Illinois Press, 1980), 286–87; Elizabeth Hubbell Schenck, *The History of Fairfield, Fairfield County, Connecticut* (New York: Published by the author, 1889), 1:72–92; Malcolm Gaskill, *Between Two Worlds: How the English Became Americans* (New York: Basic Books, 2014), 180, 182, 184, 194–95; Robert J. Taylor, *Colonial Connecticut: A History* (Millwood, NY: KTO Press, 1979), 78–79; Holdsworth, "Law and Society," 396; Demos, *Entertaining Satan*, 373. For a scholarly work that explores the connection between epidemic disease and witchcraft, see Wolfgang Behringer, "Weather, Hunger, and Fear: Origins of the European Witch-Hunts in Climate, Society, and Mentality," *German History* 13 (January 1995): 12–18.

41. Levack, *Witch-hunting in Scotland*, 7, 58, 65–68, 75; Valletta, *Witchcraft, Magic and Superstition in England*, 18–19; Gaskill, *Witchfinders*, 24–25.

42. Pestana, *The English Atlantic in an Age of Revolution*, 124, 131–39; Gura, *A Glimpse of Sion's Glory*, 204; Robert M. Bliss, *Revolution and Empire: English Politics and the American Colonies in the Seventeenth Century* (Manchester: Manchester University Press, 1990), 82.

43. Mary Beth Norton, *Founding Mothers & Fathers: Gendered Power and the Forming of American Society* (New York: Alfred A. Knopf, 1996), 81–83, 163–64; Hall, *Witch-Hunting*, 89; Hutchinson, *History of Massachusetts*, 1:187–88.

44. Karlsen, *Devil in the Shape of a Woman*, 1–2, 5, 24, 27–28, 150–52; Demos, *Entertaining Satan*, 64, 75, 87–88. For documents related to Hibbins's case, see *RMB*, 4/1:269; Hubbard, *General History of New England*, 574; Hutchinson, *History of Massachusetts*, 1:187–88.

45. Figures based on data from Demos, *Entertaining Satan*, 404–5, and my own research. Demos includes one case—that of Katherine Palmer of Wethersfield in 1660—that I do not include in my list of witchcraft cases. It is clear from a deposition Hannah Robbins gave against Palmer in 1667 that seven years earlier her father had suspected Palmer of bewitching her mother. According to her statement, Mr. Robbins prepared a written complaint but never submitted it to the court, and no formal proceedings took place against Palmer—see testimony of Alice Wakeley, SWP-CSL, no. 17.

46. For the case of William Brown, see *RQCE*, 2:36–37, and Demos, *Entertaining Satan*, 62. For information on John Godfrey's career as a witch suspect, see Demos, *Entertaining Satan*, 36–56; John Demos, "John Godfrey and his Neighbors: Witchcraft and the Social Web in Colonial Massachusetts," *WMQ* 33 (April 1976): 242–65; and Hall, *Witch-Hunting*, 115–33. For documents on the case of Winifred and Mary Holman, see Hall, *Witch-Hunting*, 134–46.

47. Demos, *Entertaining Satan*, 213–45; *REH*, 1:119–21, 128–36, 139–40, 152–55, 188–89; *RPC*, 188–89; and *PRCC* 1:572–73.

48. The Saybrook case of 1659 is referenced in Demos, *Entertaining Satan*, 404. For the case of Margaret and Nicholas Jennings, see *PRCC*, 1:338; *RPC* 238, 240; and Tomlinson, *Witchcraft Prosecution*, 76–79.

49. Paul R. Lucas, *Valley of Discord: Church and Society along the Connecticut River, 1636–1725* (Hanover, NH: University Press of New England, 1976); Robert G. Pope, *The Half-Way Covenant: Church Membership in Puritan New England* (Princeton, NJ: Princeton University Press, 1969); Gura, *A Glimpse of Sion's Glory*, 144–50.

50. Figures drawn from Demos, *Entertaining Satan*, 405, and my own research.

51. Two good narratives of the Hartford crisis can be found in Tomlinson, *Witchcraft Prosecution*, 81–114; and Walter W. Woodward, *Prospero's America: John Winthrop Jr., Alchemy, and the Creation of New England Culture, 1606–1676* (Chapel Hill: University of North Carolina Press for the OIEAHC, 2010), 230–35.

52. Tomlinson, *Witchcraft Prosecution*, 105–14.

53. Figures in this paragraph based on data from Demos, *Entertaining Satan*, 402–5, and my own research.

54. Demos, *Entertaining Satan*, 349–52, 369, 382–83. Prosecutions for occult crime appeared to have functioned as a catharsis in Bermuda in the wake of intense

religious and political conflict in the colony in the 1640s—see Bernhard, "Religion, Politics, and Witchcraft in Bermuda," 707–8—and may have played a similar role in Connecticut in the early 1660s.

55. Bliss, *Revolution and Empire*, 68, 132–52; Cressy, *Coming Over*, 256; Gaskill, *Between Two Worlds*, 217–29; Taylor, *Colonial Connecticut*, 27–29.

56. Data obtained from Demos, *Entertaining Satan*, 405–6, and my own research—Demos missed the 1665 case of John Brown of New Haven when he compiled his list of known episodes of witchcraft in seventeenth-century New England.

57. Tomlinson, *Witchcraft Prosecution*, 115–17; *NHTR*, 2:129–32.

58. For information on Massachusetts's witchcraft cases between 1665 and 1669, see Demos, *Entertaining Satan*, 405–6. For information on Susannah Martin's 1669 case and her involvement in the Salem Crisis, see *RQCE*, 4:129, 133; Emerson W. Baker, *A Storm of Witchcraft: The Salem Trials and the American Experience* (New York: Oxford University Press, 2015), 108, 199, 291; and Karlsen, *Devil in the Shape of a Woman*, 89–95.

59. Tomlinson, *Witchcraft Prosecution*, 117–18. For documents on Graves's case, see SWP-JHL, W-8 and W-9.

60. Tomlinson, *Witchcraft Prosecutions*, 118–19; *HCC*, 71–72.

61. In this context, "Presbyterian" is not a reference to a specific denomination but a style of church governance distinguished by the precedence it gave to the clergy over laymen and to the role the church played in ministering to all members of the community, whether they were full members of the church or not. In contrast, the Congregational position tended to emphasize the power and independence of congregations and the separation between church members and nonmembers. Lucas, *Valley of Discord*, 61–65, 79–80; Lipman, *The Saltwater Frontier*, 189–91; Taylor, *Colonial Connecticut*, 52–53; Stephen Foster, *The Long Argument: English Puritanism and the Shaping of New England Culture, 1570–1700* (Chapel Hill: University of North Carolina Press for the IEAHC, 1991), 177; Demos, *Entertaining Satan*, 380.

62. Valletta, *Witchcraft, Magic, and Superstition in England*, 132; Sharpe, *Instruments of Darkness*, 221–22; Sir Robert Filmer, *An Advertisement to the Jurymen of England, Touching Witches* (London: Printed by I.G. for Richard Royston, 1653), especially 9–15; Holdsworth, "Law and Society," 433–34.

2. "Being Instigated by the Devil"

1. *RPC*, 188–89; *RCA*, 3:151–52. For an account of Godfrey's long career as a witch, see John Demos, "John Godfrey and his Neighbors: Witchcraft and the Social Web in Colonial Massachusetts," *WMQ* 33 (April 1976): 242–65.

2. James Sharpe, *Instruments of Darkness: Witchcraft in Early Modern England* (Philadelphia: University of Pennsylvania Press, 1996), 60–62, 80–88; Keith Thomas, *Religion and the Decline of Magic* (New York: Charles Scribner's Sons, 1971), 436–44; *Holy Bible, King James Version* (Wichita, KS: Hartel Bible Publishers, 1970), 60—other biblical references to witches that informed new England witchcraft statutes include Leviticus 19:26, 20:27; and 2 Kings 21:6, 23:24.

3. *RPC*, 188; *RCA*, 3:151–52.

4. *REH*, 1:134–36; *RCA* 3:160–61; Demos, "John Godfrey," 252–53.

5. *REH*, 1:129, 132–33, 134; David D. Hall, *Witch-Hunting in Seventeenth-Century New England* 2nd ed. (Durham, NC: Duke University Press, 1999), 119.

6. These observations intersect with a debate over the relationship between the malefic and diabolical conceptions of witchcraft in New England. One view—advanced for example by Richard Godbeer in *The Devil's Dominion: Magic and Religion in Early New England* (New York: Cambridge University Press, 1992)—holds that the colonists' understanding of what it was to be a witch varied sharply, with elites (the clergy and political leadership) cleaving to the diabolical concept of the witch and common folk holding to the view of witchcraft as maleficium. In opposition stands the idea—expressed in Elizabeth Reis's *Damned Women: Sinners and Witches in Puritan New England* (Ithaca, NY: Cornell University Press, 1997)—that New Englanders were not so divided when it came to their thoughts on the nature of witchcraft and that elites and ordinary colonists held a largely shared outlook on the occult. My views strongly lean toward the latter interpretation.

7. Jeffrey Burton Russell, *Witchcraft in the Middle Ages* (Ithaca, NY: Cornell University Press, 1972), 65; Thomas, *Religion and the Decline of Magic*, 435–38.

8. For an example of the discussions found in early modern demonologies on how to distinguish between natural and supernatural maladies, see Richard Bernard, *A Guide to Grand Jury Men* (London: Felix Kingston, 1629), 163–70.

9. *REH*, 1:128; SWP-JHL, W-6.

10. Malcolm Freiberg, ed., *Winthrop Papers* (Boston: Massachusetts Historical Society, 1992), 6:300–302.

11. *RCNH*, 2:33–34; *RQCE*, 6:207; SWP-JHL, W-8; *REH*, 1:139–40.

12. SWP-CSL, no. 10; Samuel G. Drake, ed., *Annals of Witchcraft in New England* (Boston: W. Elliot Woodward, 1869), 247, 252; *REH*, 1:132–33.

13. *RPC*, 238, 131; R. G. Tomlinson, *Witchcraft Prosecution: Chasing the Devil in Connecticut* (Rockland, ME: Picton Press, 2012), 69–75, 117–18.

14. *RPC*, 131, 106–7; Tomlinson, *Witchcraft Prosecution*, 53–55.

15. Drake, *Annals*, 227–28; *RCNH*, 2:31; *REH* 1:134, 136; SWP-JHL, W-15; Benjamin F. Thompson, *History of Long Island* (New York: E. French, 1893), 151–53. For more on the witchcraft case of Mrs. Elizabeth Godman, see Mary Beth Norton, *Founding Mothers & Fathers: Gendered Power and the Forming of American Society* (New York: Alfred A. Knopf, 1996), 250–52.

16. *RCNH*, 2:35–36; *NHTR*, 1:250–51, 252; John Demos, "John Godfrey," 247, 249.

17. SWP-JHL, W-4, W-15; *RCNH*, 2:152.

18. SWP-JHL, W-10; Hall, *Witch-Hunting*, 100–101; SWP-CSL, no. 6.

19. James Kendall Hosmer, ed., *Winthrop's Journal, 1630–49* (New York: Charles Scribner's Sons, 1908), 2:344–45; Drake, *Annals*, 239–40; Hall, *Witch-Hunting*, 216.

20. *RCNH*, 2:30, 31–32, 33.

21. *RCA*, 3:160; Hall, *Witch-Hunting*, 102–3; Hosmer, ed., *Winthrop's Journal*, 2:345–46.

22. Joseph H. Smith, ed., *Colonial Justice in Western Massachusetts, 1639–1702: The Pynchon Court Record* (Cambridge, MA: Harvard University Press, 1961), 219–20; *NHTR*, 1:252; SWP-JHL, W-13, W-10; SWP-CSL, no. 9.

23. Drake, *Annals*, 230–31, 232–33, 243, 222–23.

24. J. H. Lefroy, ed., *Memorials of the Discovery and Early Settlement of the Bermudas or Somers Islands, 1515–1687* (London: Longmans, Green, 1879), 2:603, 604, 609–10, 614, 617–19.

25. Wolfgang Behringer, "Weather, Hunger and Fear: Origins of the European Witch-hunts in Climate, Society, and Mentality," *German History* 13 (1995): 1–27;

Carol Karlsen, *The Devil in the Shape of a Woman: Witchcraft in Colonial New England* (1987; reprint New York: W. W. Norton, 1998), 156–57—citations refer to the 1998 edition; James Sharpe, *Instruments of Darkness*, 65.

26. Hall, *Witch-Hunting*, 142; Bernard, *A Guide to Grand Jury Men*, 194; Dalton, *The Country Justice*, 341–42.

27. Bernard, *A Guide to Grand Jury Men*, 172–77. For additional discussions of the methods witches used to inflict harm, see John Gaule, *Select Cases of Conscience Touching Witches and Witchcrafts* (London: Printed by W. Wilson, 1646), 128–30; Karlsen, *Devil in the Shape of a Woman*, 7–8; and Godbeer, *The Devil's Dominion*, 38–42.

28. Gaule, *Select Cases of Conscience*, 129; RCNH, 2:32, 152.

29. NHHS, 1:255; Hall, *Witch-Hunting*, 215.

30. Lefroy, *Memorials*, 2:602, 603, 632. For a discussion of the links between speech and witchcraft, see Jane Kamesky, "Words, Witches, and Woman Trouble: Witchcraft, Disorderly Speech, and Gender Boundaries in Puritan New England," *Essex Institute Historical Collections* 128 (October 1992): 286–307, and *Governing the Tongue: The Politics of Speech in Early New England* (New York: Oxford University Press, 1999), 150–80.

31. Gaule, *Select Cases of Conscience*, 129; NHNS, 1:256–57; Hosmer, *Winthrop's Journal*, 2:344; Demos, "John Godfrey": 249; REH, 1:135–36.

32. Bernard, *A Guide to Grand Jury Men*, 202; SWP-JHL, W-7; REH, 1:134. John Demos discusses this "intruder" aspect of witchcraft in *Entertaining Satan*, 178–79.

33. Gaule, *Select Cases of Conscience*, 128–29; REH, 1:134; Hall, *Witch-Hunting*, 135; SWP-JHL, W-4; SWP-CSL, no. 10.

34. Gaule, *Select Cases on Conscience*, 129; Dalton, *The Country Justice*, 342; Hall, *Witch-Hunting*, 143. For a discussion of this sort of "image" magic, see Godbeer, *The Devil's Dominion*, 38–42.

35. Brian P. Levack, *The Witch-Hunt in Early Modern Europe*, 2nd ed. (Harlow, UK: Longman, 1995), 27–50.

36. Levack, *The Witch-Hunt in Early Modern Europe*, 27–50, 76–84; Michael Bailey, *Battling Demons: Witchcraft, Heresy, and Reform in the Late Middle Ages* (University Park: Pennsylvania State University Press, 2003), 1–10, 29–53, 139–46; Joseph Klaits, *Servants of Satan: The Age of the Witch Hunts* (Bloomington: Indiana University Press, 1985), 128–58.

37. English demonological works that advance a diabolical understanding of witchcraft include Alexander Roberts, *A Treatise of Witchcraft* (London: Nicholas Okes, 1616); Thomas Cooper, *The Mystery of Witch-craft* (London: Nicholas Okes, 1617); William Perkins, *A Discourse of the Damned Art of Witchcraft* (Cambridge: Cantrell Legge, 1618); John Cotta, *The Infallible True and Assured Witch* (London: I. L. for R. H. Thomas, 1625); and Gaule, *Select Cases of Conscience*. For information on the rise of diabolism in England, see Thomas, *Religion and the Decline of Magic*, 438–46; and Sharpe, *Instruments of Darkness*, 80–102. England's three witchcraft statues can be found in Barbara Rosen, ed., *Witchcraft in England, 1558–1618* (Amherst: University of Massachusetts Press, 1969), 53–58.

38. David D. Hall, *Witch-Hunting in Seventeenth-Century New England*, 1st ed. (Boston: Northeastern University Press, 1991), 315–16; RPC, 93.

39. PRCC 1:171; Cotton Mather, *Memorable Providences, Relating to Witchcrafts and Possessions* (1689), in *Narratives of the Witchcraft Cases, 1648–1706*, ed. George Lincoln Burr (New York: Charles Scribner's Sons, 1914), 135–36.

40. For a good summary of the elements of diabolical witchcraft, see Levack, *Witch-Hunt in Early Modern Europe*, 29–50.

41. Perkins, *A Discourse of the Damned Art of Witchcraft*, 614; Roberts, *A Treatise of Witchcraft*, 26–31; Cooper, *The Mystery of Witch-craft*, chap. 5; John Stearne, *A Confirmation and Discovery of Witchcraft* (London: Printed by William Wilson, 1648), 15.

42. Hall, *Witch-Hunting*, 119.

43. CMHS, *The Mather Papers*, 4th series (Boston: Massachusetts Historical Society, 1868), 8:468.

44. CMHS, 4th series, 8:58; Rev. John Hale, *A Modest Inquiry into the Nature of Witchcraft* (1702), in *Narratives of the Witchcraft Cases, 1648–1706*, ed. George Lincoln Burr (New York: Charles Scribner's Sons, 1914), 410.

45. Stuart Clark, "Protestant Demonology: Sin, Superstition, and Society," in *Early Modern European Witchcraft: Centers and Peripheries*, ed. Bengt Ankarloo and Gustav Henningson (New York: Oxford University Press, 1990), 45–81; Ildikó Kristóf, " 'Wise Women,' Sinners, and the Poor: The Social Background in a 16th–18th-century Calvinist City of Eastern Hungary," *Acta Ethnographica Hungarica* 37 (1991): 100–102.

46. CMHS, 4th Series, 8:468; SWP-JHL, W-1; SWP-CSL, no. 1.

47. For the high frequency with which animal familiars appeared in English witchcraft testimony, see Rosen, ed., *Witchcraft in England*. Examples of English demonologies' discussions of familiars include Bernard, *Guide to Grand Jury Men*, 109–10; Dalton, *The County Justice*, 341–42; and John Stearne, *A Confirmation and Discovery of Witchcraft*, 12.

48. Sharpe, *Instruments of Darkness*, 71–74; Hall, *Witch-Hunting*, 142–43, 103; SWP-JHL, W-1, RCNH, 2:34.

49. Sharpe, *Instruments of Darkness*, 73–74, 178–79. English demonologists who reference witch marks include Cooper, *The Mystery of Witch-craft*, 88; Perkins, *Discourse of the Damned Art of Witchcraft*, 643; Bernard, *Guide to Grand Jury Men*, 107–9; Stearne, *A Confirmation and Discovery of Witchcraft*, 42–49; and Dalton, *The Country Justice*, 342.

50. Hosmer, ed., *Winthrop's Journal*, 2:344; RCNH, 2:81–82, 84; Hall, *Witch-Hunting*, 216–17, 119; CA, 3:213.

51. SWP-JHL, W-4; RCA, 3:155–56.

52. Levack, *Witch-Hunt in Early Modern Europe*, 44–49, 7; Clark, "Protestant Demonology," 45–81. The fourth chapter of the second book of James I's *Daemonology* addresses witches' ability to fly.

53. Clark, "Protestant Demonology," 45–81; Richard Wiesman, *Witchcraft, Magic, and Religion in 17th-Century Massachusetts* (Amherst: University of Massachusetts Press, 1984), 25–26, 58–60.

54. Cooper, *Mystery of Witch-craft*, 56; Bernard, *Guide to Grand Jury Men*, 2–3, 52; Gaule, *Select Cases of Conscience*, 136.

55. Clark, "Protestant Demonology;" Godbeer, *The Devil's Dominion*, 85–106; Kristof, " 'Wise Women,' Sinners and the Poor," 101.

56. Clark, "Protestant Demonology," 62–69; Weisman, *Witchcraft, Magic, and Religion*, 54; Macfarlane, *Witchcraft in Tudor and Stuart England*, 129.

57. Bernard, *Guide to Grand Jury Men*, 151, 138–39; Perkins, *Discourse of the Damned Art of Witchcraft*, 638; Gaule, *Select Cases of Conscience*, 30–31; Roberts, *A Treatise of Witchcraft*, 62–64.

58. Weisman, *Witchcraft, Magic, and Religion*, 25–29, 58–61; Godbeer, *The Devil's Dominion*, 59–64.

59. Walter W. Woodward, *Prospero's America: John Winthrop Jr., Alchemy, and the Creation of New England Culture* (Chapel Hill: University of North Carolina Press for the OIEAHC, 2010), 215–17.

60. SWP-JHL, W-18; Drake, *Annals of Witchcraft*, 275–76.

61. Valerie A. Kivelson proposes this same understanding of the relationship between the malefic and diabolical views of witchcraft in "Lethal Convictions: The Power of a Satanic Paradigm in Russian and European Witch Trials," *Magic, Ritual, and Witchcraft* 6 (summer 2011): 38–41.

62. Rosen, *Witchcraft in England*, 57; Sharpe, *Instruments of Darkness*, 70–73, 75–78, 134–39; Fredrick Valletta, *Witchcraft, Magic and Superstition in England, 1640–70* (Burlington, VT: Ashgate, 2000), 134; Clive Holmes, "Popular Culture? Witches, Magistrates, and Divines in Early Modern England," in *Understanding Popular Culture: Europe from the Middle Ages to the Nineteenth Century*, ed. Steven L. Kaplan (Berlin: DEU Walter de Gruyter, 2012), 94, 97–101.

63. Sharpe, *Instruments of Darkness*, 66–70; Godbeer, *The Devil's Dominion*, 64–65; Homes, "Popular Culture?," 102–04.

64. David D. Hall, *Worlds of Wonder, Days of Judgement: Popular Religious Belief in Early New England* (New York: Alfred A. Knopf, 1989), 5–11; Godbeer, *Devil's Dominon*, 15–18; Virginia DeJohn Anderson, "Migrants and Motives: Religion and the Settlement of New England, 1630–1640," *NEQ* 58 (1985): 339–83.

65. Thomas, *Religion and the Decline of Magic*, 212–52; Godbeer, *The Devil's Dominion*, 31–51; Demos, *Entertaining Satan*, 81–82.

66. Bernard, *Guide to Grand Jury Men*, 184; Godbeer, *Devil's Dominion*, 42–45; Weisman, *Witchcraft, Magic, and Religion*, 40–41; Demos, *Entertaining Satan*, 182–84.

67. Drake, *Annals of Witchcraft*, 220, 249; Hale, *A Modest Inquiry*, in Burr, *Narratives of the Witchcraft Cases*, 408; RCNH, 2:224.

68. Drake, *Annals*, 240; NHNS, 1:256–57; REH, 1:133, 134.

69. David D. Hall, "Witchcraft and the Limits of Interpretation," *NEQ* 58 (June 1985): 275–77; Hall, *Worlds of Wonder*, 94; Karlsen, *Devil in the Shape of a Woman*, 4–5; Reis, *Damned Women*, 55–57.

70. The nineteen pre-1670 witchcraft suspects whose cases featured testimony evoking diabolical themes include Goody Knapp, Elizabeth Godman, Elizabeth Garlick, Judith Ayers, Nathaniel and Rebecca Greensmith, Goody Grant, Elizabeth Seager, John Brown, Katherine Harrison, Margaret Jones, Hugh Parsons, John Bradstreet, Jane Walford, Eunice Cole, Winifred and Mary Holman, John Godfrey, and Ann Burt.

71. Reis, *Damned Women*, 63, 79–83; Lauren Martin, in "The Devil and the Domestic: Witchcraft, Quarrels and Women's Work in Scotland," in *The Scottish Witch-Hunt in Context*, ed. Julian Goodare (Manchester: Manchester University Press, 2002), 73–89, also argues that the concepts of maleficium and diabolism were not mutually exclusive but often complimentary forms of evidence in Scottish witchcraft cases.

3. "A Forward, Discontented Frame of Spirit"

1. For biographical information on Mary (Bliss) Parsons, see John Demos, *Entertaining Satan: Witchcraft and the Culture of Early New England* (New York: Oxford

University Press, 1982), 257–59, 262–63. For information on Mary (Lewis) Parsons, see Samuel G. Drake, *Annals of Witchcraft in New England* (Boston, MA: W. Elliot Woodward, 1869), 66–67, 72.

2. Demos, *Entertaining Satan*, 260–62; Henry M. Burt, *The First Century of the History of Springfield: The Official Records from 1636–1736*. (Springfield, MA: Henry M. Burt, 1898), 1:73–74; Historic Northampton Museum and Education Center, ccbit. cs.umass.edu/parsons/hnmockup/famtrees/PARSONS/CHART.HTM.

3. Burt, *History of Springfield*, 1:75; Carol Karlsen, *The Devil in the Shape of a Woman: Witchcraft in Colonial New England* (1987; reprint New York: W. W. Norton, 1998), 22—citations refer to the 1998 edition; Drake, *Annals of Witchcraft*, 67; Demos, *Entertaining Satan*, 270. Documents related to Mary Bliss Parsons's 1656 and 1674–75 witchcraft cases can be found in David D. Hall, *Witch-Hunting in Seventeenth-Century New England*, 2nd ed. (Durham, NC: Duke University Press, 1999), 99–114.

4. *RCNH*, 2:29.

5. John Demos, in *Entertaining Satan*, 57–94; and Karlsen, in *The Devil in the Shape of a Woman*, 46–152, each present a comprehensive profile of New England witch suspects. My analysis builds on these previous works.

6. In *The Devil in the Shape of a Woman* (130–34), Carol Karlsen addresses the fact that much of what the historical record has to say about the accused comes from the perspective of their accusers and that just because they portray witch suspects as aggressive, envious, or deceitful does not necessarily mean that these characterizations are true; likewise, in *Entertaining Satan* (172–84) John Demos implicitly argues the same in his discussion of accusers' "fantasies" of the witch.

7. Richard Bernard, *A Guide to Grand Jury Men* (London: Printed by Felix Kingston for Edward Blackmore, 1629), 91; Thomas Cooper, *The Mystery of Witchcraft* (London: Printed by Nicholas Okes, 1617), 57; John Gaule, *Select Cases of Conscience Touching Witches and Witchcrafts* (London: Printed by W. Wilson for Richard Clutterbuck, 1646), 54–55; *RCNH*, 2:30.

8. Karlsen, *Devil in the Shape of a Woman*, 125–30, 149–50.

9. Cotton Mather, *Memorable Providences, Relating to Witchcrafts and Possessions* (1689), in *Narratives of the Witchcraft Cases, 1648–1706*, ed. George Lincoln Burr (New York: Charles Scribner's Sons, 1914), 136; John Hale, *A Modest Inquiry into the Nature of Witchcraft* (1702), in Burr, ed., *Narratives*, 410; Hall, *Witch-Hunting*, 214.

10. Hall, *Witch-Hunting*, 214; Joseph H. Smith, ed., *Colonial Justice in Western Massachusetts, 1639–1702: The Pynchon Court Record* (Cambridge, MA: Harvard University Press, 1961), 219–20; Stephen Innes, *Labor in a New Land: Economy and Society in Seventeenth-Century Springfield* (Princeton, NJ: Princeton University Press, 1983), 137–39; John Demos, "John Godfrey and his Neighbors: Witchcraft and the Social Web in Colonial Massachusetts," *WMQ* 33 (April 1976): 253–54, 261.

11. Karlsen, *Devil in the Shape of a Woman*, 128–30; Jeannette Edwards Rattray, *East Hampton History, Including Genealogies of Early Families* (Garden City, NY: Country Life Press, 1953), 71–72; *REH* 1:33–36 (quote from 36); Demos, "John Godfrey", 247.

12. Drake, *Annals*, 251, 224, 241.

13. *RCNH*, 2:30–31; James Kendall Hosmer, ed., *Winthrop's Journal, "History of New England," 1630–49* (New York: Charles Scribner's Sons, 1908), 2:345; Drake, *Annals*, 234; *RCA*, 3:161.

14. *HCC*, 147–48; SWP-JHL, W-12; Demos, "John Godfrey," 261–62; *RPC*, 28–30, 45, 88–89, 91; Demos, *Entertaining Satan*, 353.

15. Rev. Willliam Hubbard, *A General History of New England from the Discovery to 1680*, 2nd ed. (Boston: Charles C. Little & James Brown, 1848), 574; Thomas Hutchinson, *The History of the Colony of Massachusetts Bay* (London: Thomas and John Fleet, 1797), 1:187.

16. *NHTR*, 1:245–46. In "John Godfrey and His Neighbors," (248–49) John Demos discusses witch-suspects' association with shocking, mischievous speech, saying that Godfrey uttered words "that would startle, confuse, or annoy his listeners" and "flouted his community's standards of discreet conversation."

17. Hall, *Witch-Hunting*, 124; SWP-CSL, no. 3; *RCNH*, 2:31, 34.

18. *NHTR*, 1:250–51; Drake, *Annals*, 237–38.

19. *RQCE*, 1:234; *PRCC*, 1:376 (Though the court considered fining Mr. Blackleach £100 for his transgression, they only levied a £30 penalty against him after "considering some weakness that too evidently appears that he is incident unto." As to what this weakness was, the court never said.); *NHTR* 1:491; *RCNH*, 2:429; Hall, *Witch-Hunting*, 214; *RQCE*, 1:129; *REH*, 1:21.

20. Cooper, *Mystery of Witchcraft*, 57; Gaule, *Select Cases of Conscience*, 54.

21. Drake, *Annals*, 231–32, 241; *NHTR* 1:434, 443; SWP-JHL, W-11; Hall, *Witch-Hunting*, 145.

22. Karlsen, *Devil in the Shape of a Woman*, 147–49; *NHTR*, 1:245–46; SWP-CSL, no. 7; SWP-JHL, W-11.

23. Drake, *Annals*, 223–24, 237–38.

24. Virginia DeJohn Anderson, "Migrants and Motives: Religion and the Settlement of New England, 1630–1640," *New England Quarterly* 58 (September 1985): 352–53; Karlsen, *Devil in the Shape of a Woman*, 186–87. In Windsor, Connecticut, men comprised 56 percent of the population in 1640 and 53 percent by 1686: see, Linda A. Bissell, "Family, Friends, and Neighbors: Social Interaction in Seventeenth-Century Windsor" (PhD diss., Brandeis University, 1974), 41.

25. The figures concerning the proportion of male and female witches in New England are drawn from data found in Demos, *Entertaining Satan*, 402–9 and my own research. Those related to the Salem crisis are drawn from Emerson W. Baker, *A Storm of Witchcraft: The Salem Trials and the American Experience* (New York: Oxford University Press, 2015), 288–92. Malcolm Gaskill, "Witches and Witchcraft Prosecutions, 1560–1600," in *Early Modern Kent, 1540–1640*, ed. Michale Zell (Woodbridge, Suffolk, UK: Boydell Press and the Kent County Council, 2000), 257; Alan Macfarlane, *Witchcraft in Tudor and Stuart England: A Regional and Comparative Study* (New York: Harper & Row, 1970), 160.

26. My findings on the ages of accused witches contrast with Lyle Koehler's assessment that most were older and often elderly in *A Search for Power: The "Weaker Sex" in Seventeenth-Century New England* (Urbana: University of Illinois Press, 1980), 267–77, but are generally in line with those of Carol Karlsen (*Devil in the Shape of a Woman*, 64–66) and John Demos (*Entertaining Satan*, 65) when taking into account my study's different chronological focus. Macfarlane, *Witchcraft in Tudor and Stuart England*, 161; Karlsen, *Devil in the Shape of a Woman*, 69.

27. In "Family, Friends, and Neighbors," (41) Linda Bissell calculates that those between the ages of 15 and 39 constituted 50.2 percent of the population of Wind-

sor in 1640 and 41.8 percent in 1686, for an average of 46 percent. More information on the age structure of seventeenth-century New England can be found in Terry L. Anderson and Robert Paul Thomas, "White Population, Labor Force and Extensive Growth of the New England Economy in the Seventeen Century," *Journal of Economic History* 33 (September 1973): 652–53. In order to arrive at my figures drawn from Anderson and Thomas's work, I averaged together the age structure figures that they provide for both men and women.

28. This data are drawn from my analysis of the stage of the legal process—from complaint to execution—reached by each pre-1670 New England witchcraft suspect.

29. Bissell, "Family, Friends, and Neighbors," 41; Anderson and Thomas, "White Population, Labor Force, and Extensive Growth," 652–53. John Demos and Carol Karlsen also emphasize that middle age and beyond were the periods of life most associated with witchcraft, see Demos, *Entertaining Satan*, 66–68 and Karlsen, *Devil in the Shape of a Woman*, 66–71.

30. Bissell, "Family, Friends, and Neighbors," 41; Anderson and Thomas, "White Population," 652–53. John Demos notes that contemporaries also saw the age of sixty as the beginning of old age and presents data showing that, on average, during the seventeenth century 4.1 percent of the population was over sixty; see Demos, "Old Age in Early New England," *American Journal of Sociology* 84 (1978): 249, 254. Karlsen, *Devil in the Shape of a Woman*, 67–71.

31. For a discussion of how suspicions of witchcraft built up over time, see Alison Rowlands, "Witchcraft and Old Women in Early Modern Germany," *Past & Present* 173 (November 2001): 50–89. Carol Karlsen forwards the argument that older women's inability to carry out what Puritans perceived as basic female functions, such as childbearing, helps to explain why older folk were so vulnerable to accusation and that witch suspects got older as the seventeenth century advanced: see *Devil in the Shape of a Woman*, 71, 69. John Demos discusses the economic position of and social tensions concerning the elderly in "Old Age in Early New England," 266–68, 280–82.

32. Demos, *Entertaining Satan*, 68–69; Demos, "Old Age in Early New England," 266.

33. The percentages of married, widowed, and single witch suspects presented here are derived from my analysis of New England's witchcraft suspects. For a discussion of the marital status of witch suspects in early New England, see Demos, *Entertaining Satan*, 72–73; and Karlsen, *Devil in the Shape of a Woman*, 71–75.

34. Carol Karlsen addresses the issue of proportionality in her work, estimating that, on average, married women outnumbered widowed and other single adult women by a factor of four to one across the seventeenth century: see *Devil in the Shape of a Woman*, 73–74, 302–3n92. This ratio is consistent with my findings on the marital status of male and female witches compared to the general population.

35. Karlsen, *Devil in the Shape of a Woman*, 75; Demos, "John Godfrey," 258–59; Lucius R. Paige, *History of Cambridge, Massachusetts, 1630–1877* (Boston: H. O. Houghton, 1877), 587; Norbert R. Bankert, "More on the Identity of Abigail (Graves) Dibble and Her Tragic Death and Suspicions of Witchcraft," *New England Historic and Genealogical Register* 155 July (2001): 273–74; R. G. Tomlinson, *Witchcraft Prosecution: Chasing the Devil in Connecticut* (Rockland, ME: Picton Press), 60–61.

36. James T. Johnson, "English Puritan Thought on the Ends of Marriage," *Church History* 38 (December 1969): 429–36.

37. John Demos advances the notion that accused witches tended to have fewer children than the population at large: see *Entertaining Satan*, 72–73; Philip J. Greven, *Four Generations: Population, Land, and Family in Colonial Andover, Massachusetts* (Ithaca, NY: Cornell University Press, 1970), 201, 203–4. The average number of children born to married female witch-suspects in New England before 1671 is based on my analysis of existing genealogical information.

38. Tomlinson, *Witchcraft Prosecution*, 94; Demos, *Entertaining Satan*, 71; Rattray, *East Hampton History,* 71–72.

39. Anderson, "Migrants and Motives," 356–67; Alfred A. Cave, "Indian Shamans and English Witches in Seventeenth-Century New England," *Essex Institute Historical Collections* 128 (1992): 239–54.

40. Mather, *Memorable Providences*, in Burr, ed., *Narratives*, 103–4. In the past there has been much debate over whether Tituba was an African or Native American. However, the weight of evidence leans clearly toward her being the latter. Two articles that convincingly establish Tituba's identity as a Native American are Chadwick Hansen's, "The Metamorphosis of Tituba," *New England Quarterly* 47 (March 1974): 3–12; and Bernard Rosenthal's, "Tituba's Story," *New England Quarterly* 71 (June 1998): 190–205. Benjamin Ray also supports the idea that Tituba was a Native American and mentions two African-American women caught up the Salem crisis, Mary Black and Candy: see Ray, *Satan & Salem: The Witch-Hunt Crisis of 1692* (Charlottesville: University of Virginia Press, 2015), 201–5.

41. Demos, *Entertaining Satan*, 71; Karlsen, *Devil in the Shape of a Woman*, 14–18, 121–22.

42. Karlsen, *Devil in the Shape of a Woman*, 122–25; Peter Elmer, " 'Saints or Sorcerers': Quakerism, Demonology and the Decline of Witchcraft in Seventeenth-century England," in *Witchcraft in Early Modern Europe: Studies in Culture and Belief*, ed. Jonathan Barry et al. (New York: Cambridge University Press, 1996), 145–79.

43. This break down of witch suspects by wealth is based on economic data on the accused derived from sources such as surviving tax assessments and probate records. For my look at the economic status of the accused, I borrow the wealth categories established by Carol Karlsen: she identifies New Englanders with property valued at £500 or higher as upper class, those with between £200–500 as middle class, and those with less than £200 pounds as lower class—see Karlsen, *Devil in the Shape of Woman*, 79–80.

44. Demos, *Entertaining Satan*, 85; RQCE, 3:61–62, 100; Charles W. Manwaring, *A Digest of Early Connecticut Probate Records* (Hartford, CT: R. S. Peck, 1994), 1:103, 312; *RPC*, 204.

45. NHTR, 1:249; Donald L. Jacobus, ed., *History and Genealogy of the Families of Old Fairfield* (New Haven, CT: Tuttle, Morehouse, and Taylor, 1930), 1:34–35, 364–65. I came to an estimated value of William Ayers's Hartford property in 1656 by taking the assessed value of fellow Hartford resident Nathaniel Greensmith's estate in 1662 (£181, 18 shillings, and 5 pence) and his 1656 tax assessment (10 shillings and 9 pence) to arrive at a tax rate of 0.2954 percent. I then took Ayers's assessment of 3 shillings and 4 pence and divided it by that rate, giving me an estate valued at £56, 8 shillings. (Note: all cash values were translated into pence for ease of calculation: 12 pence = 1 shilling, 20 shillings = 1 pound.)

46. *RQCE* 2:215; *CCHS*, 14:496–98. In order to estimate the values of Richard Seager's estate, I followed the same process as for William Ayers—see the previous footnote.

47. Manwaring, *Early Connecticut Probate Records*, 1:121–22 (the value of Greensmith's inventory was initially valued as £137, 14s, 1d; however, later on another £44, 4s., and 4d was added for a total value of £181, 18s. 5d); *RQCE*, 2:426; Tomlinson, *Witchcraft Prosecution*, 101; Manwaring, *Early Connecticut Probate Records*, 1:158.

48. Manwaring, *Early Connecticut Probate Records*, 276, 206; Demos, *Entertaining Satan*, 353; Hall, *Witch-Hunting*, 89; Mary Beth Norton, *Founding Mothers & Fathers: Gendered Power and the Forming of American Society* (New York: Alfred A. Knopf, 1996), 81.

49. Koehler, *A Search for Power*, 281; *RCNH*, 1:105.

50. *CCHS*, 6:103; Burt, *History of Springfield*, 1:195; *RPC*, 174; *RQCE*, 2:300; *PRCC*, 1:227.

51. *PRCC*, 1:297, 428, 2:521.

52. Hall, *Witch-Hunting*, 89; James Russell Trumbull, *History of Northampton, Massachusetts* (Northampton, MA: Press of Gazette Printing Company, 1898), 1:25, 34, 107, 143; Burt, *History of Springfield*, 1:183, 217, 227.

53. *CCHS*, 6:142; Liam Connell, "'A Great or Notorious Liar': Katherine Harrison and her Neighbors, Wethersfield, Connecticut, 1668–1670," *Eras* 12 (March 2011): 3.

54. Demos, *Entertaining Satan*, 85–86; Paul Boyer and Stephen Nissenbaum, *Salem Possessed: The Social Origins of Witchcraft* (Cambridge, MA: Harvard University Press, 1974), 199–204.

55. Demos, *Entertaining Satan*, 234–35, 260–61, 356–59; E. B. O'Callaghan, *The Documentary History of the State of New York* (Albany, NY: Weed, Parsons, 1850), 2:253–54; *REH*, 1:488–91; Karlsen, *Devil in the Shape of a Woman*, 86.

56. In his *A General History of New England* (574), William Hubbard reported that Mr. Hibbins once lost £500 due to the unspecified "carelessness" of a shipmaster; and *In The History of the Colony and Province of Massachusetts Bay* (Vol. 1, 187), Thomas Hutchinson also made reference to these financial setbacks, stating that "losses in the latter part of his [William Hibbins's] life had reduced his estate."

57. Hall, *Witch-Hunting*, 215; Demos, *Entertaining Satan*, 70. For a discussion of the general European belief that witchcraft was transmitted along family lines, see Deborah Willis, "The Witch-Family in Elizabethan and Jacobean Print Culture," *Journal for Early Modern Cultural Studies* 13 (winter 2013): 4–31; and Alison Rowlands, "Gender, Ungodly Parents and a Witch Family in Seventeenth-Century Germany," *Past & Present* 232 (August 2016): 45–86.

58. The couples in question are William and Judith Ayres, Nicholas and Goody Bayley, Elizabeth and John Blackleach, Joan and John Carrington, Nathaniel and Rebecca Greensmith, Ralph and Mary Hall, Margaret and Nicholas Jennings, Margaret and Thomas Jones, Hugh and Mary Parsons, and Mary and Andrew Sanford.

59. Willis, "The Witch-Family"; Rowlands, "Gender, Ungodly Parents and a Witch Family."

60. Demos, *Entertaining Satan*, 70; Karlsen, *Devil in the Shape of a Woman*, 19–20. For the case of Winifred and Mary Holman, see Hall, *Witch-Hunting*, 134–46. For an excellent account of the events surrounding the 1682 accusation of Hannah Walford Jones, see Emerson W. Baker, *The Devil of Great Island: Witchcraft and Conflict in Early New England* (New York: Palgrave Macmillan, 2007).

61. Demos, *Entertaining Satan*, 257; Hall, *Witch-Hunting*, 108–9, 110–11; Gale Ion Harris, "William and Goodwife Ayres of Hartford, Connecticut: Witches Who Got Away," *American Genealogist* 75 (July 2000): 198.

62. John Demos has done the most to analyze the criminal background of witch suspects and its relevance to their accusations, and his observations generally parallel my own findings: see Demos, *Entertaining Satan*, 76–79.

63. *NHTR* 1:245–46; *PRCC*, 1:376–78; *RQCE*, 1:235.

64. *HCC*, 91; *RQCE*, 1:88, 164, 202, 2:375, 4:184; *REH*, 1:58–59; *RPC*, 106, 108, 132, 245, 247; Innes, *Labor in a New Land*, 136. For a discussion of the relationship between illicit speech, gender, and witchcraft in the Puritan colonies, see Jane Kamensky, *Governing the Tongue: The Politics of Speech in Early New England* (New York: Oxford University Press, 1997), 150–79.

65. *RPC*, 43, 81, 86, 96–97, 111, 171–72, 202–3; Hale, *A Modest Inquiry*, in Burr, ed., *Narratives*, 408; *RCNH*, 1:89, 105; *HCC*, 93.

66. For an overview of the prosecution of sexual crimes in early New England, see William K. Holdsworth, "Law and Society in Colonial Connecticut, 1636–1672" (PhD diss., Claremont Graduate School, 1974), 513–22. Carol Karlsen discusses sexual crimes in New England and their connection to witch-hunting in *Devil in the Shape of a Woman*, 194–96, 198–202. *RCNH*, 1:88, 89, 105; Hale, *A Modest Inquiry*, in Burr, ed., *Narratives*, 408–09; *PRCC*, 1:186–87; *HCC*, 7. The implications of the fact that all of the witch suspects accused of sexual crimes before 1670 were women is addressed in chap. 4.

67. Charles T. Libby, *Province and Court Records of Maine* (Portland: Maine Historical Society, 1931), 2:81; *RQCE*, 1:305; *HCC*, 7.

68. *RPC*, 50, 107–08; *RQCE*, 1:129, 374.

69. *RQCE*, 1:168, 179, 227–28, 265; *NHTR*, 1:434–35, 490; 2:189, 210; *RPC*, 51, 77; *RCNH*, 1:122.

70. Karlsen, *Devil in the Shape of a Woman*, 162–64; Demos, *Entertaining Satan*, 74–75; Robert Marcus and David Burner, eds., *America Firsthand* (New York: St. Martin's Press, 1989), 1:61.

71. Drake, *Annals*, 240, 236; Hall, *Witch-Hunting*, 101, 108; *RQCE*, 3:186–87.

72. Paul Boyer and Stephen Nissenbaum, *Salem-Village Witchcraft: A Documentary Record of Local Conflict in Colonial New England* (Boston: Northeastern University Press, 1972), 157, 36–52, 155, 156.

73. *NHTR*, 2:26–30, 42–44; *PRCC*, 2:323; *CCA*, 35–36.

74. *RPC*, 225, 88–89, 91; Demos, *Entertaining Satan*, 353.

75. Karlsen, *Devil in the Shape of a Woman*, 142–43. For an extensive exploration of women's activities as healers in early New England, see Rebecca J. Tannenbaum *The Healer's Calling: Women and Medicine in Early New England* (Ithaca, NY: Cornell University press, 2002).

76. David Harley, "Historians as Demonologists: The Myth of the Midwife-witch," *Society for the Social History of Medicine* 3 (1990): 1–26; Demos, *Entertaining Satan*, 80; James Sharpe, "Witchcraft and Women in 17th-century England: Some Northern Evidence," *Continuity and Change* 6 (1991): 179–99; Clive Holmes, "Women: Witnesses, and Witches," *Past & Present* 140 (1993): 65–75; and Rebecca Tannenbaum, *The Healer's Calling*, 94–97–98, 107.

77. SWP-JHL, W-16; Hall, *Witch-Hunting*, 135; Hosmer, ed., *Winthrop's Journal*, 2:344–45.

78. Tannenbaum, *The Healer's Calling*, 124–33; Demos, *Entertaining Satan*, 79–84; Mary R. O'Neil, "Missing Footprints: Maleficium in Modena," *Acta Ethnographica Hungarica* 37 (1991–92): 123–42.

79. Frederick Valletta, *Witchcraft, Magic and Superstition in England*, 1640–70 (Burlington, VT: Ashgate, 2000), 95–124; Keith Thomas, *Religion and the Decline of Magic* (New York: Charles Scribner's Sons, 1971), 212–52; Demos, "John Godfrey," 249; Hosmer, *Winthrop's Journal*, 2:344–45.

80. Demos, *Entertaining Satan*, 357; Connell, "'A Great or Notorious Liar,'" 1–29; SWP-JHL, W-11; SWP-CSL, no. 7, 8, 11, 12. For a discussion of William Lilly's *Christian Astrology*, see Thomas, *Religion and the Decline of Magic*, 284n1. For a discussion of divining magic in early New England, see Richard Godbeer, *The Devil's Dominion: Magic and Religion in Early New England* (New York: Cambridge University Press), 32–38.

4. "The More Women, the More Witches"

1. David D. Hall, *Witch-Hunting in Seventeenth-Century New England: A Documentary History, 1638–1693*, 2nd ed. (Durham, NC: Duke University Press, 1999), 87–88; RPC, 131, 251; James Kendall Hosmer, ed., *Winthrop's Journal, "History of New England," 1630–49* (New York: Charles Scribner's Sons, 1908), 2:344–46.

2. Virginia DeJohn Anderson, "Migrants and Motives: Religion and the Settlement of New England, 1630–1640," *New England Quarterly* 58 (September 1985): 352–53; Carol Karlsen, *The Devil in the Shape of a Woman: Witchcraft in Colonial New England* (1987; reprint New York: W. W. Norton, 1998), 186–87—citations refer to the 1998 edition; Linda A. Bissell, "Family, Friends, and Neighbors: Social Interaction in Seventeenth-Century Windsor" (PhD diss., Brandeis University, 1974), 41.

3. Brian P. Levack, *The Witch-Hunt in Early Modern Europe*, 2nd ed. (Harlow, UK: Longman Group, 1995), 133–34; James Sharpe, *Instruments of Darkness: Witchcraft in Early Modern England* (Philadelphia: University of Pennsylvania Press, 1996), 169; Richard Bernard, *A Guide to Grand Jury Men* (London: Felix Kingston, 1629), 87; William Perkins, *A Discourse on the Damned Art of Witchcraft* (Cambridge: Cantrell Legg, 1618), 637.

4. While the view of witch-hunting as a device of patriarchal control deployed against women was more current in witchcraft scholarship in the 1970s, more recent works—such as Marianne Hester's, "Patriarchal Reconstruction and Witch Hunting," in *Witchcraft in Early Modern Europe: Studies in Culture and Belief*, ed. Jonathan Barry et al. (New York: Cambridge University Press, 1996), 288–306—continue to promote elements of this perspective. For an example of the view that men were mostly secondary suspects, see John Demos, *Entertaining Satan: Witchcraft and the Culture of Early New England* (New York: Oxford University Press, 1982), 60–62.

5. Some of the studies that advance this point of view include Malcolm Gaskell, "The Devil in the Shape of a Man: Witchcraft, Conflict, and Belief in Jacobean England," *Historical Research* 71 (1998): 142–71; Lara Apps and Andrew Gow, *Male Witches in Early Modern Europe* (Manchester: Manchester University Press, 2003); Elizabeth J. Kent, "Masculinity and Male Witches in Old and New England, 1593–

1680," *History Workshop Journal* 60 (autumn 2005): 69–92; and Valerie Kivelson, "Male Witches and Gendered Categories in 17th-Century Russia," *Comparative Studies in Society and History* 45 (July 2003): 606–31. Quote from Christina Larner, *Witchcraft and Religion: The Politics of Popular Belief* (Oxford: Basil Blackwell, 1984), 87.

6. Scholars who have helped to bring the intersection between men's lives and witch fears into focus in New England and England include Kent, "Masculinity and Male Witches," 69–92; Erika Gasser, *Vexed With Devils: Manhood and Witchcraft in Old and New England* (New York: New York University Press, 2017); and Gaskill, "The Devil in the Shape of a Man," 142–47.

7. Carol Karlson states that 78 percent of the accused in New England during the seventeenth and early eighteenth centuries were women: see Karlsen, *Devil in the Shape of a Woman*, 47. John Demos, who only looks at cases in the seventeenth century, determined that 80 percent of the accused were female: see, Demos, *Entertaining Satan*, 61.

8. In her study of women and witchcraft in colonial New England, Carol Karlsen does more than any other scholar to analyze the different legal fates of male and female witch suspects: see *Devil in the Shape of a Woman*, 48–52.

9. Carol Karlsen documents the different qualitative treatment faced by male and female witch suspects: see *Devil in the Shape of a Woman*, 60–63. Information on the number of times individual suspects were accused of witchcraft drawn from Demos, *Entertaining Satan*, 401–9. The women who suffered repeated accusations were Alice Stratton, Elizabeth Godman, Winifred Holman, Elizabeth Seager, Mary Hall, Jane Walford, Katherine Palmer, Eunice Cole, and a woman with the last name of Evens. Winifred Holman faced three witchcraft accusations in 1659–60, while Elizabeth Seager went to trial for the crime twice in 1663 and a third time in 1665. Eunice Cole faced trial for witchcraft in 1656, 1673, and 1680. Katherine Palmer fell under suspicion in 1648, 1667, and 1672.

10. Hall, *Witch-Hunting*, 134; Demos, *Entertaining Satan*, 273–74, 505n29.

11. Karlsen, *Devil in the Shape of a Woman*, 71; Demos, *Entertaining Satan*, 67–68.

12. Carol Karlsen also discusses the relationship between witchcraft suspicions and marital status in *Devil in the Shape of a Woman*, 64–75, 301–2n88.

13. *NHTR*, 2:132.

14. Rebecca J. Tannenbaum, *The Healer's Calling: Women and Medicine in Early New England* (Ithaca, NY: Cornell University Press, 2002), 124–33; Demos, *Entertaining Satan*, 79–84; Hosmer, *Winthrop's Journal*, 2:344–45; Hall, *Witch-Hunting*, 185–88. Dr. Roger Toothaker, the only New England physician prosecuted for occult crime, was arrested during the Salem witch hunt of 1692—see, Mary Beth Norton, *In the Devil's Snare: The Salem Witchcraft Crisis of 1692* (New York: Vintage Books, 2003), 172, 182.

15. It seems that rather distinct profiles of male and female witchcraft emerged in many parts of early modern Europe. Elizabeth Kent discerns distinctly gendered patterns of witchcraft in early modern England in "Masculinity and Male Witches in Old and New England," 70–78; and Rolfe Schulte describes different types of harms associated with male witches in "Men as Accused Witches in the Holy Roman Empire" in *Witchcraft and Masculinities in Early Modern Europe*, ed. Alison Rowlands (London: Palgrave Macmillam, 2009), 52–73. In contrast, Malcolm Gaskill does not see much distinction between the misdeeds attributed to the male witch suspect

William Godfrey and those linked to female suspects: see Gaskill, "The Devil in the Shape of a Man," 161–62.

16. Although formal indictments against witches in New England invariably include references to diabolism, I have only designated a witchcraft case as having diabolical elements if it produced evidence concerning witch marks, witches' Sabbaths, familiar spirits, or a suspect's direct contact with the Devil. Forty percent of female suspects and 43 percent of male suspects from before 1670 meet this criteria. Of these, 25 percent of the men and 29 percent of the women were accused of having familiars, and 8 percent of men and 16 percent of women had testimony entered against them concerning witches' teats. Samuel G. Drake, *Annals of Witchcraft in New England* (Boston: W. Elliot Woodward, 1869), 244.

17. *NHTR*, 2:129–30; Hall, *Witch-hunting*, 87–88; *RQCE*, 4:78, 99.

18. *NHTR*, 2:129–30; Hall, *Witch-hunting*, 87–88; SWP-CSL, no. 7; Kent, "Masculinity and Male Witches," 85; Michael Bailey, *Battling Demons: Witchcraft, Heresy, and Reform in the Late Middle Ages* (College Park: Pennsylvania State University Press, 2003), 48–52; Kristen Hastrup, "Iceland: Sorcerers and Paganism," in *Early Modern European Witchcraft*, ed. B. Ankarloo and G. Henningson (New York: Oxford University Press, 1990), 383–401.

19. Drake, *Annals*, 227–28, 235.

20. Elizabeth Reis stresses how learned views of the clergy that portrayed women as physically and spiritually weak and vulnerable to the Devil's temptations and witchcraft were widely shared in New England: see *Damned Women: Sinners and Witches in Puritan New England* (Ithaca, NY: Cornell University Press, 1997), 5, 93–97, 110–11.

21. James I of England, *Daemonology in Forme of a Dialogue* (Edinburgh: Robert Waldegrave, Printer to the King's Majestie, 1597), 43–44; Perkins, *A Discourse of the Damned Art of Witchcraft*, 637; Bernard, *A Guide to Grand Jury Men*, 89; John Gaule, *Select Cases of Conscience Touching Witches and Witchcrafts* (London: W. Wilson for Richard Clutterbuck, 1646), 51–52; Thomas Cooper, *The Mystery of Witchcraft* (London: Nicholas Okes, 1617), 206; Alexander Roberts, *A Treatise of Witchcraft* (London: Printed by N.O. for Samuel Man, 1616), 40, 42–43.

22. Bernard, *Guide to Grand Jury Men*, 108; Michael Dalton, *The Country Justice* (London: Company of Stationers, 1655), 342; Clive Homes, "Women: Witnesses and Witches," *Past & Present* 140 (1993): 66, 70–71; Drake, *Annals*, 240.

23. Reis, *Damned Women*, 110–16; Lyle Koehler, *A Search for Power: The "Weaker Sex" in Seventeenth-Century New England* (Urbana: University of Illinois Press, 1980), 271–72; Karlsen, *Devil in the Shape of a Woman*, 138–41; Cotton Mather, *Memorable Providences, Relating to Witchcrafts and Possessions* (1689), in *Narratives of the Witchcraft Cases, 1648–1706*, ed. George Lincoln Burr (New York: Charles Scribner's Sons, 1914), 136; *CMHS*, 4th Series, 8:468.

24. James Sharpe, "Witchcraft and Women in Seventeenth-Century England: Some Northern Evidence," *Continuity and Change* 6 (1991): 189; Éva Pócs, "Why Witches are Women," *Acta Ethnographica Hungarica* 48 (2003): 372–79.

25. Tannenbaum, *The Healer's Calling*, 60; Karlsen, *Devil in the Shape of a Woman*, 16–18; Hall, *Witch-Hunting*, 134–43; SWP-JHL, W-8 and W-9.

26. Sharpe, "Witchcraft and Women," 186–87; Diana Purkiss, "Women's Stories of Witchcraft in Early Modern England: The House, the Body, and the Child," *Gen-*

der & History 7 (1995): 408–32; Pócs, "Why Witches are Women," 375; *NHTR* 1:245; *REH*, 1:134–36. For a discussion of female social networks and conflict in early New England, see Mary Beth Norton, *Founding Mothers & Fathers: Gendered Power and the Forming of American Society* (New York: Alfred A. Knopf, 1996), 222–39, 253–61.

27. *RCNH*, 2:81–82; R. G. Tomlinson, *Witchcraft Prosecution: Chasing the Devil in Connecticut* (Rockland, ME: Picton Press, 2012), 43–46.

28. First-generation couples in Andover, Massachusetts (who are likely representative of those throughout rural communities in early New England), bore an average of 8.3 children and an average of 7.2 of them lived at least till the age of twenty-one: see Philip J. Greven, *Four Generations: Population, Land, and Family in Colonial Andover, Massachusetts* (Ithaca, NY: Cornell University Press, 1970), 201. In contrast, based on my research, women accused of witchcraft before 1671 had an average of 4 children. Genealogical information on the witch suspects referenced in this paragraph can be found in Demos, *Entertaining Satan*, 233; *RPC*, 225, 243; Charles W. Manwaring, ed., *A Digest of Early Connecticut Probate Records* (Hartford, CT: R. S. Peck, 1904), 1:121–22, 206; Tomlinson, *Witchcraft Prosecution*, 96, *PRCC*, 1:162, 479; and Drake, *Annals*, 66.

29. Richard Baxter, *A Christian Directory* (London, 1678), 3:145–49 (quotations from 145, 147, and 149). For a similar view of a wife's duties, see Daniel Rogers, *Matrimoniall Honour* (London: Printed by Thomas Harper for Philip Nevil, 1642), 253–303.

30. Karlsen, *Devil in the Shape of a Woman*, 163–73, 180–81; Reis, *Damned Woman*, 157.

31. *REH*, 1:58; Thomas Hutchinson, *The History of the Colony of Massachusetts Bay* (London: Mr. Richardson, 1765), 1:187; quote from the church proceedings against Anne Hibbins found in Hall, *Witch-Hunting*, 89. For a discussion of Anne Hibbins's behavior in the context of early New England's gender norms, see Norton, *Founding Mothers & Fathers*, 81–83, 163–64.

32. Karlsen, *Devil in the Shape of a Woman*, 80–89, 101–13, 206–18 (reference to Hibbins on 104). For a discussion of the problems widows could pose for early New England's gender norms and social hierarchy, see Norton, *Founding Mothers & Fathers*, 138–80.

33. Manwaring, *Early Connecticut Probate Records*, 1:206; Karlsen, *Devil in the Shape of a Woman*, 84–89; Demos, *Entertaining Satan*, 355–60.

34. SWP-JHL W-12; Liam Connell, "'A Great or Notorious Liar': Katherine Harrison and her Neighbors, Wethersfield, Connecticut, 1668–1670," *Eras* 12 (March 2011): 2; *HCC*, 66–67, 101, 147–48.

35. Perkins, *A Discourse of the Damned Art of Witchcraft*, 636–37;Gaule, *Select Cases of Conscience*, 53; *RQCE*, 4:78. For male witchcraft cases on both sides of the Atlantic, see Kent, "Masculinity and Male Witches," 69–92; Gaskill, "The Devil in the Shape of a Man," 142–71; and the essays contained in Rowlands, ed., *Witchcraft and Masculinities in Early Modern Europe*.

36. Demos, *Entertaining Satan*, 60–61. Tomlinson, *Witchcraft Prosecution*, 89–93, 96–98.

37. Male suspects from before 1670 who came under suspicion as a result of accusations against their wives include Andrew Sanford, Nathaniel Greensmith, William Ayres, Thomas Jones, Nicholas Bayley, and Ralph Hall. Primary male suspects

include John Brown, William Graves, James Wakeley, Hugh Parsons, John Brad-street, William Brown, Robert Williams, Thomas Wells, and John Godfrey. For the extant documentation on the cases of John Carrington, Nicholas Jennings, and John Blackleach, see *RPC*, 92–93, 238, 240, 260–61; Matthew Grant Diary, 1637–1654, CSL; *PRCC*, 1:338; and SWP-JHL, W-1.

38. Drake, *Annals*, 66–72, 219–58; *RMB*, 3:229, 273, 4/1:47–48, 73, 96; *RPC*, 240.

39. A deposition given in March 1654 identifies Bradstreet as being twenty-four years old, which would mean that he was twenty-two or twenty-three when he was accused of witchcraft in 1652, see *RQCE*, 1:333. *RQCE*, 1:188, 227–28, 235, 265.

40. Demos, "John Godfrey," 244; Hall, *Witch-Hunting*, 119.

41. Demos, *Entertaining Satan*, 60–61; *RQCE*, 7:355–59; John Novel, ed., *Records of the Court of Assistants of the Colony of the Massachusetts Bay, 1630–1692* (Boston: Published by the County of Suffolk, 1901), 1:228–29; Tomlinson, *Witchcraft Prosecution*, 175; CA, Crimes and Misdemeanors, I (part 1), 185–86; Bernard Rosenthal et al., eds., *Records of the Salem Witch Hunt* (New York: Cambridge University Press, 2009), 193–94.

42. Tomlinson, *Witch Prosecution*, 115–17; *RCNH*, 2:429–31 (quote on 429); *NHTR*, 1:434–44, 490–94; 2:26–31, 42–44, 129–32.

43. Gaskill, "The Devil in the Shape of a Man," 151–58; Demos, "John Godfrey," 249; Rosenthal, et. al., eds., *Records of the Salem Witch Hunt*, 644–45.

44. Reis, *Damned Women*, 157; NHTR 1:434–44, 490–94, 2: 26–31, 42–44; *RQCE*, 1:374; *RPC*, 50; *RCNH*, 1:89. Richard Godbeer, "'Your Wife Will Be Your Biggest Accuser': Reinforcing Codes of Manhood at New England Witch Trials," *Early American Studies* 15 (summer 2017): 474–504.

45. The male suspects associated with disorderly speech are William Ayres (*RPC*, 132, 245, 247), John Blackleach (*PRCC*, 1:376–78), John Bradstreet (*RQCE*, 1:235), William Brown (*RQCE*, 2:36–37), Ralph Hall (*RQCE*, 1:164), James Wakeley (*RPC*, 106), and Thomas Welles (*RQCE*, 4:49–50). For cases of domestic unrest that involved James Wakeley and John Brown respectively, see *RPC*, 88–91 and *NHTR*, 2:26–31, 42–44. For a discussion of early New Englanders' expectations for fathers and husbands, see Norton, *Founding Mothers & Fathers*, 101.

46. *RPC*, 96–97, 111, 172 (William Ayers), 202–03 (Andrew Sanford), 142 (John Blackleach); Demos, *Entertaining Satan*, 353 (James Wakeley). For information on the many debt suits initiated by John Blackleach and James Wakeley, refer to the indexs of the *RPC* and the *HCC*. Elizabeth Kent notes a pattern of perceived economic misconduct among male witches in both England and New England: see, "Masculinity and Male Witches," especially 73–75. For a discussion of community interactions among men in early New England and the role honesty played in rating men's reputations, see Norton, *Founding Mothers & Fathers*, 207–22.

47. Kent, "Masculinity and Male Witchcraft," 82–83; Demos, "John Godfrey," 242–65 (quote on 247).

48. Demos, "John Godfrey," 254–55, 261–62; *RQCE*, 4:9, 78, 3:121–22.

49. Kent, "Masculinity and Male Witchcraft," 79–82; Drake, *Annals*, 239, 236–39, 241, 250, 234.

50. Drake, *Annals*, 224, 228, 230–33, 243.

51. Drake, *Annals*, 236, 241–42.

52. Demos, *Entertaining Satan*, 260–61; Joseph H. Smith, ed., *Colonial Justice in Western Massachusetts, 1639–1702: The Pynchon Court Record* (Boston: Harvard University Press, 1961), 221–22, 238, 295; Hall, *Witch-Hunting*, 101, 108–9.

53. Kevin M. Sweeny identifies John Harrison as being a shoemaker before he became a merchant in "Furniture and the Domestic Environment in Wethersfield, Connecticut, 1639–1800," in *Material Life in America, 1600–1800*, ed. Robert Blair St. George (Boston: Northeastern University Press, 1987), 267; Demos, *Entertaining Satan*, 357–58; SWP-JHL, W-16.

54. C. L'Estrange Ewen, *Witch Hunting and Witch Trials: The Indictments for Witchcraft from the Records of 1,373 Assizes held for the Home Circuit A.D. 1559–1736* (London: Kegan Paul, Trench, Trubner, 1929), 123, 125, 126, 138, 164, 169, 195, 205, 208, 233, 236, 239, 249; Sharpe, *Instruments of Darkness*, 108; Sharpe, "Witchcraft and Women," 184.

55. Virginia Bernhard, "Religion, Politics, and Witchcraft in Bermuda, 1651–1655," *WMQ* 67 (October 2010): 695–701; J. H. Lefroy, *Memorials of the Discovery and Early Settlement of the Bermudas or Somers Islands* (London: Longmans, Green, 1879), 2:603–10.

56. Ewen, *Witch Hunting and Witch Trials*, 212–65. Illustrating the ambiguous use of the term *spinster*, the 1647 indictment of Jane Lavender describes her as "spinster, wife of Francis Lavender" (Ewen, *Witch Hunting*, 233). In fact, out of the sixty-five women labeled as spinsters in Home Circuit indictments between 1625 and 1701, forty-three of them are also identified as being married. Sharpe, "Witchcraft and Women in Seventeenth-Century England," 184.

57. Of 342 witch suspects identified by Carol Karlsen, 269 were women: see *Devil in the Shape of a Woman*, 47–48. Demos, *Entertaining Satan*, 61

58. See chapter 3 for a detailed discussion of the profile of New England's witch suspects.

59. John Demos advances the notion that accused witches tended to have fewer children than the population at large: see, *Entertaining Satan*, 72–73. Genealogical information on the witch couples referenced in this paragraph can be found in *RQCE*, 1:74; Sherman W. Adams and Henry R. Stiles, *History of Ancient Wethersfield, Connecticut* (1904; reprint Camden, ME: Picton Press, 1995), 2:102; Karlsen, *Devil in the Shape of a Woman*, 116, 317n153; Demos, *Entertaining Satan*, 349, 506n40; Manwaring, *Early Connecticut Probate Records*, 1:121–22; Tomlinson, *Witchcraft Prosecution*, 96; *PRCC*, 1:162, 479; and Drake, *Annals*, 66–67. In addition to the couples mentioned in this paragraph, records indicate that the Halls may only have had one child—see E. B. O'Callaghan, *The Documentary History of the State of New York* (Albany, NY: Weed, Parsons, 1850), 2:305—and that the Jennings had two or three: *RPC*, 225, 243. Besides the previously listed sources, the genealogical website www.geni.com was also useful in tracking down the number of children born to New England's witch suspects.

Extending this analysis across the Atlantic to England may, at first glance, undermine the idea that witch couples stood out in the Puritan colonies due to their lack of children. Seventeenth-century English women gave birth an average of six or seven times. However, due to a high rate of child mortality, the average family size in England stood at just under five individuals. Taking into account that this usually included parents, this means that the average English couple raised two or three children. This would seem to indicate the New England's accused witch couples were, according to English standards, not all that unusual in terms of the number of children they had. However, the critical question is by whose standard were they being judged, England's or New England's, and it makes sense that it was the latter's. By the time witch prosecutions took off in the Puritan colonies in the 1650s, their inhabitants had been exposed to New England's different demographic environment and most likely perceived married couples with relatively large numbers of children as normative and those without as deviant. For data on household size in early modern England, see Peter Laslett, "Mean Household Size in England Since the Sixteenth Century," in *Household and Family in the Past*, ed. Laslett and Richard Wall (New York: Cambridge University Press, 1972), 126, 139; and Keith Wrightson and David Lane, *Poverty and Piety in An English Village: Terling, 1525–1700* (New York: Academic Prress, 1979), 49.

60. Greven, *Four Generations*, 201, 203–4.

61. For discussions of marriage in early modern Europe, see Lawrence Stone, *The Family, Sex, and Marriage in England, 1500–1800* (New York: Harper & Row, 1977); Eric J. Carlson, *Marriage and the English Reformation* (New York: Oxford University Press, 1994); John Witte Jr., *From Sacrament to Contract: Marriage, Religion, and Law in the Western Tradition* (Louisville, KY: Westminster John Knox Press, 1997); and Michael M. Sheehan, *Marriage, Family, and Law in Medieval Europe*, ed. James K. Farge (Toronto: University of Toronto Press, 1996).

62. John Demos, *A Little Commonwealth: Family Life in Plymouth Colony* (New York: Oxford University Press, 1970), 82–118; Edmund S. Morgan, *The Puritan Family: Religion and Domestic Relations in Seventeenth-Century New England* (New York: Harper & Row, 1966), especially 133–60; Karlsen, *Devil in the Shape of a Woman*, 162–65; William Gouge, *Of Domesticall Duties* (London, 1622), 17–18; Daniel Rogers, *Matrimoniall Honour* (London: Printed by Thomas Harper for Philip Nevil, 1642)—quote from section entitled "To the Reader."

63. For discussions of the witch as an inversion of the wife and mother, see Demos, *Entertaining Satan*, 179–81; Louise Jackson, "Witches, Wives, and Mothers: Witchcraft Persecutions and Women's Confessions in 17th-century England," *Women's History Review* 4 (1995): 71–79; Purkiss, "Women's Stories of Witchcraft in Early Modern England," 413–25; Lyndal Roper, "Witchcraft and Fantasy in Early Modern Germany," in *Witchcraft in Early Modern Europe: Studies in Culture and Belief*, eds. Jonathan Barry et. al. (New York: Cambridge University Press, 1996), 207–36; and Alison Rowlands, "Gender, Ungodly Parents and a Witch Family in Seventeenth-Century Germany," *Past & Present* 232 (August 2016): 77–78.

64. SWP-JHL, W-1; *RPC*, 257–58. The six accusations against married couples that started with suspicions against the wife include the cases of Margaret and Thomas Jones, Nicholas and Goody Bayley, William and Judith Ayers, Andrew and Mary Sanford, Rebecca and Nathaniel Greensmith, and Ralph and Mary Hall.

65. Deborah Willis, "The Witch-Family in Elizabethan and Jacobean Print Culture," *Journal for Early Modern Cultural Studies* 13 (winter 2013): 4–31; Rowlands, "Gender, Ungodly Parents, and a Witch Family in Seventeenth-Century Germany," 45–86. Among the families caught up in the Salem crisis were the Proctors, Hobbs, Wardwells, and Toothakers—see the list of Salem suspects appended to Emerson Baker's, *A Storm of Witchcraft: The Salem Trials and the American Experience* (New York: Oxford University Press, 2015), 288–92.

66. Jack P. Greene, *Pursuits of Happiness: The Social Development of Early Modern British Colonies and the Formation of American Culture* (Chapel Hill: University of North Carolina Press, 1988), 10–14, 25–26, 178; Laurel Thatcher Ulrich, *Goodwives: Image and Reality in the Lives of Women in Northern New England, 1650–1750* (New York: Vintage Books, 1991), 157.

67. Drake, *Annals*, 233.

68. The witch couples caught up in the Salem crisis include John and Elizabeth Proctor, Giles and Martha Cory, Sarah and Edward Bishop, Mary and Philip English, Roger and Mary Toothaker, Samuel and Sarah Wardwell, and William and Deliverance Hobbs: see Baker, *A Storm of Witchcraft*, 288–92.

69. For discussions of land shortages in late-seventeenth-century New England or how they intersected with witchcraft, see Kenneth A. Lockridge, "Land, Population and the Evolution of New England Society, 1630–1790," *Past & Present* 39 (April 1968): 62–80; Paul Boyer and Stephen Nissenbaum, *Salem Possessed: The Social Origins of Witchcraft* (Cambridge, MA: Harvard University Press, 1974), 123–28, 180; and Karlsen, *Devil in the Shape of a Woman*, 206–18.

5. "There Was Some Mischief in It"

1. *RCNH*, 2:224–26, 254–55, 258–63; *NHTR*, 1:317–18, 300–302.

2. Carol Karlsen calculates that out of 732 people who provided testimony against witch suspects in seventeenth- and eighteenth-century New England, 78 were bewitched accusers: see *The Devil in the Shape of a Woman: Witchcraft in Colonial New England* (1987; reprint New York: W. W. Norton, 1998), 183–85—citations refer to the 1998 edition.

3. The figure of 181 represents the number of named individuals known to have presented formal testimony against suspected witches before 1670 and does not include those who made informal accusations.

4. Carol Karlsen notes that the gap between the numbers of male and female accusers held true across the entire seventeenth and early eighteenth century, with men constituting about two-thirds of all known prosecuting witnesses; see *Devil in the Shape of a Woman*, 183–84. Samuel G. Drake, ed., *Annals of Witchcraft in New England* (Boston: W. Elliot Woodward, 1869), 230–31.

5. Out of the 181 known accusers who gave testimony before 1670, the ages of only 34 of them can be determined with any precision, and conclusions drawn from this data are thus tentative. Carol Karlsen's and Richard Weisman's findings on the ages of accusers roughly support my own; see Karlsen, *Devil in the Shape of a Woman*, 184; and Weisman, *Witchcraft, Magic, and Religion in 17th-Century Massachusetts* (Amherst: University of Massachusetts Press, 1984), 51.

6. There are 101 nonafflicted accusers whose marital status can be determined with some confidence. The three young, unwed accusers were Samuel Parsons and William Russell, both of whom were involved in the prosecution of Elizabeth Garlick in 1658—see John Demos, *Entertaining Satan: Witchcraft and the Culture of Early New England* (New York: Oxford University Press, 1982), 237—and Hannah Robbins, who spoke against Katherine Harrison in 1668—see SWP-JHL, W-7. The widowed accusers who blamed their spouses' deaths on witchcraft were Eleazer Kimberly,

Zachariah Dibble, and Arthur Howell: see SWP-CSL, no. 16; SWP-JHL, W-8 and W-9; *REH*, 1:128–30.

There is some debate over whether or not Mrs. Elizabeth Godman was widowed or a spinster when she came under suspicion for witchcraft, but the evidence points more to the latter: see Mary Beth Norton, *Founding Mothers & Fathers: Gendered Power and the Forming of American Society* (New York: Alfred A. Knopf, 1996), 250–52 and notes related to these pages.

Richard Weisman's research on the marital status of accusers in early Massachusetts roughly supports my own findings—see Weisman, *Witchcraft, Magic, and Religion*, 50—as does Carol Karlsen's—see Karlsen, *Devil in the Shape of a Woman*, 185—although her inclusion of cases related to the Salem witch crisis means that the proportion of young, single accusers is higher.

7. Karlsen, *Devil in the Shape of a Woman*, 184; Lucius Barnes Barbour, *Families of Early Hartford, Connecticut* (Baltimore, MD: Genealogical Publishing, 1977), 351; James Russell Trumbull, *History of Northampton, Massachusetts from its Settlement in 1654* (Northampton, MA: Gazette Printing Company, 1898), 1:27, 68, 107, 145.

8. Drake, *Annals*, 228–29. For the Reverend Samuel Stone's witch-hunting efforts, see Cotton Mather, *Memorable Providences, Relating to Witchcrafts and Possessions* (1689), in *Narratives of the Witchcraft Cases, 1648–1706*, ed. George Lincoln Burr (New York: Charles Scribner's Sons, 1914), 135–36; and *CMHS*, 4th Series, 8:466–69. R. G. Tomlinson, *Witchcraft Prosecution: Chasing the Devil in Connecticut* (Rockland, ME: Picton Press), 35; *REH*, 1:133.

9. *HCC*, 9–10, 52, 101, 245.

10. *RCNH*, 2:224, 258–62; *NHTR*, 1:247, 317–18, 300–302.

11. *RQCE*, 1:52, 225, 233, 428, 2:57.

12. *RQCE*, 1:29, 58, 162; Jeannette Edwards Rattray, *East Hampton History, Including Genealogies of Early Families* (Garden City, NJ: Country Life Press, 1953), 17, 71–72; Demos, *Entertaining Satan*, 236–37.

13. Demos, *Entertaining Satan*, 284. For a discussion of how knowledge of witchcraft was allegedly passed down from one generation to another within families, see Alison Rowlands, "Gender, Ungodly Parents, and a Witch Family in Seventeenth-Century Germany," *Past & Present* 282 (August 2016): 45–86; and Deborah Willis, "The Witch-Family in Elizabethan and Jacobean Print Cultures," *Journal for Early Modern Cultural Studies* 13 (winter 2013): 4–31. Alan Macfarlane also mentions that witchcraft accusations periodically emerged out of "tensions between affines—that is, between relations by marriage" but not blood: see *Witchcraft in Tudor and Stuart England: A Regional and Comparative Study* (New York: Harper & Row, 1970), 169–70. For an example of a place where witchcraft accusations did occur within families, see Valarie Kivelson, "Patrolling the Boundaries: Witchcraft Accusations and Household Strife in Seventeenth-Century Muscovy," *Harvard Ukrainian Studies* 19 (1995): 302–23.

14. Drake, *Annals*, 222–23, 227–29, 233–35, 235–37, 239–40, 240–43; SWP-JHL, W-1; CA, Crimes and Misdemeanors, 1st Series, 3: 213; SWP-JHL, W-9. The depositions collected about Sarah Dibble's alleged witch teat were part of her bid to gain a divorce from Zachary on the grounds that he had abused her and jeopardized her life by wrongly accusing her of witchcraft.

15. Demos, *Entertaining Satan*, 284–85; Lyndal Roper, "Witchcraft and Fantasy in Early Modern Germany," in *Witchcraft in Early Modern Europe: Studies in Belief and Culture*, ed. Jonathan Barry et al. (New York: Cambridge University Press, 1996), 207–36.

16. Mather, *Memorable Providences*, in *Narratives of the Witchcraft Cases*, Burr, ed., 135–36; Demos, *Entertaining Satan*, 234; *REH*, 1:135–36; David D. Hall, *Witch-Hunting in Seventeenth-Century New England*, 2nd ed. (Durham, NC: Duke University Press, 1999), 214, 222. While many of early New England's witch suspects numbered among the poorer members of their communities, besides the case of Eunice Cole, there is no evidence that they received systematic poor relief.

17. Demos, *Entertaining Satan*, 279–84; Jack P. Greene, *Pursuits of Happiness: The Social Development of Early Modern British Colonies and the Formation of American Culture* (Chapel Hill: University of North Carolina Press, 1988), 22–23.

18. Tomlinson, *Witchcraft Prosecution*, 34–35; *RPC*, 56; Hall, *Witch-Hunting*, 135–44; Demos, *Entertaining Satan*, 279–84.

19. *NHTR*, 1:251–52; *NHCR*, 2:33–34; Drake, *Annals*, 230; Tomlinson, *Witchcraft Prosecution*, 53–55.

20. Reginald Scott, *The Discovery of Witchcraft* (London: William Brome, 1584), 7.

21. Hall, *Witch-Hunting*, 214, 217; *RQCE*, 3:61–62, 100.

22. *HCC*, 71–72; *SWP-JHL*, W-1; *RPC*, 261. The two defendants in Mr. Blackleach's slander suit were John Stedman and Moses Mudge. Though their offending words are not found in surviving records, the timing of the cases and the fact that Blackleach sought the eye-popping sum of £200 in damages make it highly probable that they were accusations of witchcraft. For a discussion of the class dynamics of criminal prosecution in the Puritan colonies, see Edgar J. McManus, *Law and Liberty in Early New England: Criminal Justice and Due Process, 1620–1692* (Amherst: University of Massachusetts Press, 1993), 120–22.

23. This analysis of the witnesses involved in *Parsons v. Bridgeman* is drawn from Demos, *Entertaining Satan*, 260–65, 268. Hall, *Witch-Hunting*, 110.

24. Weisman, *Witchcraft, Magic, and Religion*, 88; Malcolm Gaskill, "Witchcraft in Early Modern Kent: Stereotypes and the Background to Accusations," in *Witchcraft in Early Modern Europe*, ed. Barry et al., 265–67; E. J. Kent, "Masculinity and Male Witches in Old and New England, 1593–1680," *History Workshop* 60 (autumn 2005): 73–75.

Recent scholarship on witchcraft in early modern Europe notes that many witchcraft cases were fought out between accusers and accused who occupied similar social strata; see Malcolm Gaskill, *Crime and Mentalities in Early Modern England* (Cambridge: Cambridge University Press, 2000), 36–38, 61; and Thomas Robisheaux, in *The Last Witch of Langenburg: Murder in a German Village* (New York: W. W. Norton, 2009), tells the fascinating tale of a witchcraft case that emerged out of tensions between villagers of roughly equal social status.

25. Henry M. Burt, *The First Century of the History of Springfield: The Official Records from 1636–1736* (Springfield, MA: Henry M. Burt, 1898), 1:190–92. Of the men who gave testimony against Hugh Parsons, 21 appear on the Springfield tax assessment taken shortly before his trial, 13 had land holding that fell within 10 acres of Parsons's, and 12 had assessment within 3 shillings of Parsons's.

26. Demos, *Entertaining Satan*, 234–37 (on page 236 Demos identifies seven of Elizabeth Garlick's nine accusers as low-status individuals); *REH*, 1:66, 79–81.

27. The importance of high-status accusers was not unique to New England but also characterized witch prosecutions in Europe; for example, see Clive Holmes, "Women: Witnesses, and Witches," *Past & Present* 140 (1993): 51–59.

28. Tomlinson, *Witch Prosecutions*, 69–72; Demos, *Entertaining Satan*, 213–20, 236–38, 288–89; *REH*, 1:128–30, 133; Hall, *Witch-Hunting*, 214, 216, 217; and Clive Holmes, "Women: Witnesses and Witches," 53–54. For information on the Gardiner family and Gardiner's Island, see Robert David Lion Gardiner, "The Gardiner Family and the Lordship and Manor of Gardiner's Island," *New York Genealogical and Bio-graphical Record* 23 (October 1892): 159–90.

29. Tomlinson, *Witch Prosecution*, 82–102, 125–27, 131–32; Demos, *Entertaining Satan*, 360–65; Carolyn S. Langdon, "A Complaint against Katherine Harrison, 1669," *Bulletin of the Connecticut Historical Society* 34 (1969): 21. Alice Wakeley, the wife of the prosperous merchant and witch suspect James Wakeley, also eventually offered testimony against Harrison: see SWP-CSL, no. 17.

30. Keith Thomas, *Religion and the Decline of Magic* (New York: Charles Scribner's Sons, 1971), 560; Weisman, *Witchcraft, Magic, and Religion*, 45, 78.

31. SWP-JHL, W-9.

32. Drake, *Annals*, 71–72, 224; Burt, *History of Springfield*, 1:73; Joseph Smith, ed., *Colonial Justice in Western Massachusetts (1639–1702): The Pynchon Court Record* (Cambridge, MA: Harvard University Press, 1961), 219–20.

All told, before 1670 there were eighteen legal proceedings for occult crime in New England for which enough depositional testimony survives to give some sense of whether or not the accused and their accusers had a history of conflict. Seven clearly reveal a background of interpersonal disputes. These cases include those of Elizabeth Garlick, William Graves, Katherine Palmer, Hugh and Mary Parsons, Eunice Cole, Winifred and Mary Holman, and John Godfrey. The cases that do not exhibit evidence of long-standing rivalries between accusers and accused include those of the Ayers, Greemsmiths, Blackleaches, Mary Barnes, James Wakeley, Elizabeth Seager, John Brown, Jane Walford, Ann Burt, Elizabeth Godman, and Katherine Harrison. The first six cases were related to the Hartford witch panic of 1662–63—an unusual and unevenly documented instance of witch-hunting that diverged somewhat from regular patterns of prosecution. Putting them aside for the moment, this leaves only four witch prosecutions in which there is no known history of conflict between accusers and the accused. It is quite possible that a pattern of contention undergirded these cases but simply did not come up in witness testimony. Indeed, accusers who wished to shield themselves against the charge that malice motivated their actions had reason to suppress such information. Finally, the cases of Elizabeth Godman and Katherine Harrison involved tensions between the accused and several witnesses, but it is not completely clear if they predated witchcraft accusations or were a product of them.

33. NHTR, 1:249–50; RCNH, 2:29.

34. *REH*, 1:140; Hall, *Witch-Hunting*, 144, 120; *RQCE*, 2:157; Otis G. Hammond, ed., *New Hampshire Court Records, 1640–1692: Court Papers, 1652–1668* (State of New Hampshire, 1943), 38, 258; *NHHS*, 1:257.

35. Demos, *Entertaining Satan*, 293–98; Karlsen, *Devil in the Shape of a Woman*, 184; Weisman, *Witchcraft, Magic, and Religion*, 44.

36. Diane Purkiss, "Woman's Stories of Witchcraft in Early Modern England: The House, the Body, the Child," *Gender & History* 7 (November 1995): 411–12; *NHHS*, 1:255; J. H. Lefroy. ed., *Memorials of the Discovery and Early Settlement of the Bermudas or Somers Islands, 1515–1687* (London: Longmans, Green, 1879), 2:610.

37. Thomas Ady, *A Candle in the Dark* (London: Robert Ibbitson, 1656), 114–15; *RCNH*, 2:35–36; Lefroy, *Memorials*, 2:621.

38. Demos, *Entertaining Satan*, 293–99; Karlsen, *Devil in the Shape of a Woman*, 184; Weisman, *Witchcraft, Magic, and Religion*, 44; Macfarlane, *Witchcraft in Tudor and Stuart England*, 173–76; Thomas, *Religion and the Decline of Magic*, 552–53, 561–66.

39. *NHTR*, 1:252; *RCNH*, 2:152; SWP-JHL, W-15; Drake, *Annals*, 229–30.

40. SWP-JHL, W-10; Demos, "John Godfrey and his Neighbors: Witchcraft and the Social Web in Colonial Massachusetts," *WMQ* 33 (April 1976): 247; Drake, *Annals*, 254–55, 256. For discussions of how early modern Europeans believed that refusing a witch what they desired could lead to magical retaliation, see Thomas, *Religion and the Decline of Magic*, 506–8, 553–58, 565–66; and MacFarlane, *Witchcraft in Tudor and Stuart England*, 104–5.

41. Demos, "John Godfrey," 247; Hall, *Witch-Hunting*, 117–18; Kent, "Masculinity and Male Witches," 81–82; Drake, *Annals*, 224, 228.

42. Demos, *Entertaining Satan*, 257–68; Hall, *Witch-Hunting*, 134–43.

43. Hall, *Witch-Hunting*, 134–43, 102–3; SWP-JHL, W-8, Tomlinson, *Witchcraft Prosecution*, 117–18; Norbert R. Bankert, "More on the Identity of Abigail (Graves) Dibble and Her Tragic Death and Suspicions of Witchcraft," *New England Historic and Genealogical Register* 155 (July 2001): 273–78.

44. Demos, *Entertaining Satan*, 352, 510n65. Mrs. Robbins's death took place shortly after giving birth to Samuel in September 1659.The infant died about two months later, and Mr. Robbins passed in June 1660. Tomlinson, *Witchcraft Prosecution*, 36; SWP-CSL, no. 16; Sherman W. Adams and Henry R. Stiles, *The History of Ancient Wethersfield, Connecticut* (1904; reprint Camden, ME: Picton Press, 1995), 2:471–72; Drake, *Annals*, 66; Benjamin F. Thompson, *History of Long Island* (New York: E. French, 1839), 151–53.

45. Thomas, *Religion and the Decline of Magic*, 535–36, 539.

46. Purkiss, "Women's Stories of Witchcraft in Early Modern England," 420–21; *REH*, 1:154–55.

47. Richard Godbeer, *The Devil's Dominion: Magic and Religion in Early New England* (New York: Cambridge University Press, 1992), 42–46; SWP-JHL, W-4. See chapter 1 for a detailed breakdown of the legal action taken against accused witches in New England before 1760.

48. Thomas, *Religion and the Decline of Magic*, 539; SWP-JHL, W-10; Drake, *Annals*, 254–55; Hall, *Witch-Hunting*, 104–6.

49. *REH*, 1:135–36; Tomlinson, *Witchcraft Prosecution*, 53–56; *RPC*, 106–7, 114, 131, 219.

50. Demos, *Entertaining Satan*, 195–97; Weisman, *Witchcraft, Magic, and Religion*, 44, 89. This same dynamic also shaped witchcraft episodes in England; see Macfarlane, *Witchcraft in Tudor and Stuart England*, 196, 204; and Thomas, *Religion and the Decline of Magic*, 555–57.

51. *NHTR*, 1:252; Hall, *Witch-Hunting*, 216.

52. Thomas, *Religion and the Decline of Magic*, 543; Hall, *Witch-Hunting*, 102.

53. Malcolm Gaskill, in "The Devil in the Shape of a Man: Witchcraft, Conflict, and Belief in Jacobean England," *Historical Research* 71 (June 1998): 162–67, explores the connection between witchcraft and personal and community conflict. For a discussion of the role of conflict in early New England, see Stephen Innes, *Labor in a New Land: Economy and Society in Seventeenth-Century Springfield* (Princeton, NJ: Princeton University Press, 1983), xvii–viii, 123–29, 171.

54. Demos, *Entertaining Satan*, 250–56; Hall, *Witch-Hunting*, 105, 110.

55. Paul R. Lucas, *Valley of Discord: Church and Society along the Connecticut River, 1636–1725* (Hanover, NH: University Press of New England, 1976), 50–51, 75–76; Homer Worthington Brainard et al., *The Gilbert Family: Descendants of Thomas Gilbert, 1582–1659 of Mt. Wollaston (Braintree), Windsor, and Wethersfield* (New Haven, CT, 1953), 20; Demos, *Entertaining Satan*, 364–65; Gaskill, "Witchcraft in Early Modern Kent," 267–68.

56. John Hale, *A Modest Inquiry into the Nature of Witchcraft* (1702), in *Narratives of the Witchcraft Cases, 1648–1706*, ed. George Lincoln Burr (New York: Charles Scribner's Sons, 1914), 409.

57. James Sharpe, *Instruments of Darkness: Witchcraft in Early Modern England* (Philadelphia: University of Pennsylvania Press, 1996), 191–93.

58. Perhaps the best and most eloquent case that the Salem crisis included acts of fraud can be found in Bernard Rosenthal, *Salem Story: Reading the Witch Trials of 1692* (New York: Cambridge University Press, 1993).

59. A number of historians have discussed witchcraft as the collective expelling of a perceived evil: see Demos, *Entertaining Satan*, 301–2; and Virginia Bernard, "Religion, Politics, and Witchcraft in Bermuda," *WMQ* 67 (October 2010): 677–708.

60. Demos, *Entertaining Satan*, 235–39. For witness testimony presented against the Parsons, see Drake, *Annals*, 219–58.

61. Lucas, *Valley of Discord*, especially chaps 1–4; Demos, *Entertaining Satan*, 340–67.

62. The points I present in this paragraph draw heavily from John Demos's analysis of the community dynamics and timing of witch prosecutions, see *Entertaining Satan*, 340–67. Bernard, "Religion, Politics, and Witchcraft in Bermuda," 677–708 (especially 707–8).

63. Thomas, *Religion and the Decline of Magic*, 566; Demos, *Entertaining Satan*, 307–9.

64. My analysis in the second half of this paragraph follows a path first outlined by John Demos, see *Entertaining Satan*, 304–5. HCC, 7; RCA 3, 153.

6. "Very Awful and Amazing"

1. SWP-JHL, W-6.

2. SWP-CSL, no. 5.

3. Due to frustrating gaps in the historical record, and barring the discovery of a trove of lost documents, it is impossible to fully recover the story of the Hartford witch hunt. Nevertheless, enough evidence survives to piece together a narrative. For recent accounts of the episode, see Walter W. Woodward, *Prospero's America: John Winthrop, Jr., Alchemy, and the Creation of New England Culture, 1606–1676* (Chapel

Hill: University of North Carolina Press for the OIEAHC, 2010), 230–37; and R. G. Tomlinson, *Witch Prosecution: Chasing the Devil in Connecticut* (Rockland, ME: Picton Press, 2012), 81–114.

4. SWP-JHL, W-6.

5. SWP-JHL, W-6.

6. SWP-CSL, no. 5; Sarah Tarlow, *Ritual, Belief, and the Dead in Early Modern Britain and Ireland* (New York: Cambridge University Press, 2002), 164–65.

7. Tomlinson, *Witchcraft Prosecution*, 85–86; Woodward, *Prospero's America*, 231–32. On the one hand, the idea that the autopsy took place on or near March 31 (five days after Elizabeth Kelly's death) is supported by the fact that Dr. Rossiter was living in Guilford, and so it would have taken time for a request for his services to reach him and for him to travel north to Hartford. On the other, the doctor had already been shuttling back and forth between his home and Hartford in order to treat the town's ailing minister, Samuel Stone, and it is possible that he was already on the scene when Elizabeth Kelly died. Nevertheless, the doctor's description of Elizabeth Kelly's corpse gives the impression that he examined a body that had been dead for several days.

8. SWP-JHL, W-5; Tomlinson, *Witchcraft Prosecution*, 85–88. Autopsies, whether related to cases of witchcraft or not, were extremely rare in early New England, and there is only one other recorded instance of the procedure in the region before the one performed on Kelly (referenced in Tomlinson). Thus, it is doubtful that Dr. Rossiter had much experience with postmortem examinations unless he obtained it before he left England for the New World.

9. Tomlinson, *Witchcraft Prosecution*, 89; SWP-CSL, no. 3 and 4.

10. *RPC*, 247; SWP-JHL, W-2; Tomlinson, *Witchcraft Prosecution*, 89–91.

11. Lucius Barnes Barbour, *Families of Early Hartford*, Connecticut (Baltimore, MD: Genealogical Publishing Company, 1977), 351; *RPC*, 237

12. Barbour, *Families of Early Hartford*, 185; CCHS 6:121, 129, 134; *CMHS*, 8:466.

13. When Anne Cole started suffering from her strange affliction remains a point of debate. Andrew and Mary Sanford came before a grand jury for witchcraft on June 6 and June 13, 1662, respectively, and their indictment accused them of having "acted things in a preternatural way beyond the course of nature to the great prejudice of the comforts of several members of this commonwealth" (*RPC*, 251). This wording implies that the couple faced trial, not for alleged crimes against a lone individual, but for bewitching a group of people. This means that their indictments must have been handed down after Anne Cole joined Elizabeth Kelly as an alleged victim of witchcraft and indicates that Cole's supposed bewitchment started sometime after March and before June. Although there is no definitive evidence that Elizabeth Kelly's death preceded Cole's affliction, circumstance points in that direction. Thus, like other narratives of the Hartford witch hunt, mine starts with Kelly's death.

14. *CMHS*, 8:466–68; Tomlinson, *Witchcraft Prosecution*, 94–95.

15. *CMHS*, 4th series, 8:466–68; Charles J. Hoadly, "A Case of Witchcraft in Hartford," *Connecticut Magazine* 5 (1899): 558–59.

16. SWP-JHL, W-4; *RPC*, 251, 132; Gale Ion Harris, "William and Goodwife Ayers of Hartford, Connecticut: Witches Who Got Away," *American Genealogist* 75

(July 2000): 198; William Deloss Love, *The Colonial History of Hartford* (Hartford, CT: Published by the author, 1904), 284.

17. Tomlinson, *Witchcraft Prosecution*, 94; *CCHS*, 6:136.

18. *CMHS*, 4th Series, 8:467–68. Whiting's narrative is rather vague about when Greensmith's turn of heart took place, but she probably gave her confession sometime in the fall of 1662.

19. *CMHS*, 4th Series, 8:467–68; *SWP-JHL*, W-1.

20. *RPC*, 251; Tomlinson, *Witchcraft Prosecution*, 92–93.

21. Tomlinson, *Witchcraft Prosecution*, 90–9; *CMHS*, 4th Series, 8:469; *RPC*, 258; Gale Ion Harris, "William and Goodwife Ayres of Hartford, Connecticut," 199–200, 205. Increase Mather, *An Essay for the Recording of Remarkable Providences* (1684), in *Narratives of the Witchcraft Cases, 1648–1706*, ed. George Lincoln Burr (New York: Charles Scribner's Sons, 1914), 21—although Mather never names William and Judith Ayers in his account, they are the only married couple who fled the Hartford hunt and so the story must refer to them.

22. *CCHS*, 24:8; *RPC*, 260–61; *HCC*, 50, 53; *PRCC*, 2:34, 59, 531; Tomlinson, *Witchcraft Prosecution*, 94, 105–6—after she won her freedom, Judith Varlett went to New Netherland where she soon married Nicholas Bayard, Governor Sturyesant's nephew.

23. Quote from William Goffe's diary in Thomas Hutchinson, *The History of the Province of Massachusetts Bay* (Boston: Thomas and John Fleet, 1797), 2:17; *RPC*, 257–58; Tomlinson, *Witchcraft Prosecution*, 97–100. In the months and years that followed, Hartford officials disposed of Nathaniel Greensmith's estate, see: *HCC*, 37, 42.

24. *RPC*, 259, 265; Tomlinson, *Witchcraft Prosecution*, 100–101; Frederick Wayne Barnes and Edna Cleo (Bauer) Barnes, eds., *Thomas Barnes, Hartford, Connecticut, 8,591 Descendants (& Spouses), 14 Generations, 1615–2001* (Baltimore, MD: Gateway Press, 2001), 1:3–4, 6–7.

25. *SWP-JHL*, W-1. On January 20, the same day that the court condemned Mary Barnes and the Greensmiths, Mr. Blackleach sued John Stedman and Moses Mudge for slander. The timing of the suits and that Blackleach demanded the massive sum of £200 pounds in damages (indicating that the offending words related to a serious matter such as accusing someone of witchcraft) makes it very likely that the legal action was related to the Hartford hunt: see *RPC*, 261.

26. *SWP-JHL*, W-1; *RPC*, 56, 161; John P. Demos, *Entertaining Satan: Witchcraft and the Culture of New England* (New York: Oxford University Press, 1982), 352–53; Gale Ion Harris, "Henry and Katherine Palmer of Wethersfield, Connecticut and Newport, Rhode Island," *The Genealogist* 17 (fall 2003): 178–80; Tomlinson, *Witchcraft Prosecution*, 110. Records show that Henry Palmer was living in Rhode Island (specifically Newport) by 1669: see *Rhode Island Court Records: Volume 2, 1662–70* (Providence: Rhode Island Historical Society, 1922), 85; and *Rhode Island Land Evidences: Volume 1, 1648–96* (Providence: Rhode Island Historical Society, 1921), 25.

27. *RPC*, 259–60; *SWP-JHL*, W-2 and W-4; Tomlinson, *Witchcraft Prosecution*, 107–8.

28. The body of scholarship on the Salem witch crisis is large and ever growing; however, three of the best and most recent studies of the hunt include Mary Beth Norton, *In the Devil's Snare: The Salem Witchcraft Crisis of 1692* (New York: Vintage Books, 2002); Emerson W. Baker, *A Storm of Witchcraft: The Salem Trials and the*

American Experience (New York: Oxford University Press, 2015); and Benjamin C. Ray, *Satan & Salem: The Witch-Hunt Crisis of 1692* (Charlottesville: University of Virginia Press, 2015). For the most thorough reconstruction of the Fairfield witch hunt, see Richard Godbeer, *Escaping Salem: The Other Witch Hunt of 1692* (New York: Oxford University Press, 2005).

29. James Sharpe, *Instruments of Darkness: Witchcraft in Early Modern England* (Philadelphia: University of Pennsylvania Press, 1996), 128–47, 98–99, 126; Malcolm Gaskill, "Witches and Witchcraft Prosecutions, 1560–1660," in *Early Modern Kent, 1540–1640*, ed. Michael Zell (Woodbridge, Suffolk: The Boydell Press, 2000), 245–46; Brian P. Levack, *Witch-hunting in Scotland: Law, Politics and Religion* (New York: Routledge, 2008), 81–97; Brian P. Levack, *The Witch-Hunt in Early Modern Europe*, 2nd ed. (London: Longman, 1995), 174–77, 211–13.

30. For discussions of religious conflict within Salem Village, see Richard Latner, "'Here Are No Newters': Witchcraft and Religious Discord in Salem Village and Andover," *NEQ* 79 (March 2006): 92–122; and Benjamin Ray, "Satan's War against the Covenant in Salem Village, 1692," *NEQ* 80 (March 2007): 69–95. See Norton, *In the Devil's Snare*, and Baker, *A Storm of Witchcraft*, for discussions of the links between the Salem panic, war, and political instability. For an in-depth study of England's East Anglian witch panic, see Malcolm Gaskill, *Witchfinders: A Seventeenth-Century English Tragedy* (Cambridge, MA: Harvard University Press, 2000). Virginia Bernard explores the ties between the English Civil War and witch-hunting in Bermuda in "Religion, Politics, and Witchcraft in Bermuda, 1651–55," *WMQ* 67 (October 2000): 677–708.

31. Robert M. Bliss, *Revolution and Empire: English Politics and the American Colonies in the Seventeenth Century* (Manchester: Manchester University Press, 1990), especially 74–87, 132–47.

32. Tomlinson, *Witchcraft Prosecution*, 81–82; Rebecca J. Tannenbaum, *The Healer's Calling: Women and Medicine in Early New England* (Ithaca, NY: Cornell University Press, 2002), 55.

33. For surviving documentation related to the Hartford Controversy, see "Papers Relating to the Controversy in the Church in Hartford, 1656–59," in *CCHS*, 2:51–125. The tale of the Hartford Controversy is long and complicated, and the most thorough treatment of the episode is found in Paul R. Lucas, *Valley of Discord: Church and Society along the Connecticut River, 1636–1725* (Hanover, NH: University Press of New England, 1976), 30–36, 43–49. Also see William K. Holdsworth, "Law and Society in Colonial Connecticut, 1636–1672" (PhD diss., Claremont Graduate School, 1974), 208–10, 215–17; and George Leon Walker, *History of the First Church in Hartford, 1633–1883* (Hartford, CT: Brown & Gross, 1884), 153–75.

34. Demos, *Entertaining Satan*, 342–45; Lucas, *Valley of Discord*, 50–51.

35. Lucas, *Valley of Discord*, 50–51, 75–76; Holdsworth, "Law and Society in Colonial Connecticut," 211. Hollister and his followers maintained a legal offensive against Reverend Russell that continued after he left Wethersfield: see *RPC*, 196–97, 202–3.

36. Homer Worthington Brainard et al., *The Gilbert Family: Descendants of Thomas Gilbert, 1582?-1659 of Mt. Wollaston (Braintree), Windsor, and Wethersfield* (New Haven, CT, 1953), 20.

37. See chapter 3 for a discussion of the age, sex, and marital status of witch suspects in New England before 1670.

38. Tomlinson, *Witchcraft Prosecution*, 85, 90, 96, 109–10; *RPC*, 81, 86, 96–97, 107–8, 111, 132, 145, 156, 171–72, 201, 202–3, 245; *PRCC*, 1:186–87; *HCC*, 44–45.

39. Charles W. Manwaring, ed., *A Digest of Early Connecticut Probate Records* (Hartford, CT: R.S. Peck, 1904), 1:121–22, 158, 276, 312; *CCHS*, 14:428–30, 496–98; Barnes, *Thomas Barnes of Hartford*, 1–4; *PRCC*, 1:227, 2:521.

40. Sharpe, *Instruments of Darkness*, 131–34. For the case of Rebecca Nurse, see Bernard Rosenthal, *Salem Story: Reading the Witch Trials of 1692* (New York: Cambridge University Press, 1993), 90–94; and Norton, *In the Devil's Snare*, 47, 61–65. For a discussion of how the Salem witch hunt paralleled more ordinary patterns of witch prosecution in New England, see Richard Latner, "The Long and Short of Salem Witchcraft," *Journal of Social History* (fall 2008): 137–56.

41. Many scholars who explore the Salem crisis have noted its unusual level of diabolical testimony, and a recent study that gives particular attention to this topic is Benjamin Ray's, *Satan & Salem*, 5, 33–34, 85–92. Sharpe, *Instruments of Darkness*, 76, 134–37.

42. *CMHS*, 8:466–69; SWP-CSL, no. 1; SWP-JHL, W-1; SWP-JHL, W-4.

43. Latner, "The Long and Short of Salem Witchcraft;" Sharpe, *Instruments of Darkness*, 128–29; Levack, *The Witch-Hunt in Early Modern Europe*, 175.

44. Brian Levack, "State-building and Witch Hunting in Early Modern Euorpe," in *Witchcraft in Early Modern Europe: Studies in Culture and Belief*, ed. Johnathan Barry et al. (New York: Cambridge University Press, 1996), 104–7. Besides Rebecca Greensmith, the other two accused witches who confessed to the crime before 1670 were Mary Johnson of Wethersfield in 1648 and Goody Bassett of Fairfield in 1651; see Tomlinson, *Witchcraft Prosecution*, 32–33, 40–42.

45. Johannes Dillinger, "The Political Aspects of German Witch Hunts," *Magic, Ritual, and Witchcraft* (summer 2009): 66–72; James Sharpe, "The Devil in East Anglia: The Matthew Hopkins Trials Reconsidered," in *Witchcraft in Early Modern Europe*, 237–39; Levack, *Witch-Hunting in Scotland*, 56.

46. Walker, *History of the First Church in Hartford*, 182–84; Barbour, *Families of Early Hartford*, 298; Love, *The Colonial History of Hartford*, 284–85; Woodward, *Prospero's America*, 233–34. Historians who study the Salem crisis invariably stress the role that civil officials and some local clergymen played in expanding and perpetuating the crisis. Recent studies which pay close attention to this issue are Ray, *Satan & Salem*, especially see 34–43, 94–102, and 144–54; and Richard Latner, "'Here Are No Newters,'" 106–16.

47. *CMHS*, 8:467–68; Cotton Mather, *Memorable Providences, Relating to Witchcrafts and Possessions* (1689), in Burr ed., *Narratives of the Witchcraft Cases*, 136.

48. *CMHS*, 8:468. That court testimony and confessions gathered during witchcraft trials were joint products of the elite and common folk was not unique to New England and shaped witch prosecutions in England and elsewhere in Europe—for example, see Clive Holmes, "Women: Witnesses and Witches," *Past & Present* 140 (1993): 45–78.

49. Norton, *In the Devil's Snare*, 20–22, 30–40; Ray, *Satan & Salem*, 44–65; Baker, *A Storm of Witchcraft*, 98–124; Godbeer, *Escaping Salem*, 35–40, 45–49.

50. Increase Mather, *Remarkable Providences*, in Burr ed., *Narratives of the Witchcraft Cases*, 18, 19; Richard Weisman, *Witchcraft, Magic, and Religion in 17th-Century*

Massachusetts (Amherst: The University of Massachusetts Press, 1984), 47–49; *CMHS*, 8:468; SWP-CSL, no. 4, 5; SWP-JHL, W-6.

51. Godbeer, *Escaping Salem*, 13–50; Rosenthal, *Salem Story*, 32–50; Ray, *Satan & Salem*, 44–65.

52. Carol Karlsen, *The Devil in the Shape of a Woman: Witchcraft in Colonial New England* (1987; reprint New York: W.W. Norton, 1998), 223–25—citations refer to the 1998 edition; Samuel G. Drake, ed., *Annals of Witchcraft in New England* (Boston: W. Elliot Woodward, 1869), 228–29; David D. Hall, *Witch-Hunting in Seventeenth-Century New England: A Documentary History, 1638–1692*, 2nd ed. (Durham, NC: Duke University Press, 1999), 188.

53. I compiled figures concerning the proportion of bewitched males and females from data found in Weisman, *Witchcraft, Magic, and Religion*, 50–51; and Karlsen, *Devil in the Shape of a Woman*, 224. In both cases, roughly 12 percent of the afflicted were male and the remaining 88 percent female. Similarly, Richard Godbeer concludes that 86 percent of the bewitched were female; see *The Devil's Dominion: Magic and Religion in Early New England* (New York: Cambridge University Press, 1992), 114.

54. Tomlinson, *Witchcraft Prosecution*, 69, 82–83. Figures on the ages of New England's bewitched are drawn from Karlsen, *Devil in the Shape of a Woman*, 224; and Weisman, *Witchcraft, Magic, and Religion*, 51. Karlsen's data shows that about half (54 percent) of the bewitched were under nineteen, while Weisman's figures (which are limited to Massachusetts) indicate that 65 percent fell into this age group. For references to the relative youth of the afflicted in England, see Sharpe, *Instruments of Darkness*, 196–97.

55. For data on the marital status of the bewitched, see Karlsen, *Devil in the Shape of a Woman*, 224. Data on ordinary accusers can be found in Karlsen, *Devil in the Shape of a Woman*, 184–85; and Weisman, *Witchcraft, Magic, and Religion*, 50–51.

56. Karlsen, *Devil in the Shape of a Woman*, 226–31. Elizabeth Kelly's parents were poor, which is borne out by the fact that her mother received support from the town of Hartford after her father's death; see *CCHS*, 6:146, 147. On the status of Branch, Knapp, and several Salem accusers as servants, see Godbeer, *Escaping Salem*, 3; Demos, *Entertaining Satan*, 127; Karlsen, *Devil in the Shape of a Woman*, 227–28.

57. Karlsen, *Devil in the Shape of a Woman*, 230–31; Keith Thomas, *Religion and the Decline of Magic* (New York: Charles Scribner's Sons, 1971), 480–81; Godbeer, *The Devil's Dominion*, 107; Mather, *Remarkable Providences*, in Burr, ed., *Narratives of the Witchcraft Cases*, 18; *CMHS*, 8:466; *CCHS*, 6:152.

58. SWP-JHL, W-6; *CMHS*, 8:467–68; Demos, *Entertaining Satan*, 99–111; Godbeer, *Escaping Salem*, 13–32; Ray, *Satan & Salem*, 44–65.

59. Holmes, "Women: Witnesses and Witches," 59–65; Michael Dalton, *The Country Justice* (London: Company of Stationers, 1655), 343.

60. David Harley provides an excellent discussion of the distinctions between obsession and possession, the difficulties contemporaries had in distinguishing between the two, and how the process of diagnosis could have significant implications for witch-hunting: see Harley, "Explaining Salem: Calvinist Psychology and the Diagnosis of Possession," *AHR* 101 (April 1996): 307–30. On the connection early modern English folk made between possession, obsession, and witchcraft, see Sharp, *Instruments of Darkness*, 190–93; and Keith Thomas, *Religion and the Decline of Magic*, 477–92. For the references to Katherine Branch, see SWP-JHL, W-19.

61. Harley, "Explaining Salem," 311–12.

62. Frederick Valetta, *Witchcraft, Magic and Superstition in England, 1640–70* (Burlington, VT: Ashgate, 2000), 44–45; Harley, "Explaining Salem," 312–16.

63. Harley, "Explaining Salem," 316–22; Demos, *Entertaining Satan*, 99–111.

64. For commentary on the upstanding Christian character of Anne Cole and her family, see John Whiting's letter to Increase Mather in *CMHS*, 8:466–67.

65. Godbeer, *The Devil's Dominion*, 108; *CMHS*, 8:468; Demos, *Entertaining Satan*, 100–101, 119–21. On March 20, 1692, the Reverend Deodat Lawson preached as a guest minister in Salem Village's meetinghouse, and during the service Abigail Williams and Goody Bathshua Pope interrupted him during his prayers and sermon; see Norton, *In the Devil's Snare*, 55.

66. Demos, *Entertaining Satan*, 159–60; Karlsen, *Devil in the Shape of a Woman*, 244–48.

67. Karlsen, *Devil in the Shape of a Woman*, 248, 251; Holmes, "Woman: Witnesses and Witches," 59–65.

68. Godbeer, *The Devil's Dominion*, 108–9, 117.

69. The exception in the Salem episode was Ann Putnam Jr. who, like Anne Cole, came from a prominent and pious family. In 1706 Putnam made a public confession to the members of the Salem Village church concerning her role in the Salem trials—she died unmarried in 1715: see Richard Godbeer, ed., *The Salem Witch Hunt: A Brief History with Documents* (Boston: Bedford/St. Martins, 2011), 176–77; and Norton, *In the Devil's Snare*, 310–11.

70. Tomlinson, *Witchcraft Prosecution*, 105; Hutchinson, *History of Massachusetts*, 2:17; Increase Mather, *An Essay for the Recording of Illustrious Providences* (Boston: Printed by Samuel Green, 1684), 75, 128.

7. "According to God's Law"

1. *RPC*, 259–60; *SWP-JHL*, W-2.

2. *HCC*, 7, 48–49, 50, 61–62; *PRCC*, 2:531.

3. William Perkins, *A Discourse on the Damned Art of Witchcraft* (Cambridge: Cantrell Legge, Printer to the University of Cambridge, 1618), 642.

4. James Sharpe and Richard Godbeer note how elite and popular conceptions of witchcraft often clashed during court proceedings in England and New England: see Sharpe, *Instruments of Darkness: Witchcraft in Early Modern England* (Philadelphia: University of Pennsylvania Press, 1996), 232–33; and Godbeer, *The Devil's Dominion: The Devil's Dominion: Magic and Religion in Early New England* (New York: Cambridge University Press, 1992), 153–78.

5. Brian P. Levack, *The Witch-Hunt in Early Modern Europe*, 2nd ed. (Harlow, UK: Longman, 1995), 69–71.

6. Richard Weisman, *Witchcraft, Magic, and Religion in Seventeenth-Century Massachusetts* (Amherst: University of Massachusetts Press, 1984), 10–11; Levack, *Witch-Hunt in Early Modern Europe*, 71–76; John Tedeschi, "Inquisitorial Law and the Witch," in *Early Modern European Witchcraft: Centers and Peripheries*, ed. Bengt Ankarloo and Gustav Henningsen (New York: Oxford University Press, 1990), 83–115; Michael D. Bailey, "The Age of Magicians: Periodization in the History of European Magic," *Magic, Ritual, and Witchcraft* 3 (summer 2008): 10–13; Matteo Duni, *Under the Devil's*

Spell: Witches, Sorcerers and the Inquisition in Renaissance Italy (Florence: Syracuse University in Florence, 2007), 13–14.

7. Levack, *Witch-Hunt in Early Modern Europe*, 76–84; Tedeschi, "Inquisitorial Law and the Witch," 97–103; Joseph Klaits, *Servants of Satan: The Age of the Witch Hunts* (Bloomington: Indiana University Press, 1985), 128–58.

8. Levack, *Witch-Hunt in Early Modern Europe*, 73–74; Sharpe, *Instruments of Darkness*, 214–15; Malcolm Gaskill, *Witchfinders: a Seventeenth-Century English Tragedy* (Cambridge, MA: Harvard University Press, 2005), 106–7.

William Perkins was one English demonologist who opened the door to torture. He advised that firm and persistent questioning was the best way to gather information from a suspect and asserted that torture could be used "upon strong and great presumptions going before, and when the party is obstinate": see Perkins, *Discourse on the Damned Art of Witchcraft*, 643. Writing at midcentury, the jurist Sir Robert Filmer attempted to close the door to this exception, arguing that torture was illegal in all court proceedings except for cases of treason: see Filmer, *An Advertisement to the Jurymen of England, Touching Witches* (London: Printed by I.G. for Richard Royston, 1653), 10.

9. Brian P. Levack, "State-building and Witch Hunting in Early Modern Europe," in *Witchcraft in Early Modern Europe: Studies in Culture and Belief*, ed. Jonathan Barry et al. (New York: Cambridge University Press, 1996), 96–115; Johannes Dillinger, "The Political Aspects of German Witch Hunts," *Magic, Ritual, and Witchcraft* (summer 2009): 62–81; Brian P. Levack, *Witch-hunting in Scotland: Law, Politics, and Religion* (New York: Routledge, 2008), 2–3, 24–30.

10. Sharpe, *Instruments of Darkness*, 214–15; Levack, "State-building and Witch Hunting," 108–12.

11. Gail Sussman Marcus, " 'Due Execution of the Generall Rules of Righteousness': Criminal Procedure in New Haven Town and Colony, 1638–1658," in *Saints and Revolutionaries: Essays on Early American History*, ed. David D. Hall, John M. Murrin, and Thad W. Tate (New York: W. W. Norton, 1984), 102–3, 117–20, 128–29; John M. Murrin, "Magistrates, Sinners, and a Precarious Liberty," in *Saints and Revolutionaries*, 168, 182; Edgar J. McManus, *Law and Liberty in Early New England: Criminal Justice and Due Process, 1620–1692* (Amherst: University of Massachusetts Press, 1993), 107–8.

12. William K. Holdsworth, "Law and Society in Colonial Connecticut, 1636–1672" (PhD diss., Claremont Graduate School, 1974), 475–79; Levack, "State-building and Witch Hunting," 109–10; McManus, *Law and Liberty in Early New England*, 94–97; Nathan Matthews, "The Results of the Prejudice against Lawyers in Massachusetts in the 17th Century," *Massachusetts Law Quarterly* 13 (1928): 73–94; Jack P. Greene, *Pursuits of Happiness: The Social Development of Early Modern British Colonies and the Formation of American Culture* (Chapel Hill: The University of North Carolina Press, 1988), 178.

13. Marcus, "Due Execution of the Generall Rules of Righteousness," 127; Murrin, "Magistrates, Sinners, and a Precarious Liberty," 176.

14. Richard Bernard, *A Guide to Grand Jury Men* (London: Felix Kyngston, 1629), 213.

15. McManus, *Law and Liberty*, 33, 132–33; Weisman, *Witchcraft, Magic, and Religion*, 12–13.

16. McManus, *Law and Liberty*, 17, 76, 82–87, 99–100, 103, 105–6; Holdsworth, "Law and Society," 148, 149–55, 161, 370–71, 406–7, 452–59, 93–94; Murrin, "Magistrates, Sinners, and a Precarious Liberty," 152–206.

Before the 1690s, the New England colonies lacked county sheriffs, which meant that all local law enforcement was thrust on town constables. They had to cooperate in order to extradite a suspect from one jurisdiction to another, and all of the New England colonies, with the exception of Rhode Island, had extradition agreements with one another. This helps explain why fleeing from one colony to another, and especially to Rhode Island, was often an effective strategy for witch suspects to escape prosecution: see McManus, *Law and Liberty*, 58–59, 65.

While the early Puritan colonies did eventually allow for defendants to retain a lawyer in civil litigation, they banned defense counsel in serious criminal cases. What appears as a wrong-way-round practice is explained by the fact that in medieval England one of the disabilities that came with being charged with the original felony, treason, was the loss of any legal counsel. This practice may have then simply been extended to other felonies such as witchcraft: see, McManus, *Law and Liberty*, 93–94.

17. McManus, *Law and Liberty*, 167, 171, 173–74, 176–78; CCA, 10–11.

18. Richard Weisman notes that "in purely formal terms, legal action against witchcraft . . . cannot be distinguished from legal action against other capital offenses" and that "only in the informal spheres of judicial conduct—in the methods of discovery, arrest, and detection and the weighing of evidence—was the special character of the crime perforce acknowledged": see Weisman, *Witchcraft, Magic, and Religion*, 15.

19. RQCE, 2:157–58; David D. Hall, *Witch-Hunting in Seventeenth-Century New England*, 2nd ed. (Durham, NC: Duke University Press, 1999), 134–35; McManus, *Law and Liberty*, 59, 90.

20. McManus, *Law and Liberty*, 90–91; Bradly Chapin, *Criminal Justice in Colonial America, 1606–1660* (Athens: University of Georgia Press, 1983), 33, 34. Several historians have argued that one of reasons why the Salem witch hunt spun out of control was the magistrates' willingness to condemn the accused for crimes that were not relevant to the charges laid out in their indictments: see Bernard Rosenthal, *Salem Story: Reading the Witch Trials of 1692* (New York: Cambridge University Press, 1993), 191; and Benjamin C. Ray, *Satan & Salem: The Witch-Hunt Crisis of 1692* (Charlottesville: University of Virginia Press, 2015), 160.

21. RPC, 92–93; RMB, 4/1:96.

22. Michael Dalton, *The Country Justice* (London: Company of Stationers, 1655), 344.

23. RMB, 4/1:96; RCA, 3:151; RPC, 92–93, 188–89, 238. Edgar McManus reflects on how in New England the "source of the mischief, not the mischief itself" was the critical aspect in witchcraft charges: see *Law and Liberty*, 133.

24. McManus, *Law and Liberty*, 97–98, 92–94.

25. Holdsworth, "Law and Society," 162–64; SWP-JHL, W-2; Chapin, *Criminal Justice in Colonial America*, 46; PRCC 1, 84–85.

26. Levack, *Witch-Hunt in Early Modern Europe*, 90–91. The trial of Rebecca and Nathaniel Greensmith illustrates the short period of time that usually separated a conviction and execution for witchcraft; see RPC, 257–58, 259, 265. For the post-trial phase of Hugh Parson's case, see: RMB, 3:273, 4/1: 96. For the post-trial review of

Elizabeth Seager's case, see *HCC*, 50, 61–62. For the post-trial review of Katherine Harrison's verdict, see Carolyn S. Langdon, "A Complaint against Katherine Harrison, 1669," *Bulletin of the Connecticut Historical Society* 34 (1969): 20–21; *CCA*, 10–11; SWP-JHL, W-18; *PRCC*, 2:132.

27. For New Haven's witchcraft cases, see R. G. Tomlinson, *Witchcraft Prosecution: Chasing the Devil in Connecticut* (Rockland, ME: Picton Press, 2012), 60–69; *RCNH*, 2:29–36, 151–52; and *NHTR* 1:245–46, 249–52, 256–58, 264.

28. Holdsworth, "Law and Society," 163–67, 469; Homer Worthington Brainard et al., *The Gilbert Family: Descendents of Thomas Gilbert, 1582?–1659 of Mt. Wollaston (Braintree), Windsor, and Wethersfield* (New Haven, CT, 1953), 18.

29. Holdsworth, "Law and Society," 401–2, 469; McManus, *Law and Liberty*, 100.

30. The statistics on legal action concerning occult crime contained in this paragraph are drawn from my own research and information contained in John Demos, *Entertaining Satan: Witchcraft and the Culture of Early New England* (New York: Oxford University Press, 1982), 402–6.

31. The figures on witch-hunting in Massachusetts between 1657 and 1670 are based on my own research and data contained in Demos, *Entertaining Satan*, 404–6.

32. Holdsworth, "Law and Society," 470–71, 526, 581; SWP,-JHL, W-2

33. Holdsworth, "Law and Society," 143–44, 402–3; Lucius Barnes Barbour, *Families of Early Hartford, Connecticut* (Baltimore, MD: Genealogical Publishing Company, 1977), 279, 702–03.

34. Holdsworth, "Law and Society," 402–6; Tomlinson, *Witchcraft Prosecution*, 178–79, 182.

35. Holdsworth, "Law and Society," 492–93; Tomlinson, *Witchcraft Prosecution*, 183–85.

36. Tomlinson, *Witchcraft Prosecution*, 183–84.

37. Walter W. Woodward, *Prospero's America: John Winthrop, Jr., Alchemy, and the Creation of New England Culture, 1606–1676* (Chapel Hill: University of North Carolina Press for the OIEAHC, 2010), 210–52, especially 223–24; Tomlinson, *Witchcraft Prosecutions*, 185; Holdsworth, "Law and Society," 523–25.

38. Woodward, *Prospero's America*, 228–30, 234–37, 238–51; Holdsworth, "Law and Society," 519–25; *RPC*, 188–89, 240; *HCC*, 50, 61–62.

39. Malcolm Gaskill provides good discussion of the legal and evidentiary context of English witch-hunting in "Witchcraft and Evidence in Early Modern England," *Past & Present* 198 (February 2008): 33–70.

40. John Cotta, *The Infallible True and Assured Witch* (London: I.L. for R.H., 1625), 124.

41. Perkins, *Discourse of the Damned Art of Witchcraft*, 642–43; Dalton, *The Country Justice*, 342–43; Bernard, *Guide to Grand Jury Men*, 201–6 (quote on 202).

42. James I of England, *Deamonologie* (Edinburgh: Robert Walde-grave, 1597), 80–81; Clive Holmes, "Women: Witnesses and Witches," *Past & Present* 140 (1993): 69; Sharpe, *Instruments of Darkness*, 218.

43. James I, *Deamonologie*, 80–81; Keith Thomas, *Religion and the Decline of Magic* (New York: Charles Scribner's Sons, 1971), 220; Sarah Tarlow, *Ritual, Belief and the Dead in Early Modern Britain and Ireland* (New York: Cambridge University Press, 2011), 164–65; John Gaule, *Select Cases of Conscience Touching Witches and Witchcrafts*

(London: W. Wilson for Richard Clutterbuck, 1646), 80–81; Dalton, *The Country Justice*, 343.

44. Perkins, *Discourse of the Damned Art of Witchcraft*, 643–44; Bernard, *Guide to Grand Jury Men*, 207–8, 210–11; Cotta, *The Infallible True and Assured Witch*, 127–31, 138–39, 145.

45. James I, *Deamonologie*, 79–80; Dalton, *The Country Justice*, 342; Bernard, *Guide to Grand Jury Men*, 205–6; Cotta, *The Infallible True and Assured Witch*, 21; Sharpe, *Instruments of Darkness*, 223–26; Gilbert Geis and Ivan Bunn, *A Trial of Witches: A Seventeenth-Century Witchcraft Trial* (New York: Routledge, 1997), especially 66, 88–89.

46. Dalton, *The Country Justice*, 343.

47. Dalton, *Country Justice*, 342; Bernard, *Guide to Grand Jury Men*, 217; Gaule, *Select Cases of Conscience*, 78–79.

48. Holmes, "Women: Witnesses and Witches," 66, 69–71; Levack, *Witch-hunting in Scotland*, 73; Gaskill, *Witchfinders*, 42, 89–90.

49. Sharpe, *Instruments of Darkness*, 72–73; Holmes, "Women: Witnesses and Witches," 70; James I, *Deamonologie*, 80; Perkins, *Discourse of the Damned Art of Witchcraft*, 643; Cooper, *The Mystery of Witchcraft*, 275; Bernard, *Guide to Grand Jury Men*, 214–15.

50. Bernard, *Guide to Grand Jury Men*, 215; Dalton, *The Country Justice*, 342.

51. Perkins, *Discourse of the Damned Art of Witchcraft*, 643; Cooper, *The Mystery of Witchcraft*, 275; Gaule, *Select Cases of Conscience*, 80; Cotta, *The Infallible True and Assured Witch*, 89–92; James I, *Deamonologie*, 80; Bernard, *Guide to Grand Jury Men*, 214–16; Dalton, *The Country Justice*, 342 (both quotes in the last sentence are from Dalton).

52. Perkins, *Discourse of the Damned Art of Witchcraft*, 644; Bernard, *Guide to Grand Jury Men*, 220–21; Cooper, *Mystery of Witchcraft*, 277; Dalton, *Country Justice*, 343; Cotta, *Infallible True and Assured Witch*, 95; Sir Robert Filmer, *An Advertisement to the Jurymen of England, Touching Witches* (London: Printed by I.G. for Richard Royston, 1563), 12–13.

53. Perkins, *Discourse of the Damned Art of Witchcraft*, 642; Dalton, *The Country Justice*, 343; Filmer, *Advertisement to the Jurymen of England*, 12; James I, *Deamonologie*, 79; Bernard, *Guide to Grand Jury Men*, 218.

54. Perkins, *Discourse of the Damned Art of Witchcaft*, 644–45; Cotta, *Infallible, True and Assured Witch*, 22.

55. McManus, *Law and Liberty*, 133, 138.

56. Holdsworth, "Law and Society," 400.

57. SWP, JHL, W-2; John Demos, "John Godfrey and his Neighbors: Witchcraft and the Social Web in Colonial Massachusetts" *WMQ* 33 (April 1976): 247; *NHCR*, 2: 32; Bernard, *Guide to Grand Jury Men*, 202.

58. Perkins, *Discourse of the Damned Art of Witchcraft*, 643; Bernard, *Guide to Grand Jury Men*, 209–10; Increase Mather, *An Essay for the Recording of Remarkable Providences* (1684), in *Narratives of the Witchcraft Cases, 1648–1706*, ed. George Lincoln Burr, (New York: Charles Scribner's Sons, 1914), 21; SWP-JHL, W-2; Liam Connell, "'A Great or Notorious Liar': Katherine Harrison and her Neighbors, Wethersfield, Connecticut, 1668–70," *Eras* 12 (March 2011): 10.

59. SWP-JHL, W-34; SWP-CSL, no. 22; J. H. Lefroy, *Memorials of the Discovery and Settlement of the Bermudas or Somers Islands, 1515–1687* (London: Longmans, Green,

1879), 2:602–3. For references to the "blood cry" version of the touch test, see SWP-CSL, no. 5 and SWP-JHL, W-8 and W-9.

60. Drake, *Annals*, 252–53; *REH*, 1:132; SWP-JHL, W-10.

61. Woodward, *Prospero's America*, 240–43; Holdsworth, "Law and Society," 520–21; Connell, "'A Great or Notorious Liar,'" 9–10.

62. SWP-JHL, W-18.

63. SWP-JHL, W-18.

64. Woodward, *Prospero's America*, 243–51; Connell, "'A Great or Notorious Liar,'" 11–14; Tomlinson, *Witchcraft Prosecution*, 132–34. It is unclear if the judges who oversaw the Salem witch trials were familiar with the conclusions Connecticut's clerical commission reached in the late 1660s, but what the crisis of 1692 provided was an episode where *groups* of afflicted accusers corroborated each other's spectral assaults. This, in theory, provided the judges with a pretext to argue that the testimony satisfied the two-witness rule.

65. Thomas Hutchinson, *The History of the Colony of Massachusetts Bay*, 2nd ed. (London: Mr. Richardson, 1765), 1:187–88; SWP-JHL, W-5.

66. *RMB*, 2:242; Drake, *Annals*, 241, 244; *RQCE*, 3:4; *NHCR*, 2:87.

67. Rebecca J. Tannenbaum, *The Healer's Calling: Women and Medicine in Early New England* (Ithaca, NY: Cornell University Press, 2002), 94–98; Cornelia Hughes Dayton, *Women before the Bar: Gender, Law, and Society in Connecticut, 1639–1789* (Chapel Hill: University of North Carolina Press for the IEAHC, 1995), 21. There is no recorded instance of a physical examination of a male suspect for witch marks before 1670, but the records of the Salem witch trials of 1692 indicate that physicians oversaw panels of male searchers: see Bernard Rosenthal, ed., *Records of the Salem Witch Hunt* (New York: Cambridge University Press, 2009), 363–64.

68. *RCNH*, 2:81–82; James Kendall Hosmer, ed., *John Winthrop's Journal, 1630–49* (New York: Charles Scribner's Sons, 1908), 2:345; Hutchinson, *History of the Colony of Massachusetts Bay*, 1:187.

69. For references to searches for witch marks on Bermuda, see Lefroy, *Memorials*, 2:602–3, 606, 610–11, 617, 622, 623, 626, 629 (quote from 606).

70. Drake, *Annals*, 240, 253–54; Hall, *Witch-Hunting*, 104.

71. Perkins, *Discourse of the Damned Art of Witchcraft*, 642–43; Cooper, *Mystery of Witchcraft*, 275; Gaule, *Select Cases of Conscience*, 80; Bernard, *Guide to Grand Jury Men*, 212–14; Dalton, *Country Justice*, 342.

72. Kendall, ed., *John Winthrop's Journal*, 2:344; *RCNH*, 2:81–82, 84.

73. The pre-1670 witch suspects who confessed were Mary Johnson, Goody Basset, and Rebecca Greensmith. For Goody Glover's trial, see Cotton Mather, *Memorable Providences* (1689), in *Narratives of the Witchcraft Cases, 1648–1706*, ed. George Lincoln Burr (New York: Charles Scribner's Sons, 1914), 103–5. For English authors who took a cautious approach to confessions, see Cotta, *Infallible, True and Assured Witch*, 95–96; Perkins, *Discourse of the Damned Art of Witchcraft*, 644; Filmer, *Advertisement to the Jurymen of England*, 12–13.

74. For English writers who believed that an accusation of a person contained in another witch suspect's confession was a valid form of convictive evidence, see James I, *Deamonologie*, 79; and Bernard, *Guide to Grand Jury Men*, 218; SWP-JHL, W-1.

75. McManus, *Law and Liberty*, 35–36; Marcus, "Due Execution of the Generall Rules of Righteousness," 111–12; SWP-JHL, W-2; Drake, *Annals*, 233.

76. Dayton, *Women before the Bar*, 30; Holdsworth, "Law and Society," 528–29; McManus, *Law and Liberty*, 110, 137; Marcus, "Due Execution of the Generall Rule of Righteousness," 111–16; John Winthrop, *The History of New England from 1630–1649*, ed. James Savage (Boston: Thomas B. Wait and Son, 1826), 2:47.

77. SWP-JHL, W-18; Holdsworth, "Law and Society," 530; Woodward, *Prospero's America*, 244–45.

78. Godbeer, *Devil's Dominion*, 154–58; Weisman, *Witchcraft, Magic, and Religion*, 98–100, 105–6.

Conclusion

1. The depositions related to Ann Burt's witchcraft case can be found in David D. Hall, ed., *Witch-Hunting in Seventeenth-Century New England: A Documentary History, 1638–1693*, 2nd ed. (Durham, NC: Duke University Press, 1999), 185–88; and the *RQCE*, 4:207–9. The original documents are in the Essex County Court Papers, 15:61–1, 62–1, 62–2, 63–1, 63–2 at the Essex Institute in Salem, MA. For a reference to Ann Burt's death, see *RQCE*, 5:204.

2. Hall, *Witch-Hunting*, 185–88.

3. *RQCE*, 4:208.

4. J. H. Lefroy, ed., *Memorials of the Discovery and Early Settlement of the Bermudas or Somers Islands, 1515–1687* (London: Longmans, Green, 1879), 2:630; H. R. McIlwaine, ed., *Minutes of the Council and General Court of Colonial Virginia* (Richmond: Virginia State Library, 1924): 509; C. L'Estrange Ewen, ed., *Witch Hunting and Witch Trials: The Indictments for Witchcraft from the Records of 1373 Assizes held for the Home Circuit, AD 1559–1736* (London: Kegan Paul, Trench, Trubner, 1929), 256.

5. Virginia Bernhard, "Religion, Politics, and Witchcraft in Bermuda, 1651–55," *WMQ* 67 (October 2010): 677–708. Twelve out of Bermuda's nineteen witchcraft cases took place in the 1650s: see Lefroy, *Memorials*, 602–32.

6. The four formal complaints of witchcraft in the Chesapeake include those against William Harding, Barbara Wingborough, and Alice Stephens of Virginia in 1656, 1657, and 1668 respectively; see "Witchcraft in Virginia," *WMQ* 1 (January 1893): 127–29; and H. R. McIlwaine, ed., *Minutes of the Council and General Court of Colonial Virginia.* (Richmond, VA: Virginia State Library, 1924), 506, 509. Regarding the witchcraft case of Elizabeth Bennett of Maryland in 1665, see J. Hall Pleasants, ed., *Archives of Maryland* (Baltimore: Maryland Historical Society, 1932), 49:476, 486, 508. On the relationship between the Chesapeake colonies, Puritanism, and England's Commonwealth government, see Babette M. Levy, "Early Puritanism in the Southern and Island Colonies," *Proceedings of the American Antiquarian Society* 52 (1960): 93–147, 201–39; Robert M. Bliss, *Revolution and Empire: English Politics and the American Colonies in the Seventeenth Century* (Manchester: Manchester University Press, 1990); and Carla Gardina Pestana, *The English Atlantic in an Age of Revolution, 1640–1661* (Cambridge, MA: Harvard University Press, 2004).

7. Hall, *Witch-Hunting*, 186–88.

8. See John Demos, *Entertaining Satan: Witchcraft and the Culture of Early New England* (New York: Oxford University Press, 1982), 57–94; Carol Karlsen, *The Devil in the Shape of a Woman: Witchcraft in Colonial New England* (1987; reprint New York: W.

W. Norton, 1998), 46–76, 117–52—citations refer to the 1998 edition; and chapter 3 of this study for discussions of the social profile of witch suspects.

9. *RQCE*, 5:203–4; Demos, *Entertaining Satan*, 81–84; Karlsen, *Devil in the Shape of a Woman*, 142–43; Mary R. O'Neil, "Missing Footprints: Maleficium in Modena," *Acta Ethnographica Hungarica* 37 (1991–92): 123–42.

10. Demos, *Entertaining Satan*, 76–79; *RQCE*, 1:9–10, 56.

11. Ann Burt was married twice and her first husband's name was Roger Bassett; see Charles E. Banks, *The Planters of the Commonwealth* (Baltimore, MD: Genealogical Publishing Company, 1961), 164; *RQCE*, 2:250, 265, 282, 329–30.

12. *RQCE*, 4:208; Hall, *Witch-Hunting*, 185–86. The scholarship on the social context of witchcraft accusations is far too extensive to summarize here; however, a few of the most relevant studies are Demos, *Entertaining Satan*, 275–312; Karlsen, *Devil in the Shape of a Woman*, 182–221; Keith Thomas, *Religion and the Decline of Magic* (New York: Charles Scribner's Sons, 1971), 535–69; and Malcolm Gaskill, "The Devil in the Shape of a Man: Witchcraft, Conflict, and Belief in Jacobean England," *Historical Research* 71 (June 1998): 142–71.

13. For a comprehensive assessment of how gender intersected with witchcraft accusations aimed at women in early New England, see Karlsen, *Devil in the Shape of a Woman*. Several studies that explore witch-hunting in early modern Europe observe that communities directed witch fears at women because their day-to-day responsibilities (i.e., childcare, healing, and neighborhood exchange) crossed paths with areas of life often associated with witchcraft. They include Éva Pócs, "Why Witches Are Women," *Acta Ethnographica Hungarica* 48 (2003): 367–83; James Sharpe, "Witchcraft and Women in Seventeenth-Century England: Some Northern Evidence," *Continuity and Change* 6 (1991): 179–99; and Lauren Martin, "The Devil and the Domestic: Witchcraft, Quarrels and Women's Work in Scotland," in *The Scottish Witch-Hunt in Context*, ed. Julian Goodare (Manchester: Manchester University Press, 2002), 73–89.

14. For discussions of the social profile and character of those who accused others of witchcraft in early New England, see Karlsen, *Devil in the Shape of a Woman*, 183–85; Demos, *Entertaining Satan*, 151–57; and chapter 5 of this study.

15. *The Colonial Society of Massachusetts, Collections: Records of the Suffolk County Court, 1671–1680, Part 1* (Boston: Published by the Colonial Society of Massachusetts, 1933), 29:114–15. Ann Burt was not the only resident of Lynn to become a target of Dr. Reed's witch-finding efforts, and in 1680 he lodged a witchcraft complaint against Margaret Gifford, but like Burt she avoided conviction: see *RQCE*, 7:405.

16. Bernard Rosenthal et al., eds., *Records of the Salem Witch Hunt* (New York: Cambridge University Press, 2009), 239–40, 270, 272, 274, 298, 776; Mary Beth Norton, *In The Devil's Snare: The Salem Witchcraft Crisis of 1692* (New York: Vintage Books, 2003), 113–14, 371n2, 375n26; Enders A. Robinson, *The Devil Discovered: Salem Witchcraft 1692* (Prospect Heights, IL: Waveland Press, 1991), 106, 346–47.

17. *RQCE*, 4:207, 209; Hall, *Witch-Hunting*, 185–86. The distinctions between witch panics and ordinary witchcraft cases are addressed in chapter 6 of this book. For discussions of the social profile of regular and bewitched accusers and the sorts of evidence they presented, see Karlsen, *Devil in the Shape of a Woman*, 183–85, 222–51; Demos, *Entertaining Satan*, 157–65; and chapters 5 and 6 of this study.

18. Demos, *Entertaining Satan*, 406–7. One of the unlucky few accused of witchcraft in the 1670s was Mary Ingham of Scituate—her arrest set off Plymouth's only

witch prosecution. The other three people to face the courts for occult crime between 1671 and 1678 were Eunice Cole, Anna Edmunds, and Mary (Bliss) Parsons.

19. Demos, *Entertaining Satan*, 407. For an account of the connected witch trials of Caleb Powell and Elizabeth Morse, see Hall, *Witch-Hunting*, 230–59.

20. Demos, *Entertaining Satan*, 407–08.

21. For the Salem crisis, see Benjamin C. Ray, *Satan & Salem: The Witch-hunt Crisis of 1692* (Charlottesville: University of Virginia Press, 2015). For the Fairfield hunt, see Richard Godbeer, *Escaping Salem: The Other Witch Hunt of 1692* (New York: Oxford University Press, 2005).

22. Karlsen, *Devil in the Shape of a Woman*, 142.

23. Demos, *Entertaining Satan*, 408–9. The cases of Crotia and the Benhams are discussed in R. G. Tomlinson, *Witchcraft Prosecution: Chasing the Devil in Connecticut* (Rockland, ME: Picton Press, 2012), 165–67; and Karlsen, *Devil in the Shape of a Woman*, 44, 52. For documents concerning Hugh Crotia, see CA, Crimes & Misdemeanors, Series 1, 1:185–86.

24. Karlsen, *Devil in the Shape of a Woman*, 45; and Tomlinson, *Witchcraft Prosecution*, 167–68. For documents related to the cases of Clother, Brown, and Spencer, see CA, Crimes & Misdemeanors, Series 1, 2:73–76, 398–401.

Bibliography

Manuscript Collections

Connecticut State Library, Hartford, CT
    Connecticut Archives, 1629–1856, bulk 1628–1820 (RG 001:010).
        Crimes and Misdemeanors, 1st Series, 1662/63–1789, Vols. 1–3.
    Matthew Grant Diary, 1637–1654.
    Samuel Wyllys Papers.
John Hay Library, Brown University, Providence, RI
    Samuel Wyllys Papers, 1638–1737.

Contemporary Publications

Ady, Thomas. *A Candle in the Dark: or, a Treatise Concerning the Nature of Witches and Witchcraft*. London: Robert Ibbitson, 1656.

Baxter, Richard. *Christian Directory*. Vol. 3. London: Printed by Robert White for Nevill Simmons, 1678.

Bernard, Richard. *A Guide to Grand Jury Men*. London: Felix Kyngston, 1629.

Cooper, Thomas. *The Mystery of Witch-craft Discovering, the Truth, Nature, Occasions, Growth and Power Thereof*. London: Nicholas Okes, 1617.

Cotta, John. *The Infallible True and Assured Witch: or, The Second Edition of the Tryall of Witch-craft*. London: I.L. for R.H. Thomas, 1625.

Dalton, Michael. *The Countrey Justice*. London: Company of Stationers, 1655.

Filmer, Robert. *An Advertisement to the Jurymen or England, Touching Witches. Together with a Difference between An English and Hebrew Witch*. London: Printed by I.G. for Richard Royston, 1653.

Gaule, John. *Select Cases of Conscience Touching Witches and Witchcrafts*. London: W. Wilson for Richard Clutterbuck, 1646.

Glanvill, Joseph. *Saducismus Triumphatus: Or, Full and Plain Evidence Concerning Witches and Apparitions*. London: Printed for A. L., 1700.

Gouge, William. *Of Domesticall Duties*. London: Printed by John Haviland for William Bladen, 1622.

Hale, John. *A Modest Inquiry into the Nature of Witchcraft* (1702). In *Narratives of the Witchcraft Cases, 1648–1706*, edited by George Lincoln Burr, 395–432. New York: Charles Scribner's Sons, 1914.

Hopkins, Matthew. *The Discovery of Witches*. London: Printed for R. Royston, 1647.

Hubbard, William. *A General History of New England from the Discovery to 1680*. 2nd ed. Boston: Charles C. Little and James Brown, 1848.

Hutchinson, Thomas. *The History of the Province of Massachusetts Bay*. 3 vols. London: M. Richardson, 1765.

James I of England. *Daemonologie, in Forme of a Dialogue*. Edinburgh: Printed by Robert Walde-grave, 1597.

The Lawes against Witches, and Conjuration. And Some Brief Notes and Observations for the Discovery of Witches. London: Printed for R.W., 1645.

Mather, Cotton. *A Brand Plucked out of the Burning* (1693). In *Narratives of the Witchcraft Cases, 1648–1706*, edited by George Lincoln Burr, 253–88. New York: Charles Scribner's Sons, 1914.

——. *Magnalia Christi Americana; or, The Ecclesiastical History of New England*. Vol. 2. New York: Russell & Russell, 1967.

——. *Memorable Providences Relating to Witchcraft and Possessions* (1689). In *Narratives of the Witchcraft Cases, 1648–1706*, edited by George Lincoln Burr, 89–144. New York: Charles Scribner's Sons, 1914.

Mather, Increase. *An Essay for the Recording of Illustrious Providences*. Boston: Printed by Samuel Green, 1684.

——. *An Essay for the Recording of Remarkable Providences* (1684). In *Narratives of the Witchcraft Cases, 1648–1706*, edited by George Lincoln Burr, 1–38. New York: Charles Scribner's Sons, 1914.

Perkins, William. *A Discourse on the Damned Art of Witchcraft*. Cambridge: Printed by Cantrell Legge, 1618.

Potts, Thomas. *The Wonderfull Discoverie of Witches in the Countie of Lancaster*. London: Printed by W. Stansby for John Barnes, 1613.

Roberts, Alexander. *A Treatise of Witchcraft. Wherein Sundry Propositions are Laid Downe, Plainly Discovering the Wickedness of that Damnable Art*. London: Nicholas Okes, 1616.

Rogers, Daniel. *Matrimoniall Honour*. London: Printed by Thomas Harper for Philip Nevel, 1642.

Scott, Reginald. *The Discovery of Witchcraft*. London: William Brome, 1584.

Stearne, John. *A Confirmation and Discovery of Witchcraft*. London: Printed by William Wilson, 1648.

A True and Exact Relation of the Severall Informations, Examinations, and Confessions of the Late Witches, Arraigned and Executed in the County of Essex. London: Printed by M.S. for Henry Overton and Benj. Allen, 1645.

A True Relation of the Arraignment of Thirty Witches at Chelmsford in Essex. London: Printed by I.H., 1645.

Published Collections of Records and Documents

Banks, Charles E, ed. *The Planters of the Commonwealth*. Baltimore, MD: Genealogical Publishing Company, 1961.

Burt, Henry M., ed. *The First Century of the History of Springfield: The Official Records from 1636–1736*. Vol. 1. Springfield, MA: Henry M. Burt, 1898.

Collections of the Connecticut Historical Society. Vol. 2. "Records of the Hartford Controversy." Hartford, CT: Connecticut Historical Society, 1870.

——. Vol. 14. "Original Distribution of the Lands in Hartford among the Settlers, 1639" and "Early Hartford Vital Records." Hartford, CT: Connecticut Historical Society, 1912.

——. Vol. 22. "Records of the Particular Court of Connecticut, 1639–1663." Hartford, CT: Connecticut Historical Society, 1928.

——. Vol. 24. "Hoadley Memorial: Early Letters and Documents Relating to Connecticut, 1643–1709." Hartford, CT: Connecticut Historical Society, 1932.

Collections of the Massachusetts Historical Society. 4th Series, Vol. 7. "The Winthrop Papers." Boston: Massachusetts Historical Society, 1865.

——. 4th Series, Vol. 8. "The Mather Papers." Boston: Massachusetts Historical Society, 1868.

Collections of the New Hampshire Historical Society. Vol. 1. Concord, NH: Jacob B. Moore, 1824.

The Colonial Society of Massachusetts, Collections: Records of the Suffolk County Court, 1671–1680, Part 1. Vol. 29. Boston: Published by the Colonial Society of Massachusetts, 1933.

Dexter, Franklin Bowditch, ed. *New Haven Town Records.* Vols. 1 (1649–62) and 2 (1662–84). New Haven, CT: New Haven Colony Historical Society, 1917 and 1919.

Dow, George Francis, ed. *Records and Files of the Quarterly Courts of Essex County.* 9 vols. Salem, MA: Essex Institute, 1911–75.

Drake, Samuel G., ed. *Annals of Witchcraft in New England.* Boston: W. Elliot Woodward, 1869.

Ewen, C. L'Estrange, ed. *Witch Hunting and Witch Trials: The Indictments for Witchcraft from the Records of 1,373 Assizes held for the Home Circuit A.D. 1559–1736.* London: Kegan Paul, Trench, Trubner, 1929.

Farrand, Max, ed. *The Laws and Liberties of Massachusetts, 1648.* Cambridge, MA: Harvard University Press, 1929.

Fogg, John S.H. "Witchcraft in New Hampshire in 1656." *New England Historical and Genealogical Register* 42 (1889): 181–83.

Freiberg, Malcolm, ed. *Winthrop Papers.* 6 vols. Boston: Massachusetts Historical Society, 1992.

Hall, David D., ed. *The Antinomian Controversy, 1636–1638, A Documentary History.* Durham, NC: Duke University Press, 1990.

——., ed. *Witch-Hunting in Seventeenth-Century New England: A Documentary History, 1638–1692.* 1st ed. Boston: Northeastern University Press, 1991.

——., ed. *Witch-Hunting in Seventeenth-Century New England: A Documentary History, 1638–1692.* 2nd ed. Durham, NC: Duke University Press, 1999.

Hallett, A.C. Hollis, ed. *Bermuda under the Somers Islands Company, 1612–1684: Civil Records.* Vol. 1 (1612–1669). Pembroke, Bermuda: Juniperhill Press & Bermuda Maritime Museum Press, 2005.

Hammond, Otis G., ed. *New Hampshire Court Records, 1640–1692.* State of New Hampshire, 1943.

Hedges, Henry Parsons, ed. *Records of the Town of East Hampton, Long Island, Suffolk County, NY.* Vol. 1. Sag Harbor, NY: John H. Hunt, Printer, 1887.

Hoadly, Charles J., ed. *Records of the Colony or Jurisdiction of New Haven, 1653–1662.* Hartford, CT: Case, Lockwood, 1858.

——, ed. *Records of the Colony and Plantation of New Haven, 1639–1649.* Hartford, CT: Case, Tiffany, 1857.

Hosmer, James Kendall, ed. *Winthrop's Journal, "History of New England," 1630–49.* 2 vols. New York: Charles Scribner's Sons, 1908.

Langdon, Carolyn S. "A Complaint against Katherine Harrison." *Connecticut Historical Society Bulletin* 34 (1969): 18–25.

Lefroy, J. H., ed. *Memorials of the Discovery and Early Settlement of the Bermudas or Somers Islands, 1515–1687.* Vol. 2. London: Longmans, Green, 1879.

Libby, Charles T., ed. *Province and Court Records of Maine.* Portland: Maine Historical Society, 1931.

Manwaring, Charles W., ed. *A Digest of Early Connecticut Probate Records*, Vol. 1. Hartford, CT: R.S. Peck, 1904.

McIlwaine, H. R., ed. *Minutes of the Council and General Court of Colonial Virginia.* Richmond: Virginia State Library, 1924.

Noble, John, and John F. Cronin, eds. *Records of the Court of Assistants of the Colony of Massachusetts Bay, 1630–1692.* 3 vols. Boston: Published by the County of Suffolk, 1901–28.

Novel, John, ed. *Records of the Court of Assistants of the Colony of the Massachusetts Bay, 1630–1692.* 3 vols. Boston: Published by the County of Suffolk, 1901.

Pleasants, J. Hall, ed. *Archives of Maryland.* Vol. 49. *Proceedings of the Provincial Court of Maryland, 1663–1666.* Baltimore: Maryland Historical Society, 1932.

——, ed. *Archives of Maryland.* Vol. 53. *Proceedings of the County Court of Charles County, 1658–1666 and Manor Court of St. Clements Manor, 1659–1672.* Baltimore: Maryland Historical Society, 1936.

O'Callaghan, E. B. *The Documentary History of the State of New York.* Vol. 2. Albany, NY: Weed, Parsons, 1850.

Records, Town of Brookhaven up to 1800. Patchogue, NY: Printed at the Office of the "Advance," 1880.

Rhode Island Land Evidences. Vols. 1 (1648–96) and 2 (1662–70). Providence: Rhode Island Historical Society, 1921 and 1922.

Rosen, Barbara, ed. *Witchcraft in England, 1558–1618.* Amherst: University of Massachusetts Press, 1969.

Rosenthal, Bernard, et al., eds. *Records of the Salem Witch Hunt.* New York: Cambridge University Press, 2009.

Shurtleff, Nathaniel B., ed. *Records of the Governor and Company of Massachusetts Bay in New England.* Vols. 1 (1628–41), 2 (1642–49), 3 (1644–57) and 4/1 (1650–60). Boston: Press of William White, 1853 and 1854.

Smith, Joseph H. Smith, ed., *Colonial Justice in Western Massachusetts, 1639–1702: The Pynchon Court Record.* Boston: Harvard University Press, 1961.

Turnbull, J. Hammond, ed. *The Public Records of the Colony of Connecticut.* Vols. 1 (prior to May 1665) and 2 (1665–78). Hartford, CT: Brown and Parsons, 1850 and F. A. Brown, 1852.

Ullmann, Helen Schatvet, ed. *Colony of Connecticut, Minutes of the Court of Assistants, 1669–1711.* Boston: New England Historic Genealogical Society, 2009.

——, ed. *Hartford County, Connecticut, County Court Minutes: Volumes 3 and 4, 1663–1689 and 1697.* Boston: New England Historical and Genealogical Society, 2005.

Waters, Stanly. "Witchcraft in Springfield, MA." *New England Historical and Genealogical Register* 35 (1881): 152–55.

Winthrop, John. *The History of New England from 1630–1649.* Vol. 2. Edited by James Savage. Boston: Thomas B. Wait and Son, 1826.

"Witchcraft in Virginia." *WMQ* 1 (January 1893): 127–29.

Secondary Sources

Adams, Sherman W., and Henry R. Stiles. *History of Ancient Wethersfield, Connecticut.* 2 vols. New York: The Grafton Press, 1904 / Reprint by Camden, ME: Picton Press, 1995.

Allen, David Grayson. *In English Ways: The Movement of Societies and the Transferal of English Local Law and Custom to Massachusetts Bay.* Chapel Hill: University of North Carolina Press for the IEAHC, 1981.

Anderson, Terry L., and Robert Paul Thomas. "White Population, Labor Force, and Extensive Growth of the New England Economy in the Seventeenth Century." *Journal of Economic History* 33 (September 1973): 634–67.

Anderson, Virginia DeJohn. "Migrants and Motives: Religion and the Settlement of New England, 1630–1640." *NEQ* 58 (September 1985): 339–83.

Apps, Lara, and Andrew Gow. *Male Witches in Early Modern Europe.* Manchester: Manchester University Press, 2003.

Bailey, Michael D. "The Age of Magicians: Periodization in the History of European Magic." *Magic, Ritual, and Witchcraft* 3 (summer 2008): 1–28.

——. *Battling Demons: Witchcraft, Heresy, and Reform in the Late Middle Ages.* University Park: Pennsylvania State University Press, 2003.

Baily, Paul, ed. *Long Island: A History of Two Great Counties, Nassau and Suffolk.* Vol. 1. New York: Lewis Historical Publishing, Company, 1949.

Baker, Emerson W. *The Devil of Great Island: Witchcraft and Conflict in Early New England.* New York: Palgrave MacMillan, 2007.

——. *A Storm of Witchcraft: The Salem Trials and the American Experience.* New York: Oxford University Press, 2015.

Bankert, Norbert R. "More on the Identity of Abigail (Graves) Dibble and Her Tragic Death and Suspicions of Witchcraft." *NEHGR* 155 (July 2001): 273–78.

Banks, Charles Edwards. "Scotch Prisoners Deported to New England by Cromwell, 1651–52." *Proceedings of the Massachusetts Historical Society.* 3rd Series, 61 (October 1927–June 1928): 4–29.

Barbour, Lucius Barnes. *Families of Early Hartford, Connecticut.* Reprint, Baltimore, MD: Genealogical Publishing Company, 1977.

Barnes, Frederic Wayne, and Edna Cleo (Bauer) Barns, eds. *Thomas Barnes, Hartford, Connecticut, 8,591 Descendants (and Spouses), 14 Generations, 1615–2001.* 2 vols. Baltimore, MD: Gateway Press, 2001.

Beal, Richard Davis. "The Devil in Virginia in the Seventeenth Century." *Virginia Magazine of History and Biography* 65 (April 1957): 131–49.

Behringer, Wolfgang. "Weather, Hunger and Fear: Origins of the European Witch-Hunts in Climate, Society and Mentality." *German History* 13 (January 1995): 1–27.

Bernhard, Virginia. "Religion, Politics, and Witchcraft in Bermuda, 1651–55." *WMQ* 67 (October 2010): 677–708.

Bickford, Christopher P. *Farmington in Connecticut*. Canaan, NH: Phoenix Publishing for the Farmington Historical Society, 1982.

Bissell, Linda A. "Family, Friends, and Neighbors: Social Interaction in Seventeenth-Century Windsor." PhD diss., Brandeis University, 1973.

——. "From One Generation to Another: Mobility in Seventeenth-Century Windsor, Connecticut." *WMQ* 31 (January 1974): 79–110.

Bliss, Robert M. *Revolution and Empire: English Politics and the American Colonies in the Seventeenth Century*. Manchester: Manchester University Press 1990.

Boyer, Paul, and Stephen Nissenbaum. *Salem Possessed: The Social Origins of Witchcraft*. Cambridge, MA: Harvard University Press, 1974.

Brainard, Homer W., et al. *The Gilbert Family: Descendants of Thomas Gilbert*. New Haven, CT, 1953.

Breen, T. H. "Persistent Localism: English Social Change and the Shaping of New England Institutions." *WMQ* 32 (1975): 3–28.

Bremer, Francis J. *Congregational Communion: Clerical Friendship in the Anglo-American Puritan Community, 1610–1692*. Boston: Northeastern University Press, 1994.

Briggs, Robin. *Witches and Neighbors: The Social and Cultural Context of European Witchcraft*. New York: Viking, 1996.

Burt, Henry M. *The First Century of the History of Springfield*. Vol. 1. Springfield, MA: Henry M. Burt, 1898.

Butler, Jon. "Two 1642 Letters from Virginia Puritans." *Proceedings of the Massachusetts Historical Society* 84 (1972): 99–109.

Carlson, Eric J. *Marriage and the English Reformation*. New York: Oxford University Press, 1994.

Cave, Alfred A. "Indian Shamans and English Witches in Seventeenth-Century New England." *Essex Institute Historical Collections* 128 (October 1992): 239–54.

Chapin, Bradley. *Criminal Justice in Colonial America, 1606–1660*. Athens: The University of Georgia Press, 1983.

Clark, Bertha W. "Rhode Island Woods on Long Island." *American Genealogist* 39 (July 1963): 129–40.

Clark, Stuart. "The 'Gendering' of Witchcraft in French Demonology; Misogyny or Polarity?" *French History* 5 (1991): 426–37.

——. "Protestant Demonology: Sin, Superstition, and Society." In *Early Modern European Witchcraft: Centers and Peripheries*, edited by Bengt Ankarloo and Gustav Henningson, 45–81. New York: Oxford University Press, 1990.

Cohen, Ronald D. "The Hartford Treaty of 1650: Anglo-Dutch Cooperation in the Seventeenth Century." *New York Historical Society Quarterly Bulletin* 53 (September 1969): 311–32.

Connell, Liam. "'A Great or Notorious Liar': Katherine Harrison and her Neighbours, Wethersfield, Connecticut, 1668–1670." *Eras* 12 (March 2011): 1–29

Cressy, David. *Coming Over: Migration and Communication between England and New England in the Seventeenth Century*. Cambridge: Cambridge University Press, 1987.

Davies, Kathleen M. "The Sacred Condition of Equality: How Original Were Puritan Doctrines of Marriage?" *Social History* 2 (May 1977): 563–80.

Davis, Richard Beale. "The Devil in Virginia in the Seventeenth Century." *Virginia Magazine of History and Biography* 65 (April 1957): 131–49.

Dayton, Cornelia Hughes. *Women before the Bar: Gender, Law, and Society in Connecticut, 1639–1789*. Chapel Hill: University North Carolina Press for the IEAHC, 1995.

Demos, John. *Entertaining Satan: Witchcraft and the Culture of Early New England*. New York: Oxford University Press, 1982.

——. "John Godfrey and his Neighbors: Witchcraft and the Social Web in Colonial Massachusetts." *WMQ* 33 (April 1976): 242–65.

——. *A Little Commonwealth: Family Life in Plymouth Colony*. New York: Oxford University Press, 1970.

——. "Old Age in Early New England." *American Journal of Sociology* 84 (1978): 248–87.

Dillinger, Johannes. "The Political Aspects of German Witch Hunts." *Magic, Ritual, and Witchcraft* 3 (summer 2009): 62–81.

Drake, Frederick C. "Witchcraft in the American Colonies, 1647–62." *American Quarterly* 20 (winter 1968): 694–725.

Duni, Matteo. *Under the Devil's Spell: Witches, Sorcerers, and the Inquisition in Renaissance Italy*. Florence: Syracuse University in Florence, 2007.

Elmer, Peter. "'Saints or Sorcerers': Quakerism, Demonology, and the Decline of Witchcraft in Seventeenth-Century England." In *Witchcraft in Early Modern Europe: Studies in Culture and Belief*, edited by Jonathan Barry et al., 145–79. Cambridge: Cambridge University Press, 1996.

Fischer, David Hackett. *Albion's Seed: Four British Folkways in America*. New York: Oxford University Press, 1989.

Foster, Stephen. *The Long Argument: English Puritanism and the Shaping of New England Culture, 1570–1700*. Chapel Hill: University of North Carolina Press for the IEAHC, 1991.

——. "New England and the Challenge of Heresy, 1630–1660: The Puritan Crisis in Transatlantic Perspective." *WMQ* 38 (1981): 624–60.

Fowler, David H. "Connecticut's Freemen: The First Forty Years." *WMQ* 15 (July 1958): 312–33.

Games, Alison. *Migration and the Origins of the English Atlantic World*. Cambridge, MA: Harvard University Press, 1999.

Gardina, Carla Pestana. *The English Atlantic in an Age of Revolution, 1640–1661*. Cambridge, MA: Harvard University Press, 2004.

Gardiner, Robert David Lion. "The Gardiner Family and the Lordship and Manor of Gardiner's Island" *New York Genealogical and Biographical Record* 23 (October 1892): 159–90.

——. "Gardiner's Island." *New York History* 14 (January 1933): 53–60.

Gaskill, Malcolm. *Between Two Worlds: How the English Became Americans*. New York: Basic Books, 2014.

——. *Crime and Mentalities in Early Modern England*. Cambridge: Cambridge University Press, 2000.

——. "The Devil in the Shape of Man: Witchcraft, Conflict, and Belief in Jacobean England." *Historical Research* 71 (June 1998): 142–71.

——. "Witchcraft in Early Modern Kent: Stereotypes and the Background to Accusations." In *Witchcraft in Early Modern Europe: Studies in Belief and Culture*, edited by Jonathan Barry et al., 257–87. New York: Cambridge University Press, 1996.

——. "Witchcraft and Evidence in Early Modern England." *Past & Present* 198 (February 2008): 33–70.

——. "Witches and Witchcraft Prosecutions, 1560–1660." In *Early Modern Kent, 1540–1640*, edited by Michael Zell, 245–77. Woodbridge, Suffolk, UK: The Boydell Press and The Kent County Council, 2000.

——. *Witchfinders: a Seventeenth-Century English Tragedy*. Cambridge, MA: Harvard University Press, 2005.

Gasser, Erika. *Vexed With Devils: Manhood and Witchcraft in Old and New England*. New York: New York University Press, 2017.

Gates, Gillman. *Saybrook at the Mouth of the Connecticut*. New Haven, CT: Wilson H. Lee, 1935.

Geis, Gilbert, and Ivan Bunn. *A Trial of Witches: A Seventeenth-Century Witchcraft Trial*. New York: Routledge, 1997.

Gerrard, Christopher et al., eds. *Lost Lives, New Voices: Unlocking the Stories of the Scottish Soldiers from the Battle of Dunbar, 1650*. Havertown, PA: Oxbow Books, 2018.

Godbeer, Richard. *The Devil's Dominion: Magic and Religion in Early New England*. New York: Cambridge University Press, 1992.

——. *Escaping Salem: The Other Witch Hunt of 1692*. Oxford: Oxford University Press, 2005.

——. "'Your Wife Will Be Your Biggest Accuser': Reinforcing Codes of Manhood at New England Witch Trials." *Early American Studies* (summer 2017): 474–504.

Goodheart, Lawrence B. *The Solemn Sentence of Death: Capital Punishment in Connecticut*. Amherst: University of Massachusetts Press, 2011.

Greene, Jack P. *Pursuits of Happiness: The Social Development of Early Modern British Colonies and the Formation of American Culture*. Chapel Hill: University of North Carolina Press, 1988.

Greven, Philip J. *Four Generations: Population, Land, and Family in Colonial Andover, Massachusetts*. Ithaca, NY: Cornell University Press, 1970.

Griswold, Glenn E., comp. *The Griswold Family, England—America*. Rutland, VT: The Griswold Family Association of America, 1943.

Gura, Philip. *A Glimpse of Sion's Glory: Puritan Radicalism in New England, 1630–1660*. Middletown, CT: Wesleyan University Press, 1984.

Hall, David D. *A Reforming People: Puritanism and the Transformation of Public Life in New England*. New York: Alfred A. Knopf, 2011.

——. "Witchcraft and the Limits of Interpretation." *NEQ* 58 (June 1985): 253–81.

——. "A World of Wonders: The Mentality of the Supernatural in Seventeenth-Century New England." In *Seventeenth-Century New England*, edited by David D. Hall et al., 239–74. Boston: The Colonial Society of Massachusetts, 1984.

——. *Worlds of Wonder, Days of Judgement: Popular Religious Belief in Early New England*. Cambridge, MA: Harvard University Press, 1989.

Hansen, Chadwick. "The Metamorphosis of Tituba." *NEQ* 47 (March 1974): 3–12.

Harley, David. "Explaining Salem: Calvinist Psychology and the Diagnosis of Posses-sion." *American Historical Review* 101 (April 1996): 307–30.

——. "Historians as Demonologists: The Myth of the Midwife-witch." *Society for the Social History of Medicine* 3 (April 1990): 1–26.

Harris, Gale Ion. "Henry and Katherine Palmer of Wethersfield, Connecticut and Newport, Rhode Island." *The Genealogist* 17 (fall 2003): 175–85.

——. "The Later Career of William and Judith Ayres, Escaped Witches from Hart-ford, Connecticut." *American Genealogist* 75 (October 2000): 301–9.

——. "William and Goodwife Ayres of Hartford, Connecticut: Witches Who Got Away." *The American Genealogist* 75 (July 2000): 197–205.

Hastrup, Kristen. "Iceland: Sorcerers and Paganism." In *Early Modern European Witch-craft: Centers and Peripheries*, edited by Bengt Ankarloo and Gustav Henning-son, 383–401. New York: Oxford University Press, 1999.

Hedges, Henry P. *A History of the Town of East-Hampton, New York*. Sag Harbor, NY: J. H. Hunt, 1897.

Hester, Marianne. "Patriarchal Reconstruction and Witch Hunting." In *Witchcraft in Early Modern Europe: Studies in Culture and Belief*, edited by Jonathan Barry et al., 288–306. New York: Cambridge University Press, 1996.

Hoadly, Charles J. "A Case of Witchcraft in Hartford." *Connecticut Magazine* 5 (1899): 557–61.

Holbrook, Jay Mack. *Connecticut Colonists: Windsor 1635–1703*. Oxford, MA: Holbrook Research Institute, 1986.

Holdsworth, William K. "Adultery or Witchcraft? A New Note on an Old Case in Connecticut." *NEQ* 48 (September 1975): 394–401.

——. "Law and Society in Colonial Connecticut, 1636–1672." PhD diss., Claremont Graduate School, 1974.

Holmes, Clive. "Popular Culture? Witches, Magistrates, and Divines in Early Mod-ern England." In *Understanding Popular Culture: Europe from the Middle Ages to the Nineteenth Century*, edited by Steven L. Kaplan, 85–112. Berlin: DEU Walter de Gruyter, 2012.

——. "Women: Witnesses and Witches." *Past & Present* 140 (1993): 45–78.

Huntington, E. B. *History of Stamford, Connecticut*. Stamford, CT: Published by the author, 1868.

Innes, Stephen. *Labor in a New Land: Economy and Society in Seventeenth-Century Spring-field*. Princeton, NJ: Princeton University Press, 1983.

Jackson, Louise. "Witches, Wives, and Mothers: Witchcraft Persecutions and Wom-en's Confessions in Seventeenth-Century England." *Women's History Review* 4 (1995): 63–83.

Jacobus, Donald L. "Connecticut Witches." *New Haven Genealogical Magazine* 4 (Sep-tember 1926): 951–58.

——. ed. *History and Genealogy of the Families of Old Fairfield*. Vol. 1. New Haven, CT: Tuttle, Morehouse & Taylor, 1930.

James, Edward W. "Grace Sherwood, the Virginia Witch." *WMQ* 3 (October 1894, January 1895, and April 1985): 96–101, 190–92, 242–45.

Jarvis, Michael J. "'In the Eye of All Trade': Maritime Revolution and the Transformation of Bermudian Society, 1612–1800," PhD diss., College of William and Mary, 1998.

Johnson, James T. "The Covenant Idea and the Puritan View of Marriage." *Journal of the History of Ideas* 32 (January–March 1971): 107–18.

———. "English Puritan Thought on the Ends of Marriage." *Church History* 38 (December 1969): 429–36.

Judd, Sylvester. *History of Hadley: Including the Early History of Hatfield, South Hadley, Amherst, and Granby, Massachusetts.* Northampton, MA: Printed by Metcalf, 1863.

Kamensky, Jane. *Governing the Tongue: The Politics of Speech in Early New England.* New York: Oxford University Press, 1999.

———. "Words, Witches, and Woman Trouble: Witchcraft, Disorderly Speech, and Gender Boundaries in Puritan New England." *Essex Institute Historical Collections* 128 (October 1992): 286–307.

Karlsen, Carol F. *The Devil in the Shape of a Woman: Witchcraft in Colonial New England.* 1987; reprint New York: W. W. Norton, 1998. Page references are to the 1998 edition.

Kent, Elizabeth J. "Masculinity and Male Witches in Old and New England, 1593–1680." *History Workshop Journal* 60 (2005): 69–92.

Kibby, Ann. "Mutations of the Supernatural: Witchcraft, Remarkable Providences, and the Power of Puritan Men." *American Quarterly* 34 (summer 1982): 125–48.

Kittredge, George Lyman. *Witchcraft in Old and New England.* New York: Russell & Russell, 1929.

Kivelson, Valerie A. "Lethal Convictions: The Power of a Satanic Paradigm in Russian and European Witch Trials." *Magic, Ritual, and Witchcraft* 6 (summer 2011): 34–61.

———. "Male Witches and Gendered Categories in Seventeenth-Century Russia." *Comparative Studies in Society and History* 45 (July 2003): 606–31.

———. "Patrolling the Boundaries: Witchcraft Accusation and Household Strife in Seventeenth-Century Muscovy." *Harvard Ukrainian Studies* 19 (1995): 302–23.

Klaits, Joseph. *Servants of Satan: The Age of the Witch Hunts.* Bloomington: Indiana University Press, 1985.

Koehler, Lyle. *A Search for Power: The "Weaker Sex" in Seventeenth-Century New England.* Urbana: University of Illinois Press, 1980.

Kristóf, Ildikó. "'Wise Women,' Sinners, and the Poor: The Social Background in a 16th-18th-century Calvinist City of Eastern Hungary." *Acta Ethnographica Hungarica* 37 (1991): 93–119.

Larner, Christina. *Enemies of God: The Witch Hunt in Scotland.* Baltimore, MD: Johns Hopkins University Press, 1981.

———. *Witchcraft and Religion: The Politics of Popular Belief.* Oxford: Basil Blackwell, 1984.

Laslett, Peter. "Mean Household Size in England since the Sixteenth Century." In *Household and Family in Past Time,* edited by Peter Laslett and Richard Wall, 125–58. Cambridge: Cambridge University Press, 1972.

Latner, Richard. "'Here Are No Newters': Witchcraft and Religious Discord in Salem Village and Andover." *NEQ* 79 (March 2006): 92–122.

——. "The Long and Short of Salem Witchcraft." *Journal of Social History* (fall 2008): 137–56.

Leites, Edmund. "The Duty to Desire: Love, Friendship, and Sexuality in Some Puritan Theories of Marriage." *Journal of Social History* 15 (spring 1982): 383–408.

Levack, Brian. "State-building and Witch Hunting in Early Modern Europe." In *Witchcraft in Early Modern Europe: Studies in Belief and Culture*, edited by Jonathan Barry et al., 96–115. New York: Cambridge University Press, 1996.

——. *The Witch-Hunt in Early Modern Europe*. 2nd ed. New York: Longman, 1995.

——. *Witch-hunting in Scotland: Law, Politics and Religion*. New York: Routledge, 2008.

Levermore, Charles H. "Witchcraft in Connecticut, 1647–1697." *New Englander* 44 (1885): 806–10.

Levy, Babette M. "Early Puritanism in the Southern and Island Colonies" *Proceedings of the American Antiquarian Society* 52 (1960): 69–348.

Lipman, Andrew Charles. *The Saltwater Frontier: Indians and the Contest for the American Coast*. New Haven, CT: Yale University Press, 2015.

Lockridge, Kenneth A. "Land, Population, and the Evolution of New England Society, 1630–1790." *Past & Present* 39 (April 1968): 62–80.

Love, Rev. William Deloss. *The Colonial History of Hartford*. Hartford, CT: Published by the author, 1914.

Lucas, Paul R. *Valley of Discord: Church and Society along the Connecticut River, 1636–1725*. Hanover, NH: University Press of New England, 1976.

Macfarlane, Alan. *Witchcraft in Tudor and Stuart England: A Regional and Comparative Study*. New York: Harper & Row, 1970.

Marcus, Gail Sussman. "'Due Execution of the Generall Rules of Righteousness': Criminal Procedure in New Haven Town and Colony, 1638–1658." In *Saints and Revolutionaries: Essays on Early American History*, edited by David D. Hall, John. M. Murrin, and Thad W. Tate, 99–137. New York: W. W. Norton, 1984.

Martin, Lauren. "The Devil and the Domestic: Witchcraft, Quarrels, and Women's Work in Scotland." In *The Scottish Witch-Hunt in Context*, edited by Julian Goodare, 73–89. Manchester: Manchester University Press, 2002.

Matthews, Nathan. "The Results of the Prejudice against Lawyers in Massachusetts in the Seventeenth Century." *Massachusetts Law Quarterly* 13 (1928): 73–94.

McManus, Edgar J. *Law and Liberty in Early New England: Criminal Justice and Due Process, 1620–1692*. Amherst: University of Massachusetts Press, 1993.

Mercer, Julia E. *Bermuda Settlers of the 17th Century: Genealogical Notes from Bermuda*. Baltimore, MD: Genealogical Publishing Company, 1982.

Midelfort, H. C. Erik. "Witch Craze? Beyond the Legends of Panic." *Magic, Ritual, and Witchcraft* 6 (summer 2011): 11–33.

Moran, Gerald F. "Religious Renewal, Puritan Tribalism, and the Family in Seventeenth-Century Milford, Connecticut." *WMQ* 36 (1979): 236–54.

Morgan, Edmund S. *The Puritan Family: Religion and Domestic Relations in Seventeenth-Century New England*. New York: Harper & Row, 1966.

Murrin, John M. "Coming to Terms with the Salem Witch Trials." *Proceedings of the American Antiquarian Society* 110 (2000): 309–47.

——. "Magistrates, Sinners, and a Precarious Liberty: Trial by Jury in Seventeenth-Century New England." In *Saints and Revolutionaries: Essays on Early American History*, edited by David D. Hall, John M. Murrin, and Thad W. Tate, 152–206. New York: W. W. Norton, 1984.

Norton, Mary Beth. *Founding Mothers and Fathers: Gendered Power and the Forming of American Society.* New York: Alfred A. Knopf, 1996.

———. *In the Devil's Snare: The Salem Witchcraft Crisis of 1692.* New York: Vintage Books, 2003.

O'Neil, Mary R. "Missing Footprints: Maleficium in Modena." *Acta Ethnographica Hungerica* 37 (1991/92): 123–42.

Paige, Lucius R. *History of Cambridge, Massachusetts, 1630–1877.* Boston: O. H. Houghton, 1877.

Parke, Francis Neal. "Witchcraft in Maryland." *Maryland Historical Magazine* 31 (December 1936): 271–98.

Pestana, Carla Gardina. *The English Atlantic in an Age of Revolution, 1640–1661.* Cambridge, MA: Harvard University Press, 2004.

——. *Protestant Empire: Religion and the Making of the British Atlantic World.* Philadelphia: University of Pennsylvania Press, 2009.

Peters, Edward. *The Magician, the Witch, and the Law.* Philadelphia: University of Pennsylvania Press, 1978.

Peterson, Mark A. *The Price of Redemption: The Spiritual Economy of Puritan New England.* Stanford, CA: Stanford University Press, 1997.

Phelps, Vergil V. "The Pastor and Teacher in New England." *Harvard Theological Review* 4 (July 1911): 388–99.

Pócs, Éva. "Why Witches are Women." *Acta Ethnographica Hungarica* 48 (2003): 367–83.

Pope, Robert G. *The Half-Way Covenant: Church Membership in Puritan New England.* Princeton, NJ: Princeton University Press, 1969.

Purkiss, Diane. "Women's Stories of Witchcraft in Early Modern England: The House, the Body, the Child." *Gender & History* 7 (1995): 408–32.

Rattray, Jeannette Edwards. *East Hampton History, Including Genealogies of Early Families.* Garden City, NY: Country Life Press, 1953.

Ray, Benjamin C. *Satan and Salem: The Witch-Hunt Crisis of 1692.* Charlottesville: University of Virginia Press, 2015.

——. "Satan's War against the Covenant in Salem Village, 1692." *NEQ* 80 (March 2007): 69–95.

Reis, Elizabeth. *Damned Women: Sinners and Witches in Puritan New England.* Ithaca, NY: Cornell University Press, 1997.

Richardson, Douglas. "The English Origin of Thomas Gilbert of Braintree, Mass., and Wethersfield. Conn." *American Genealogist* 67, no. 3 (1992): 161–66.

Robinson, Enders A. *The Devil Discovered: Salem Witchcraft 1692.* Prospect Heights, IL: Waveland Press, 1991.

Robisheaux, Thomas. *The Last Witch of Langenburg: Murder in a German Village.* New York: W. W. Norton, 2009.

Roper, Lyndal. "Witchcraft and Fantasy in Early Modern Germany." In *Witchcraft in Early Modern Europe: Studies in Culture and Belief*, edited by Jonathan Barry et al., 207–36. New York: Cambridge University Press, 1996.

Rosenthal, Bernard. *Salem Story: Reading the Witch Trials of 1692*. New York: Cambridge University Press, 1993.

——. "Tituba's Story." *NEQ* 71 (June 1998): 190–205.

Ross, Christina. "Calvinism and the Witchcraft Persecution in England." *Journal of the Presbyterian Historical Society of England* 12 (May 1960): 21–28.

Rowlands, Alison. "Gender, Ungodly Parents, and a Witch Family in Seventeenth-Century Germany." *Past & Present* 232 (August 2016): 45–86.

——. *Witchcraft and Masculinities in Early Modern Europe*. London: Palgrave, 2009.

——. "Witchcraft and Old Women in Early Modern Germany." *Past & Present* 173 (November 2001): 50–89.

——. "Witchcraft and Popular Religion in Early Modern Rothenburg od der Tauber." In *Popular Religion in Germany and Central Europe*, edited by Bob Scribner and Trevor Johnson, 101–17. New York: Palgrave, 1996.

Russell, Jeffrey Burton. *Witchcraft in the Middle Ages*. Ithaca, NY: Cornell University Press, 1972.

Savage, James. *A Genealogical Dictionary of the First Settlers of New England*. 4 vols. Boston: Little, Brown, 1860.

Schenck, Elizabeth Hubbell. *The History of Fairfield, Fairfield County, Connecticut*. Vol. 1. New York: Published by the author, 1889.

Schulte, Rolf. "Men as Accused Witches in the Holy Roman Empire." In *Witchcraft and Masculinities in Early Modern Europe*, edited by Alison Rowlands, 52–73. New York: Palgrave Macmillan, 2009.

Scisco, Louis Dow. "The First Church in Charles County." *Maryland Historical Magazine* 23 (1925): 155–62.

Sharpe, James. "The Devil in East Anglia: the Matthew Hopkins Trials Reconsidered." In *Witchcraft in Early Modern Europe: Studies in Culture and Belief*, edited by Jonathan Barry et al., 237–54. Cambridge: Cambridge University Press, 1996.

——. *Instruments of Darkness: Witchcraft in Early Modern England*. Philadelphia: University of Pennsylvania Press, 1996.

——. "Witchcraft and Women in Seventeenth-century England: some Northern Evidence." *Continuity and Change* 6 (1991): 179–99.

Sheehan, Michael M. *Marriage, Family and Law in Medieval Europe*. Edited by James Farge. Toronto: University of Toronto Press, 1996.

Stiles, Henry Reed. *The History of Ancient Windsor*. 2 vols. 1891; reprint Somersworth, NH: New Hampshire Publishing Company, 1976.

Stone, Lawrence. *The Family, Sex, and Marriage in England, 1500–1800*. New York: Harper & Row, 1977.

Sweeny, Kevin M. "Furniture and the Domestic Environment in Wethersfield, Connecticut, 1639–1800." In *Material Life in America, 1600–1800*, edited by Robert Blair St. George, 261–90. Boston: Northeastern University Press, 1987.

Talmadge, Arthur White. *The Talmadge, Tallmadge, and Talmage Genalogy*. New York: Grafton Press, 1909.

Tannenbaum, Rebecca J. *The Healer's Calling: Women and Medicine in Early New England*. Ithaca, NY: Cornell University Press, 2002.

Tarlow, Sarah. *Ritual, Belief and the Dead in Early Modern Britain and Ireland*. New York: Cambridge University Press, 2011.

Taylor, Robert J. *Colonial Connecticut: A History*. Millwood, NY: KTO Press, 1979.

Tedeschi, John. "Inquisitorial Law and the Witch." In *Early Modern European Witchcraft: Centers and Peripheries*, edited by Bengt Ankarloo and Gustav Henningsen, 83–115. New York: Oxford University Press, 1990.

Thomas, Keith. *Religion and the Decline of Magic*. New York: Charles Scribner's Sons, 1971.

Thompson, Benjamin F. *History of Long Island*. New York: E. French, 1839.

Thompson, Roger. *Mobility and Migration: East Anglian Founders of New England, 1629–1640*. Amherst: University of Massachusetts Press, 1994.

Tomlinson, R. G. *Witchcraft Prosecution: Chasing the Devil in Connecticut*. Rockland, ME: Picton Press, 2012.

Trevor-Roper, H. R. "The European Witch-Craze of the Sixteenth and Seventeenth Centuries." In *The Crisis of the Seventeenth Century: Religion, the Reformation, and Social Change*, edited by H. R. Trevor-Roper, 83–178. Indianapolis, IN: Liberty Fund, 1967.

Trumbull, J. H., ed. *Memorial History of Hartford County, Connecticut, 1633–1884*. 3 vols. Hartford, CT, 1886.

Trumbull, James Russell. *History of Northampton, Massachusetts*. Vol. 1. Northampton, MA: Press of Gazette Printing Company, 1898.

Ulrich, Laurel Thatcher. *Good Wives: Image and Reality in the Lives of Women in Northern New England, 1650–1750*. New York: Vintage Books, 1980.

Valletta, Frederick. *Witchcraft, Magic, and Superstition in England, 1640–70*. Burlington, VT: Ashgate, 2000.

Waite, Gary K. "Irrelevant Interruption or Precipitating Cause? The Sixteenth-Century Reformation(s) and the Revival of the European Witch Hunts." In *Chasses aux Sorcières et Demonologie*, edited by George Modestin et al., 223–42. Firenze: Sismel, 2010.

Walinski-Kiehl, Robert. "Godly States: Confessional Conflicts and Witch-hunting in Germany." *Mentalities* 5 (1988): 13–25.

Walker, George L. *History of the First Church in Hartford, 1633–1883*. Hartford, CT: Brown & Gross, 1884.

Weisman, Richard. *Witchcraft, Magic, and Religion in 17th-Century Massachusetts*. Amherst: University of Massachusetts Press, 1984.

Wilcoxson, William Howard. *History of Stratford, Connecticut, 1639–1939*. Stratford, CT: Stratford Tercentenary Commission, 1939.

Willis, Deborah. "The Witch-Family in Elizabethan and Jacobean Print Culture." *Journal for Early Modern Cultural Studies* 13 (winter 2013): 4–31.

Winship, Michael Paul. *Making Heretics: Militant Protestantism and Free Grace in Massachusetts, 1636–1641*. Princeton, NJ: Princeton University Press, 2002.

Witte, John, Jr. *From Sacrament to Contract: Marriage, Religion, and Law in the Western Tradition*. Louisville, KY: Westminster John Knox Press, 1997.

Wrightson, Keith, and David Levine. *Poverty and Piety in an English Village, Terling, 1525–1700*. New York: Academic Press, 1979.

Woodward, Walter W. *Prospero's America: John Winthrop, Jr., Alchemy, and the Creation of New England Culture, 1606–1676*. Chapel Hill: University of North Carolina Press for the OIEAHC, 2010.

Index

CPSIA information can be obtained
at www.ICGtesting.com
Printed in the USA
LVHW111655020920
664879LV00006B/68